The Fujifilm X100VI

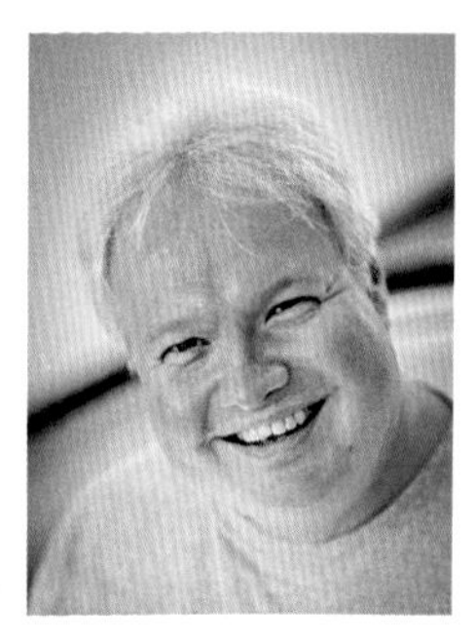

Rico Pfirstinger studied communications and has been working as a journalist, publicist, and photographer since the mid-'80s. He has written numerous books on a diverse range of topics, from computing technology to digital desktop publishing to sled dog racing. He worked as the department head of special assignments for Hubert Burda Media in Munich, Germany, and he also served as chief editor for a winter sports website.

After eight years as a freelance film critic in Los Angeles, Rico now lives in Germany and devotes his time to digital photography and compact camera systems.

Rico writes the popular X-Pert Corner blog and leads workshops called Fuji X Secrets where he offers insights, tips, and tricks on using the Fujifilm X-series cameras. He is also a regular contributor in the Gear Talk section of *FUJI-LOVE* magazine.

Rico Pfirstinger

The Fujifilm X100VI

130 X-Pert Tips to Get the Most
Out of Your Camera

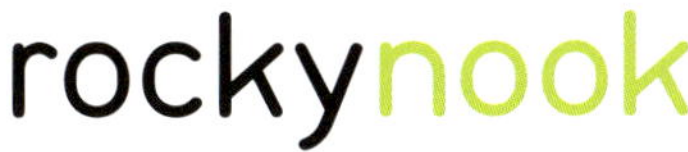

The Fujifilm X100VI
130 Tips to Get the Most Out of Your Camera
Rico Pfirstinger

Project editor: Maggie Yates
Project manager: Lisa Brazieal
Marketing coordinator: Koryn Olage
Layout and type: Petra Strauch
ISBN: 979-8-88814-273-8
1st Edition (1st printing, January 2025)
©2025 Rico Pfirstinger
All images ©Rico Pfirstinger unless otherwise noted

Rocky Nook Inc.
1010 B Street, Suite 350
San Rafael, CA 94901
USA

www.rockynook.com

Distributed in the UK and Europe by Publishers Group UK
Distributed in the U.S. and all other territories by Publishers Group West

Library of Congress Control Number: 2024944378

Printed in Dubai

Table of Contents

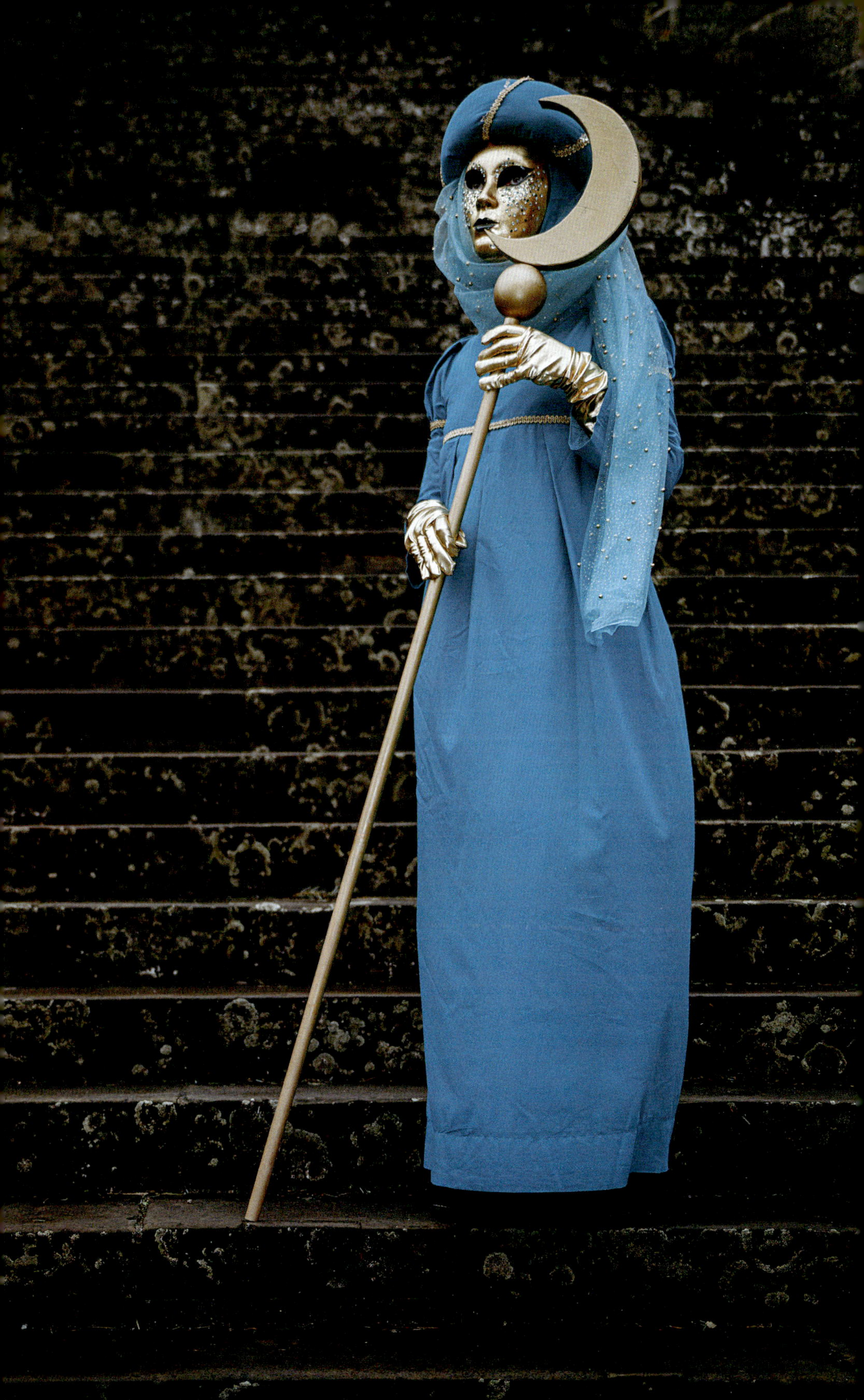

1. YOUR FUJIFILM X100VI

To start off, here's a brief overview of the buttons and controls on your Fujifilm X100VI:

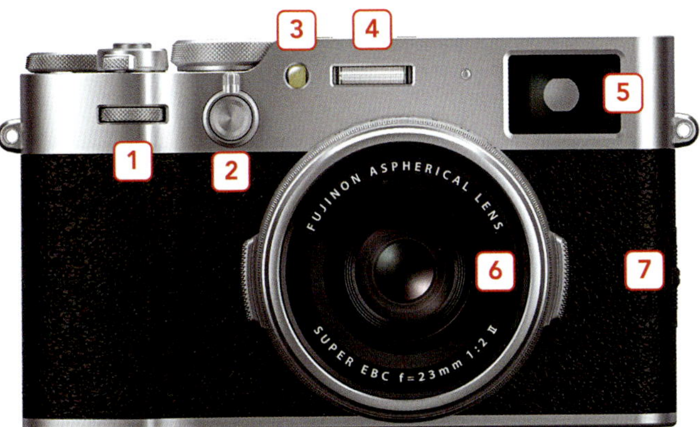

Fig. 1: X100VI frontal view: front command dial with integrated button (1), viewfinder selector with integrated Fn button (2), AF assist lamp / self-timer indicator lamp (3), built-in flash (4), hybrid viewfinder (5), 23mmF2 lens (6), focus selector at the side of the body (7)

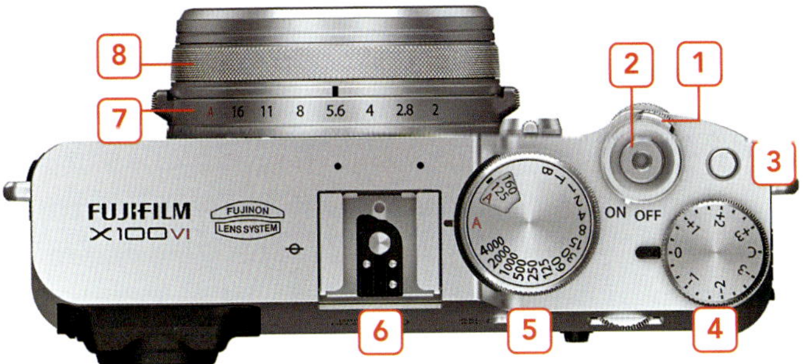

Fig. 2: X100VI top view: on/off switch (1), shutter release button (2), Fn button (3), exposure compensation dial (4), shutter speed dial with integrated ISO dial (5), hot shoe (6), aperture ring (7), focus ring (8)

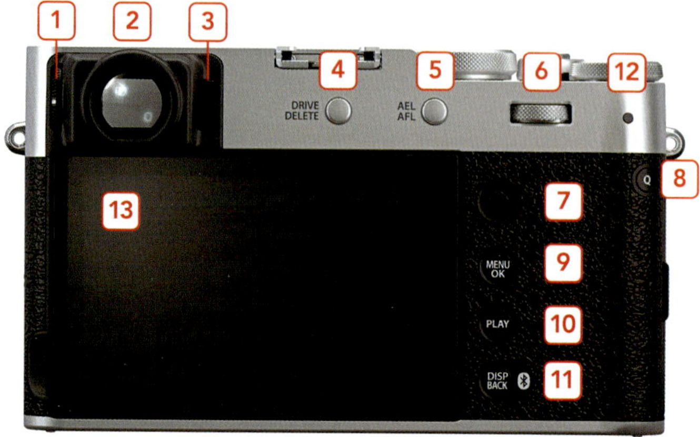

Fig. 3: X100VI rear view: diopter adjustment dial (1), hybrid view-finder (2), eye sensor (3), DRIVE/DELETE button (4), AE-L/AF-L button (5), rear command dial with integrated button (6), focus stick with integrated button (7), Q button for Quick menu (8), MENU/OK button (9), playback button (10), DISP/BACK button (11), status indicator lamp (12), LCD monitor (13)

In this first chapter, we will cover basics you should know about your camera, lens, and accessories.

| TIP 1 | RTFM! Read The Fuji Manual! |

In case you have misplaced your user manual, or you want to update to a newer edition of a manual, you can obtain downloadable PDF versions [1] in various supported languages. You will also find supplementary material that covers new features and changes based on firmware updates.

Please do yourself a favor and thoroughly study this manual to get acquainted with the functions of your X100VI. This book doesn't replace the X100VI camera manual; it serves as an *enhancement* and offers valuable tips and background information about using the various features and functions of the X100VI to make the most of your equipment.

Please note that this book is exclusively about using the camera for photography and doesn't include content about the camera's video features.

<table><tr><td>Spare batteries and third-party knockoffs</td><td>TIP 2</td></tr></table>

The X100VI is a compact camera, which means that its rechargeable battery is also rather small. Depending on how you use your camera, a fully charged battery will last for a few hundred shots.

I recommend setting the camera to one of its three Boost modes (SET UP > POWER MANAGEMENT > PERFORMANCE > BOOST) for maximum autofocus speed and the best overall performance.

Please note:

- The X100VI features an accurate battery indicator with five bars and a percentage display.

- In shooting mode, the percentage display is only available in the INFO display. To activate the INFO display, (repeatedly) press the DISP/BACK button until the INFO display appears. In playback mode, the percentage indicator is also available in the INFO display, which can be accessed by repeatedly moving the focus stick upward.

- When the battery indicator shows one remaining red bar, it's almost time to replace the battery.

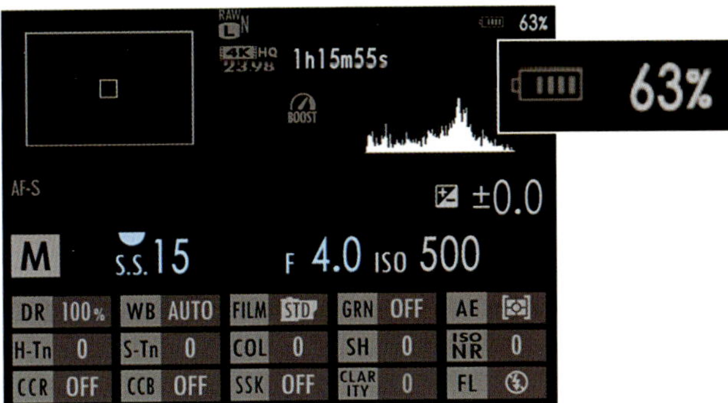

Fig. 4: In concert with original Fujifilm NP-W126S batteries, the INFO display of your X100VI features an accurate **battery power indicator**. In shooting mode, it can be accessed by repeatedly pressing the DISP/BACK button.

Your X100VI is using NP-W126S rechargeable batteries. You should not use older NP-W126-type batteries (without the "S"). Using the older type or unsuitable third-party knockoffs may impact the camera's performance.

The X100VI issues a warning when it detects an older NP-W126 battery. However, some third-party knockoffs simply *pretend* to be NP-W126S equivalents to circumvent this warning and trick you into believing that you bought a quality product.

You can obtain NP-W126S batteries from Fujifilm, or you can use compatible products from a variety of third-party vendors. Most aftermarket batteries do not offer the same quality, safety, and capacity as the more expensive Fujifilm batteries. You are likely to experience inaccurate battery life displays, and the camera may unexpectedly switch off with an empty battery even though the indicator showed there was some power left.

Also, many knockoffs don't feature an internal temperature sensor, so the camera or charger won't adjust the current to avoid overheating or damaging the battery. Instead, these batteries trick the camera or charger into believing that the battery temperature is always perfect. As a result, such batteries tend to become defective more frequently. A typical phenomenon of this is battery inflation ("swelling"), making it hard to remove a stuck battery from the camera slot.

Note: If you store your camera for several days (or longer) without a charged battery, the X100VI's built-in emergency power source may run out of juice, and all camera and user settings will reset to factory conditions.

TIP 3	Chargers and power supplies

The X100VI supports USB-C to power/charge the camera and to communicate with external devices. It's compatible with pretty much any USB power supply, so feel free to use the devices that you already use to power or charge your smartphone, tablet, or laptop. This includes car adapters and power banks that offer USB charging.

You can also use your computer's USB port as a power supply to charge the battery or to power the camera when it is on. To avoid confusion, have a look at NETWORK/USB SETTING > USB POWER SUPPLY SETTING, where you can manually select the role of the USB-C port when the camera is switched on and connected to a computer. You can force the port to act as a power supply only (POWER SUPPLY ON/COMM OFF) or as a mere communications link (POWER SUPPLY OFF/COMM ON). In most cases, the AUTO setting will do the job.

You can charge batteries in-camera or with an external charger. Fujifilm's official charger is the BC-W126S, which is on the large and expensive side. Personally, I use the Nitecore FX1, a small dual battery charger that works with any USB-A power source and features a display that shows the charging status, the charging current, and the temperature measured by the battery's internal sensor.

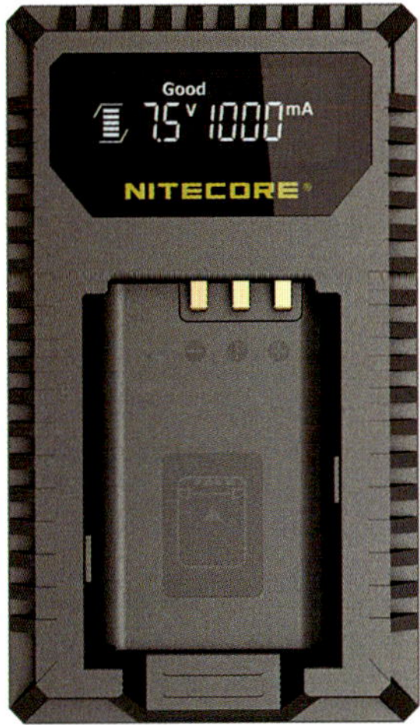

Fig. 5: The **Nitecore FX1** is my preferred external charger for Fujifilm's NP-W126S batteries.

<table>
<tr><td>**TIP 4**</td><td>**Which memory cards to use**</td></tr>
</table>

Boost your camera and relieve its built-in buffer memory by using the fastest UHS-I memory cards available. Fast memory cards give your camera an overall speed boost in shooting mode *and* in playback mode. Almost everything becomes snappier and more reactive.

Fujifilm entertains a website showing recommended memory cards that have been tested to be compatible with your camera [2].

Important: The X100VI doesn't support the faster UHS-II SD card standard, so using such cards is not only a waste of money, it could also result in subpar performance. A very fast UHS-II card isn't necessarily very fast in its UHS-I fallback mode.

Personally, I have been using SanDisk Extreme Pro UHS-I SD cards for many years. They offer an actual maximum write speed of approximately 90 MB/s. I say *actual* because newer incarnations of this card claim speeds up to 200 MB/s. Caveat: This speed boost only works in concert with a proprietary card reader and it refers to reading data, not writing it. So, when it comes to using them in your X100VI, newer versions of the card labeled "200 MB/s", "170 MB/s" or "100 MB/s" aren't writing your images faster than older ones labeled "95 MB/s".

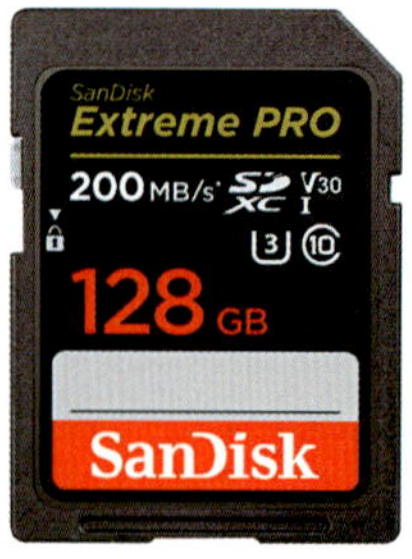

Fig. 6: Using a **fast UHS-I card** is essential to avoid data transmission bottlenecks. If money is an issue, you should always put speed before size. 128 GB conveniently hold more than 2500 RAW/JPEG pairs.

Where to find the latest firmware   **TIP 5**

- To check which firmware version is installed in your camera, switch the camera on while pressing and holding the DISP/BACK button.

- You can find and download the latest firmware versions for your camera online [3], where you can also find current versions of Fuji's application software, such as RAW File Converter EX [4].

- A step-by-step guide illustrating the firmware upgrade process is available online [5]. At Fujifilm's support website, macOS [6] and Windows [7] users can also find detailed firmware download instructions for their operating systems.

- If you can't find a new firmware version on Fuji's firmware update page, there's a good chance that your web browser is still caching an older version of this page. In this case, either delete your browser cache or force your browser to reload the webpage from the server.

Updating your firmware   **TIP 6**

- Make sure that your computer doesn't change the name of firmware files you download due to naming conflicts caused by previous firmware versions that are still residing in your download folder. The correct file name of the camera firmware for your X100VI is always FPUPDATE.DAT.

- Your battery should be fully charged when updating your firmware.

- Always copy new firmware files for your camera into the top directory of your SD memory card, and always use cards that have been freshly formatted in your camera.

After you have copied the firmware to the card, make sure to properly unmount the card from your computer before removing it.

■ To start the update process for your camera, switch it on while pressing and holding the DISP/BACK button and follow the instructions on the screen. If your camera is already on, you can use this menu command: SET UP > USER SETTING > FIRMWARE UPDATE.

■ Never switch the camera off during the update process. The camera will tell you when the update is complete. Only then can you safely switch it off.

| TIP 7 | Wireless firmware updates using Bluetooth and Wi-Fi |

Since your camera supports Bluetooth, you can perform wireless firmware updates using your smartphone or tablet and Fujifilm's free XApp [8], which is available for iOS and Android.

When your X100VI is paired with a wireless device via the XApp, the app will announce the availability of new camera firmware and offer to download it to your smartphone or tablet. From there, the firmware file is transferred to the camera via the camera's Wi-Fi hotspot.

Using the XApp is a convenient option for users who want to install new firmware without accessing a personal computer.

| TIP 8 | Use Boost mode! |

In its default NORMAL performance setting, the X100VI operates with limited performance to conserve power. To enjoy the camera's full capabilities, it's necessary to select SET UP > POWER MANAGEMENT > PERFORMANCE > BOOST. You can also program one of the camera's Fn or Touch-Fn buttons to activate Boost mode. Since the X100VI consumes more power in Boost mode, it's smart to always have replacement batteries at hand.

Boost mode offers better autofocus performance and a higher frame rate in the electronic real-time live view. In the X100VI, there are four different Boost mode options:

- EVF/LCD LOW LIGHT PRIORITY is a new setting that optimizes the live view for very dark scenes by reducing the frame rate. In situations that require long exposure times or very high ISO settings, this results in a clearer and more realistic live view image with less noise. In situations like this, the live view image can easily start to blur due to a massively decreased frame rate, so using the camera on a tripod is advisable.

- EVF/LCD RESOLUTION PRIORITY optimizes the resolution of the live view image. This mode is ideal for landscapes, portraits, etc.—pretty much everything that isn't very dark or involves high-speed action.

- EVF FRAME RATE PRIORITY (100P) increases the frame rate of the EVF to 100 fps. This can be useful for action scenes with moving subjects and/or panning shots.

Important: When the camera is set to ECONOMY mode, it will enter an energy saving mode after several seconds of user inactivity. This results in a dramatic reduction of the live view's frame rate and brightness. As soon as a button is pushed or a dial is turned, the live view goes back to normal. Also note that the frame rate and brightness reduction in ECONOMY mode don't occur when the camera is connected to an external USB-C power source.

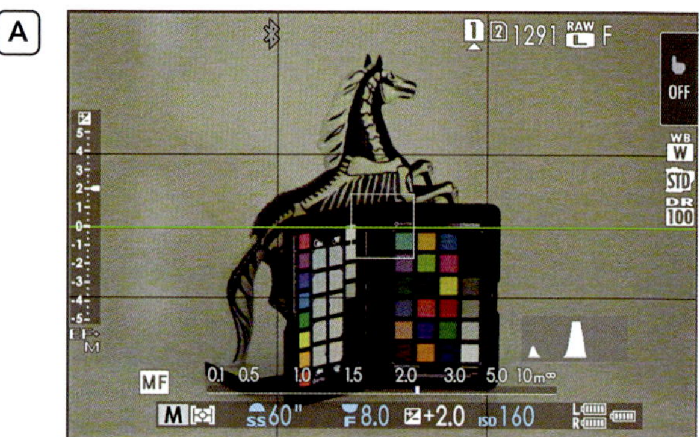

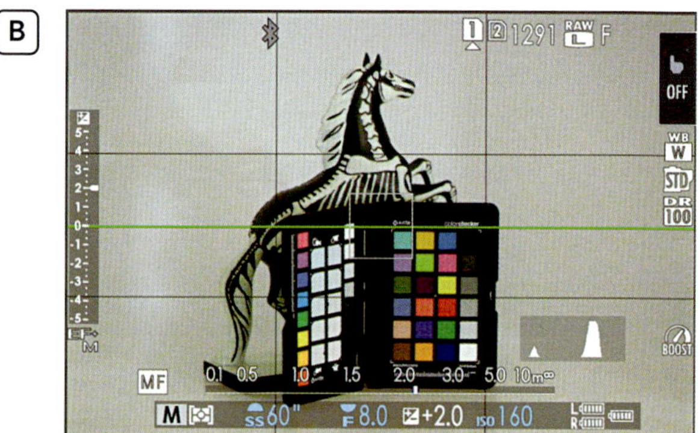

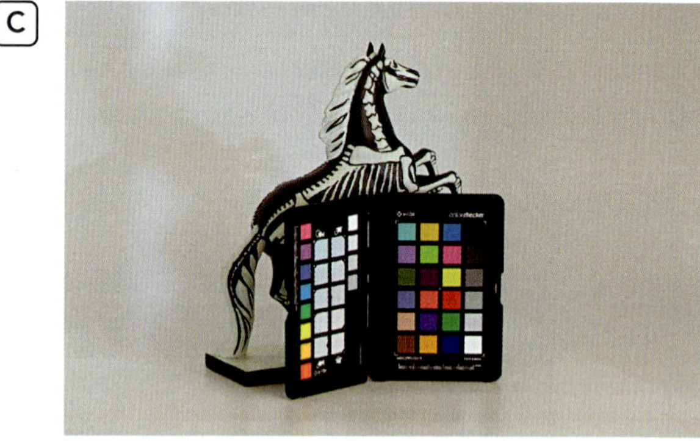

Fig. 7: This example illustrates the **difference between NORMAL and EVF/LCD LOW LIGHT PRIORITY BOOST** performance settings. I was pointing the camera at a dimly lit scene with a manual exposure setting of 60 sec. In NORMAL mode (**A**), the live view appears very noisy. It's also underexposed and doesn't correctly simulate the set exposure. In EVF/LCD LOW LIGHT PRIORITY BOOST mode (**B**), the live view looks much clearer, and this time, the exposure simulation is quite realistic. The final image (**C**) is the actual straight-out-of-camera JPEG that the camera produced after taking the shot.

Obviously, EVF/LCD LOW LIGHT PRIORITY BOOST mode is preferable in extreme low-light situations. However, we should still be careful: If you further reduce the incoming light and increase the exposure time to compensate, even EVF/LCD LOW LIGHT PRIORITY BOOST mode may not be capable of correctly simulating the resulting image brightness in the live view. Of course, this also applies to long daytime exposure shots that are taken with very strong neutral density (ND) filters.

<table><tr><td>**Keeping the sensor clean**</td><td>TIP 9</td></tr></table>

Select SET UP > USER SETTING > SENSOR CLEANING > OK to momentarily activate the built-in cleaning mechanism that helps loosen dust particles. By default, this mechanism will be employed when you switch *off* the camera. I recommend setting the camera to also activate this mechanism when the X100VI is switched *on*: to do this, select SET UP > USER SETTING > SENSOR CLEANING > WHEN SWITCHED ON > ON.

<table><tr><td>**Pixel mapping**</td><td>TIP 10</td></tr></table>

Your X100VI includes an automatic pixel-mapping feature. To use it, select IMAGE QUALITY SETTING > PIXEL MAPPING. Pixel mapping detects defective pixels on your sensor and maps them out, meaning they are interpolated with the information of adjacent pixels. Since the number of hot pixels increases with sensor temperature, pixel mapping is only available when the camera hasn't already heated up.

Please note that a few defective pixels are perfectly normal in every digital camera. As the sensor ages (even when the camera is not in use), the number of dead pixels increases. In addition to the manufacturing process, defective pixels are also caused by cosmic radiation. For example, frequently taking your camera on long-haul flights will increase the risk.

Knowing all this, it's a good idea to regularly use the pixel-mapping function to keep the defective pixel map inside your camera up to date. It takes just a few seconds.

<table><tr><td>TIP 11</td><td>Using IBIS</td></tr></table>

The X100VI offers In Body Image Stabilization (IBIS) to prevent camera shake and blurry images in situations that require you to take handheld shots at a slower-than-usual shutter speed.

IBIS is controlled through the camera menu. In SHOOTING SETTING > IS MODE, you can choose between two basic IBIS modes:

- **IS mode 1** (CONTINUOUS) is the default setting. It's always stabilizing the image, even when you are just looking through the viewfinder before you press the shutter button.

- **IS mode 2** (SHOOTING ONLY) engages only when you fully depress the shutter button to take an image (or half-press the button in AF-C mode).

These are my recommendations for using IBIS:

- When you are using very fast shutter speeds that don't require image stabilization, you can safely turn IBIS off to eliminate it as a potential interference. That said, I didn't switch off the IBIS in concert with fast shutter speeds during my testing, and I haven't experienced any issues.

- Turn off IBIS when you are working from a good tripod or with shutter speeds that are slower than a second. Of course, this decision very much depends on the sturdiness of the tripod, prevailing wind conditions, and vibrations caused by traffic. Shooting in "vibrant" cities, one encounters many situations in which leaving IBIS on is a good idea, even with the sturdiest of tripods.

- You might also want to switch IBIS off for panning shots in case you find it difficult to smoothly track your subject with IBIS turned on.

- IBIS (especially mode 2) is known to interfere with long time exposures on tripods that last several seconds or minutes, so I strongly recommend turning it off for long exposures of more than a second.

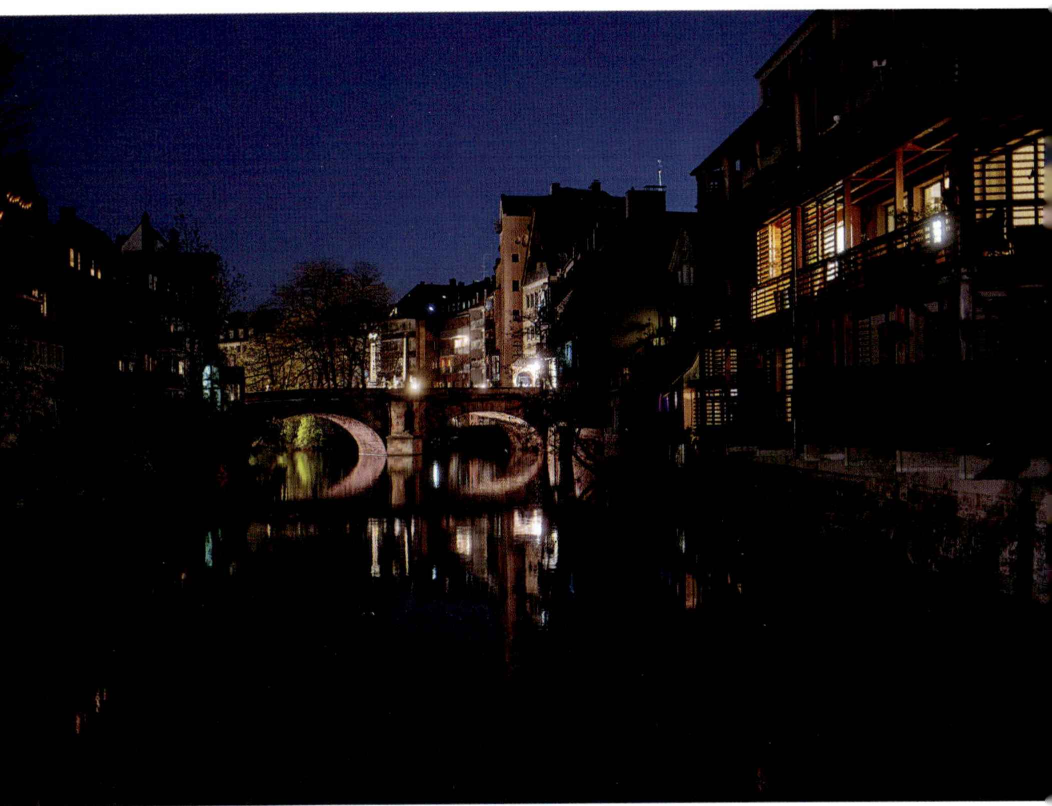

Fig. 8: IBIS in action: Thanks to image stabilization, I could use a shutter speed of 1/2 sec. for this handheld night shot. The IBIS was able to successfully compensate for camera shake caused by my hands.

<table>
<tr><td>TIP 12</td><td>Wide-angle and tele conversion lenses</td></tr>
</table>

The X100 series is famous for its built-in 23mmF2 lens. Many things changed and improved during the journey from the X100 Classic to the X100VI, but the focal length (which corresponds to a 35mm lens in full-frame terms) and brightness of the lens remained the same.

For added flexibility, you can attach wide (WCL-X100 & WCL-X100II) or tele conversion lenses (TCL-X100 & TCL-X100II) to your X100VI. The WCLs convert the focal length of the X100VI to 19mm, the TCLs turn it into a 33mm outfit. In full-frame equivalency terms, this corresponds to 28mm and 50mm lenses. Adding a WCL or TCL doesn't impact the speed of the resulting lens, so the aperture numbers on your camera remain valid.

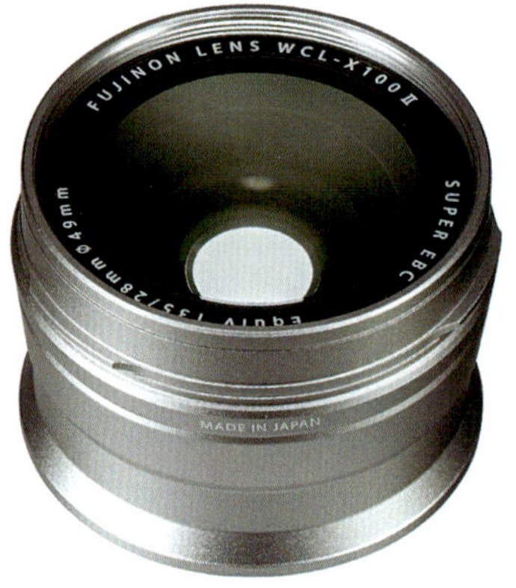
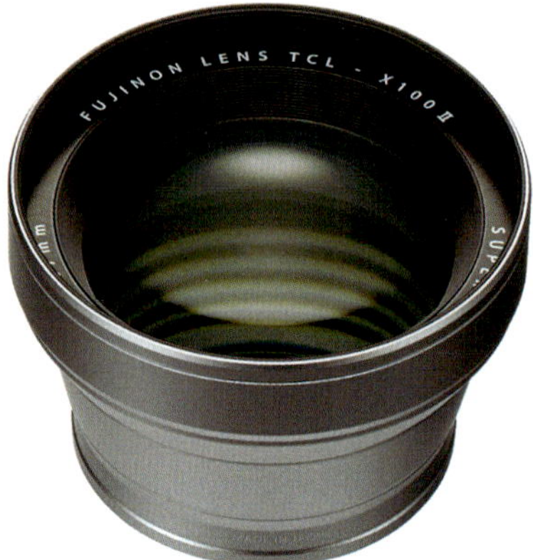

Fig. 9: The **WCL-X100(II) and TCL-X100(II)** conversion lenses are screw-mount adapters that connect directly to the built-in 23mmF2 lens of your X100VI.

Optically, there is *no* difference between the older and the newer "type II" versions of the wide and tele conversion adapters. It's just a matter of convenience—the newer versions are automatically recognized by the X100VI when you attach and remove them from the camera's lens, the older are not. Instead, you must go to the SHOOTING SETTING > CONVERSION LENS menu and tell the camera when you attach or remove an older conversion lens (WIDE, TELE, or OFF).

If you already own a legacy WCL-X100 or TCL-X100 converter from a previous X100 series camera, you can keep using it. Just don't forget to tell the camera when a conversion lens has been attached or removed. Here's why:

- The WCL and TCL conversion lenses require custom digital lens corrections for distortion, vignetting, and chromatic aberration. These corrections can only be properly applied (or stored in the RAW metadata) if the camera knows that a WCL or TCL has been attached.

- When you attach a first-generation WCL or TCL and forget to tell the camera, the X100VI will apply the wrong correction data and image quality will suffer.

- The same happens when you remove a first-generation WCL and TCL and forget to tell the camera. The X100VI still believes that a conversion lens is attached and acts accordingly; the wrong lens correction data will be used and image quality will suffer.

- Telling the camera about a WCL or TCL also adjusts the size and position of the bright frame and AF frames in the optical viewfinder (OVF). It also adjusts the electronic distance and depth-of-field scales in the viewfinder or LCD monitor.

- IBIS relies on knowing the effective focal length of the camera's lens.

The newer type-II conversion lenses can save you from forgetting to tell the camera about attaching or removing WCLs and TCLs. If you are a frequent user of a first-generation WCL or TCL, I recommend adding the CONVERSION LENS menu option to the camera's MY MENU for quick and easy access. You can edit the MY MENU with SET UP > USER SETTING > MY MENU SETTING.

Please note that conversion lenses like the TCL-X100II can mask the internal flash.

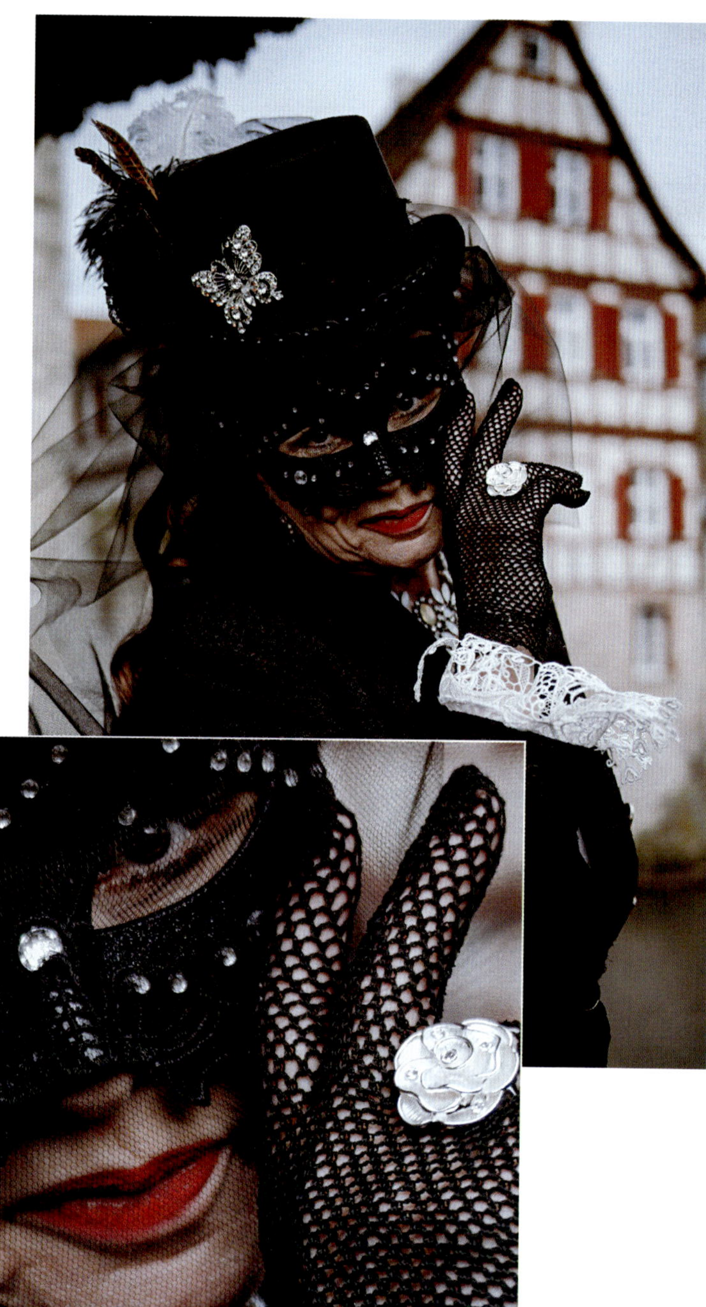

Fig. 10: I like using my old **TCL-100** (originally obtained for my X100 Classic) for portrait work with the X100VI. Shot wide-open at f/2, the resolution is perfectly adequate for 40 MP, yet not too harsh or clinical, as illustrated by this straight-out-of-camera (SOOC) JPEG.

What you should know about digital lens corrections	TIP 13

Most modern lenses achieve their optimal image quality through a combination of optical and digital corrections. Corrections are mostly applied to the three following phenomena:

- **Vignetting:** This effect results in a loss of brightness from center to corner. Vignetting [9] is more pronounced at large (open) apertures.

- **Distortion:** There are pincushion- and barrel-type distortions [10], both of which make straight lines seem curved. The lens in your X100VI has already been optically corrected for distortion.

- **Chromatic aberration:** Chromatic aberration [11] results in color fringing. This effect can be corrected (or mitigated) with apochromatic lenses, or digitally corrected during RAW conversion.

Some camera makers rely on dedicated correction profiles that must be provided by each RAW converter maker. Fujifilm isn't one of these companies: all current Fujifilm cameras store digital corrections as metadata in the RAW file. RAW converters can access this lens-specific metadata and use it to apply appropriate corrections. This way, the built-in RAW converter and external RAW conversion software, such as Lightroom or Capture One, can use the metadata in the RAW file to correct or mitigate vignetting, distortion, and chromatic aberration.

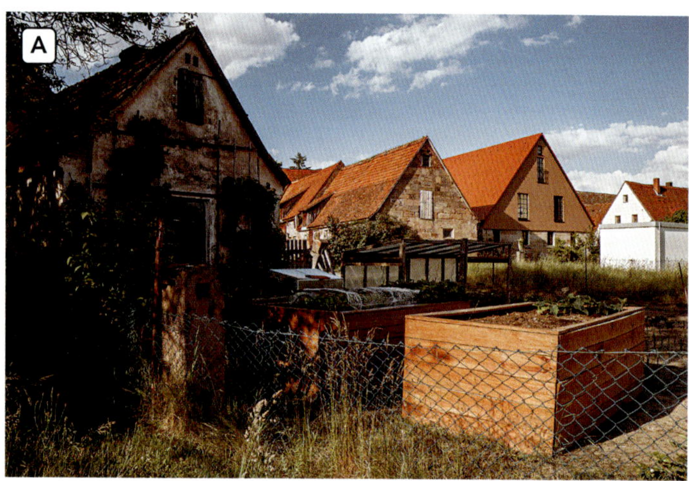

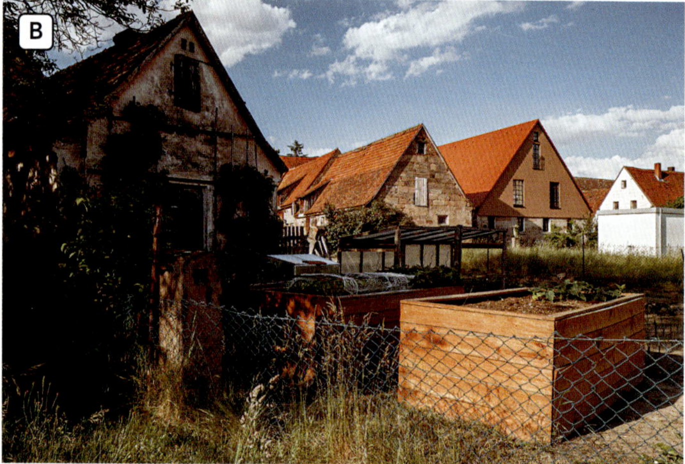

Fig. 11: This example was taken with an WCL-X100 conversion lens. In image **A**, the **digital lens correction metadata** was ignored. As a result, there's visible barrel distortion caused by the WCL. Image **B** shows the same shot, but this time with digital lens correction metadata, which is automatically applied to in-camera JPEGs and by compatible RAW converters such as Adobe Lightroom.

TIP 14	Use a lens hood!

The X100VI doesn't come with an included lens hood. However, there are several offerings from Fujifilm and aftermarket manufacturers. Apart from its optical benefits (especially the reduction of flare in backlit scenes), a lens hood protects the lens and the front glass element from damage.

Lens hoods can pose problems, too: they make the lens appear bigger than it is, and they can shade the camera flash or the autofocus assist light.

My personal choice of lens hood is the original Fujifilm LH-X100. This hood comes with an AR-X100 adapter ring and is compatible with the WCL-X100 and WCL-X100II wide-angle conversion lenses. Thanks to the AR-X100, it is also compatible with standard 49mm lens caps that I prefer over the clumsy and easy-to-lose metal cap that comes with the camera.

If you like the Fujifilm LH-X100 but find it too expensive, you might want to have a look at third-party knockoffs like the JJC LH-X100 that includes a JJC LA-49X100 adapter ring. Like the original, this affordable alternative is available in silver or black.

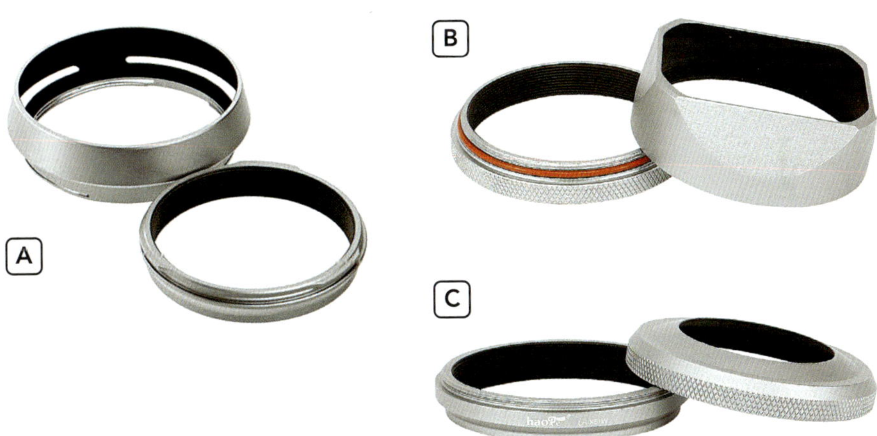

Fig. 12: Different **lens hood** styles: The LH-X100 from Fujifilm (**A**) and the LH-X54 from Haoge (**B**). The LH-X100 and its knockoffs are compatible with the WCL-X100(II) wide-angle conversion lens. If you are a frequent user of the X100VI's internal flash, you might want to consider a super-slim lens hood like the Haoge LH-X51 (**C**).

A stylish third-party alternative to the LH-X100 is the LH-X54 lens hood from Haoge. Like the original LH-X100, it is available in black and silver to match the color of your X100VI. It also comes with an adapter ring that serves the same purpose as the AR-X100 and allows connecting filters with a 49mm thread. However, due to the inward shape of the hood, standard 49mm lens caps don't fit when the LH-X54 lens hood is screwed on.

Like conversion lenses, lens hoods can mask the internal flash, so you may want to remove them in this case. The Haoge LH-X54 is more flash-friendly than the LH-X100 from Fujifilm or JJC. That said, it still adds a visible shadow to the lower part of the image. If you heavily rely on the built-in flash, you might want to have a look at a super-slim option like the Haoge LH-X51.

TIP 15 Lens protection filters

Digital cameras like the X100VI don't require the UV or skylight filters that used to be very popular in the days of analog film photography. This means that a permanently affixed filter has no optical purpose on your X100VI, and only serves as protective glass and weather sealing. Additional glass can have a detrimental effect on image quality, especially for night photographs or images shot against a bright light source. Filters increase the chance of ghosting, unwanted reflections, and a loss of contrast.

I recommend using protective glass only in situations that require this additional protective layer. In most situations, a metal lens hood like the LH-X100 should provide sufficient protection. If you still decide to use a filter, make sure to choose a high-quality product. With the PRF-49 (available in black and silver), Fujifilm offers a high-quality protective filter for your X100VI and the WCL-X100(II). There's also a 67mm filter that fits the TCL-X100(II).

Like its predecessor, the X100VI is weather resistant, meaning it is sealed against moisture and dust. However, the free-moving front lens element is a weak spot. To achieve *full* weather sealing, the front lens element must be covered with either a screw-in filter (via an AR-X100 or compatible adapter ring) or with a WCL/TCL conversion lens. Any 49mm screw-in filter will do the job, including popular diffusion filters such as Tiffen Black Pro Mist or Glimmerglass.

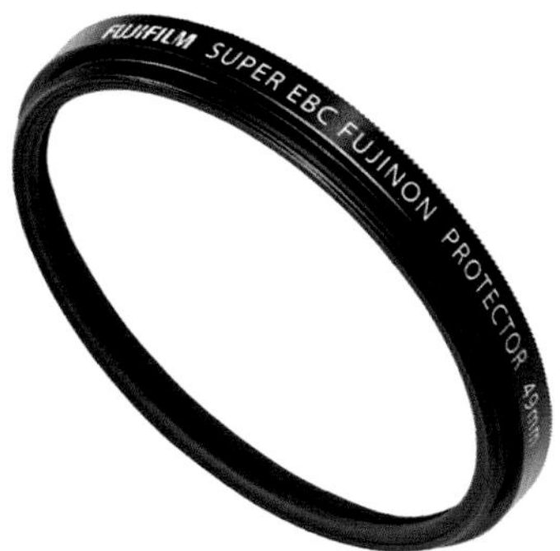

Fig. 13: In terms of image quality, the **Fujifilm PRF-49** protection filter is the best way to render the X100VI fully weather-sealed. To match your camera's color, it is available in silver and black versions.

Important: The X100VI uses screw-in filters with a diameter of 49mm, such as the Fujifilm PRF-49S. However, to install a 49mm filter on the camera's 23mmF2 lens, you must use an AR-X100 (or compatible) adapter ring which is not included with the X100VI. It is part of the LH-X100 lens hood package, though. If you use a WCL-X100(II) or TCL-X100(II) conversion lens, you can directly attach filters with diameters of either 49mm or 67mm—no adapter ring required. Never install filters directly on the 23mmF2 lens without a suitable adapter ring, as this may damage its autofocus mechanism.

<table><tr><td>TIP 16</td><td>**Remote shutter release options**</td></tr></table>

Now and then you may encounter situations that require you to remotely release the shutter to avoid vibration. A quick-and-dirty method is using the camera's self-timer with a delay of either two or ten seconds, although a better way is using a remote shutter release. Your X100VI features different options to connect remote shutter releases:

- A mechanical thread in the shutter button allows you to connect a traditional mechanical cable release.

- You can connect electronic remote shutter releases to the camera's microphone port (a 2.5mm input). This port uses a popular Canon remote shutter release standard. One of many compatible options is Fujifilm's own RR-100 trigger. However, my personal preference is the sleek and affordable Canon RS-60 E3.

- Bluetooth-equipped phones and tablets running the Fujifilm XApp, or compatible Bluetooth devices like Fujifilm's tripod grip TG-BT1.

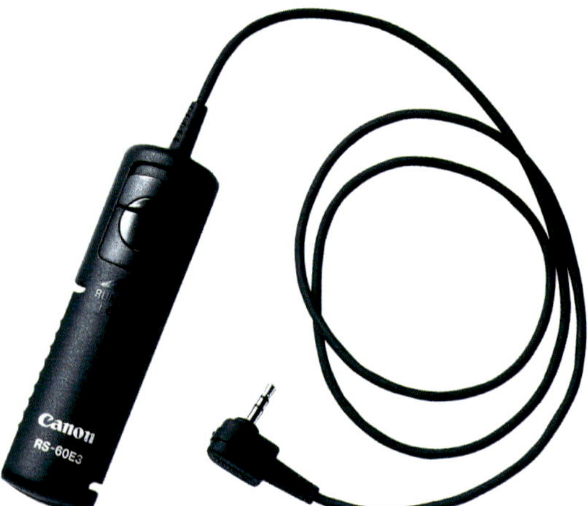

Fig. 14: The **Canon RS-60 E3** is my preferred electronic cable release for Fujifilm cameras with an RR-100 port.

TIP 17

In my opinion, a good handgrip can make a big difference. For the X100VI, I can recommend the SmallRig 4555 grip. It comes with an integrated Arca Swiss tripod plate and an L-shaped handle bead that, in my opinion, really improves the handling of the camera. You still have full access to the battery and memory card compartment.

Not a SmallRig fan? A similar product to the SmallRig 4555 is the JJC HG-X100VI. Both grips are available in silver or black.

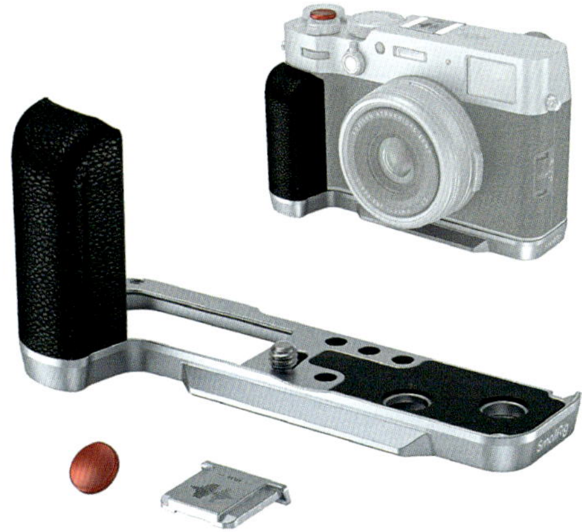

Fig. 15: The **SmallRig 4555** is my preferred handgrip for the X100VI. It comes with a few extras: a flash hot shoe cover and a red quick release button. Be cautious of the latter, though: Quick release buttons can cause severe damage to your camera as they sometimes get stuck in photo bags, literally ripping the shutter button out of the camera body when you remove it from the bag.

Rectangular filter holder and filters

TIP 18

If you want to use ND filters, graduated ND filters or a polarizer with your X100VI, I can recommend the NiSi filter system that was specifically designed for the X100 series. You can attach the filter holder directly to the 23mm lens (no adapter ring required). The filter holder accepts up to two rectangular filters at the same time, and there's a nice selection of small and affordable high-quality filters available. I recommend the "Professional Kit" that comes with a carry case and a useful selection of filters that include a circular polarizer, a Natural Night filter, a 3-stop ND, and a 3-stop GND filter.

You can then add more filters to your collection, like 6-stop and 10-stop ND filters that can be very useful for long exposures in bright daylight. In my tests, the ND filters' color tint was easy to correct in Lightroom to match it with an unfiltered shot, and infrared light was effectively filtered. Of course, rectangular ND filters can be combined with the X100VI's built-in 4-stop ND filter.

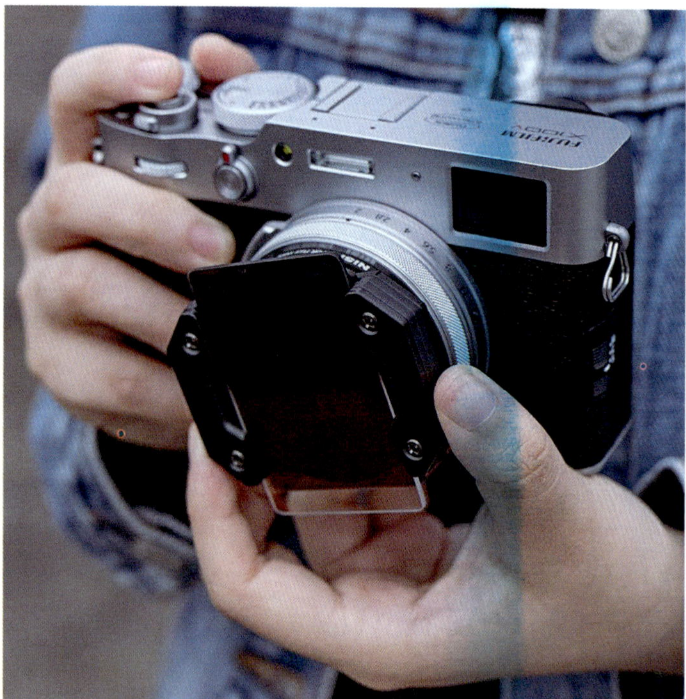

Fig. 16: The **NiSi filter system** was designed for the X100 series and is my recommended choice for the X100VI. It is small and affordable, and unlike the much larger and more expensive 100mm and 150mm filter systems for my X and GFX cameras, I happily bring the NiSi system along on trips. I have bought a complete set of filters, and everything fits in two palm-sized carrying cases.

<table><tr><td>Diffusion filters</td><td>TIP 19</td></tr></table>

The X100VI is very popular on TikTok, YouTube and with content creators who advocate a retro chic that emulates the analog film shooting experience. With its retro-style handling, 20 film simulations and a large array of JPEG settings, the X100VI is the perfect camera for this. You can create looks that mimic grainy prints with a strong '70s and '80s vibe, and you can do so straight out of camera.

There's one "problem," though: The modern lens in the X100VI is very refined, sharp, and delivers good contrast. After all, it was designed for the camera's 40 MP APS-C sensor. To achieve a believable retro look with diminished contrast, having a certain amount of organic softness and halation is a bonus. This is where diffusion filters come into play: Not only do they soften harsh details (great for portraits), but they also add a glow to bright highlights and reduce the contrast between adjacent bright and dark parts of a scene.

These filters are quite popular for movie making, where directors of photography often face a similar dilemma: The sensors of modern digital movie cameras are too "good" and too "clinical." Hence, it's no surprise that professional (and quite expensive) diffusion filters like Black Pro-Mist or Glimmerglass (both from The Tiffen Company) have become more popular than ever. It's about the beauty of imperfection.

You can easily find YouTubers and influencers who permanently shoot with Tiffen Glimmerglass 1, basically using it as an always-on protection filter to fully weather-seal their X100V or X100VI. I've tried this approach but found that it would only serve me well if I wanted to shoot soft (and possibly grainy) retro images all the time. However, I want to be more flexible. Here's what I'm using my Tiffen Glimmerglass 1 filter for:

- Portrait shoots. The filter maintains fine detail but enhances the skin by softening blemishes.

Fig. 17: These straight-out-of-camera (SOOC) JPEGs illustrate my use-cases for a diffusion filter on the X100VI. All eight samples were shot with a 49mm **Tiffen Glimmerglass 1** filter without external processing or corrections. Everything—including cropping and resizing—happened in-camera. In the context of this book, "100% created in-camera without external processing" is what I mean when I refer to "SOOC" or straight out of camera.

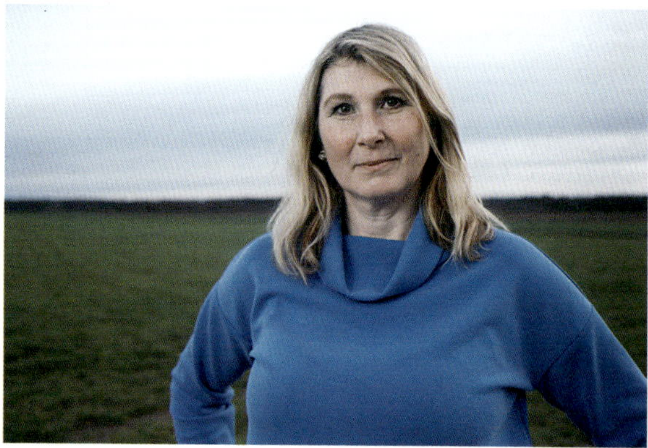

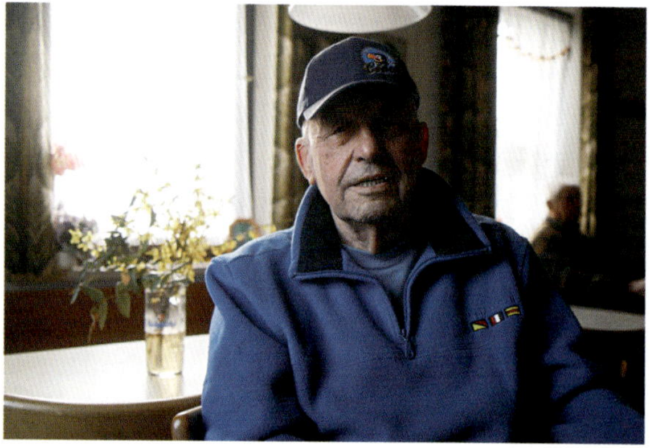

- Night scenes with specular highlights. Scenes with bright city lights and harsh contrast become more atmospheric.

- High-contrast scenes that benefit from a mellow, organic look and atmosphere, for example an indoor shoot with light falling in through windows.

While it's possible to create diffusion effects digitally in Photoshop, it's easier and more fun to do it in-camera. For me, it's a more pleasant and hands-on experience. It's the real thing vs. digital effects.

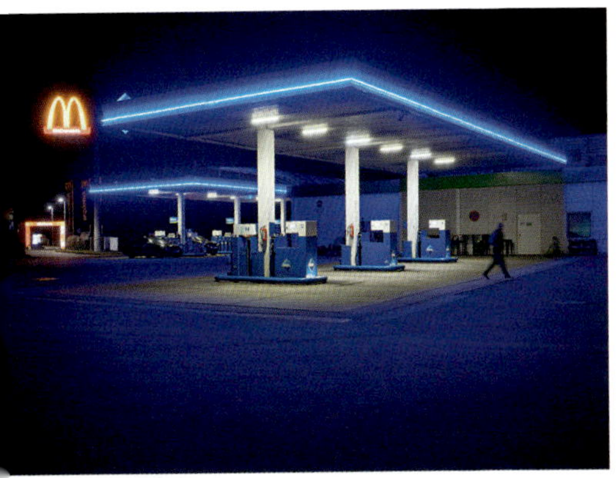

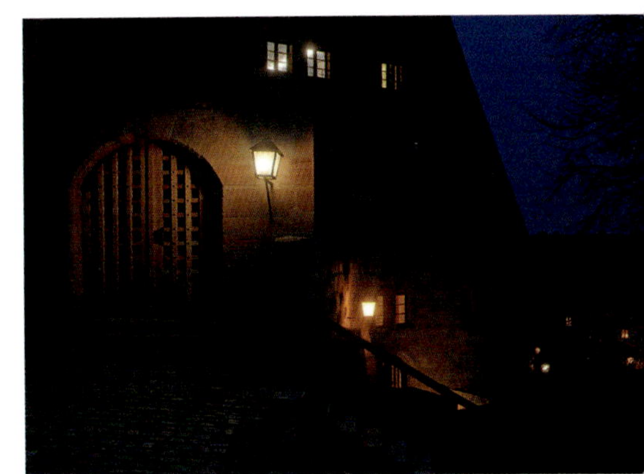

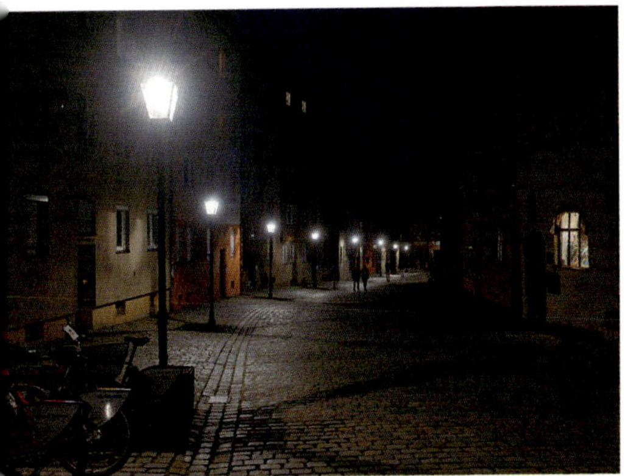

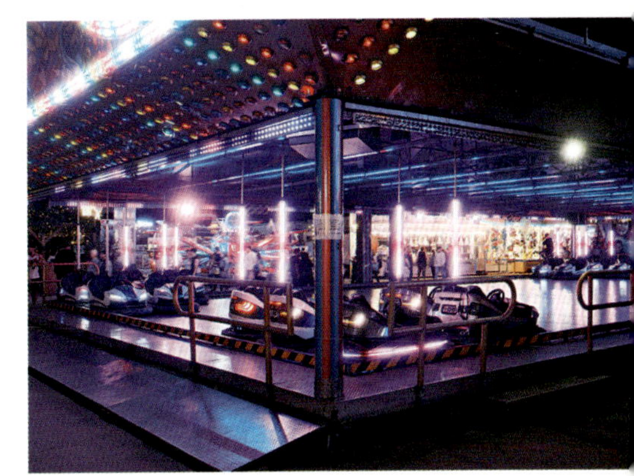

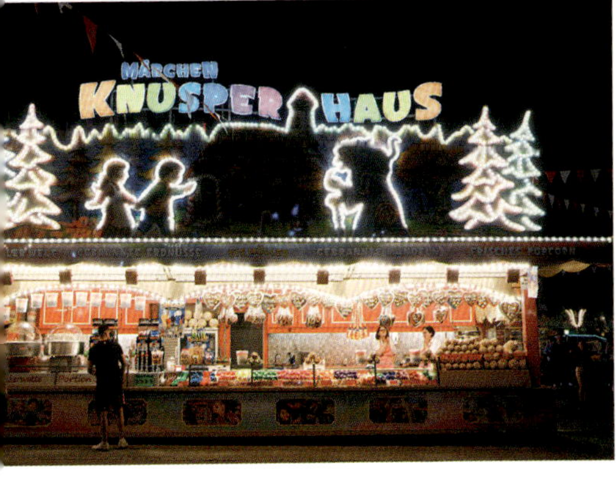
MÄRCHEN
KNUSPER HAUS

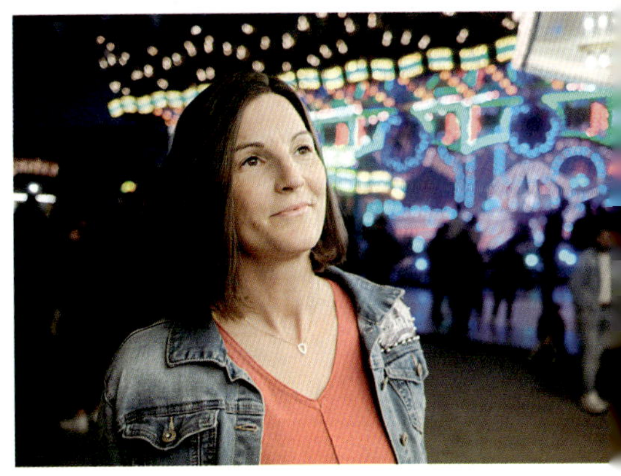

<table>
<tr><td>TIP 20</td><td>Fisheye Fun</td></tr>
</table>

Want to try something crazy? Get a fisheye lens adapter! I bought a cheap one on Amazon with a 58mm thread, so I also needed a step-up ring from 49mm to 58mm. This 0.25x "Minadax" adapter was even available in silver to fit the color of my X100VI.

On APS-C and in concert with the 23mm lens, it produces an *almost* circular image that's best covered with a 5:4 aspect ratio in your image size settings. Connect it to a WCL-X100(II), and you get a fully circular result that is best covered with a square (1:1) aspect ratio.

In case you forgot: You can adjust the aspect ratio and resolution of your JPEGs in the IMAGE QUALITY SETTING > IMAGE SIZE menu.

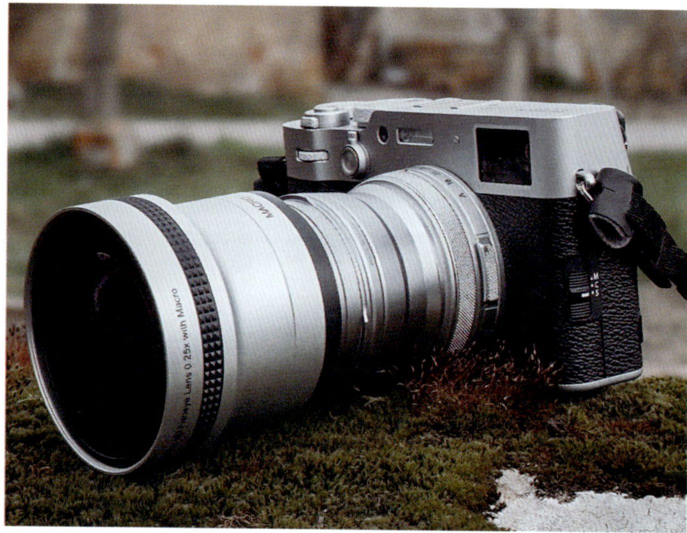

Fig. 18: This contraption is my X100VI with a WCL-X100, 49-to-52-to-58mm step-up rings and a cheap **"Minadax" 0.25x fisheye adapter** that I found on Amazon.

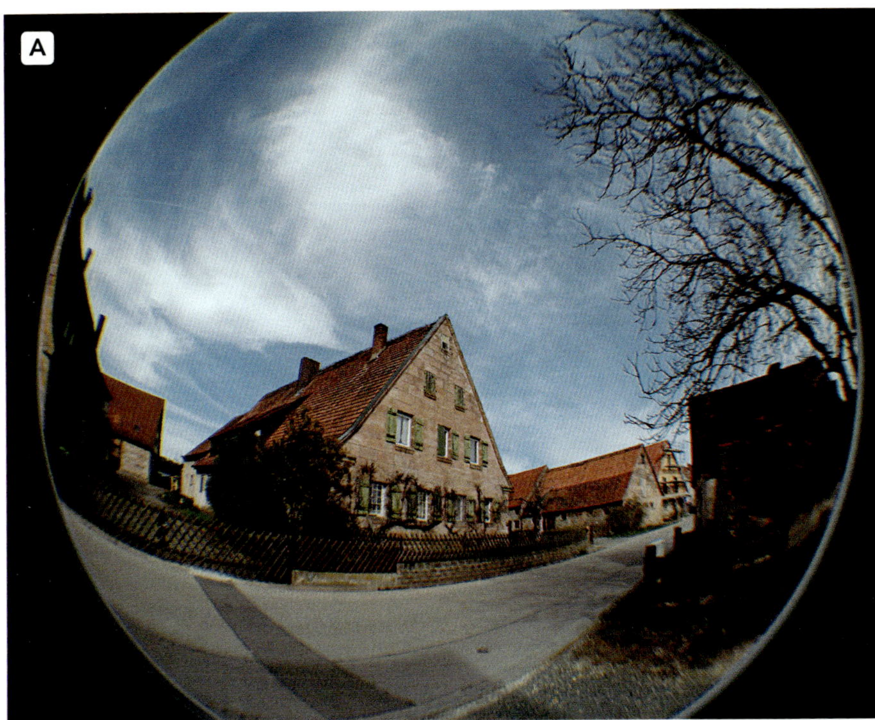

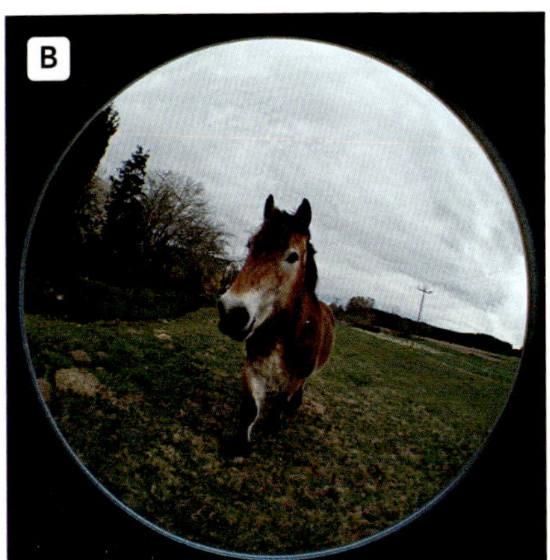

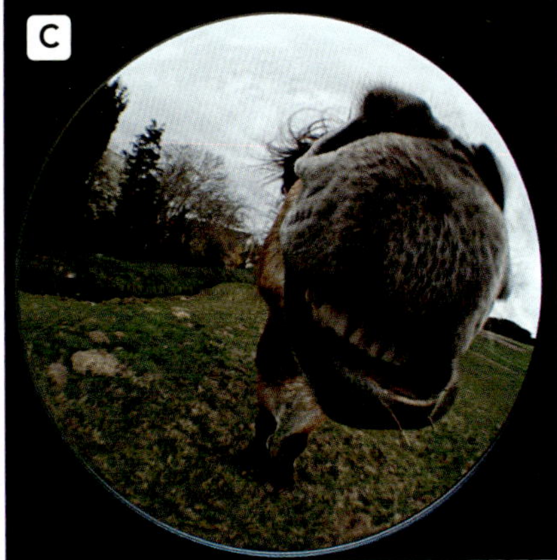

Fig. 19: With the **fisheye adapter**, image quality is nothing to write home about. Like Instax, it's all about the fun. Attached to the lens (via an AR-X100-compatible adapter ring), the fisheye adapter works best with a 5:4 aspect ratio (image **A**). In concert with a WCL-X100(II), you get fully circular results (images **B** and **C**) that work best with a square output. All these samples are straight-out-of-camera (SOOC) JPEGs. And yes, autofocus works flawlessly with this weird combo.

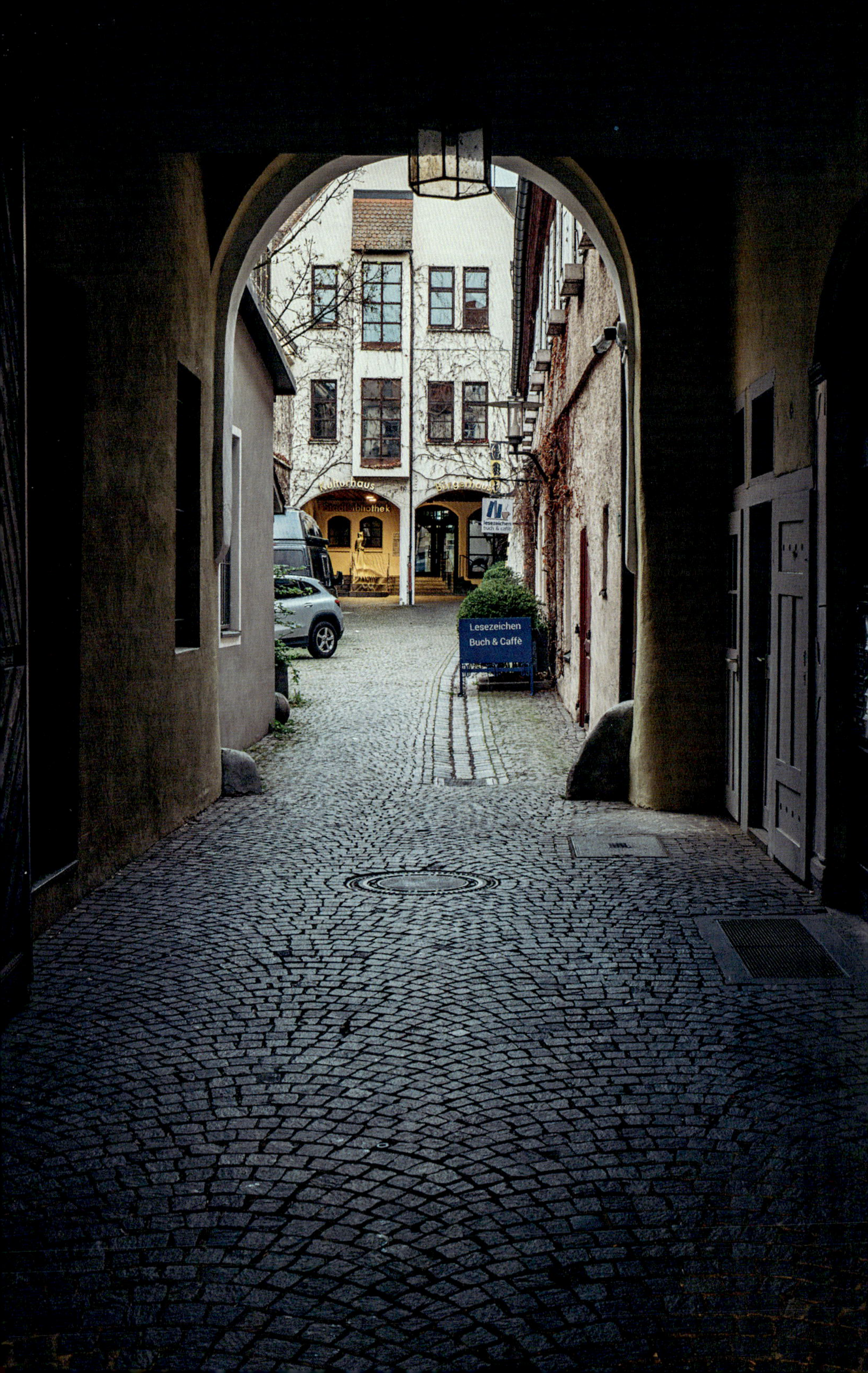

Kulturhaus
Stadtbibliothek
Bürgerhaus
Lesezeichen
buch & caffè
Lesezeichen
Buch & Caffè

2. USING THE FUJIFILM X100VI

2.1 READY, SET, GO!

New users often ask how to find the perfect settings for their camera. Short answer: there are no perfect settings. If they existed, Fuji could have saved us the trouble of navigating the menu options and simply implemented those "ideal settings" as the factory default.

That said, allow me to suggest some basic settings that are meant to provide good overall performance along with as much flexibility and user-friendliness as possible.

- Many settings (such as film simulation modes, color saturation, contrast, sharpness, noise reduction, film grain effect, etc.) belong in the "JPEG settings" category. They don't affect the RAW files but only affect the straight-out-of-camera JPEGs that are generated during RAW conversion. These settings aren't global or camera-specific—they are *image-specific,* and each image can be adjusted individually.

- In addition to the recommended standard settings, there are many shortcuts and key combinations that can make selecting the optimal camera settings for any situation much easier.

<table>
<tr><td>TIP 21</td><td>Recommended settings for your X100VI</td></tr>
</table>

There is no perfect set of basic camera settings that could suit all users in all situations. However, the following settings will allow you to use the X100VI in a flexible manner with good overall performance:

- Select **FINE+RAW** or **NORMAL+RAW** under IMAGE QUALITY SETTING > IMAGE QUALITY. This will get you high-resolution out-of-camera JPEGs (digital prints) *and* flexible RAW files (digital negatives). Using the RAW files, you can create a variety of diverse JPEGs with different looks and settings using the camera's built-in RAW converter (PLAYBACK MENU > RAW CONVERSION). Specifically, you can adjust JPEG parameters such as white balance, film simulation, contrast, brightness, noise reduction, and color saturation. This enables you to create different versions of a shot from a single RAW file; for example, you can make color and black-and-white versions of the same image, including different contrast settings. You don't have to worry about finding the perfect JPEG settings prior to taking a shot because you can always change and optimize those settings afterward in the camera's internal RAW converter.

- Do *not* use the HEIF format, at least for now. Instead, set IMAGE QUALITY > SELECT JPEG/HEIF to JPEG. Theoretically, the HEIF format is the superior choice: it's smaller and offers a higher bit-depth with less compression artifacts than JPEG. However, Fujifilm's HEIF format appears to be incompatible with many applications and operating systems. For example, macOS and iOS change the tonality (contrast, colors) of imported Fujifilm HEIF files, so your images look different (as in, worse) than they looked in-camera. This appears to be a specific issue with Fujifilm's version of 10-bit HEIF images. Also, functions such as Clarity or Adobe RGB aren't available in concert with the HEIF format.

- Make sure to use the **mechanical shutter** as your default shutter setting by selecting SHOOTING SETTING > SHUTTER TYPE > MS. Using of the electronic shutter (ES) can create all kinds of issues and should be limited to situations that require high burst rates up to 20 fps or shutter speeds faster than 1/4000 sec. You can also select M+E in SHUTTER TYPE if you want the X100VI to automatically switch from MS to ES when the shutter speed exceeds 1/4000 sec., or if the aperture setting requires it to preserve the bokeh quality.

- As a typical standard setting, most photographers use **single shot drive** (select STILL IMAGE in the menu of the DRIVE button) and **single shot autofocus** (AF-S; select S with the focus selector at the side of the camera).

- The most flexible AF mode setting is **ALL** (AF/MF SETTING > AF MODE > ALL), so please use this mode as your default setting. This way, you can seamlessly cycle between Single Point, Zone, and Wide/Tracking AF modes simply by changing the AF frame size (press the focus stick and change the AF frame size with the rear command dial).

- Speaking of the **focus stick**: It's very important that you set it to PUSH > EDIT FOCUS AREA and to TILT > DIRECT AF POINT SELECTION. Please note that this is *not* the camera's default setting. However, only this setting ensures that the X100VI behaves like previous X100 series cameras and unleashes all its focus control features. All focus-related tips in this book are based on this focus stick configuration. To access the focus stick configuration page, simply press and hold the stick until the configuration page appears.

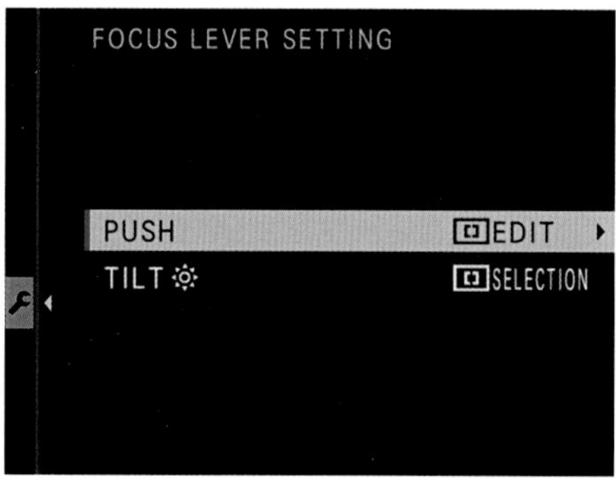

Fig. 20: It's vital that you **configure the focus stick** as pictured here. To do so, press and hold the focus stick until the FOUS LEVER SET-TING page appears.

- Set your X100VI to **Boost mode** for maximum performance by selecting SET UP > POWER MANAGEMENT > PERFORMANCE > BOOST. This option is *not* enabled by default, so you must manually select it. Only Boost mode unleashes the full potential of the camera, offering the fastest available live view readout (EVF FRAME RATE PRIORITY) and best autofocus performance (all Boost mode options). Boost mode also uses up more energy, so make sure to always carry one or two fully charged replacement batteries.

- Set **Focus Priority** via AF/MF SETTING > RELEASE/FOCUS PRIORITY > FOCUS for both AF-S and AF-C. Focus Priority makes sure that the camera records a picture only when the autofocus thinks that it has locked onto a target. In RELEASE mode, the camera will take the shot even if the autofocus couldn't lock on a target or hasn't finished focusing. Please note that if you are using AF+MF mode, the autofocus will always operate with release priority. That's why my recommended default setting for AF/MF SETTING > AF+MF is OFF.

- If you want to quickly take a series of single shots, I recommend selecting SET UP > SCREEN SET-UP > IMAGE

DISP. > OFF to not interrupt your flow. However, I *normally* set **Image Display** to the shortest available time span of 0.5 SEC. I like to see a quick preview of the final image that represents the camera's exposure and dynamic range (DR & DR-P) settings. To cancel an ongoing image preview and continue shooting, simply half-press the shutter button.

■ Activate the **eye sensor** in the SET UP > SCREEN SET-UP > VIE MODE SETTING menu, which will allow the camera to automatically switch between the viewfinder and the LCD screen depending on which view is in use. There's also an alternative mode called VIEWFINDER ONLY + EYE SENSOR, which is an energy-saving mode. This mode can make it more difficult to operate the camera because the LCD won't be available for changing menus while in shooting mode.

■ For **exposure metering**, I recommend using MULTI metering as your default mode. Intelligent matrix metering usually delivers results that don't require a massive amount of exposure correction. You can select the metering mode in SHOOTING SETTING > PHOTOMETRY, and you can also put this function in the Quick menu or My Menu. That said, if you are like me and shoot everything in manual exposure mode, SPOT metering is usually a better choice.

■ Set **white balance** to Auto via IMAGE QUALITY SETTING > WHITE BALANCE > AUTO to let the camera determine and set the correct white balance for a scene. Since you are shooting FINE+RAW or NORMAL+RAW, you can always adjust the white balance later, either with the camera's built-in RAW converter or with external RAW conversion software such as Lightroom. That said, AUTO will deliver very good results in most scenarios.

- Set **Dynamic Range** by selecting IMAGE QUALITY SET-TING > DYNAMIC RANGE > DR100% as your default setting. If you require more highlight dynamic range (DR) for a specific subject to avoid blown highlights, you can manually set DR200% (for *one* extra stop of dynamic range in the highlights) or DR400% (for *two* extra stops of dynamic range in the highlights). Setting DYNAMIC RANGE to AUTO is *not* recommended. Extending the dynamic range can bring back texture to otherwise blown-out areas of your shot (such as in white clouds on a sunny day).

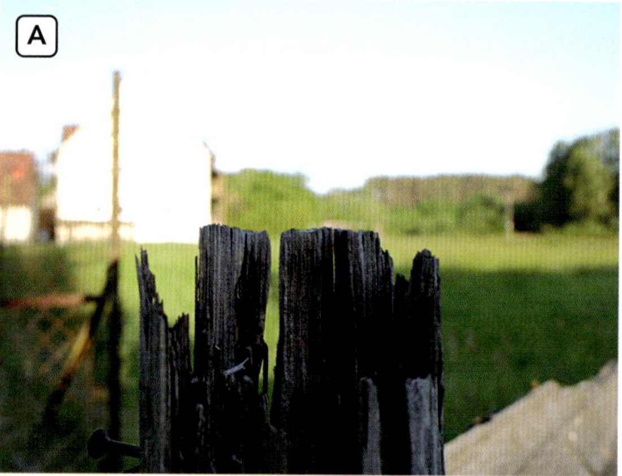

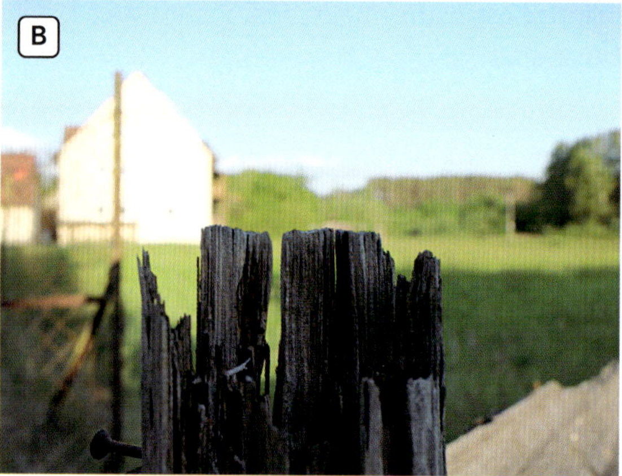

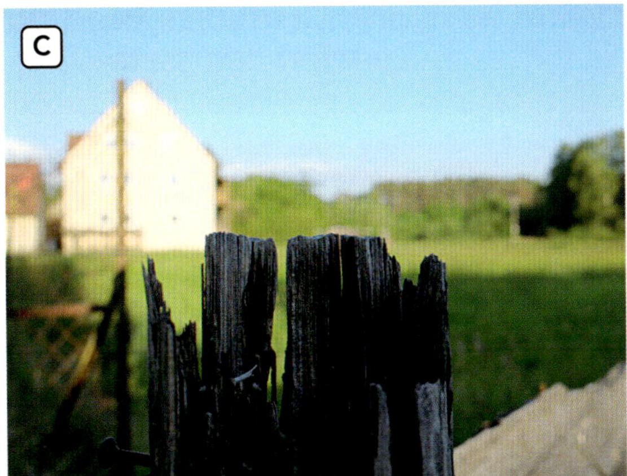

Fig. 21: All Fujifilm X cameras feature a powerful and often misunderstood **DR function** that can increase highlight dynamic range by up to two full stops (EV). The default setting is DR100% (**A**). Seeing blown-out highlights that you do not like? Increase dynamic range to DR200% (**B**) or DR400% (**C**) to get an extra one or two stops worth of highlight detail.

- Do you sometimes shoot with very slow shutter speeds lasting several seconds? In this case, I recommend setting IMAGE QUALITY SETTING > LONG EXPOSURE NR > ON to improve the quality of your results. In this **Long Exposure** mode, the camera performs a so-called dark-frame subtraction [12] to reduce noise and eliminate hot pixels. With this process, the total exposure time is at least doubled because the camera is taking the shot twice: once normally and once with a closed shutter curtain. The second shot is then subtracted from the first to improve the overall result.

- I recommend *not* using the AUTO setting for the **brightness control for the EVF** because it tends to show an overly bright live view image in bright sunlight and a subdued image when it's dark. Instead, I select SET UP > SCREEN SET-UP > EVF BRIGHTNESS > MANUAL > 0.

- In this book, we assume that **SHUTTER AF** and **SHUTTER AE** (in the SET UP > BUTTON DIAL SETTING menu) are both set to ON. This ensures that autofocus and exposure (including the working aperture) are locked when you half-press the shutter button in AF-S mode, so the camera is primed for the least possible shutter lag once you fully press the shutter button. In AF-C mode, SHUTTER AF ON means the AF keeps tracking a subject while the shutter button is half-pressed or pressed, and SHUTTER AE ON makes sure the exposure is locked as long as you half-press or press the shutter button.

- I select SET UP > BUTTON DIAL SETTING > COMMAND DIAL SETTING > *front command dial* 1 > F (aperture) and COMMAND DIAL SETTING > *rear command dial* > S.S. (shutter speed). All related recommendations in this book are based on this setting. In the same menu, my settings for *front command dial* 2 and *front command dial* 3 are ISO and EXPOSURE COMPENSATION, respectively. This means you can cycle between aperture, ISO, and exposure compensation settings by pressing the front command dial. Of course, you are free to set-up your X100VI differently. Just remember which dial is supposed to perform a specific function that I mention in this book.

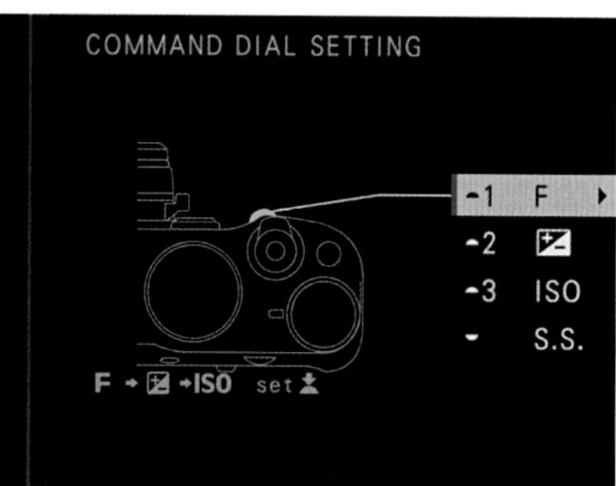

Fig. 22: This screenshot illustrates my recommended **command dial settings** for the X100VI.

- **Auto-ISO** is a convenient option with three presets that can be selected by setting the ISO dial to "A" and selecting one of three Auto-ISO choices (AUTO1–3) with SHOOTING SETTING > ISO AUTO SETTING. For each Auto-ISO preset, you can adjust DEFAULT SENSITIVITY (I suggest 125), MAX. SENSITIVITY (I suggest 12800) and MIN. SHUTTER SPEED. Don't worry: even at the upper limit of ISO 12800, images made with the X-Trans sensor are quite good. When you are using Auto-ISO, you should pick a suitable minimum shutter speed with MIN. SHUTTER SPEED. A popular setting for the minimum shutter speed is 1/60 sec., but you can change this parameter to anything between 30 sec. and 1/2000 sec. With fast-moving objects, faster speeds are recommended to avoid unwanted motion blur. My typical minimum shutter speed settings for AUTO1, AUTO2, and AUTO3 are AUTO, 1/125 sec., and 1/500 sec.

- By pressing the DISP/BACK button, you can choose between two live view display modes: one with and one without an **information overlay**. The overlay option offers essential tools like the electronic level, the live histogram, or the electronic distance and DOF scale. To choose which elements you want displayed, select SET UP > SCREEN SET-UP > DISP. CUSTOM SETTNG. Then select either the optical viewfinder (OVF) or electronic live view (EVF/LCD) and pick the desired elements from the list. Make sure to enable the live histogram! Please note that you can select the display mode *independently* for the viewfinder (EVF or OVF) and the LCD. Pressing the DISP/BACK button only affects the currently active view (either the viewfinder or the rear LCD). To change the display mode of the viewfinder, it must be active when you press the DISP/BACK button—this means you must be looking through the viewfinder while the eye sensor is active.

<table>
<tr><td>TIP 22</td><td>Avoiding the camera menus: practical shortcuts for your X100VI</td></tr>
</table>

Navigating nested camera menus can be cumbersome. That's why the X100VI offers the Quick menu (Q button) and user configurable Fn keys that can provide direct access to important and frequently used camera functions and settings.

The X100VI also offers seven custom user settings (C1 through C7) that can hold sets of frequently used camera configurations. You can select one of these sets via the Quick menu or an appropriately configured Fn button. Unlike earlier models, the X100VI treats C1 through C7 like actual camera modes, so you can change your global camera configuration by selecting one of the 7 custom modes.

Finally, the X100VI offers the MY MENU settings, where you can arrange frequently used menu items on two configurable menu pages for quick and easy access.

Please note that the X100VI offers two full sets of MY MENU, Quick menu, and custom settings: one for photography and one for video. Depending on the status of your camera (MOVIE mode is selected or not selected in the DRIVE button menu), the X100VI provides the matching set of shortcuts and settings.

Sadly, there is only one set of Fn and T-Fn function buttons, so you can't allocate different assignments for still photography and video.

Speaking of shortcuts—there are plenty, and most of them are available at your fingertips:

- Pull up the Quick menu, then press and hold the Q button again for a few seconds to directly open the configuration menu for your custom user settings (C1 to C7).

- Press and hold the Q button while the Quick menu is *not* open to directly access the Quick menu configuration page. In this mode, you can customize the Quick menu to meet your personal requirements. You can assign one of more than two dozen different settings to any of the 16 available Quick menu elements.

- Press and hold the MENU/OK button to enable the selective function lock. Press and hold the MENU/OK button again to remove the lock. When the lock is active, a yellow padlock symbol is displayed. You can configure the selective function lock in SET UP > BUTTON/DIAL SETTING > LOCK > FUNCTION SELECTION. This is an easy way to temporarily lock specific camera functions or controls and protect them from accidental changes during shooting.

- To see where the Fn buttons are located and what's assigned to each of them, simply press and hold the DISP/ BACK button. In this menu, you can also reassign all Fn buttons.

- To confirm a new menu selection in shooting mode, you can either press the MENU/OK button or half-press the shutter button.

- Half-press the shutter button to switch from playback mode back to shooting mode.

- Half-press the shutter button during an ongoing image preview (SET UP > SCREEN SET-UP > IMAGE DISP.) to immediately cancel the preview.

- Half-press the shutter button for a few seconds to wake-up the camera from sleep mode.

- In AF-S shooting mode (with Single Point AF) or MF mode, press the rear command dial to zoom into the currently active AF frame. When zoomed-in, you can choose between several magnification levels by turning the command dial. Please note that this magnifier tool (FOCUS CHECK) is the default configuration for the rear command dial Fn button. If you assign a different function to the R-DIAL Fn button, this useful zoom shortcut won't be available. Please note that the magnifier shortcut isn't available in AF-S / Single Point AF mode when Pre-AF is on.

- Press and hold the rear command dial in MF mode to cycle between the available manual focus assist modes, such as standard, focus peaking, digital microprism, and digital split image.

- You can move the selected AF frame or zone around with the focus stick. Press the DISP/BACK button to reset the position of the AF frame or AF zone to the center. You can change the size of the selected AF frame or zone by turning one of the command dials. To reset the size of the AF frame or zone to default, press the rear command dial.

- Press and hold the focus stick in shooting mode to access the focus stick options. Make sure to enter the configuration that I recommended in the previous tip: PUSH > EDIT FOCUS AREA and TILT > DIRECT AF POINT SELECTION. This is *not* the factory default setting. However, this setting is required to properly use and benefit from several tips in this book.

- While in shooting mode, press the focus stick to access the FOCUS AREA configuration screen. Here, you can use the focus stick to move the active focus frame or zone, and you can change their size by turning one of the command dials. In this configuration screen, you can press DISP/BACK to center the focus frame or zone. Please note that this shortcut only works with the proper focus stick configuration that I have just described.

- In playback mode (while viewing an image), use the front command dial to browse through the images that are on file.

- During playback, you can turn the rear command dial to zoom in and out of an image. By pressing the DISP/BACK button, you can directly return to the standard-size view. Press the rear command dial or the focus stick to zoom in to a 100% view of a shot. You can then zoom in even further by turning the rear command dial. When you are zoomed in, pressing the dial again returns the camera to its regular view, displaying the full image.

- While displaying a RAW image in playback mode, you can press the Q button to directly access the built-in RAW converter. This function allows you to create new JPEG versions of your image with different settings.

- In playback mode, move the focus stick upward to view the first of three information pages that show the histogram and additional shooting parameters, including the position of the focus point.

- For direct access to the format menu, press and hold the DRIVE/DELETE button and the rear command dial together for about three seconds.

- Pull the viewfinder selector to the right to switch between the optical viewfinder (OVF) and the electronic viewfinder (EVF). Please note that the OVF is only available when the electronic level is off or in 2D mode. It's not available in concert with the level's 3D setting.

- Pull the viewfinder selector to the left to switch the Electronic Range Finder (ERF) window in the OVF on or off.

- In ERF mode (Electronic Range Finder), press the rear command dial to change the magnification level of the small ERF window in the lower-right corner of the OVF display. You can cycle between a full view and several magnification levels.

<table><tr><td>**TIP 23**</td><td>**Suggested Fn button assignments**</td></tr></table>

Smart assignment of your X100VI's Fn buttons will save you cumbersome trips to the camera menu. To display and change the assignment of all Fn buttons in one convenient menu, press and hold the DISP/BACK button in shooting mode until the configuration page called Bluetooth & FUNCTION (Fn) SETTING appears.

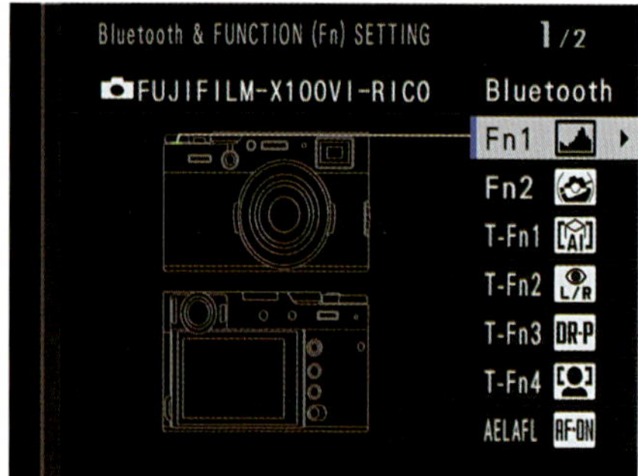

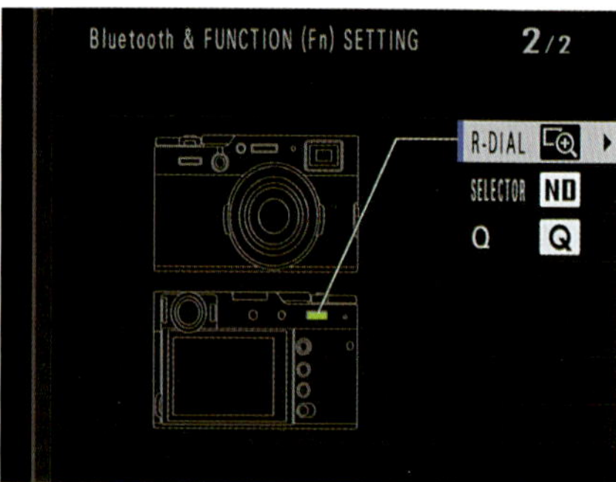

Fig. 23: Pressing and holding the DISP/BACK button for a few seconds leads directly to the FUNCTION (Fn) SETTING page, where you can configure the **function button assignment** of your X100VI.

Here are my suggested Fn button assignments:

- *Fn1:* **HISTOGRAM.** Your X100VI features an RGB live histogram with live overexposure warnings, also known as "blinkies." The only way to access this essential feature is via an Fn or a Touch-Fn button, so please make sure it is assigned to one. Personally, I am using Fn1.

- *Fn2:* **ELECTRONIC LEVEL SWITCH.** In addition to the regular single-axis indicator, the X100VI offers a dual-axis electronic level display ("3D level"). The dual-axis indicator helps you correctly align the camera to avoid non-parallel vertical lines, especially in city and architecture shots. Like the RGB histogram, this feature is accessible only via an Fn or a Touch-Fn button. Please note that the 3D level disables the OVF and forces the EVF.

- *Touch-Fn1:* **SUBJECT DETECTION ON/OFF.** This setting allows you to quickly switch the subject detection autofocus on and off.

- *Touch-Fn2:* **RIGHT/LEFT EYE SWITCH.** This touch function button lets you switch eyes in face/eye detection autofocus mode.

- *Touch-Fn3:* **DYNAMIC RANGE or D RANGE PRIORITY.** Fujifilm cameras offer a very powerful and high-quality DR function to extend the highlight dynamic range of an image, so it's a very good idea to keep this function right at your fingertips. You can choose between the regular DR function and the more extensive DR-P option. Personally, I opted for DR-P because only DR-P STRONG gives me all internal RAW converter options.

- *Touch-Fn4:* **FACE DETECTION ON/OFF.** This touch function button turns face/eye detection autofocus quickly on and off.

- *AEL/AFL:* **AF-ON.** Sadly, there's only one button for Exposure Lock and AF-Lock or Back Button Focusing (AF-ON). My choice is AF-ON. Please note that with this setting, this button will automatically change to Instant-AF in manual focus mode.

- *R-DIAL:* **FOCUS CHECK.** Pressing the rear command dial also serves as an Fn button. The factory default setting is FOCUS CHECK, which allows you to zoom into the live view image on the electronic viewfinder or LCD monitor. Since this is an important and convenient function, I do not recommend changing this default assignment. Please note that all related tips in this book assume that FOCUS CHECK is assigned to the rear command dial button.

- *SELECTOR:* **ND FILTER.** The built-in ND filter of the X100VI darkens the lens by 4 EV (or stops) and is quite useful to reduce the shutter speed in bright light and during flash photography, especially when you are shooting with a wide-open aperture. To quickly engage or disengage the built-in ND filter, I assign it to an Fn button, where I can instantly toggle it on and off. To engage or disengage the ND filter, tilt the viewfinder selector to the right and hold it there for a few seconds.

- *Q: **QUICK MENU**. Fujifilm also allows the Q button to serve as an Fn button. That said, I am happy with its position and don't want to change it.

| TIP 24 | Recommended My Menu and Quick menu configuration |

To keep the shooting process effortless and free of interruptions, it's vital to assign frequently used functions to Fn buttons so they are immediately accessible. Sadly, the number of Fn buttons on the X100VI is quite limited.

Luckily, we also have My Menu and the Quick menu (Q button) to quickly access frequently used functions and menus that didn't fit into the remaining Fn buttons.

- To configure **My Menu**, select SET UP > USER SETTING > MY MENU SETTING, where you can add new items, rank existing items (change their position in My Menu), or remove items from the menu.

- To configure the **Quick menu**, press and hold the Q button until the Quick menu configuration page appears, where you can change each of the 16 slots and assign them either a new function or no function at all (NONE). If you don't see 16 slots in the Quick menu, make sure to set BUTTON DIAL SETTING > EDIT/SAVE QUICK MENU > 16 SLOTS.

The following figures illustrate my personal My Menu and Quick menu settings. Neither are set in stone.

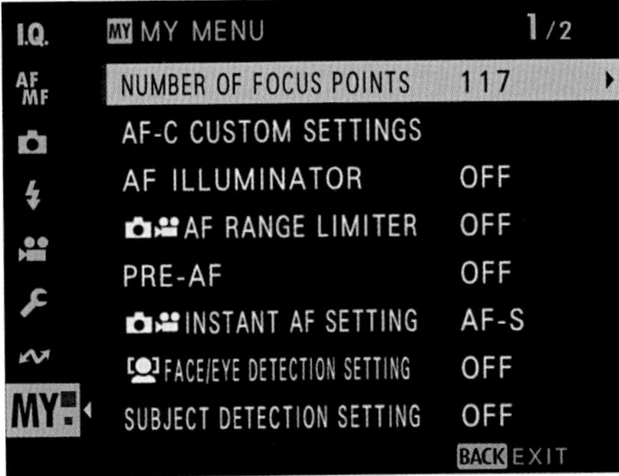

Fig. 24: My Menu consists of two menu pages with a total of 16 possible entries. I use the first page to quickly change and review focus related settings.

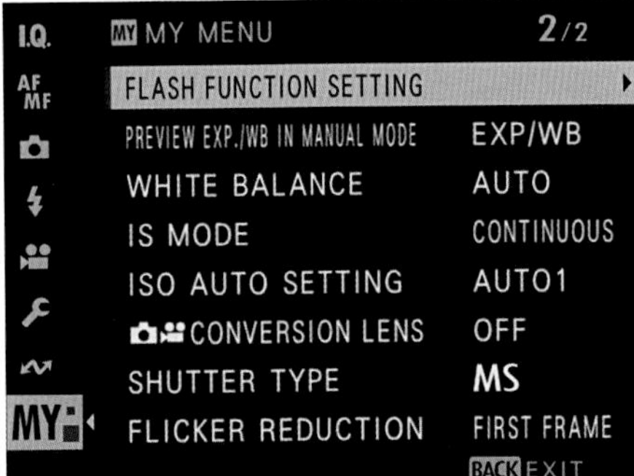

Fig. 25: The second page of my personal **My Menu** is reserved for exposure settings as well as general settings such as IS mode, conversion lens settings, shutter type, and flash configuration.

Please note that manual exposure mode **M** must be enabled to access the PREVIEW EXP./WB IN MANUAL MODE setting.

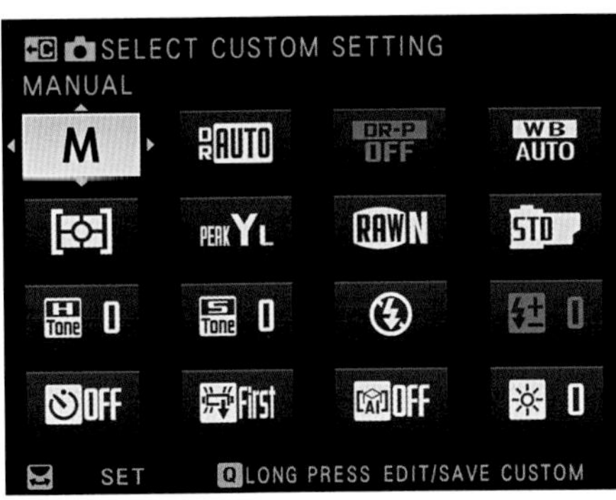

Fig. 26: The **Quick menu** page of my X100VI: Among other things, I want to have direct access to DR and DR-P, flicker reduction, MF Assist options as well as face/eye detection and subject detection settings.

TIP 25 | Working with custom settings

Beginning with the X-S10, Fujifilm changed their custom settings to "global" camera configurations that contain most camera settings. Examples of X cameras with global custom settings are the X-S10, X-S20, X-E4, X-H2, X-H2S, GFX100, GFX100II, GFX100S, GFX100SII, GFX50SII, X-T5, X-T50, and, of course, the X100VI.

My recommendation is to set up global custom settings for specific shooting scenarios. That way, you can quickly prime your camera for different scenes and subjects. For example, you could set up custom settings for portrait, landscape, action, or long exposure shots. In my experience, it's also useful to set IMAGE QUALITY SETTING > AUTO UPDATE CUSTOM SETTING to ENABLE. This allows you to select a custom setting as your starting point, then fine-tune it for the actual situation at hand. Any changes you make will automatically update that custom setting and refine it.

Of course, too much refining might eventually carry you away from your original custom sets for action, portrait, landscape, etc.—but that doesn't have to be an issue. You can save a copy of all your camera settings (including all your "generic" custom settings) on your Mac or PC with the free FUJIFILM X Acquire app [13]. That way, you can modify, adapt, and refine your initial custom settings at will during a shoot. When you are finished shooting a job, simply restore your previously saved full camera settings (including your original custom settings) with FUJIFILM X Acquire. You can even go further and use FUJIFILM X Acquire to swap between different sets of custom settings. After all, 2 × 7 sets (7 sets for video and 7 sets for still photography) may not be sufficient to cover all your shooting needs.

If you don't have access to a computer, you can also use the free Fujifilm XApp [14] on your smartphone or tablet to save and restore complete camera configurations.

To create a custom setting, select IMAGE QUALITY SETTING > EDIT/SAVE CUSTOM SETTING > CREATE NEW at one of the seven available slots. This saves your current camera settings in this slot. You can name a custom setting by selecting it and choosing EDIT CUSTOM NAME.

Sadly, the X100VI stops short of saving *all* camera settings in a custom setting slot. To see what parameters can be saved, you can create a new or select an existing custom setting with IMAGE QUALITY SETTING > EDIT/SAVE CUSTOM SETTING and then pick EDIT/CHECK. The camera will now show you all available menu items. Items that cannot be saved in a custom setting are grayed out. In addition to this, you cannot save settings that can also be accessed via "analog" dials and switches. Hence, aperture, shutter speed, ISO, exposure mode, exposure compensation, DRIVE button menu settings, and focus mode aren't part of global custom settings.

To activate a specific custom setting, you can either visit the Quick menu or use IMAGE QUALITY SETTING > SELECT CUSTOM SETTING. You can also assign the custom settings selection to an Fn button (SELECT CUSTOM SETTING) or configure an Fn button to immediately select Custom Setting 1 when that button is pressed (RECALL CUSTOM 1 SETTING). The latter can be helpful in situations that require you to immediately switch to a different camera configuration, for example one for sudden action shot opportunities. To reassign Fn buttons, press and hold the DISP/BACK button until the configuration page appears.

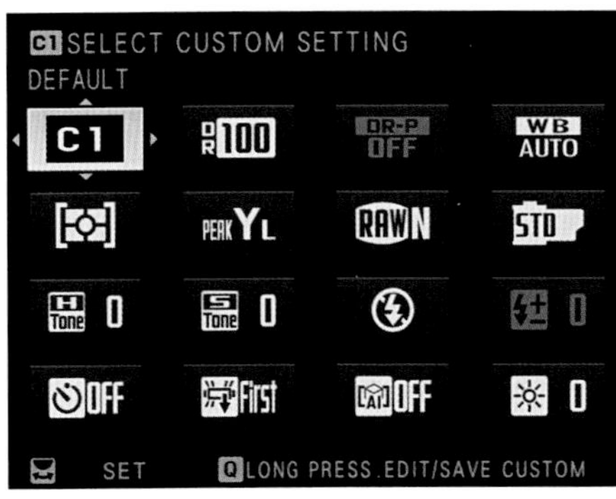

Fig. 27: You can select and activate your **custom settings** in the upper-left slot of the Quick menu. Please note that global custom settings extend far beyond the settings that are displayed in the Quick menu. To see what parameters can be saved, you can create a new or select an existing custom setting with IMAGE QUALITY SETTING > EDIT/SAVE CUSTOM SETTING and then select EDIT/CHECK.

Important: If you are a friend of film simulation "recipes," you will find that the new global custom settings aren't ideal if you want to use them to store different recipes. That's because in addition to the JPEG settings of your recipe, global custom settings also store and recall a plethora of other camera settings that you probably don't want to change when you are switching to a different recipe. As an alternative, consider applying recipes after the fact with X RAW STUDIO [15], where you can store a virtually unlimited number of recipes and apply them to any number of images with just a few clicks.

| TIP 26 | Shoot FINE+RAW or NORMAL+RAW! |

Should you shoot RAW [16] or JPEG [17]? The best option is to use both formats by setting IMAGE QUALITY SETTING > IMAGE QUALITY > FINE+RAW (or NORMAL+RAW). It doesn't matter if you consider yourself a diehard RAW shooter or a JPEG/HEIF shooter.

This is how **RAW shooters** benefit from shooting FINE+RAW or NORMAL+RAW:

- During external RAW processing, the camera-made JPEG can be used as a (sometimes hard-to-beat) reference image.

- Checking critical focus is only possible at 100% magnification, which only a full-size JPEG can provide. The JPEG that's embedded in the RAW file for preview purposes is too small. Make sure you select one of the available L (Large) options under IMAGE QUALITY SETTING > IMAGE SIZE.

- The IMAGE SIZE menu isn't available in RAW-only mode. Different image formats, such as 1:1 or 16:9, are only available in JPEG/HEIF-only mode or FINE+RAW (or NORMAL+ RAW) mode. Autofocus and exposure metering adapt to the currently selected format (aspect ratio) and deliver more accurate readings when you are shooting with odd formats like 1:1. No worries, though: the RAW image is always recorded in the sensor's native 3:2 format, so you don't lose any image information.

This is how **JPEG shooters** benefit from shooting FINE+RAW or NORMAL+RAW:

- Nobody is capable of always setting the *perfect* shooting parameters (exposure, white balance, and dynamic range, as well as JPEG parameters such as film simulation, color, sharpness, noise reduction, shadow and highlight contrast, grain effect, etc.) in advance. FINE+RAW solves this problem by allowing you to change and adjust those settings *after* the fact, either with the built-in RAW converter or with external RAW conversion software. This means you can worry about those JPEG settings later and concentrate on more important aspects of your shot, such as focusing, framing, and timing.

- Even if you chose the perfect settings in advance, it's possible that you'd like to have more than one version of a shot, such as a color version and a black-and-white version, or versions with different color film simulations. Again, FINE+RAW (or NORMAL+RAW) does the trick because you can use the built-in RAW converter to create (and compare) different JPEG, HEIF, or TIFF versions of a shot.

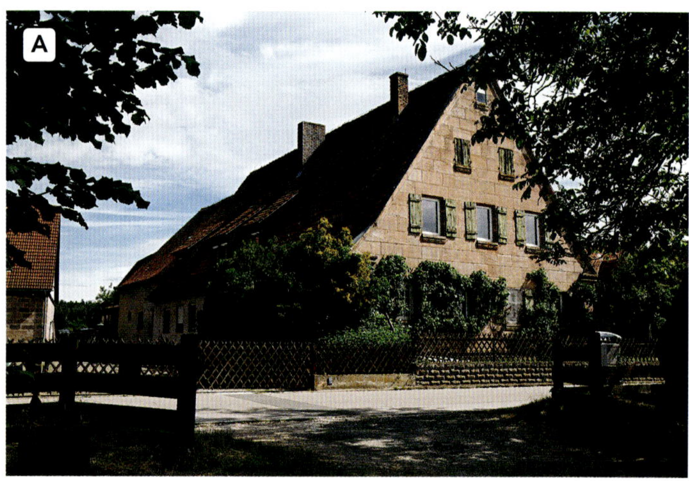

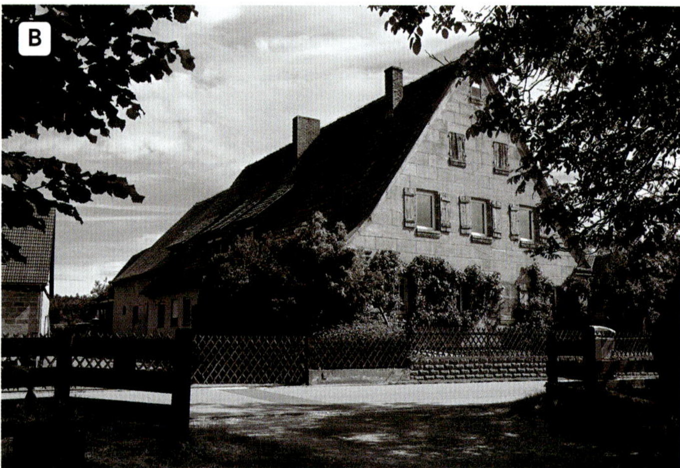

Fig. 28: The X100VI features a **built-in RAW converter** that allows you to quickly create different straight-out-of-camera (SOOC) versions of a shot and save them in formats like JPEG, HEIF, and TIFF. It only takes a few seconds to adjust exposure, contrast settings, and noise reduction of a color image (**A**), or to create a black-and-white version (**B**). All you need is the shot's RAW file.

- Progress is continually being made in the digital domain. Things that appear impossible today may be a reality in just a few years. It's perfectly feasible that future RAW converters will be able to extract much better image quality from your RAW files than is possible with today's cameras and RAW processors. It pays to be prepared by archiving the RAW files of your valuable shots. Storage space is cheap; some of your images may be priceless. For example, new AI-based demosaicing, sharpening, and denoising algorithms are now able to produce great results from shots that were considered unusable just a few years ago.

- Your skills may improve as well! Several months or a few years from now, you may be more adept at using post-processing software than you are today. Wouldn't it be sad if you couldn't revisit great shots of the past and process them in a better way? Don't forget, only RAW files contain the full potential of an image. JPEGs and HEIFs are a processed and compressed subset with limited latitude for post-processing. RAW files feature much better tonality and dynamic range. Using the built-in RAW converter of your X100VI isn't more complex or complicated than using the camera's JPEG settings in the shooting menu (which should be familiar to you as a JPEG shooter).

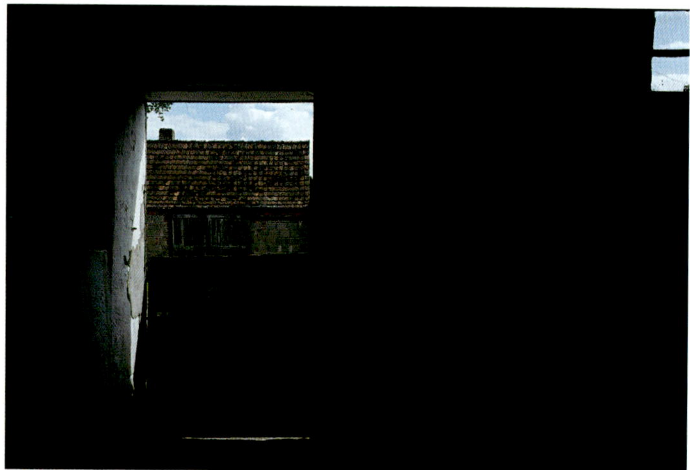

Fig. 29: X-series cameras feature competent JPEG engines with terrific film simulations, but that doesn't mean **JPEG-only shooting** is the best way to go. This JPEG illustrates the limited dynamic range of regular straight-out-of-camera DR100% JPEGs, which often render high-contrast scenes with either blown out highlights or blocked shadows—or both. There is no meaningful way to restore what has been lost in processing this JPEG. However, you can instead process the RAW file of this shot.

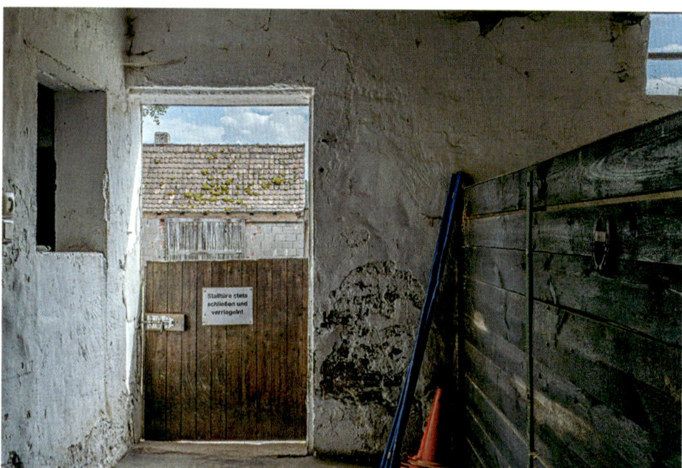

Fig. 30: This is a Lightroom-processed version of the **RAW file** of the previous shot, showcasing the superior dynamic range of the camera's original sensor data. Despite their small size and affordable price, your Fujifilm APS-C camera offers a dynamic range that rivals or even surpasses that of some modern full-frame cameras, but you need the RAW file to unlock that potential.

As you can see, FINE+RAW is the best and most flexible choice. The one detrimental aspect of using FINE+RAW (or NORMAL+RAW) is that it results in larger amounts of data being recorded. This doesn't matter much in practical terms, since your camera can quickly transfer large amounts of data to the memory card. Just make sure to use a fast card.

Let me use this opportunity to address a widespread misconception: RAW files aren't images that you can directly look at. RAWs contain image *data* that still must be *interpreted* or *processed* into an actual image—either in-camera or with external software. Every digital image (including the live view on the monitor, JPEGs from the camera, or TIFF files from Lightroom) is the result of such a translation.

A JPEG shooter who doesn't keep RAW files must settle for only one of the countless possible interpretations of RAW data into an image, and it's extremely unlikely this single JPEG or HEIF from the camera is the best of all possible versions of that image. Basically, discarding the RAW file turns your X camera into an instant camera: you only get one (most likely not the best) image per shot.

*Important: I recommend **not** using the HEIF format to replace JPEGs. Though better than JPEG in theory, there are several severe compatibility issues with Fujifilm's specific HEIF files and standard software, and even entire operating systems like macOS and iOS. Until those have been resolved, choose JPEG in the IMAGE QUALITY SETTING > SELECT JPEG/HEIF menu.*

Compressed or uncompressed RAW files?	TIP 27

The X100VI offers you a choice of uncompressed and compressed RAW files (IMAGE QUALITY SETTING > RAW RECORDING). Lossless compression cuts the size of RAW files roughly in half, so you can store more of them on a memory card or your computer. The compression also helps speed up camera processes: it takes longer to fill the fast camera buffer, and since the files are smaller, they take less time to transfer to the memory card.

It's important to note that Fujifilm's standard RAW compression is lossless, so there's no difference in image quality between uncompressed and lossless compressed RAWs. The format is widely supported, and RAW converter manufacturers can obtain a free SDK from Fujifilm to support compressed RAW file formats.

The X100VI also offers a RAW format with *lossy* compression (COMPRESSED). This option shaves another 25% off the size of a lossless compressed RAW. However, lossy compression means that some image information is discarded. This may become an issue with shots that require extensive post-processing. In my experience, there's no visible difference, though. If you need fast continuous burst rates or want to conserve storage space, switching from LOSSLESS COMPRESSED to COMPRESSED makes sense. Personally, COMPRESSED has become my default setting.

Windows users should always install the latest version of RAW FILE CONVERTER EX, even if you never intend to use it. This software is available as a free download [18]. It installs a codec that allows Windows to display thumbnail images of compressed Fuji RAW files anywhere on your PC.

TIP 28	Picking different image aspect ratios

The full resolution of the X100VI (almost 40 megapixels) is available only in its native image format (3:2). However, using a different image aspect ratio (such as 1:1 or 16:9) can still be reasonable. For example, some people prefer to view their images on a 16:9 HD television, while others are fans of the classic (square) medium format look.

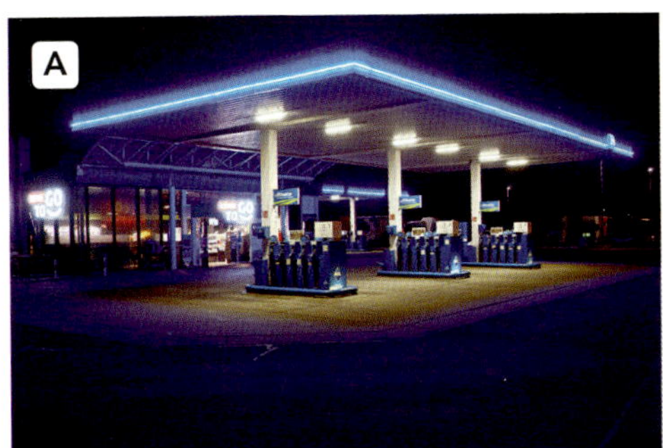

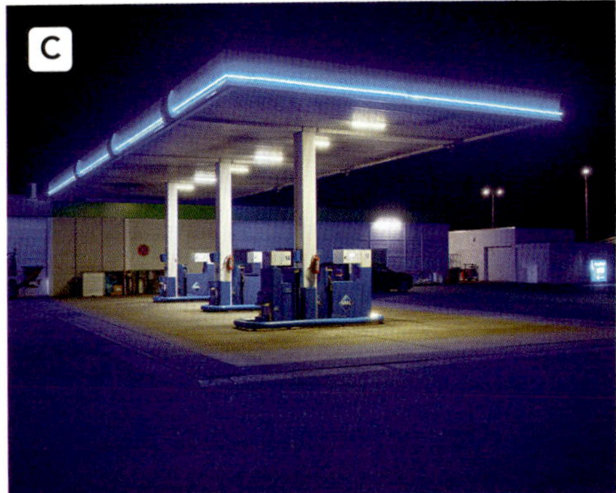
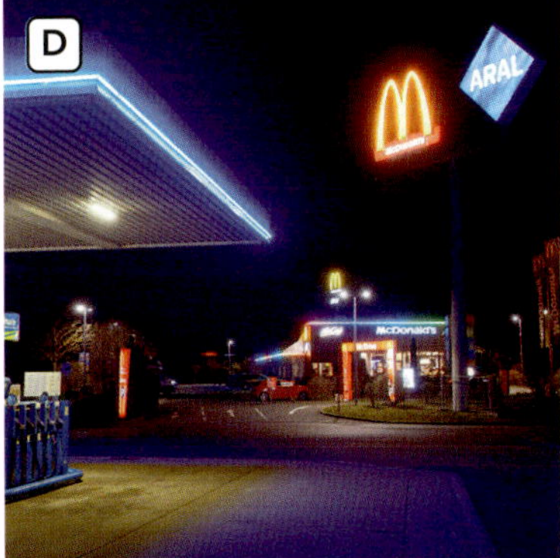

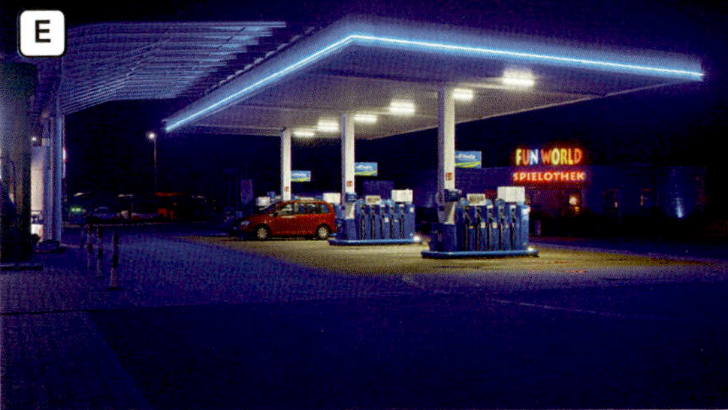

Fig. 31: The X100VI supports five different **aspect ratios** and three resolutions for JPEG output. These SOOC JPEG sample images are using IMAGE SIZE formats 3:2 (**A**), 4:3 (**B**), 5:4 (**C**), 1:1 (**D**), and 16:9 (**E**).

No matter what format (aspect ratio) and resolution you choose in IMAGE QUALITY SETTING > IMAGE SIZE, it will only affect the JPEGs coming from your camera. RAW files are always recorded in full resolution in the native 3:2 sensor format. This means that if you kept your RAW files, you could generate new full-size 3:2-format JPEGs with the built-in RAW converter or an external RAW processor.

If you want to compose shots in alternative formats, you should select the desired format in the shooting menu. Here's why:

- The live view in the viewfinder or on the LCD will automatically adjust to the new format, making it easier to compose an image.

- The camera's autofocus frames will adapt to the selected image format.

- The camera's exposure metering and live histogram are based on what's displayed in the live view. Changing the aspect ratio will enhance metering accuracy for the respective format.

TIP 29	The magical half-press

A basic rule for successfully using mirrorless cameras is minimizing the delay between pressing the shutter button and the camera taking the image. It's about not missing the decisive moment due to shutter lag.

It's up to you to anticipate these decisive moments. By half-pressing the shutter button, you are preparing the camera: exposure and autofocus (unless you are using AF-C) will be set and locked, and the lens aperture will move to its working position. The camera is now ready to record an image with minimal shutter lag—all that's left to do is to fully press the already half-pressed shutter button at the right instant.

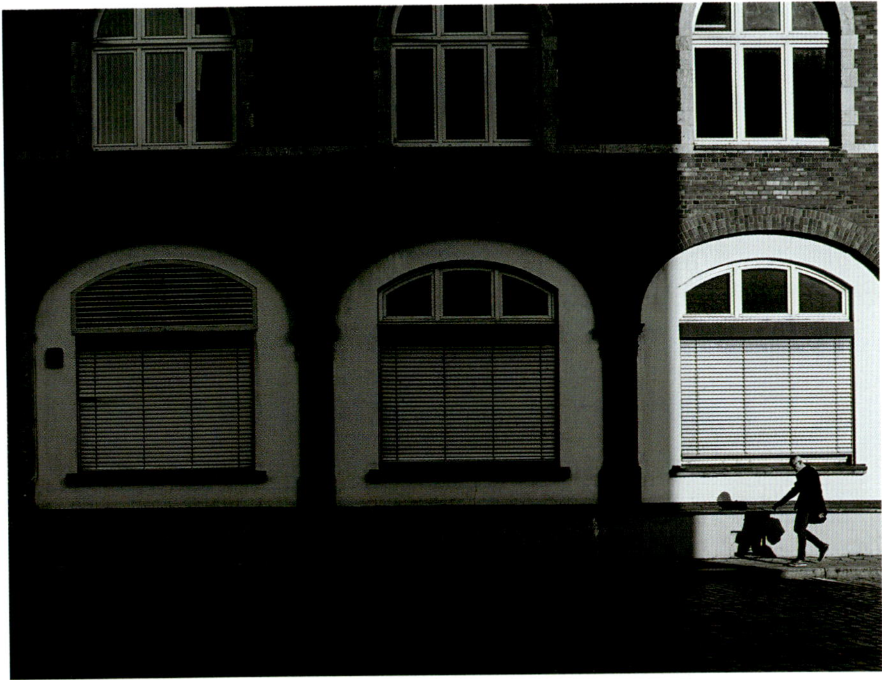

Fig. 32: To make sure your camera is ready when you are, it's useful to **prime the camera** by half-pressing the shutter button.

Don't forget that priming the camera by half-pressing the shutter button only works if SHUTTER AE and SHUTTER AF are set to ON in the SET UP > BUTTON DIAL SETTING menu for AF-S and AF-C.

2.2 MONITOR AND VIEWFINDER

The X100VI features a high-resolution hybrid viewfinder (EVF = Electronic Viewfinder; OVF = Optical Viewfinder) along with an LCD monitor. Both can be used for image composition and playback.

<table><tr><td>TIP 30</td><td>**Make use of the eye sensor!**</td></tr></table>

In the SET UP > SCREEN SET-UP > VIEW MODE SETTING menu, you can activate the built-in eye sensor for shooting mode and playback mode. The camera will then automatically switch to whichever view (the viewfinder or the LCD screen) is in use when you are taking and reviewing images or use the camera menu.

Please note that the camera is smart enough to automatically deactivate the eye sensor when the LCD screen has been horizontally unfolded to view it from above.

<table><tr><td>TIP 31</td><td>**Instant review**</td></tr></table>

To instantly review an image right after you take it, you can select SET UP > SCREEN SET-UP > IMAGE DISP. and then set a display period of 0.5 SEC, 1.5 SEC, or CONTINUOUS. The image will always be displayed in the currently active view (LCD or viewfinder).

You can immediately cancel an image review to continue shooting by half-pressing the shutter button. With the CONTINUOUS option, you can also zoom into the image: pressing the rear command dial will directly zoom to the highest available magnification.

In situations that require you to take a series of shots in quick succession, it may be advisable to switch image review off. To do so, select SET UP > SCREEN SET-UP > IMAGE DISP. > OFF. With image review off, you can still check your latest shot by pressing the playback button.

Please don't forget that the maximum image magnification (to check critical focus) is only available when the camera is set to record RAW *and* JPEG/HEIF files in size L.

Instant review also works when you are shooting with the optical viewfinder (OVF). Here, you can choose between a full-size view (the camera automatically switches to EVF mode to display the image) or a small-size view in the electronic rangefinder (ERF) window. Select your choice in SET UP > SCREEN SET-UP > OVF, IMAGE DISP., where you can choose between FULL SCREEN and SMALL WINDOW.

The DISP/BACK button can be tricky!	TIP 32

The DISP/BACK button serves two different purposes:

- As a BACK button, it returns the camera to a higher menu or selection level without saving any changes you may have made in the menu sub-level.

- As a DISPLAY button, it changes the display mode of the currently active view (LCD monitor or viewfinder).

It's important to remember that changing the display mode only affects the currently active view. For example, to change the display mode of the EVF, the EVF must be in use when you press the DISP/BACK button. This means that when you are using the eye sensor, you must look through the EVF or OVF while you are pressing the DISP/BACK button. If you don't, you will only change the display mode of the LCD monitor.

When the camera is in shooting mode, the viewfinder (OVF and EVF) and the LCD monitor can each use different display modes at the same time.

In playback mode, the EVF and LCD are synched to the same display mode. In this case it doesn't matter which view (EVF or LCD) is active when you change the display mode with the DISP/BACK button.

If you select a display with information overlays in shooting mode, you can choose which elements will appear in the viewfinder or on the LCD monitor. Select SET UP > SCREEN SET-UP > DISP. CUSTOM SETTING, and then check the items that you want displayed on the OVF and EVF/LCD.

TIP 33 | WYSIWYG—What You See Is What You Get!

The EVF and LCD monitor of the X100VI operate in WYSIWYG mode [19]: What You See Is What You Get. This means that the viewfinder and monitor are always trying to display a live view [20] that closely resembles the resulting JPEG or HEIF image. The live view simulates exposure, colors, contrast, and white balance and, in some cases, dynamic range. When you half-press the shutter button, the camera will set the selected working aperture, so the live view will then also display a preview of the depth of field.

The live view's exposure simulation is quite helpful because it allows you to recognize exposure problems *before* you take the picture. Please note that the live histogram is always based on the contents of the current live view image.

The live view's WYSIWYG simulation is available in all four of the camera's exposure modes: program AE **P**, aperture priority AE **A**, shutter priority AE **S**, and manual exposure mode **M**.

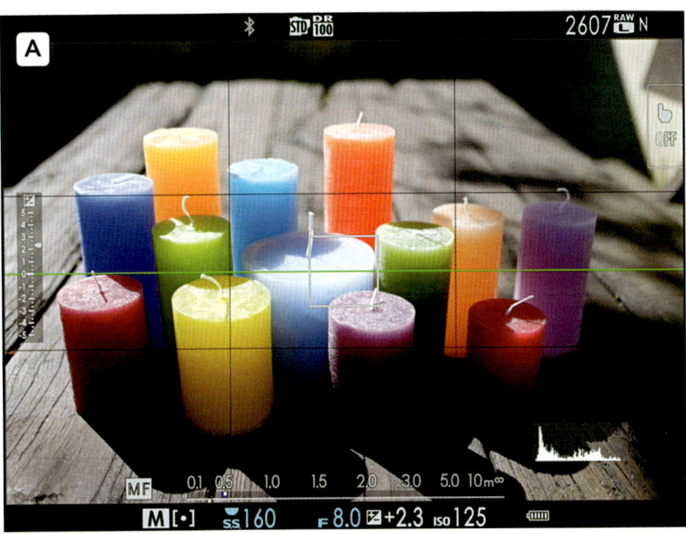

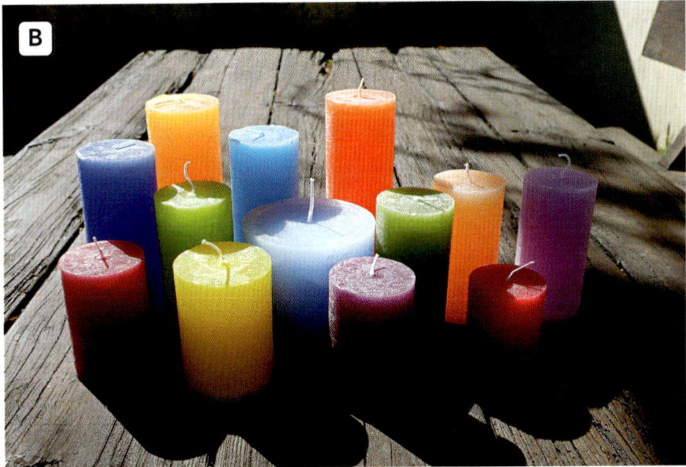

Fig. 33: WYSIWYG: This example illustrates how closely the live view (**A**) represents the JPEG taken by the camera (**B**). The live view doesn't just simulate exposure, white balance, film simulation, and other JPEG settings, it also previews *fixed* dynamic range settings like DR400% or DR-P STRONG. Please note that a preview of the correct depth-of-field (DOF) is only available when the shutter is half-pressed, or the camera's DOF preview function is engaged.

In manual exposure mode **M**, the X100VI allows you to switch off the live view exposure simulation by selecting SET UP > SCREEN SET-UP > PREVIEW EXP./WB IN MANUAL MODE > OFF. This way, the camera will always display a usable live view image in manual exposure mode, regardless of the selected exposure parameters (shutter speed, aperture, and ISO). Basically, the live view is switched to AE mode while the camera remains in manual exposure mode. This can be useful in a studio setting with flash photography. For example, you may want to eliminate the surrounding-light component by stopping down the aperture and fully illuminating your subject with strobes.

Please note that in this mode, both the live view and the live histogram aren't representing the actual exposure of your image, so don't forget to switch the exposure simulation back on if you want to work with a proper exposure simulation and live histogram in manual mode **M**.

The live view's exposure simulation may be restricted in situations with very low light and slow shutter speeds of several seconds—the live view and the live histogram may appear darker than the actual result. In such scenarios, you should set the camera to BOOST mode with EVF/LCD LOW LIGHT PRIORITY (SET UP > POWER MANAGEMENT > EVF/LCD BOOST SETTING > EVF/LCD LOW LIGHT PRIORITY). You may also first take a test shot and review it in playback mode. The information display (which you can select with the DISP/BACK button) will show you a playback histogram of the recorded JPEG image. This includes a preview with "blinkies," which indicate blown (overexposed) highlights.

TIP 34	Using the Natural Live View

The so-called Natural Live View disables the WYSIWYG simulation of JPEG settings such as Film Simulation, Tone Curve, or Color. Instead, it will display a rather flat live view image with increased dynamic range in the highlights and shadows, and with colors that are supposed to resemble what our eyes would see through an optical viewfinder. It will also set the live view to Auto white balance, so there will be no simulation of any white balance custom settings or presets. However, all current JPEG and white balance settings will still be applied to the *actual image* that is recorded.

To set the camera to Natural Live View mode, select SET UP > SCREEN SET-UP > NATURAL LIVE VIEW > ON. This setting enables generic-looking previews for color, black-and-white, and sepia shots that do *not* reflect the look of the actual JPEG results.

Let's not forget that your X100VI sports a hybrid viewfinder with an *actual* OVF, which is basically what the Natural Live View aims to simulate.

*Important: The Natural Live View of the X100VI extends highlight dynamic range by two stops, rendering the live view and live histogram highly inaccurate when shooting with DR100%, DR200%, or DR-AUTO dynamic range settings as well as DR-P WEAK or DR-P AUTO. Do **not** engage the Natural Live View if you want to use the live view and/or the live histogram to judge and set the correct exposure!*

Using the OVF	TIP 35

As mentioned above, the "real" Natural Live View of the X100VI is the optical viewfinder (OVF). Unlike DSLRs, the OVF in the X100VI isn't of the TTL type, since it's sitting on a different optical axis than the lens. This results in parallax error [21], which is more pronounced as the distance between the camera and the subject decreases.

The X100VI tries to compensate for the parallax effect by shifting and resizing the bright frame and the focus frame position in the OVF depending on the set focus distance. This results in an offset of the bright frame and focus frames to the lower-right.

If you want to see the maximum parallax-induced offset at the OVF's recommended minimum focus distance of approximately 50cm, select AF/MF SETTING > CORRECTED AF FRAME > ON. This will display a second AF frame (or AF zone) next to the regular frame, with an offset to the lower-right. This second frame represents the parallax-corrected focus frame position for the 50cm minimum distance.

If you focus closer than the recommended OVF minimum focus distance of approximately 50cm, the green AF frame confirmation will move past the corrected AF frame to the lower right. Under such circumstances, focusing turns into a parallax-induced lottery, so better switch to the EVF.

The bright frame in the OVF supports focal lengths of 19mm, 23mm, or 33mm. The camera will adjust the size of the bright frame based on your SHOOTING SETTING > CONVERSION LENS settings (or automatically when a new "type-II" WCL or TCL conversion lens is attached).

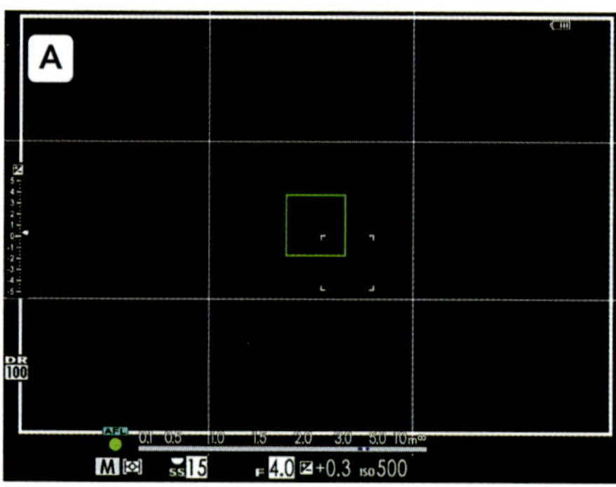

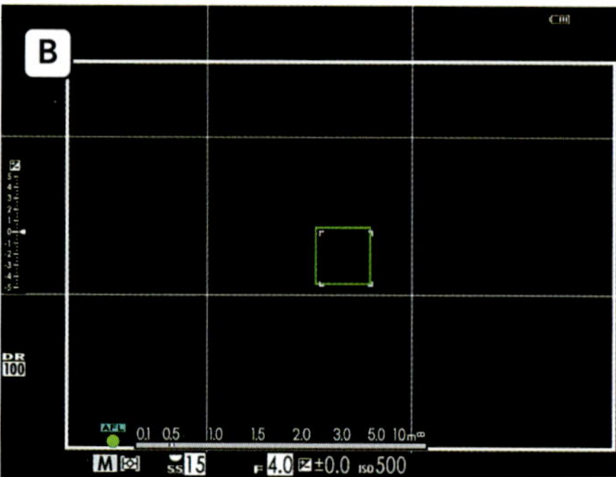

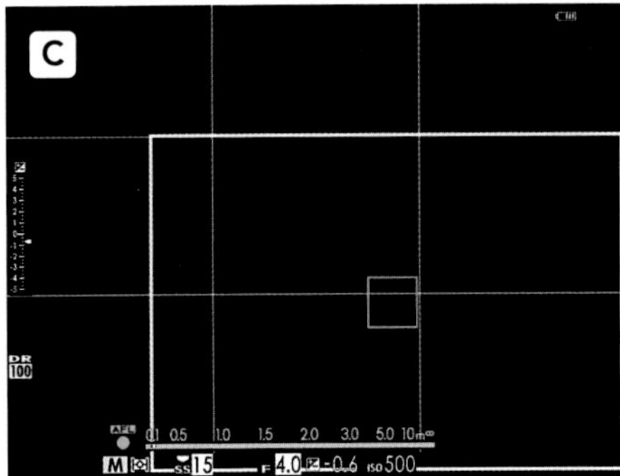

Fig. 34: Like every optical viewfinder that isn't exactly mounted on the optical axis, the OVF of the X100VI is prone to parallax error. This error increases with decreasing focusing distance, hence the recommendation to use the EVF for close-ups and short-distance shots.

That said, the camera tries to compensate parallax error by shifting the bright frame along with the focus frame when the autofocus has determined the distance between the camera and the subject.

With AF/MF SETTING > CORRECTED AF FRAME > ON, the OVF displays a helpful second focus frame that represents the parallax offset at a distance of 50 cm (**A**). As the focusing distance decreases and nears 50 cm, the actual focus frame and the 50 cm frame meet at the same position (**B**).

Below 50 cm, there's only one AF frame visible, along with a huge bright frame correction (**C**). This example shows a focusing distance of 10 cm.

Please note that the focus frame wasn't moved with the focus stick between images A, B, an C. All position changes are due to the camera's automatic parallax correction based on different focusing distances.

The OVF offers several pros and cons. Let's start with the cons:

- Parallax error: Since the OVF and the lens occupy different optical axes, the OVF (and hence the photographer looking through it) is seeing a different image than the camera. This difference grows more pronounced as the focus distances shortens. While the X100VI makes every effort to correct this parallax effect by adjusting the bright frame and focus frames in the OVF, this only works after the actual focus distance has been determined. Also, the OVF shouldn't be used below a focus distance of approximately 50 cm.

- The undesirable parallax effect also means that the position of the focus frames isn't as accurate as we'd like them to be. That's why there's only one Single Point focus frame size in OVF mode (there are six sizes in EVF mode). Allowing different focus frame sizes in the OVF display would imply a degree of focus accuracy that simply doesn't exist. If you need pin-point focus accuracy, use the EVF or the rear LCD.

- No WYSIWYG: The OVF display represents how the human eye sees the world, which is quite different from what the camera sees. This means that your images will look different from what you saw in the OVF when you took the picture.

That said, the OVF also has its benefits:

- No display lag: While the EVF in your X100VI exhibits a very short display lag, the optical viewfinder has no time lag at all. This is useful in situations where a fast reaction is more important than pin-point focus frame accuracy.

- Early-warning effect: Since the OVF usually displays a larger image area than the actual bright frame, you get an early warning when a subject enters the scene. This can be useful during action or street photography. However, the bright frame covers only 92% (or less) of the actual image. For an accurate 100% view, switch to the EVF.

- Easy contrast: Through the OVF, we see the world with our own eyes, and our brain automatically adjusts high-contrast scenes, so we don't perceive blocked shadows and blown highlights. This can be useful in situations with high contrast.

- No blackout: The electronic live view suffers from a brief blackout period after each shot, which is particularly problematic in burst mode. Even at 3 fps (CL), there's still a short blackout phase that can make it difficult to keep your eye on moving subjects. Luckily, there's no blackout at all when you are looking through the OVF. This can come in handy when you are shooting moving subjects in burst mode.

- Saving power: If you are exclusively using the OVF (without the ERF), the camera's battery will last longer.

<table><tr><td>Using the ERF</td><td>TIP 36</td></tr></table>

The ERF (Electronic Range Finder) expands the optical viewfinder's scope by adding a tiny EVF window in the lower-right corner of the OVF. That way, the ERF brings some of the benefits of the EVF to the OVF.

To turn the ERF on or off, pull the viewfinder selector briefly to the left. The small ERF window offers multiple view modes: a full view of the scene and several magnification (zoom) levels. You can cycle through these view modes by briefly pressing the rear command dial. In cases of the zoom modes, the magnified area always corresponds with the position of the active focus frame. This can help you determine the gravity of the parallax effect before you focus on a specific element in your scene.

In manual focus (MF) mode, the ERF supports focus assistants such as "digital split image" or "focus peaking". You can cycle through the focus assistants and the standard view by pressing and holding the rear command dial.

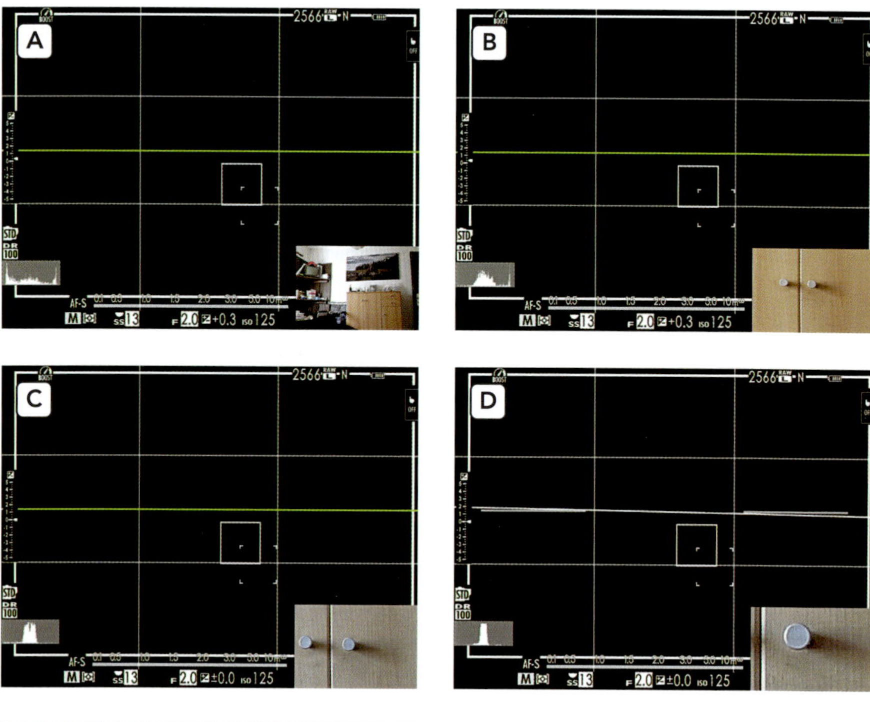

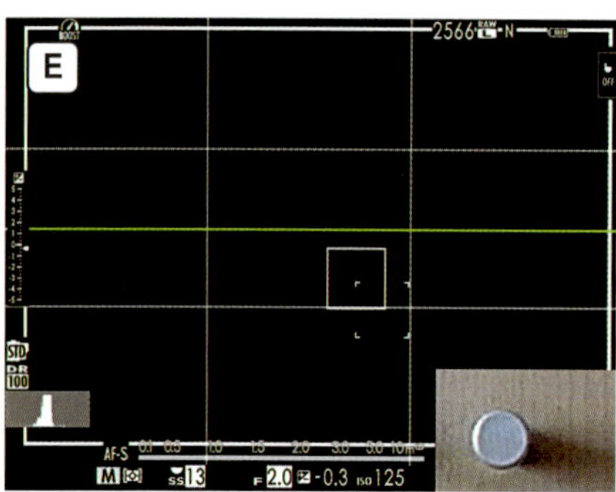

Fig. 35: The ERF is a small EVF window that is displayed in the lower-right corner of the OVF (image **A**). By pressing the rear command dial, there are several magnification levels at your disposal (images **B** to **E**) that can help you pinpoint a target.

However, using ERF magnification slows down the autofocus, and the live histogram display is limited to the magnified area.

However, the ERF also bears several issues:

- There is a noticeable decrease in autofocus performance when the ERF is used in one of its magnified views. To achieve normal AF performance, you should only use the ERF's full-image view.

- At any ERF magnification level, the live histogram in the OVF doesn't represent the full image but only the magnified image portion displayed in the ERF. To benefit from a live histogram that represents the complete scene, you should switch to the ERF's full image view by briefly pressing the rear command dial until the desired mode appears.

- Please note that the ERF is only available in AF-S mode combined with Single Point AF, and in manual focus (MF) mode. You can also use the ERF in AF-C mode combined with Single Point AF, but only without any magnification levels.

Using the LCD touchscreen	TIP 37

The X100VI features a touchscreen that can perform several functions in shooting mode and playback mode. To use the touchscreen, make sure to select SET UP > BUTTON/DIAL SETTING > TOUCH SCREEN SETTING > *Camera* TOUCH SCREEN SETTING > ON.

In *shooting mode,* you can use the touchscreen to pick a focus frame or zone; to autofocus with the selected focus frame or zone; or to autofocus and shoot with the selected focus frame or zone. These are your options (AF/MF SET-TING > TOUCH SCREEN MODE):

- **AREA:** Select a focus frame or zone by tapping once on the LCD touchscreen.

- **AF:** Tap on the LCD touchscreen to pick a focus frame or zone and trigger the autofocus. In MF mode, this option will focus the camera using Instant AF.

- **SHOT:** Tap on the touchscreen to select a focus area or zone, trigger the autofocus through this frame or zone, and take a picture without further delay. In MF mode, this option will immediately take a shot without (re-) focusing.

- **OFF:** Temporarily disable shooting with the touchscreen. This prevents you from accidentally triggering any of the three other touchscreen functions.

Apart from focusing and triggering the camera, the touchscreen offers several additional functionalities:

- In *playback mode,* you can use the touchscreen like a smartphone to browse through images. You can also zoom in and out of an image by double-tapping, or by pinching the image with two fingers. To use the touchscreen in playback mode, make sure to select SET UP > BUTTON/DIAL SETTING > TOUCH SCREEN SETTING > *Playback* TOUCH SCREEN SETTING > ON.

- You can still use the touchscreen when you are shooting with the electronic viewfinder (EVF). In this usage scenario, the touchscreen works like a trackpad that allows you to blindly move the focus frame. To define the active touchscreen area for EVF operation, select SET UP > BUTTON/DIAL SETTING > TOUCH SCREEN SETTING > EVF TOUCH SCREEN AREA SETTINGS. You will be given a choice of seven active areas and OFF.

- You can also double tap the touchscreen in shooting and playback mode to zoom into the picture. This function has the same effect as pressing the rear command dial in its default FOCUS CHECK configuration. To make sure this feature is available to you in shooting mode, select SET UP > BUTTON/DIAL SETTING > TOUCH SCREEN SETTING > *Camera* DOUBLE TAP SETTING > ON. Double tap also works when you are looking through the EVF if you have defined an active touchscreen area for EVF operation.

- Finally, the touchscreen gives you access to four virtual Fn buttons, so-called Touch-Fn or T-Fn buttons. You can "press" one of these virtual buttons by flicking your finger left, right, up, or down on the screen. You can assign new T-Fn functions by pressing and holding the DISP/

BACK button until the FUNCTION (Fn) SETTING screen appears. Please note that T-Fn buttons are available only if SET UP > BUTTON/DIAL SETTING > TOUCH SCREEN SETTING > *T-Fn* TOUCH FUNCTION is set to ON.

2.3 EXPOSING RIGHT

It's not the job of the camera to find and set the correct exposure; it's the job of the photographer. That said, the X100VI features the usual set of AE (auto exposure) modes: aperture priority **A**, shutter priority **S**, and program AE **P**.

- **Aperture priority A** automatically sets a suitable shutter speed to match a preset aperture based on your exposure.

- **Shutter priority S** automatically sets a suitable aperture to match a preset shutter speed based on your exposure.

- **Program AE P** automatically sets a suitable aperture and shutter speed combination based on your exposure.

- **Auto-ISO** can contribute a suitable ISO setting (within predefined limits). In digital cameras, ISO is the level of signal amplification applied to an image that has been recorded by the camera's sensor. ISO impacts the brightness of the final image (JPEG/HEIF/TIFF and the camera's WYSIWYG live view).

Auto exposure (AE) modes are typically set with the aperture ring on the lens and the shutter speed dial on the camera body: Pre-selecting an aperture and setting the shutter speed dial to "A" activates *aperture priority* mode. Selecting "A" on the aperture ring in concert with a specific shutter speed activates *shutter priority* mode. Finally, selecting "A" on both the lens and the shutter speed dial selects *program AE*.

It is important to understand that these auto exposure (AE) modes (including Auto-ISO) are not responsible for correctly exposing images: exposure is *always* the responsibility of the photographer. AE modes automatically fill variables (such as the shutter speed in aperture priority **A**) in a way that matches the exposure *you* have set. Auto exposure will only deliver good results if the photographer is exposing correctly.

Exposing correctly—how does this work?

Don't panic! Unlike conventional DSLR cameras, your mirrorless X100VI makes things easy. Four different metering modes (multi, spot, center-weighted, and average), the WYSIWYG live view, and the live (RGB) histogram help you determine the correct exposure for any given scene. If you shoot in one of the three AE modes, the most important tool is the exposure compensation dial, which allows you to correct the metered exposure up to ±3 EV in convenient steps of 1/3 EV. EV means Exposure Value, and 1 EV is equivalent to one full aperture stop. The correct exposure isn't what the camera is metering, it's what *you* make of the metering by adjusting the exposure compensation dial or with manual exposure settings.

TIP 38	Choosing the right metering method

There are up to four different metering methods available to measure the amount of light that goes through the lens and hits the image sensor:

- **Average** metering calculates an unweighted average of the total light that hits the entire sensor area.

- **Spot** metering considers only a tiny percentage of the sensor area. The metering area typically covers a standard-sized focus frame in the center of the image. Alternatively, you can link spot metering directly to the size and position of the active focus frame (in SINGLE POINT AF or MF mode).

- **Center-weighted** metering is a cross between average and spot metering. While it encompasses the entire image area, it puts special emphasis on the image center.

- **Multi** or **matrix** metering calculates a weighted average of the total light that hits the sensor. The weighting is a result of 256 metering areas (the matrix) that the camera evaluates and compares to typical scenarios, which is why multi metering is considered "smarter" than the other methods. For example, multi metering is designed to recognize when you are shooting against the sun.

Average, spot, and center-weighted metering return exposure recommendations based on middle gray. In other words, when you take a picture of a black wall and then a picture of a white wall with auto exposure (AE), the results will both look middle gray. This means:

- If you want the black wall to look black in the resulting image, you must manually adjust the exposure downward.

- If you want the white wall to look bright white in the resulting image, you must manually adjust the exposure upward.

Fig. 36: This illustration shows a black sheet of paper and a white sheet of paper. Both were photographed with the camera's spot metering without any exposure correction. As you can see, the camera delivered a **middle-gray exposure** in both cases. To get an image that reflects the actual brightness of a subject, the metered exposure must be adjusted.

Fujifilm recommends a correction of +1 EV when you are shooting in snowfields, or −2/3 EV when you are shooting subjects in spotlight. Instead of following these rules, I recommend a more precise and methodical course of action using the live view and the live histogram. To minimize corrective adjustments, it's best to select a metering method that fits the subject and the job at hand:

- **Multi** metering is a general-purpose method. Since it is supposed to be "smarter" than the other methods, there's a chance you won't have to apply (m)any corrective adjustments to the proposed exposure.

- **Average** and, to a lesser degree, **center-weighted** metering are rather neutral metering methods that will likely stay more consistent despite small changes in composition (or framing) than multi metering and spot metering. I recommend average metering if you want to take a series of shots of the same subject under similar conditions in one of the auto exposure (AE) modes. In such cases, average metering will help you keep the exposure consistent.

- **Spot** metering bases its measurements on one spot in the overall image. This means you must work very precisely to make sure you are metering the appropriate part (spot) of the scene. The resulting exposure recommendation will expose this spot with middle-gray brightness. For example, if you spot meter a backlit face against the sun, the metered exposure will display the face with middle-gray brightness (or zone V in the famous Ansel Adams zone system [22]). If that's too dark for your taste, you can use the exposure compensation dial to lift the exposure by +1/3 EV or +2/3 EV. On the other hand, if the person has dark skin, you may want to reduce the exposure with a correction in the opposite direction. It's up to you to choose the zone (brightness) of the spot-metered part of the image.

Spot metering is the most powerful and challenging metering method. It's useful when the light is very difficult—too difficult for multi and average metering. Typical examples are isolated bright objects in front of a dark background (and vice versa), such as a spot-lit musician or an actor on an otherwise dark stage, or strongly backlit subjects. Whenever your exposure must be spot on, spot metering is your friend.

With that said, it's obvious that spot metering requires you to meter very precisely. Even minute changes in the camera's direction can lead to dramatic changes in the metered result. Therefore, it can be useful to combine spot metering with the camera's AE-Lock function. AE-L will lock your exposure to prevent it from changing when you alter your composition, or when your subject starts to move away from your metering spot.

The best way to use spot metering is in manual exposure mode M. In this mode, metering doesn't affect the exposure because you are manually setting all three exposure parameters (shutter speed, aperture, and ISO). Spot metering in manual mode lets you determine the brightness level of any part of your image for any set exposure: The exposure scale in the viewfinder or LCD tells you exactly how much brighter or darker than middle gray (zone V) the spot metered object will appear in your shot (either ±3 EV or ±5 EV, depending on your exposure compensation dial mode setting).

Don't forget to *disable* Auto-ISO in manual mode M. If you don't, the camera will still operate in some kind of AE mode (I call it "misomatic"); in this mode, the ISO setting will be the exposure variable that's automatically adjusted.

Important: Multi, average, center-weighted, and spot metering are automatically disabled when face/eye detection or subject detection is switched on. In this case, the camera uses a modified version of multi metering that puts particular emphasis on the area of a detected face. When no faces are detected, the camera always reverts to regular multi metering as a fallback mode, which may be different from the exposure metering mode that you had selected before you switched on face/eye or subject detection.

| **TIP 39** | Linking spot metering to focus frames |

Traditionally, spot metering covers the center of the image with an area that's about as large as a standard-sized focus frame. However, by selecting AF/MF SETTING > INTERLOCK SPOT AE & FOCUS AREA > ON, you can link the spot metering area to the position and size(!) of the active focus frame in Single Point AF and MF mode.

This is a very useful feature if you are using one of the camera's many off-center AF frames, since it's likely that your focus area covers the same part of your subject that is also relevant for exposure metering (such as the brightly lit face of a musician or stage actor who is standing in front of a dark background).

If you want to decouple spot metering from the AF area and limit it to the very center of the frame, make sure to select AF/MF SETTING > INTERLOCK SPOT AE & FOCUS AREA > OFF.

Always remember that the camera will not interlock spot metering with the focus area if you set it to either Zone AF or Wide/Tracking AF. Interlocking only works in concert with Single Point AF or manual focus (MF) mode. And don't forget that spot metering is automatically disabled when either subject detection or face/eye detection are active.

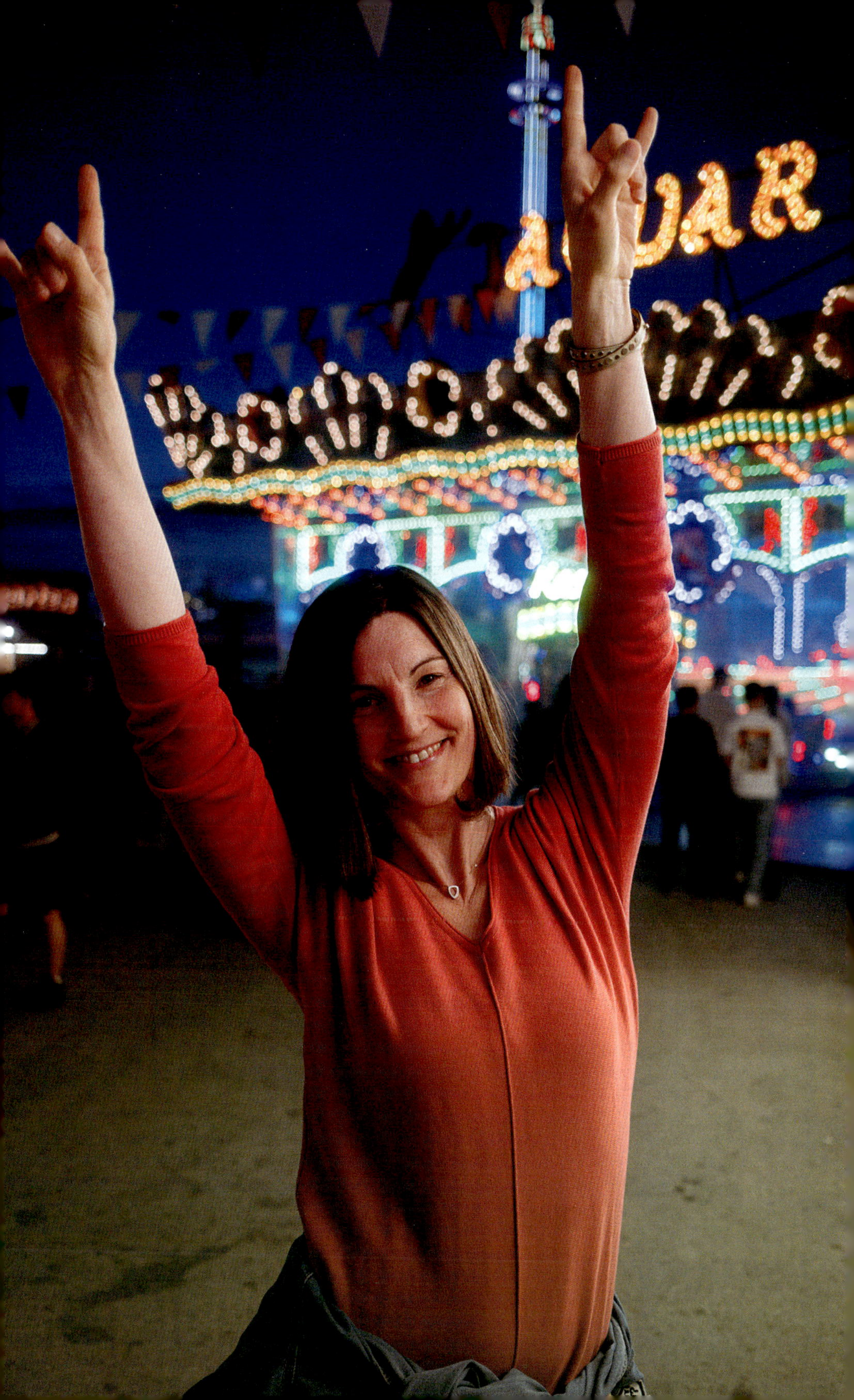

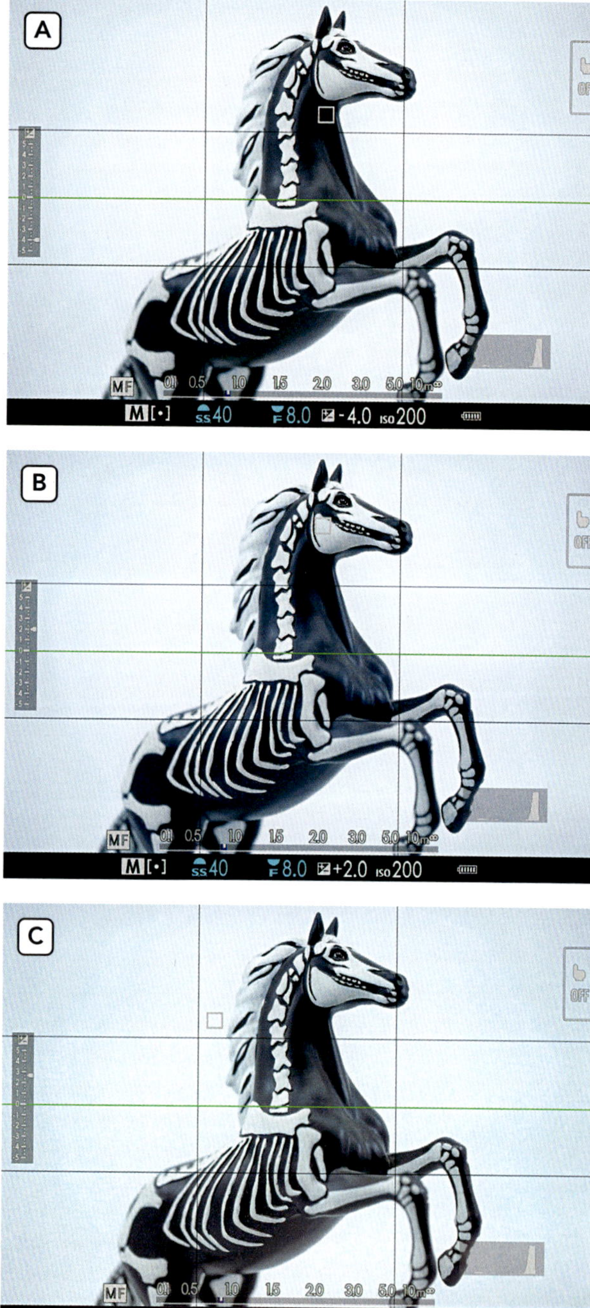
A
MF 0.1 0.5 1.0 1.5 2.0 3.0 5.0 10 m ∞
M [•] ss 40 F 8.0 ☒ -4.0 iso 200
OFF

B
MF 0.1 0.5 1.0 1.5 2.0 3.0 5.0 10 m ∞
M [•] ss 40 F 8.0 ☒ +2.0 iso 200
OFF

C
MF 0.1 0.5 1.0 1.5 2.0 3.0 5.0 10 m ∞
M [•] ss 40 F 8.0 ☒ +2.6 iso 200
OFF

Fig. 37: Spot metering and manual exposure mode: Metering different parts of an image is easy with spot metering. Simply set an exposure (aperture, shutter speed, and ISO), and then point the small spot-metering area at different parts of the scene. The exposure scale in your live view tells you the brightness of any metered spot, with 0 representing middle gray (zone V in the Ansel Adams zone system). To make things easier and most effective, interlock spot metering with the size and position of the currently active focus frame and select the smallest available focus frame size in AF-S or MF mode.

In this example, I spot metered the darkest part of the model horse at –4 EV (**A**), its brightest part at +2 EV (**B**), and the brightest overall part of the scene at +2.66 EV (**C**). This means that the dynamic range of this scene comprises less than 7 EV (2.66 + 4 = 6.66), a range that fits neatly into a regular DR100% JPEG image.

Using the live view and live histogram	TIP 40

Unlike optical viewfinders in DSLRs, the electronic live view of modern mirrorless cameras like your X100VI provides an accurate simulation of the resulting JPEG image. The live preview encompasses color, contrast, exposure, and effect settings.

In standard display mode, this WYSIWYG preview is complemented by a live histogram [23]. I strongly recommend using the live histogram because it provides a useful overview of the brightness distribution in your scene. It also helps you identify areas of over- and underexposure in advance, so you can take corrective measures:

- If bars are piling up like a bell curve at the right end of the histogram, but are cut off mid-peak, parts of your shot will be overexposed with blown highlights. If this affects important parts of your image, you should correct the exposure downward. Alternately, you can expand the shot's dynamic range by selecting DR200% or DR400% in the respective menu.

- If the histogram leans to the left, leaving plenty of unused space on the right, the shot might end up underexposed. In this case, you can adjust the exposure upward.

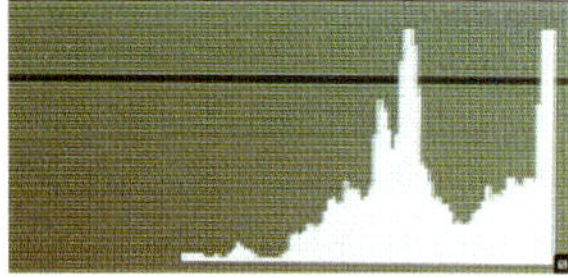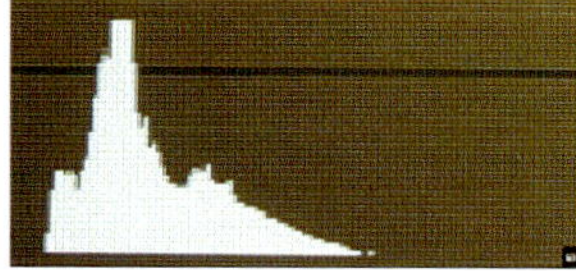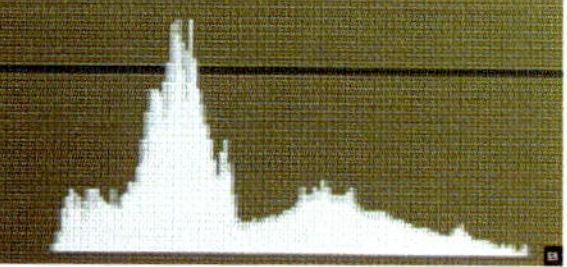

Fig. 38: Three **live histograms** that show overexposure, underexposure, and a balanced exposure of the same scene.

The histogram provides a technical representation of the live view simulation. When the Natural Live View is turned off, both the live view and the live histogram will reflect the current JPEG settings of the camera (white balance, film simulation, color, highlight and shadow contrast, etc.). For example, the VELVIA film simulation delivers more contrast and more saturated colors than ETERNA, and this is reflected in the live view and the live histogram.

It's important to note that the live view and live histogram also represent (simulate) the effect of manual DR200% or DR400% dynamic range settings. However, if you set the camera to DR-AUTO, the live view and live histogram will always display a DR100% preview. DR-P WEAK and DR-P STRONG are also simulated, with DR-P AUTO always showing a DR-P WEAK preview.

The X100VI also offers an **RGB histogram** [24], which is available only by assigning it to an Fn or Touch-Fn button. The RGB histogram is once again based on the current live view image, so it represents the resulting JPEG image. In fact, the color histogram displays four different histograms at once: overall luminance distribution (a larger version of the standard histogram) and separate histograms for the three color channels: red, green, and blue. That way, you can immediately recognize clipping of individual color channels in your JPEG. For example, shooting a red rose, the red channel is the first to clip and, thus, lose texture.

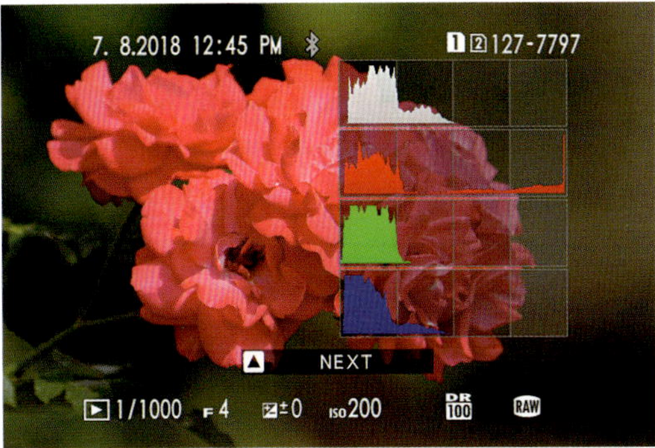

Fig. 39: The **RGB histogram** of this image of a rose illustrates how the red channel is already clipping (indicated by the peaking line at the right edge of the red channel histogram), while green, blue, and overall luminance are barely touching the right half of the histogram. Please note that if the Natural Live View is turned off, the histogram always reflects the current JPEG settings (film simulation, contrast settings, color saturation setting, etc.).

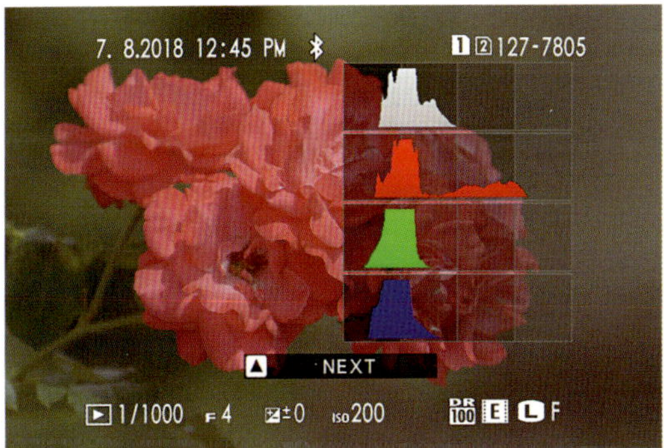

Fig. 40: This is the same RAW image, but this time processed with flat JPEG settings: Eterna film simulation, Shadow Tone Curve –2, Highlight Tone Curve –2, and Color –4. These settings reflect **the flattest possible color profile** you can achieve in your X100VI, and there's now plenty of additional headroom in the shadows and highlights. Thanks to the much higher dynamic range of the flat JPEG, there's also no clipping of the red channel in the histogram. This flat JPEG reflects the dynamic range of the actual RAW file much better than the camera's default JPEG settings, and many RAW shooters use these or similar flat JPEG settings in concert with the RGB histogram because it makes it easier to determine the optimal exposure, which is right at the sensor's saturation limit.

The RGB histogram also includes "blinkies," which are live overexposure or clipping warnings. If bright parts of your scene start to blink in RGB histogram mode, the blinking areas will be blown out in the resulting JPEG (i.e., losing texture and detail). The blinkies make it easy to set an exposure where important highlights are protected (i.e., not blinking in the RGB histogram view).

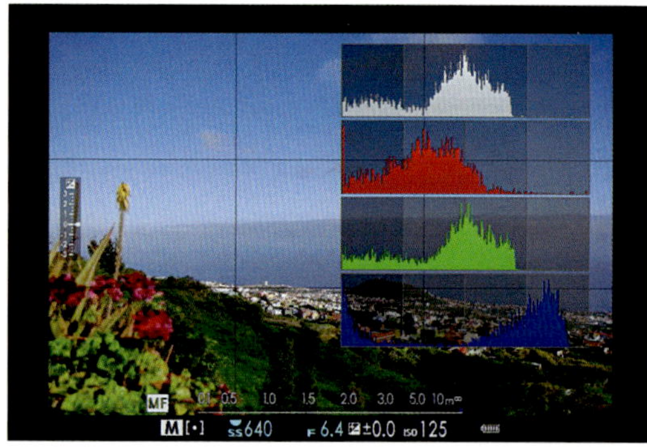

Fig. 41: In shooting mode, the **RGB histogram** displays a proper representation of the live view contents. This includes exposure, film simulation, contrast / tone curve, dedicated DR / DR-P settings, color saturation, and effect settings like Color Chrome. If parts of your scene are overexposed, the RGB histogram display will show them blinking. Please note that in shooting mode, the RGB histogram can only be activated via a properly configured Fn button or Touch-Fn gesture.

TIP 41	Auto exposure (AE) with modes **P**, **A**, and **S**

The three auto exposure modes of your X100VI are **P** (program AE), **A** (aperture priority), and **S** (shutter priority).

A brief reminder:

- **Program AE P** will automatically set a suitable aperture and shutter-speed combination.

- **Aperture priority A** will automatically set a suitable shutter speed to match a preset aperture.

- **Shutter priority** **S** will automatically set a suitable aperture to match a preset shutter speed.

To take a picture in one of these modes, you can follow these steps:

- Meter the exposure with one of the metering modes: multi, center-weighted, average, or spot.

- After metering, adjust the exposure to taste using the exposure compensation dial. Use the live view and the histogram to determine the best setting. Remember: it's not the camera that's setting the exposure; it's you. Don't blindly follow what the camera is proposing. Instead, always keep an eye on the live view and the live histogram.

- When you half-press the shutter button, your exposure will be locked as long as you keep the button half-pressed. As long as the shutter button remains half-pressed, you can adjust the framing or composition of your shot without changing the exposure. For this to work, make sure that SET UP > BUTTON/DIAL SETTING > SHUTTER AE is set to ON for both AF-S/MF and AF-C.

- To take the shot, fully press the shutter button.

Metering and exposure are two different things. After metering a scene, it is the photographer who sets the actual exposure with the exposure compensation dial:

- **Metering** is performed using either multi, center-weighted, average, or spot metering.

- Use the **exposure compensation dial** to adjust the metering result. Use the information from the live view and live histogram to adjust the exposure. Of course, there are instances where the initial metering is already spot-on and matches your desired exposure, so you won't have to apply any further correction.

- **Expose** the image using one of three AE modes: aperture priority, shutter priority, or program AE.

If you set the exposure compensation dial to its C position, exposure compensation will be performed by one of the command dials with an extended range of ±5 EV instead of ±3 EV. To configure a specific command dial to serve as your exposure compensation dial, go to the SET UP > BUTTON/ DIAL SETTING > COMMAND DIAL SETTING screen.

Using auto exposure (AE) modes, the live view will always show the calculated exposure brightness, even when this exposure cannot be realized due to technical limits. For example, the aperture cannot open beyond its maximum "wide open" setting. If the camera's AE encounters such a limit, the affected exposure parameter (aperture or shutter speed) will be displayed in red, meaning that the camera has calculated an exposure parameter setting that isn't practically available. However, the live view acts as if that practical limit didn't exist.

In manual exposure mode, the live view always represents the actual exposure if SET UP > SCREEN SET-UP > PREVIEW EXP./WB IN MANUAL MODE is set to PREVIEW EXP./WB.

TIP 42	Using manual exposure M

In manual exposure mode, you manually specify all three exposure parameters: aperture, shutter speed, and ISO amplification. For this to work, Auto-ISO must be turned off. Otherwise, ISO would become an exposure variable that the camera would automatically fill.

For the live view and live histogram to correctly display the set exposure in manual mode, make sure that SET UP > SCREEN SET-UP > PREVIEW EXP./WB IN MANUAL MODE > PREVIEW EXP./WB is set. I recommend setting the metering to spot metering.

Here's how you can expose in manual mode:

- Select and set an aperture and shutter speed that suits your subject and image idea. Aperture controls the depth of field [25]; shutter speed controls the amount of motion blur [26] and camera shake in your exposure.

- Next, select an ISO value that will yield the desired brightness in your shot. You can (and should) use the live view and live histogram to find a suitable setting. As usual, try not to blow out important highlights. The live histogram is your friend.

- You can check specific parts of your scene by spot metering them. The exposure scale in the live view screen tells you how much above or below middle gray (zone V) the spot-metered selection will be exposed. This tool helps you ensure that important parts of your image (such as skin tones or snow) will be exposed exactly like you want them to be.

- Finally, you may want to readjust or fine-tune aperture, shutter speed, and ISO according to your metering. Once everything is set, you can take the shot(s).

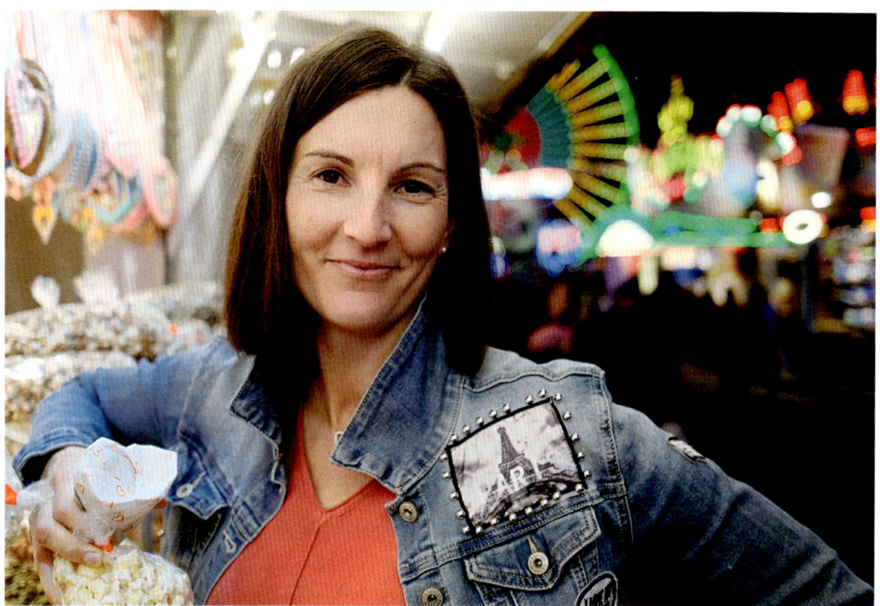

Fig. 42: I shoot in **manual exposure mode** almost all the time. And maybe you should too. Not only can the camera make fewer mistakes when you are in charge, but manual mode also gives you full control over aperture (depth of field), shutter speed (motion blur, camera shake), and ISO (noise level, effective dynamic range).

Manual mode also ensures that multiple shots of a scene will have the same consistent exposure, because the exposure doesn't change unless *you* change it. It also forces you to think about your actual exposure parameters: Why are you using a particular setting for aperture, shutter speed, and ISO?

Thanks to the WYSIWYG nature of mirrorless cameras, manual exposure mode can help you avoid unpleasant surprises: You *set* the exposure with the dials, you *see* the exposure in the live view, and you *get* the exposure you set and saw in your JPEG.

The SOOC JPEG in this example was shot manually with available light.

Important: The available maximum shutter speed of the mechanical shutter depends on the set aperture and can range between 1/2000 sec. (f/2 to f/2.5) and 1/4000 sec. (f/4.5 to f/16). It's possible that the manually selected shutter speed is faster than the camera's available maximum speed for the set aperture. If that's the case, the selected shutter speed will be displayed in red. You can safely use shutter speeds beyond the available maximum mechanical shutter speed by engaging the electronic shutter, or you can deploy the built-in ND filter and at the same time reduce the shutter speed by four stops without changing the exposure. In manual exposure mode, the X100VI will still honor "illegal" shutter speeds (shutter speeds that are displayed in red), but the resulting image may suffer from degraded bokeh.

Using aperture priority **A**　　　　　　　　　　　　　　**TIP 43**

In aperture priority AE [27], you manually set the aperture [28], and the camera automatically selects a suitable shutter speed based on your chosen exposure (as set with the exposure compensation dial). Which aperture should you select? Let's look at some basics:

■ As the aperture gets smaller (the aperture number gets bigger), your depth of field [29] (DOF) increases. DOF is the zone in front of and behind the focus plane that appears in perfect focus in your resulting image. In standard display mode, the viewfinder and LCD offer a focus and DOF bar that displays the focus distance and the calculated depth-of-field zone that surrounds it.

■ A fast lens like the 23mmF2 in your X100VI can exhibit a tight DOF when used wide open, so it's possible, for instance, in a portrait shot, for only one of the subject's eyes to be perfectly in focus. If that's the case, you can stop down the lens or change the position of your subject so that both eyes are the same distance from the camera.

■ Stopping down a lens beyond f/8 leads to increased diffraction blur [30] across the image area. While the larger depth of field increases the in-focus zone, maximum detail is reduced. In other words, when you shoot with f/16, there's a good chance that your scene will be in focus from front to back. However, its overall crispness will be lower than it would be at f/8. The built-in Lens Modulation Optimizer (LMO) in your X100VI can compensate for diffraction blur to a degree, but its effect only extends to JPEGs from the camera, including those created by the built-in RAW converter. External RAW converters don't support the LMO.

Important: The available maximum shutter speed of the mechanical shutter depends on the set aperture and can range between 1/2000 sec. (f/2 to f/2.5) and 1/4000 sec. (f/4.5 to f/16). When you shoot wide open or with a high ISO setting, it's possible that the calculated shutter speed is faster than the camera's available maximum speed. If that's the case, the available shutter speed will be displayed in red (overexposure warning). You can use shutter speeds beyond the available maximum mechanical shutter speed by engaging the electronic shutter, or you can deploy the built-in ND filter to reduce the shutter speed by four stops without changing the exposure.

TIP 44 Using shutter priority **S**

Shutter priority AE [31] works like aperture priority, except you are manually setting a shutter speed [32], and the camera automatically selects a fitting aperture value based on your exposure.

Setting the right shutter speed is dependent on two factors:

- Motion blur [33]: The faster your subject is moving, the faster your shutter speed must be in order to avoid shots with motion blur. This doesn't mean that motion blur is always bad; it can be used as a conscious choice to add dynamic punch to your image. For instance, panning [34] the camera in sync with a moving subject blurs the background behind that subject. Motion blur can be a benefit of long exposures [35]—exposure times of several seconds or minutes can smoothen water surfaces, blur cloudy skies, or add star trails.

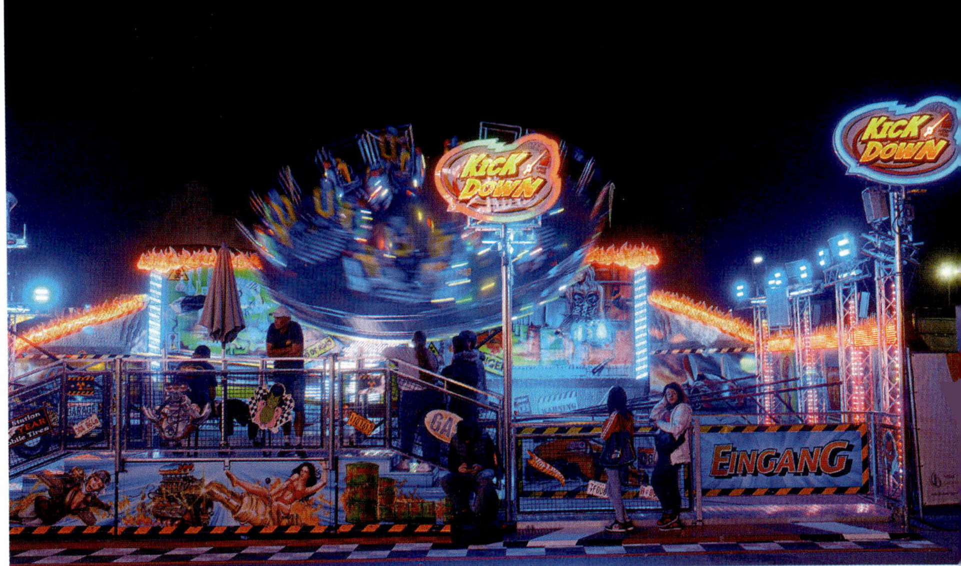

Fig. 43: In this handheld SOOC JPEG shot of a moving ride, **motion blur** was a conscious choice. The selected shutter speed of 1/8 sec. was slow enough to illustrate the motion of the ride. At the same time, it was fast enough to avoid camera shake which would have blurred the non-moving parts, as well.

- Blur due to camera shake [36]: if you don't hold the camera steady when you take a shot, the resulting image can be blurred. The IBIS can help, or you can put the camera on a tripod or a solid surface and use the self-timer or a remote shutter release to take the shot.

If you set a very slow shutter speed or choose a high ISO setting in shutter priority mode, it's possible that even the smallest aperture opening of your lens will still be too large to avoid overexposure. In this case, the aperture value will be displayed in red.

Since your camera features a dedicated shutter speed dial, you can use it to quickly change the shutter speed in full-stop increments. You can also use the command dial to fine-tune your selection in 1/3 EV intermediate steps.

Hint: Setting the shutter speed dial to **T** (Time) allows you to select the *full* range of available shutter speeds (in 1/3 EV increments) by turning a command dial. You can assign shutter speed control to one of the command dials in SET UP > BUTTON/DIAL SETTING > COMMAND DIAL SETTING. Personally, I always assign shutter speed control to the rear command dial.

Important: *As previously mentioned, the available maximum shutter speed of the mechanical shutter depends on the set aperture and can range between 1/2000 sec. (f/2 to f/2.5) and 1/4000 sec. (f/4.5 to f/16). It's possible that the selected shutter speed is faster than the camera's available maximum speed for the calculated aperture. If that's the case, the selected shutter speed will be displayed in red. You can safely use shutter speeds beyond the available maximum mechanical shutter speed by engaging the electronic shutter, or you can deploy the built-in ND filter and, at the same time, reduce the shutter speed by four stops without changing the exposure. In shutter priority and manual exposure mode, the X100VI will still honor "illegal" shutter speeds (shutter speeds that are displayed in red), but the resulting image may suffer from degraded bokeh.*

TIP 45	Using program AE **P** and program shift

In program AE, the camera will automatically pick aperture *and* shutter speed settings that correspond to your set exposure. This mode can be useful for inexperienced photographers or in situations when you don't have the time to manually adjust the aperture or shutter speed.

Like in aperture priority AE, the slowest possible shutter speed in program AE is limited to a maximum duration of 30 seconds. When this (in concert with an already wide-open aperture) isn't long enough to achieve the set exposure, the camera will display a red underexposure warning when you half-press the shutter release button.

Even in program AE, you can influence shutter speed and aperture to a degree by using program shift. Program shift allows you to select more suitable combinations of aperture and shutter speed compared to the one originally proposed by the camera's program. You can cycle through various combinations of apertures and shutter speeds that all result in the same exposure. When the camera is in program AE mode, you can activate program shift by turning the command dial that is otherwise responsible for adjusting the shutter speed.

Let's say you are shooting a portrait. It's a bright day, so program AE offers a shutter speed of 1/500 sec. with an aperture of f/4. However, you prefer to shoot the portrait wide open at f/2 to achieve a blurrier background. In this situation, you have two choices: you can either switch to aperture priority mode by manually setting an aperture of f/2, or you can use program shift by turning the command dial until the aperture display shows f/2. Opening the aperture two stops, from f/4 to f/2, won't change the original exposure because program shift will automatically adjust the shutter speed two stops from 1/500 sec to 1/2000 sec.

Important: *Program shift is only available when certain conditions are met. It's not available if DYNAMIC RANGE or D RANGE PRIORITY are set to AUTO, or if a TTL flash is in use.*

Playing it safe with auto exposure bracketing	TIP 46

As you know by now, the automatic exposure (AE) modes **P**, **A**, and **S** are merely responsible for automatically filling exposure variables. The exposure itself is the responsibility of the photographer. You can use metering (multi, center-weighted, average, or spot), the live view, and the live histogram to determine the correct exposure.

Nobody is perfect! If you want to play it safe, auto exposure bracketing [37] can be a helpful feature. AE BKT takes a series of at least two shots in quick succession, each with a different exposure (known as exposure bracketing). With this method, there will often be one shot with normal exposure, one underexposed shot, and one overexposed shot.

Exposure bracketing is especially useful with subjects that don't move much. After you've taken the shot, you can decide which of the differently exposed versions you want to keep.

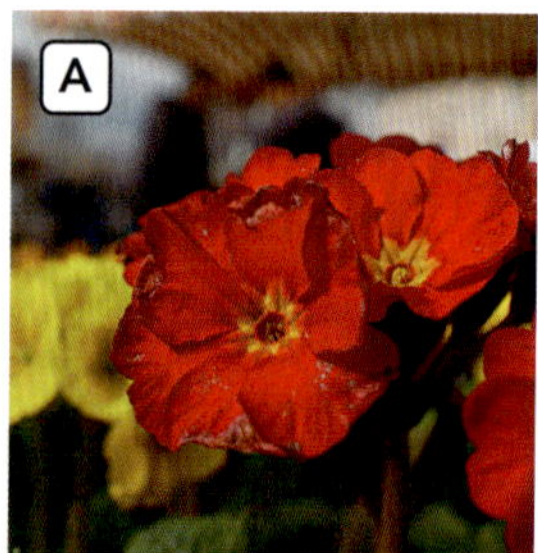
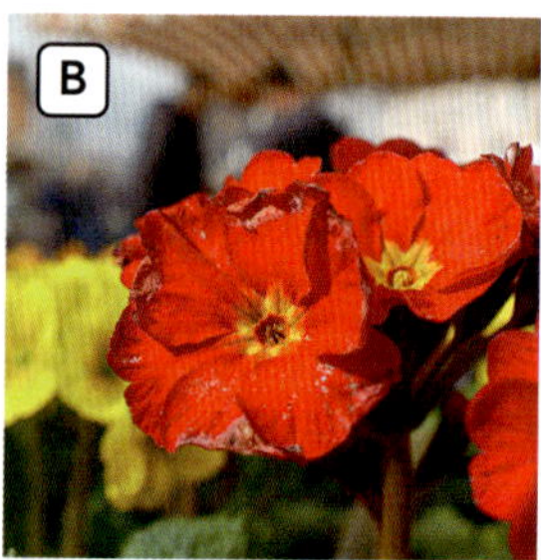
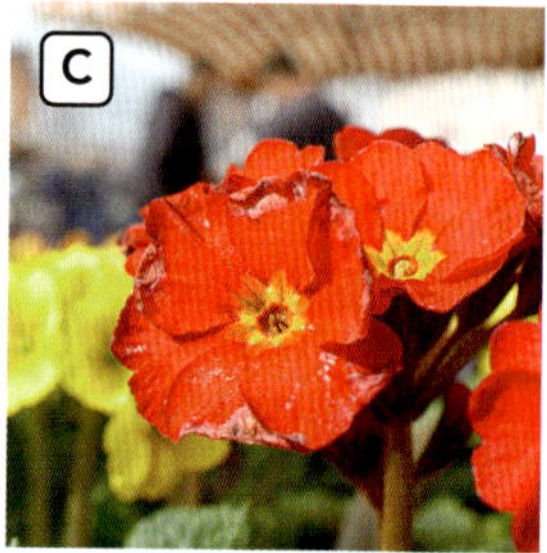

Fig. 44: Auto exposure bracketing automatically takes two or more images with varying exposure. Contrary to its name, AE bracketing even works in manual exposure mode, so you can manually set an exposure (aperture, shutter speed, ISO) you think is right, and AE bracketing will give you additional options with different shutter speeds that are brighter and/or darker than your original exposure. In this example, image **B** shows the originally set exposure. Image **A** was bracketed 2/3 EV darker, and image **C** was bracketed 2/3 EV brighter.

You can activate AE BKT by selecting it in the DRIVE button menu. In the regular camera menu, you can configure the AE bracketing parameters such as the exposure difference between images (SHOOTING SETTING > AE BKT SETTING).

| Long exposures | TIP 47 |

Long exposures can lead to impressive results. Fireworks, night shots, water surfaces, stars, or clouds: exposure times of several seconds or minutes capture the course of time in a single photograph. Of course, this only works if you put the camera on a tripod or a solid surface.

You have two basic options:

- Set the shutter-speed dial to **T** (Time) and then use the rear command dial to set the shutter speed. To avoid camera shake, use a remote shutter release or the self-timer to take the shot.

- Set the shutter speed dial to **B** (Bulb), then press and hold the shutter for as long as you want the camera to expose. Obviously, it makes sense to use a (tethered or wireless) remote shutter release that can be locked for the duration of the shot.

For good-quality results, make sure to set IMAGE QUALITY SETTING > LONG EXPOSURE NR > ON. By doing so, the camera will perform a dark-frame subtraction [38] depending on what ISO and exposure time you used. Dark-frame subtraction doubles the effective exposure duration, so be patient.

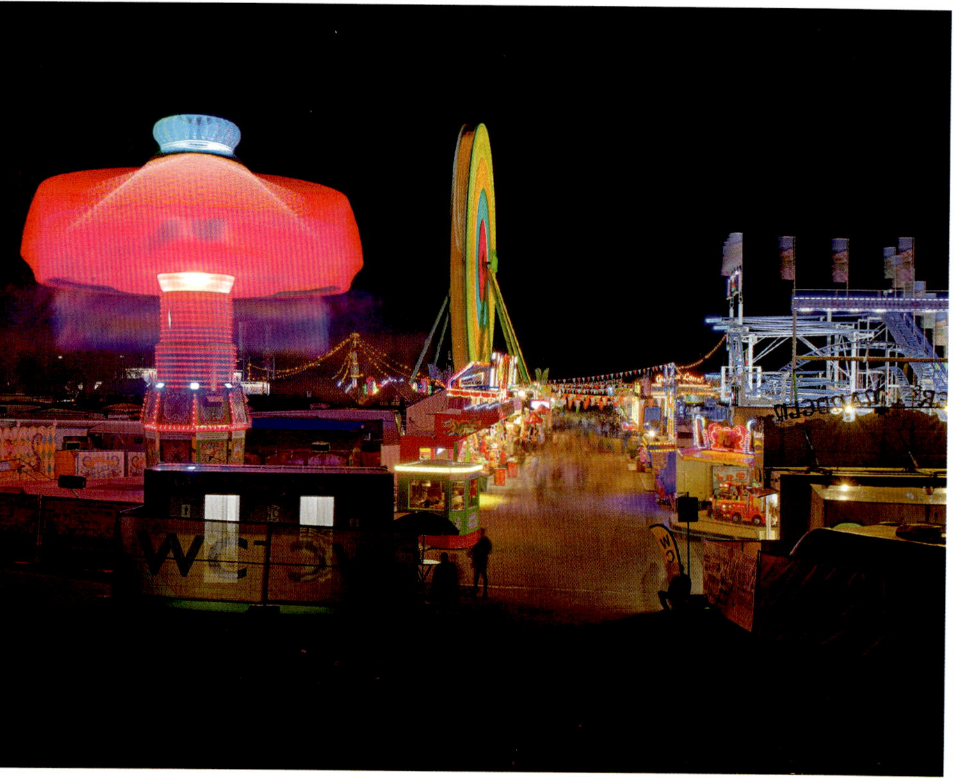

Fig. 45: A **long exposure** of 40 sec. taken in T mode (SOOC JPEG). Make sure to use a solid tripod and a remote shutter release for this kind of shot. IBIS should either be in Continuous mode or turned off.

TIP 48	Long exposures in bright daylight

To achieve long exposure times under normal daylight conditions, you can't just stop down the lens—even at f/16 and ISO 125, your shutter speed would still be too fast. Besides, diffraction blur is kicking it around f/8, so stopping down way beyond this point is only recommended when it cannot be avoided.

To realize long shutter speeds in good light, it's best to use a so-called ND filter [39], or Neutral Density filter. This is a fancy name for a gray filter that you can put in front of the lens to block a portion of the light from reaching the sensor.

For example, a filter with an ND 3.0 specification will extend your exposure time by a factor of about 1000 (or 10 f-stops/EV). This means that by using such a filter, a scene that would normally require a shutter speed of 1/50 sec. at f/8 can be shot at the same aperture with an exposure time of 20 seconds.

However, there's a catch: since your X100VI is equipped with a rather weak infrared cut filter in front of the sensor, long exposures (typically one minute or longer) in bright daylight should be performed with a regular neutral density (ND) filter and a dedicated IR cut filter in front of the lens. This will help you avoid false colors. A few ND filters (like my rectangular NiSi filters for the X100 series) already include an IR cut filter.

As you know, your X100VI also comes with a built-in ND filter that you can deploy in the camera menu or with a Fn button. It's an ND 1.2, meaning the exposure time for any given aperture will be extended by four f-stops (EV). Feel free to combine the built-in ND filter with an external ND filter: the number of f-stops will simply add up. For example, combining am external 10-stop ND filter with the built-in 4-stop ND filter will extend your exposure time by 14 stops.

Please keep in mind that every optical filter has the potential to add undesirable effects such as reflections, flare, or ghost images. This includes the camera's built-in ND filter, and particularly applies to night scenes with a bright street and city lights.

Finally, don't forget that you need an AR-X100 adapter ring to attach a regular 49mm filter on the camera's built-in 23mmF2 lens. Don't try to attach filters directly to the lens.

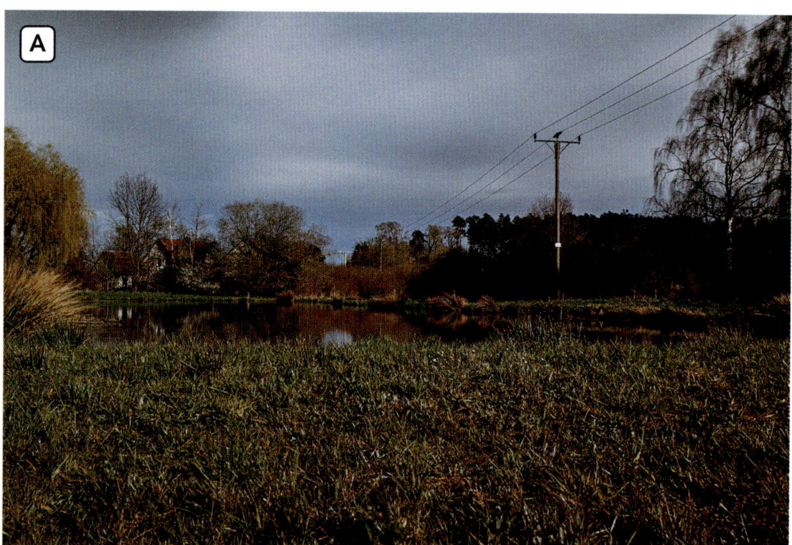

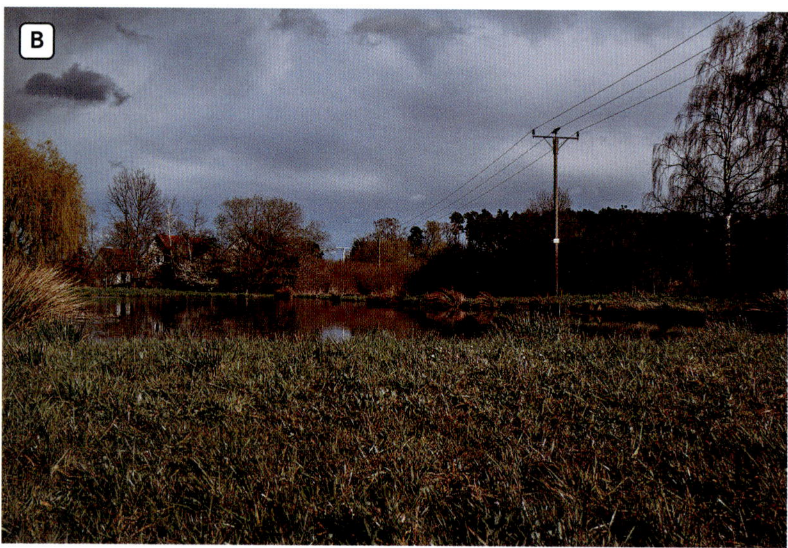

Fig. 46: This **long daylight exposure** lasted 50 seconds at f/8 and ISO 125 (image **A**) and was made possible by combining the camera's built-in 4-stop ND filter with a 10-stop rectangular NiSi filter that was made for the X100 series. For comparison, image **B** shows the unfiltered version with f/8 and 1/320 sec. (14 stops faster), also at ISO 125. As you can see, the long exposure not only blurs the moving clouds and water surface but also tree branches and vegetation that were moving in the wind.

The meaning of ISO in the digital realm is often misunderstood. Unlike film, higher ISO settings *don't* increase the sensor's sensitivity. The sensor in your X100VI is calibrated to a native ISO 125 (based on the popular SOS standard) [40], and this remains the same no matter what ISO you set.

To be clear, there's no difference between taking a shot with f/5.6 and 1/60 sec. at either ISO L (64) or at ISO H (51200). In both cases, the sensor is exposed to the exact same amount of light (or photons) due to the fixed f/5.6 and 1/60 sec. setting. The amount of light that hits the sensor (the actual exposure) is solely determined by aperture and shutter speed.

So, what exactly is ISO doing? ISO determines the amount of *signal amplification* that's applied to the image. ISO 125, the sensor's native setting, is the camera's basic calibration (base ISO). At ISO 250, the signal (or sensor data) is amplified by one aperture stop (1 EV) to brighten the image and increase its exposure. At ISO 500, the amplification amounts to two stops (2 EV), and so on. At ISO 12800, the additional amplification of the light recorded by the sensor amounts to almost seven stops. It's not surprising that image quality decreases when ISO amplification increases because noise and artifacts are amplified along with the actual image data.

The amplification we are talking about means brightening the image by increasing its exposure. This concept of amplification isn't limited to the camera itself by setting the ISO—it's also part of the entire workflow from in-camera exposure via RAW file (digital negative) to the final JPEG, HEIF, or TIFF file (digital print). If you are familiar with RAW converters such as Lightroom, you know there's an exposure slider. Moving this slider to the left or right changes the exposure (and hence the ISO brightness) of an image after the fact.

If you take a shot with an ISO 500 setting, you're telling the camera's Auto Exposure (AE) to expose the image two stops darker than it would at its base ISO of 125, then to amplify (brighten) that image two stops to compensate for the underexposure.

Regarding image quality and ISO, there's a basic rule: lower ISO settings lead to higher-quality results—hence the general recommendation to keep the ISO settings as low as possible. However, we obviously can't shoot with base ISO all the time, especially in low-light situations.

There are two basic methods to amplify a digital image:

- **Analog/digital hybrid amplification** *prior* **to writing the RAW file:** This method applies a mix of analog and digital signal processing to amplify or push the image to the brightness level that corresponds to the camera's ISO setting. The digitized result of this amplification/ multiplication process is then saved as a RAW file.

- **Digital amplification (push)** *after* **writing the RAW file:** This method changes the brightness of an image during RAW processing, *after* the RAW file has been generated. Metadata (i.e., instructions) in the RAW file tell the RAW converter what to do. You can also use the camera's built-in RAW converter to adjust the effective brightness (and hence, effective ISO) of an image after it has been recorded, or simply by adjusting your external RAW con- verter's exposure slider during RAW processing.

Digital amplification (i.e., multiplication) during RAW processing is beneficial because it's reversible. If the digital amplification (exposure) was too strong (leading to blown highlights), you can always pull it back again to reduce it. If it was too weak, you can push it up. ISO (i.e., exposure am- plification) is a volatile aspect of the photographic process because it can be applied *anytime:* prior to writing the RAW file, and later during RAW processing.

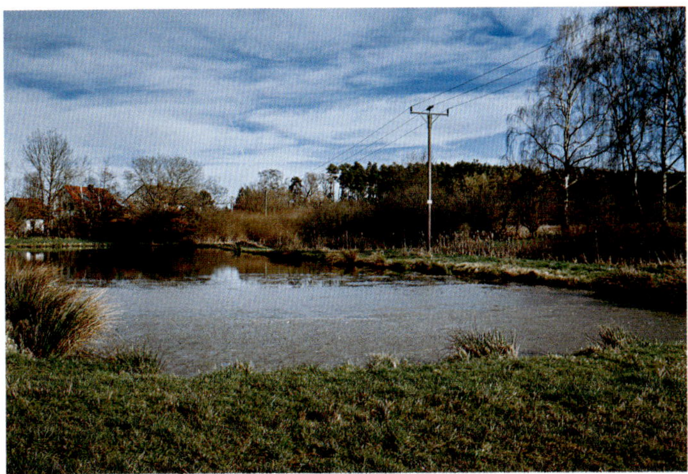

Fig. 47: ISO-less sensor (1): This shot was taken at ISO 2000, with classic analog/digital in-camera amplification. The ISO 2000 result was then burned into the RAW file and the RAW converted to a JPEG.

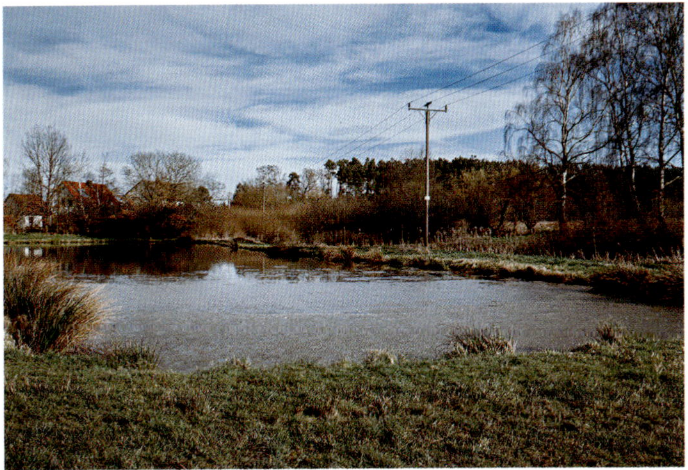

Fig. 48: ISO-less sensor (2): This shot was also *effectively* taken at ISO 2000. However, it was shot with an ISO 125 base setting, using the same aperture and shutter speed as the previous image, effectively underexposing it four stops (4 EV). The amplification from ISO 125 to ISO 2000 took place digitally during RAW conversion, simply by moving the exposure slider in Adobe Lightroom 4 EV to the right, thus compensating for the underexposure.

The sensor in your X100VI is a so-called ISO-less sensor. This means there's no significant quality difference between conventional signal amplification prior to writing a RAW file and digital amplification later during RAW conversion. This is great, because it allows you to digitally increase the ISO (i.e., brightness/exposure) of your shots during RAW processing, either in-camera or with external software such as Lightroom. Pushing the exposure up later in your RAW converter won't look much different from choosing a higher ISO setting when you take the shot.

Fig. 49: ISO-less sensor (3): This is the same as the previous shot that was recorded as an ISO 125 RAW file—but without the push of 4 EV that effectively turned it into an image with ISO 2000 brightness.

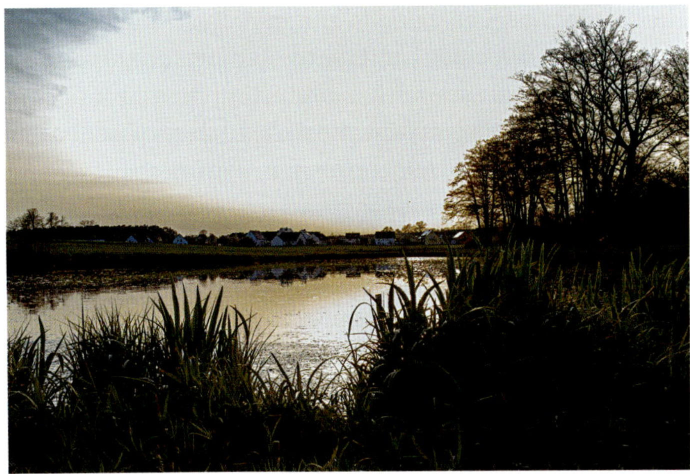

Fig. 50: ISO-less sensor (4): This image was taken at ISO 2000. The exposure was set for the foreground. As you can see, the sky is blown and couldn't be recovered during RAW conversion.

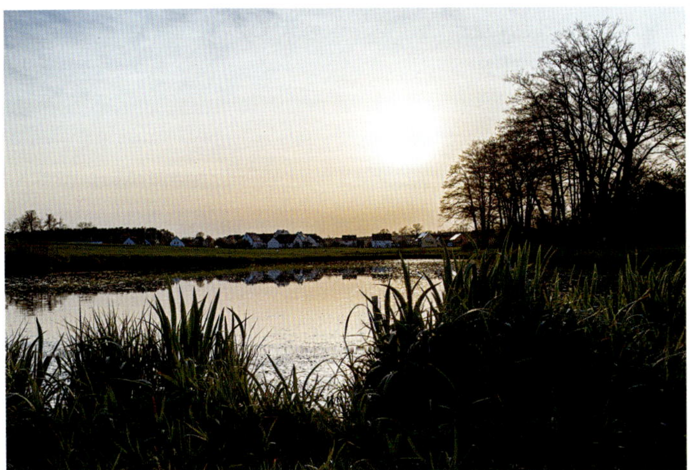

Fig. 51: ISO-less sensor (5): This image was taken at ISO 125, with otherwise the same exposure settings (aperture and shutter speed) as the previous ISO 2000 shot. I also used the same Lightroom development settings as before, with only one difference: the exposure slider was moved 4 EV to the right. This effectively pushes the image data to ISO 2000. Image quality in the shadows and midtones is very similar, but the highlights (sky and clouds) are now fully intact.

The ISO-less sensor extends the dynamic range of your X100VI. You can now confidently expose for the critical highlights in your scene, thus protecting them from being blown. In step two, you raise the dark (underexposed) parts of the image during RAW conversion. Raising shadows and midtones doesn't produce more visible noise than using a higher ISO setting in the first place.

Of course, it also depends on your RAW converter and how competent it is at raising shadows. Pushing your exposure by 4 EV or even 5 EV is possible if your converter plays along. Basically, you don't just need an ISO-less sensor, you also need an "ISO-less RAW converter."

With Adobe Lightroom, my best experience regarding massive exposure push operations has been with Iridient X-Transformer [41] as an intermediary. X-Transformer not only performs better demosaicing than Lightroom's standard algorithm, it also produces a linear DNG file that is better suited for strong push operations in Lightroom than the original RAF file.

Even better results with very little noise can often be achieved by pushing and processing linear DNG files that were generated with Adobe Lightroom's new AI denoise/demosaicing function. However, this option may produce color shifts and other artifacts with certain shots, so your mileage may vary.

Another alternative is DxO PureRAW [42], an AI-based demosaicing option that also exports linear DNG files and works standalone or as a Lightroom plug-in. Color fidelity in concert with push operations is quite good and you can adjust the amount of detail smoothing.

<table><tr><td>**What you should know about extended ISO**</td><td>**TIP 50**</td></tr></table>

You have probably noticed that in addition to the standard ISO settings (ISO 125 to ISO 12800), your X100VI offers three additional settings: L (64), H (25600), and H (51200).

- **H means High**: In these modes, image data is digitally amplified further. This enormous amplification leads to a visible decrease in image quality. While ISO 25600 is still quite usable (especially for black-and-white JPEGs using the ACROS film simulation), ISO 51200 is only for emergencies.

- **L means Low**: In ISO L (64) mode, an ISO 125 RAW is over-exposed by one stop. During RAW conversion, the JPEG is pulled down one stop and saved, resulting in an ISO 64 JPEG file. A digital pull is the direct opposite of a digital push operation: Digital pull decreases the exposure of the resulting image. The ISO L (64) RAW and JPEG files contain one stop *less* dynamic range than normal ISO 125 files. This means bright areas like clouds in the sky can easily appear blown out. On the other hand, ISO L (64) can add contrast and punch to scenes with dull lighting and little contrast.

Fig. 52: Extended ISO L can add punch thanks to its decreased dynamic range. To pull it off, set your camera to manual exposure mode, select base ISO 125, and expose the scene to the highlights using the live view and live histogram. Exposing to the highlights means that the brightest, important parts of the scene are exposed as bright as possible, but without clipping (i.e., losing highlight detail). After the exposure to the highlights is manually set, change the ISO setting from 125 to L (64) without changing aperture or shutter speed. This will increase the contrast of the image by darkening the shadows and midtones one stop, while bright highlights remain where they were.

Extended ISO L is great for subjects with little contrast (image **A**), or in situations where you want to emphasize and maximize the contrast (image **B**).

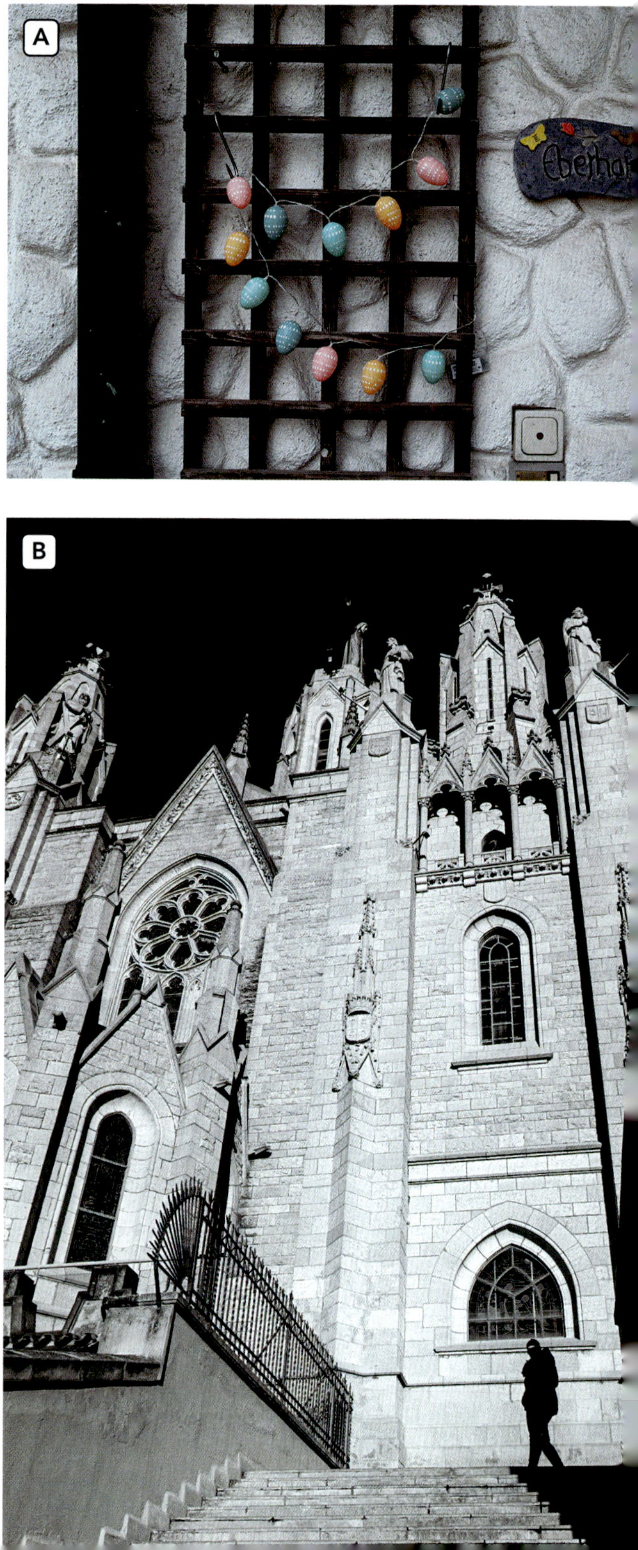

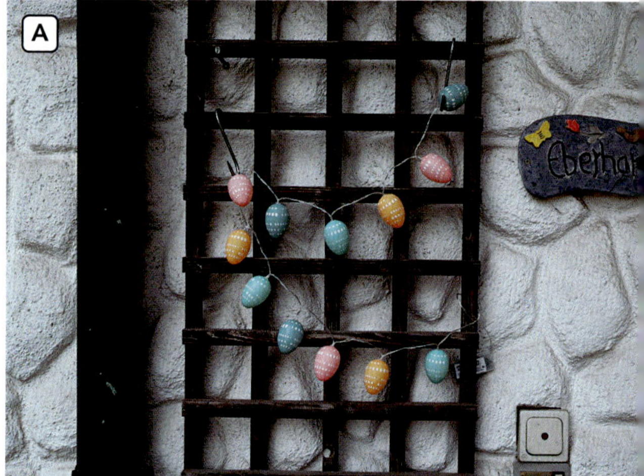

While shooting in extended ISO L diminishes highlight dynamic range, this fact is *not* reflected in the live view and live histogram. This means the live view and live histogram become pretty much useless for determining the correct exposure to the highlights when you are using ISO L. Only when you half-press and hold the shutter button to lock the exposure will the live view adapt, but at that stage there is no histogram available.

Practically, this means it's not recommended that you use extended ISO L in one of the auto exposure (AE) modes: **P**, **A**, and **S**. Instead, you should first set the correct exposure to the highlights in manual mode **M** at ISO 125 using the live view and live histogram, and then change the ISO setting to ISO L (64) without further adjustments to shutter speed and aperture. This will keep your highlights intact and will add contrast to the image by lowering the midtones and shadows to the new ISO L (64) settings.

The X100VI also offers extended ISO L (100) and ISO L (80) settings, which are derived from ISO 200 and ISO 160 by first overexposing the shot one stop and then pulling it back down one stop during RAW conversion to match the brightness of the selected ISO L setting of 100 or 80. Doing so deducts one stop of dynamic range. I strongly advise against using these two additional extended ISO L settings.

Important: *Extended ISO settings are only available when the mechanical shutter (MS) is selected.*

Auto-ISO and minimum shutter speed	TIP 51

You can automate the task of selecting the best (or lowest) possible ISO setting for any given shooting situation. Auto-ISO is an option with up to three configurable presets (AUTO1, AUTO2, and AUTO3) that can be configured in the ISO menu of your camera (SHOOTING SETTING > ISO AUTO SETTING):

- DEFAULT SENSITIVITY: This is the lower ISO limit. The camera will always try to use this ISO setting if the other parameters permit it.

- MAX. SENSITIVITY: This is the upper ISO limit. The camera's Auto-ISO will never go beyond this level.

- MIN. SHUTTER SPEED: Auto-ISO will automatically increase the ISO setting (up to the MAX. SENSITIVITY threshold) when the minimum shutter speed cannot be realized. There's also an AUTO setting here: If you set MIN. SHUTTER SPEED to AUTO, the camera will adjust the minimum shutter speed depending on the current focal length, using the formula *Minimum Shutter Speed = [1 ÷ (Focal Length × 1.5)] sec.* With the 23mmF2 prime lens of your X100VI without a WCL or TCL, the AUTO setting delivers a minimum shutter speed setting of 1/34 sec. Activating the digital teleconverter doesn't affect the AUTO setting for the minimum shutter speed, but using a WCL or TCL does.

Obviously, MIN. SHUTTER SPEED is only relevant in auto exposure (AE) modes **A** and **P**, because you set the shutter speed manually in modes **M** and **S**. Auto-ISO minimum shutter speed makes sure that within the lower and upper ISO limits, the camera will always use a shutter speed that is at least as fast as the set minimum shutter speed.

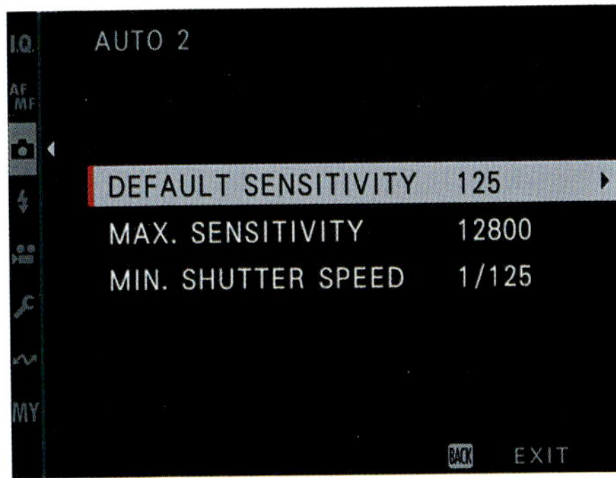

Fig. 53: Auto-ISO works with an ISO range between DEFAULT SEN-SITIVITY (the ISO floor) and MAX. SENSITIVITY (the ISO ceiling). It will always try to keep ISO as close to the floor as possible, but only if the resulting shutter speed isn't slower than the set MIN. SHUTTER SPEED.

Here's an example: Let's say you are shooting in mode **A** (aperture priority) in bright light conditions using f/5.6. Auto-ISO is set to ISO 125 as the lower limit and ISO 12800 as the upper limit. You have set 1/125 sec. as your minimum shutter speed, because you want to avoid motion blur while taking pictures of people walking in the street.

If the scene is brightly lit, there is no problem. The camera will use ISO 125 with shutter speeds at least as fast as 1/125 sec. However, as the sun sets and it becomes impossible to successfully use 1/125 sec. at f/5.6 and ISO 125, Auto-ISO will increase the ISO to ensure the shutter speed doesn't drop below 1/125 sec. This automatic adjustment continues as the light conditions deteriorate until Auto-ISO reaches the upper ISO limit (in our case, ISO 12800). What now? Since the camera can't increase the ISO any further, it will start to reduce the shutter speed to values slower than 1/125 sec. to still ensure a correct exposure.

In mode **S** (shutter priority), the photographer sets the shutter speed. In this mode, Auto-ISO will increase the ISO setting only when the aperture is already wide open and can't be opened further. This can be a problem with the fast lens in your X100VI. When shot wide open at f/2, the depth of field can be quite limited. This is why Auto-ISO is better suited for modes **P** or **A**.

TIP 52   Auto-ISO in manual mode M: the "misomatic" mode

Manual mode in tandem with Auto-**ISO** provides another auto**MATIC** exposure mode: the so-called "**misomatic**" mode. In this mode, you preselect the aperture and shutter speed, and the camera automatically selects a suitable ISO setting that matches the exposure that has been determined by the currently active metering mode.

To be useful in a misomatic setup, Auto-ISO should be able to use the full ISO bandwidth, so you should configure it with the camera's base ISO 125 as the lower limit and the highest available upper limit (ISO 12800).

Misomatic gives you full manual control over aperture (depth of field) and shutter speed (motion blur and camera shake). You can tailor shutter speed and aperture to the requirements of the task at hand; there will be no surprises. At the same time, you still enjoy the comfort of automatic exposure (AE).

Misomatic also allows you to adjust the camera-metered exposure with the exposure compensation dial. For this to be effective, it's even more important to set the Auto-ISO DEFAULT SENSITIVITY as low as possible and the MAX. SENSITIVITY as high as possible.

If you don't want to spend time with exposure compensation while you are in misomatic mode, you can use Fuji's DR function as a workaround by selecting DR200% in concert with the misomatic. This setting is your insurance against accidental overexposure by the camera's AE, because it gives you at least one stop of extra latitude for after-the-fact overexposure corrections with the internal or an external RAW converter. To correct a poor auto-exposure after the fact, you can use the PUSH/PULL PROCESSING function of the camera's internal RAW converter, or move the exposure slider of your external RAW processing software.

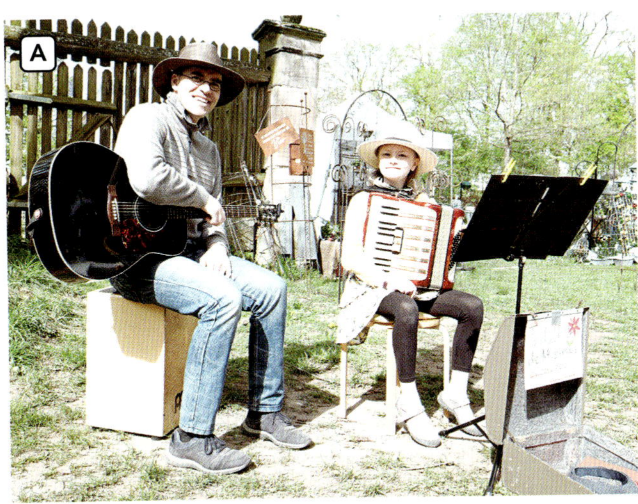

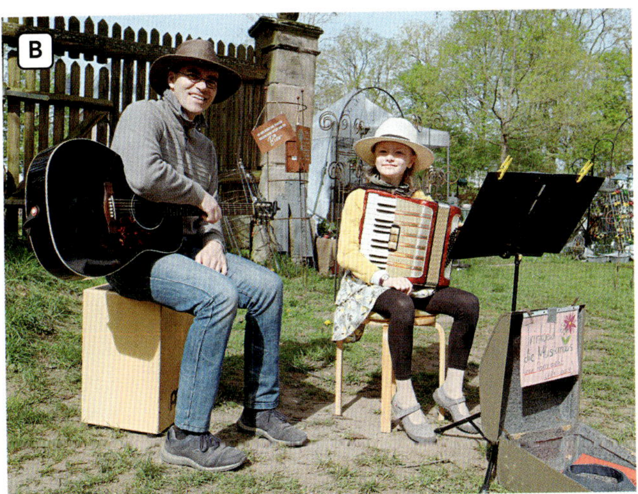

Fig. 54: Misomatic mode combines manual exposure with Auto-ISO. It can be helpful in situations with quickly and suddenly changing light conditions, such as with concerts and other stage events, sporting events, action shots, and street photography. Basically, it's about situations that don't leave you enough time to manually adjust the exposure, and where catching the decisive moment is your priority. In misomatic mode, you can set the desired depth of field (aperture) and motion blur (shutter speed), while the camera auto-exposes the images by applying the right amount of ISO amplification. To protect against accidental overexposure (**A**), you can buy "insurance" by setting the camera to DR200% or DR400% in misomatic mode. This way, overexposure can be corrected during RAW conversion (**B**).

Don't forget: ISO is just an amplification of the image signal. Using misomatic mode, the amount of light that reaches the sensor is solely determined by your manual aperture and shutter speed settings. It always stays the same, regardless of the automatic ISO setting chosen by the camera. In misomatic mode, the only exposure variable is the amount of signal amplification (i.e., ISO); and with an ISO-less sensor, this variable can also be adjusted later during RAW conversion. In this context, choosing DR200% ensures there's more leeway for after-the-fact exposure corrections.

> **TIP 53** **Extending the dynamic range**

If the dynamic range of a scene surpasses the dynamic range of the camera's sensor or image processing, one—or both—of the following phenomena occur:

- The highlights of the image are blown out or appear too bright (overexposed).

- Midtones appear too dark (underexposed), and shadows lose detail in dark areas.

In both cases, the shot's exposure is out of balance. Sadly, it's very difficult (if not impossible) to restore detail in blown highlights. It's much easier to lift underexposed midtones and blocked shadows. This procedure is called *tone mapping*, and it's the only way to access the full potential of a modern digital camera's dynamic range. Tone mapping reassigns certain tonal values of the original exposure, either by employing a tone curve or by using a more complex procedure known as *adaptive* tone mapping, which takes the brightness of neighboring pixels into account.

To record the full tonal range of a high-contrast scene, it's best to expose the image in a way that preserves the color and texture of its important bright parts. Of course, doing so can lead to an image with underexposed midtones and blocked shadows that needs further processing to look natural, realistic, and pleasing. You can correct these issues with most external RAW converters.

While every RAW converter is different, most programs offer functions to selectively manipulate the exposure of a shot after the fact. For example, you can change the overall exposure with the exposure slider, and you can restore blown highlights with a highlight recovery slider. Most converters also offer sliders that only target shadow tones.

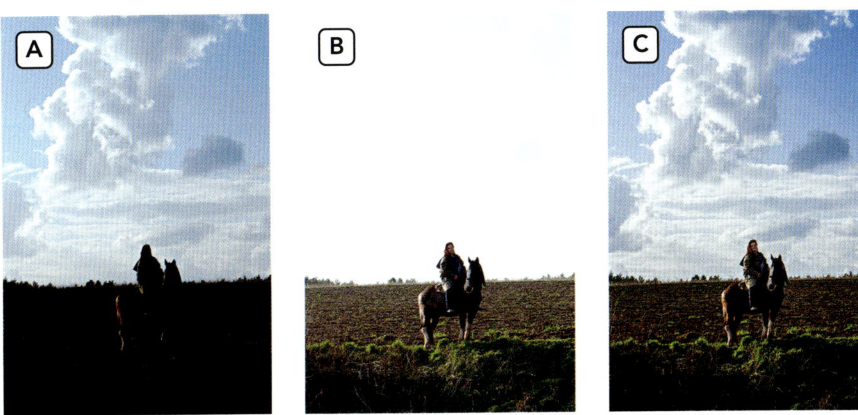

Fig. 55: In many instances, the **dynamic range** of a standard (DR100%) JPEG is smaller than the dynamic range of the scene, so no matter how you expose the scene in your camera, some parts of the resulting image will end up either too dark or too bright (or both). Here's a practical example:

Image **A** was exposed to the highlights, showing color and texture in the blue sky and white clouds. However, the darker foreground is clearly underexposed, resulting in blocked shadows. Horse and rider are almost reduced to a silhouette.

Image **B** depicts the same scene, but this time it was exposed about two stops (EV) brighter, removing blocked shadows and adding detail to the main subject. However, the cloudy blue sky is now overexposed and has all but disappeared.

This is a Catch-22, because no matter how you expose this scene, the standard JPEG from the camera will always display essential parts either too dark or too bright. Quite obviously, different parts of this scene require different exposures. To pull this off, we can use the RAW file of image A, which was exposed to preserve the clouds and the sky. By applying tone mapping in a modern RAW converter, we selectively push (brighten) shadows and midtones without further brightening the highlights of the clouds and sky. We can even add additional contrast to the clouds and darken the sky a bit. Image **C** shows the result out of Adobe Lightroom, where different pixels received different levels of (after-the-fact) amplification.

The built-in DR function of your X100VI can help you automate the tone mapping procedure. It works in two stages:

- The RAW file is exposed one (DR200%) or two stops (DR400%) darker than indicated to preserve bright highlights of a scene that would otherwise be clipped and lost.

- During the RAW conversion in the camera, the under-exposed shadows and midtones are digitally amplified by one (DR200%) or two stops (DR400%) to restore their natural brightness, while the (already correctly exposed) highlights are mostly left alone to preserve them.

The resulting JPEG from the camera has undergone a selective exposure correction. The DR function restores the shadows and midtones of a shot that was initially exposed one or two stops darker to preserve the highlights of the scene. Looking at the resulting JPEGs, this leads to an effective gain in dynamic range (DR): one additional stop of highlight DR at DR200%, and two stops of additional highlight DR at DR400%.

In DR-Auto mode, the camera will automatically select a suitable DR setting. Please note that in this mode, the X100VI will only choose either DR100% (no highlight DR expansion) or DR200% (one stop of highlight DR expansion). DR400% (two stops of highlight DR expansion) is available only when it is manually selected.

You can change the DR settings of your camera in the Quick menu or by selecting IMAGE QUALITY SETTING > DYNAMIC RANGE and then either AUTO, DR100%, DR200%, or DR400%.

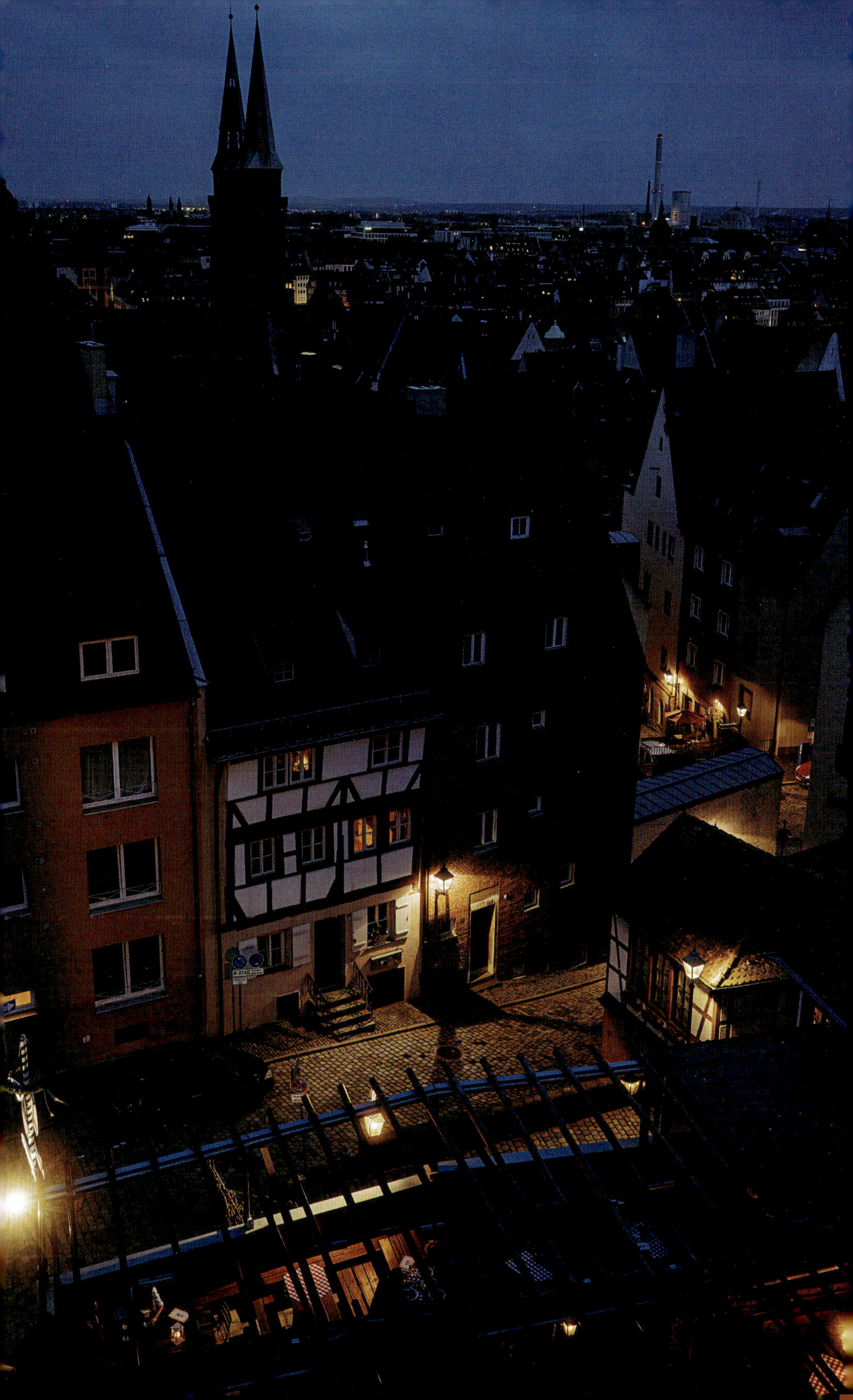

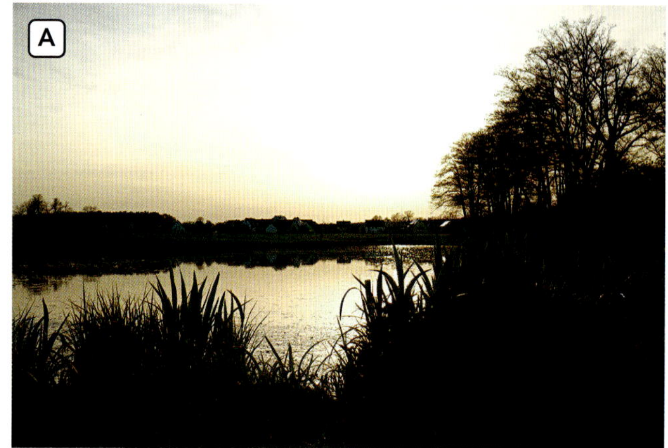

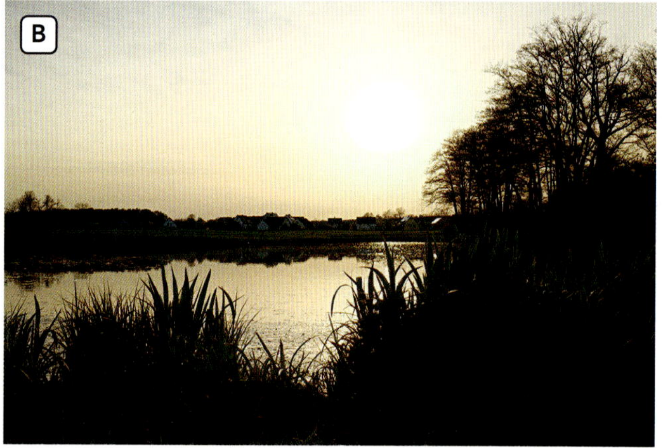

Fig. 56: These examples show the same shot with DR100% (image **A**) and DR400% (image **B**). At DR100%, the dark foreground is correctly exposed, but the much brighter colors in the sky are blown out because they were outside of the camera's dynamic range. In the DR400% version of the shot, the exposure (brightness) of the foreground didn't change, however, the sunset sky is now accurately colored and textured.

To pull this off, the camera exposed the DR400% RAW file two stops (EV) darker than indicated, and then boosted shadows and midtones two stops brighter during RAW conversion. The result is a **DR400% JPEG** with 2 EV of extended highlight dynamic range. Image **C** illustrates the shot as it was taken at the RAW level, before the DR function's camera-internal tone mapping was applied.

All images are SOOC JPEGs.

Extending the dynamic range for RAW shooters	TIP 54

RAW shooters mostly set the camera to DR100% and perform the tone mapping of their shots later during RAW processing. The normal strategy is to expose toward the critical highlights of a high-contrast scene, making sure that there's sufficient color texture in the bright parts of the shot. This can result in an image with dark midtones and blocked shadows. However, while blown highlights are difficult, or even impossible, to restore, blocked shadows can be lifted (pushed) later. Balanced results from scenes with a very high dynamic range can be achieved in almost any good external RAW conversion software.

Here's what to do:

- Use the live view and live histogram to adjust the exposure in a way that ensures the important highlights of your scene are not blown out. This will preserve the highlights, but it may also lead to darkened midtones and blocked shadows, which you must deal with later during the RAW conversion of your shot.

- After taking the shot, enhance darkened shadows and midtones by selectively lifting the exposure in your RAW conversion software. For example, you could first lift the overall exposure and then restore the highlights with a highlight-recovery slider, or you could lift only the shadow tones with a shadow-tone slider. You can also combine both methods: Many RAW converters are quite flexible and offer several sliders to selectively change the exposure. Lightroom and Adobe Camera RAW (ACR), for example, feature five different controls (exposure, whites, blacks, shadows, and highlights) to perform this task. Whenever you change an exposure slider, you are effectively changing the ISO of any part of the image that is affected by that slider. However, in the digital domain of the RAW conversion stage, nothing is lost, and everything is fully reversible. *Selectively* changing the exposure of an image is known as tone mapping.

- Don't forget that the DR function (including DR-P) also affects the RAW file. This means that any highlights that the DR function rescued in the JPEG and the live view have also been protected in the RAW data. After importing such a RAW file into software like Lightroom, you can easily restore these highlights.

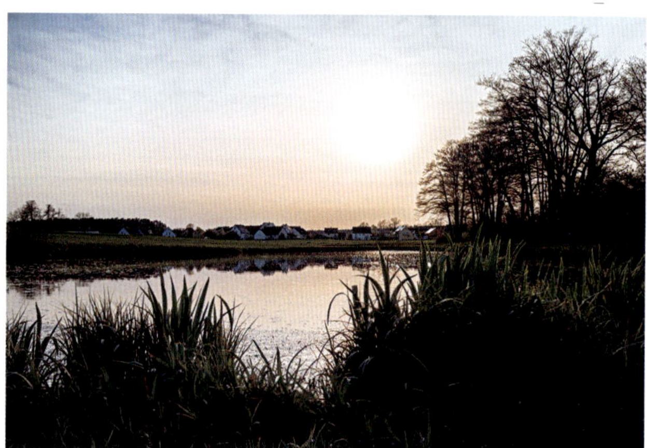

Fig. 57: For this example, I processed the **DR400% RAW file** from our previous tip in Adobe Lightroom to take advantage of its broader functionality. As you can see, the RAW file retains the highlights because it was exposed two ISO stops darker than its on-face ISO value indicates.

| JPEG settings for RAW shooters | TIP 55 |

The previous tip explained the procedure to capture and process scenes with high dynamic range. Since our exposure relies on the live view and the live histogram, it's useful to find camera settings that force the live histogram and live view to display as much dynamic range as possible. After all, we are shooting RAW and aren't really interested in the JPEGs from the camera, so we want the live view and live histogram to closely represent the data that will be recorded in the RAW files. This goal can be achieved by choosing JPEG settings in the IMAGE QUALITY SETTING menu that display as much dynamic range as possible:

- Set FILM SIMULATION to ETERNA. This setting results in JPEGs with less contrast than the other film simulation modes.

- Set TONE CURVE > HIGHLGHTS (HIGHLIGHT TONE) to −2. This setting lowers the highlight contrast of the JPEG in the live view and in the live histogram.

- Set TONE CURVE > SHADOWS (SHADOW TONE) to −2. This setting reduces the shadow contrast of the JPEG in the live view and the live histogram.

- If you are shooting scenes with bright and saturated tones of red, blue, or green, you can also dial back the COLOR setting.

The JPEG settings listed above give you a live view and live histogram with maximum dynamic range. JPEGs that are generated with these settings may look flat, but we usually don't intend to keep them anyway. We are only interested in the RAW file, which isn't affected by JPEG settings. However, the live view and live histogram *are* affected, and a flat live view image with a correspondingly flat live histogram is exactly what we want. It helps us to better fine-tune our exposure to preserve important highlights.

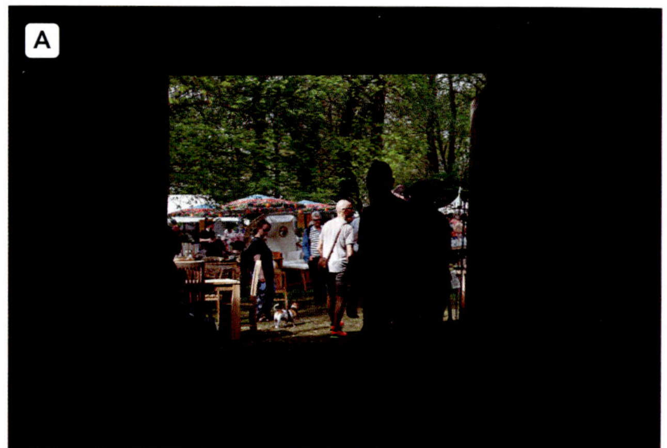

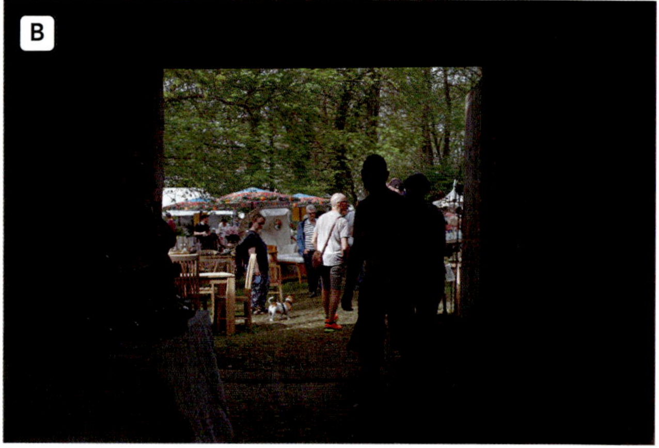

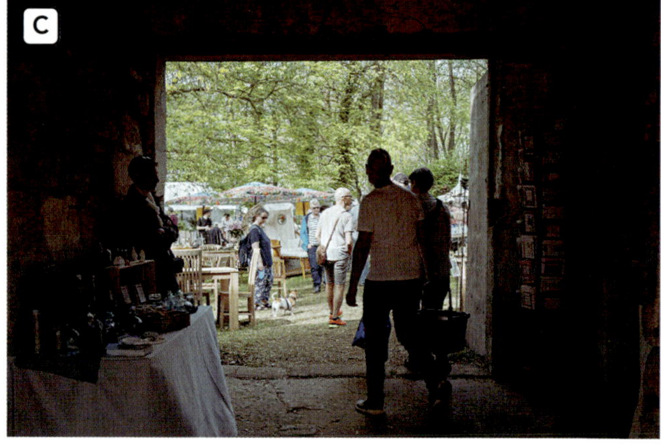

Fig. 58: These examples were all taken using the same exposure settings (ISO, aperture, and shutter speed). The exposure was geared toward the highlights of the sunlit parts behind the much darker foreground.

Image **A** shows how the live view (or JPEG) of the correctly exposed scene looks with the camera's Provia factory setting and DR100%. While the sunny background is nicely lit, the dark parts are hard to make out. It is difficult to frame this shot.

Image **B** depicts the same scene with the same exposure settings, but this time I used **JPEG settings for RAW shooters** (Eterna, Shadow Tone –2, Highlight Tone –2). These settings deliver a flat live view image (or JPEG) with less contrast and significantly more dynamic range than the camera's default settings. Using flat JPEG settings can be helpful when you compose high-contrast scenes. You can expose to preserve important highlights but still see what you are shooting. Remember: JPEG settings don't affect the RAW data—they only affect how the RAW data is processed in the live view and the resulting SOOC JPEG image.

Image **C** is the result after processing (tone mapping) the RAW file in Adobe Lightroom with a Kodak Gold 200 legacy film profile from RNI.

<table>
<tr><td>Extending the dynamic range for JPEG shooters</td><td>TIP 56</td></tr>
</table>

If you prefer to work with JPEGs that come directly from your camera (or want to shoot and keep RAWs *and* JPEGs), you can use Fuji's powerful DR function to capture scenes with high dynamic range. As you know, the DR function employs a two-stage process: reducing the ISO exposure at the RAW level to preserve critical highlights, and then lifting dark shadows and midtones to restore their brightness (exposure) back to realistic-looking levels.

You can simply set the camera to DR-Auto (not recommended), or manually set DR200% or DR400% (recommended) when you take pictures of high-contrast scenes. Remember that DR200% requires a minimum ISO setting of one stop (1 EV) above your camera's base ISO 125, while DR400% requires a minimum ISO setting of two stops (2 EV) above base ISO. This is because the shadows and midtones in your scene will eventually be amplified by one (DR200%) or two (DR400%) ISO stops when the JPEG is created during

RAW conversion. In the case of your X100VI, this means that DR200% requires at least ISO 250, and DR400% requires at least ISO 500.

What if we don't want to just *guess* what DR setting is optimal for any given scene? Can't we use the camera's metering to determine *exactly* how much DR expansion is required? Yes, we can! Here's how:

- To begin with, let's set the camera to DR100% and expose toward the critical highlights of a scene, just like a RAW shooter would do. Assuming you are shooting in one of the AE modes, this will often require you to turn the exposure compensation dial in the negative direction until the live view and live histogram display the scene without blown highlights.

- Next, turn the exposure compensation dial in the oppo- site (positive) direction until the shadows and midtones are displayed as bright as you want them to appear in the final image. Here's the important part: When you turn the exposure compensation dial up again, count the number of clicks it takes to reach the target brightness of your scene. One, two, or three clicks mean you should set the camera from DR100% to DR200% for one stop of additional highlight dynamic range. More than three clicks mean you should use DR400%. More than six clicks mean that highlights may be blown even when you set DR400%, so you might want to avoid overcompensating beyond six clicks. As you know, each click of the exposure compensation dial equals 1/3 EV (or a third of a stop).

The above describes the procedure for any of your camera's auto exposure (AE) modes **P**, **A**, and **S**, including *miso- matic* mode. Don't compensate with more than six 1/3 EV clicks (that's a total of 2 EV), or your resulting JPEG will be overexposed in the very highlights that you were trying to protect. Instead, try to reduce the shadow contrast by set- ting SHADOW TONE −1 or SHADOW TONE −2. You can also try a film simulation with less contrast, such as Pro Neg. Std or Eterna.

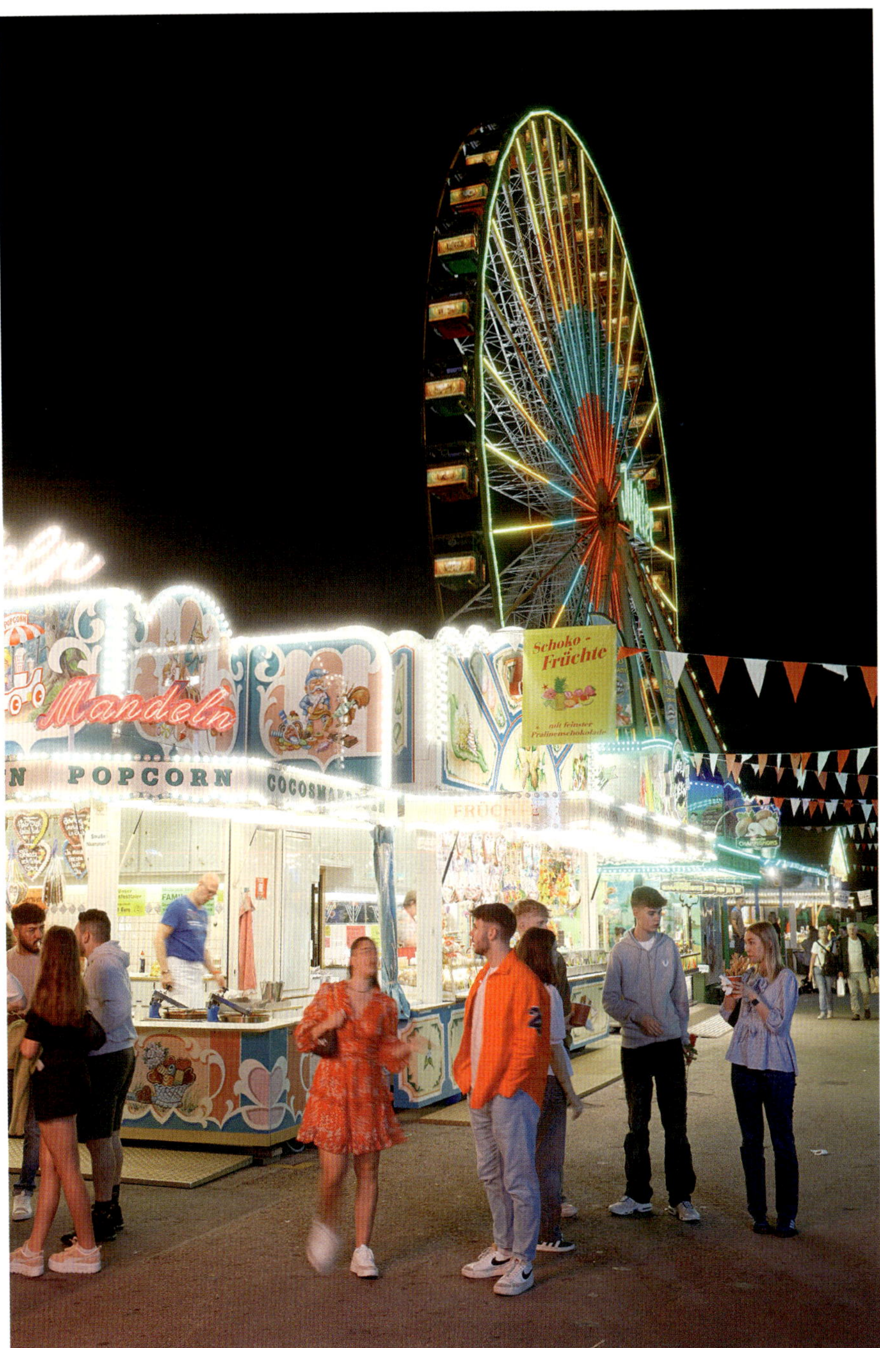

Fig. 59: Night scenes with bright lights and high contrast can benefit from a fixed **DR400%** setting to preserve color and texture in the
highlights (Nostalgic Neg., DR400%, SOOC JPEG).

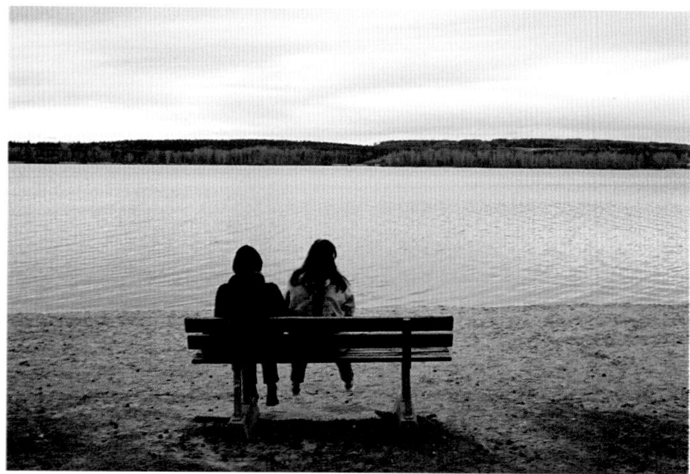

Fig. 60: On the other hand, there are instances where you may want to maintain high contrast and concentrate on the bright parts of a high-contrast scene. In such cases, a fixed **DR100%** setting is in order while you are exposing to the critical highlights (Acros, DR100%, SOOC JPEG).

The two above examples illustrate that DR-Auto is not a "smart" setting; it cannot predict what the photographer has in mind.

*Important: The X100VI simulates the effect of manually selected DR200% and DR400% dynamic range settings in the live view and live histogram. However, automatic DR expansion via DR-Auto is **not** simulated in the live view. Instead, the live view and live histogram will display a DR100% simulation, even when DR-Auto eventually decides to take the shot at DR200%.*

In extended ISO L settings, the live view and live histogram wrongly show the dynamic range of a regular ISO setting, giving you the false impression of one stop more highlight dynamic range than what is available. Only when you lock the exposure by half-pressing the shutter button will the live view change to display the recorded dynamic range. However, at this stage, there's no live histogram available.

High-contrast scenes: Using the DR function to the benefit of RAW shooters TIP 57

Fujifilm's DR function works by reducing the *actual* ISO of the RAW file one (DR200%) or two (DR400%) stops below the *indicated* ISO level. If you set ISO 500 and DR400% and take a picture, the RAW file of the image will be recorded with ISO 125—two stops darker than it appears in the live view or in the camera's resulting JPEG. Underexposing an image by one or two stops means that one or two stops of additional bright highlights are protected.

In other words, when the DR function is active, the camera's built-in RAW converter (which is also known as the JPEG engine) pushes the shadows and midtones of the underexposed RAW data one (DR200%) or two (DR400%) stops up to ensure that the live view and the resulting JPEG match the indicated ISO setting. It won't push the brightest highlights, though.

For example, if you set ISO 500 and DR400%, the RAW data will be recorded with ISO 125 (to protect two stops of highlights), but the built-in JPEG engine of the camera will make sure the shadows and midtones of the live view and the resulting JPEG image are pushed back up two stops to ISO 500 to compensate for the RAW file's underexposure. However, the brightest highlights of the JPEG will remain at ISO 125.

This is why the minimum ISO settings for DR200% and DR400% in cameras with a base ISO of 125 (like your X100VI) are ISO 250 and ISO 500, respectively. Remember that per definition and convention, ISO settings only apply to the JPEGs generated in the camera, not to the RAW files. It's perfectly normal for the RAW data to be recorded darker or brighter than the indicated ISO level because all ISO settings apply only to JPEGs and the live view, not to RAW data.

Understanding this, it becomes clear that in the X100VI with base ISO 125, extended ISO L (64) is doing just the opposite of the DR function: it records RAW data one stop brighter at ISO 125, while the JPEG engine pulls down (darkens) the live view and the resulting JPEG one stop to simulate and match the indicated ISO L (64) setting. Overexposing an image one stop brighter in the RAW than it appears in the live view and JPEG also means that one stop of highlight dynamic range is cut off and lost, so selecting ISO L (64) has the same effect as a DR50% setting would have (if that setting officially existed).

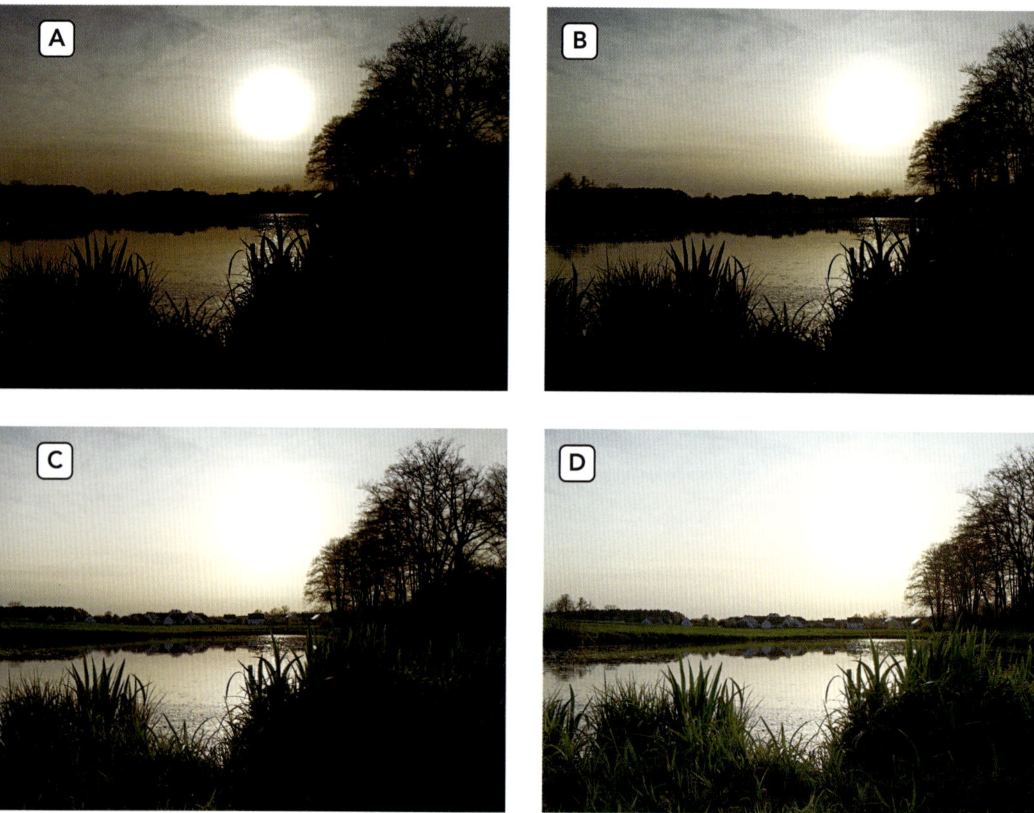

Fig. 61: In this example, I took four images using the same exposure settings: aperture f/11 and shutter speed 1/400 sec. The only differences were **four equivalent ISO and DR settings** that neutralized each other at the RAW level: Image **A** shows the JPEG that resulted from ISO L (64) / DR50%, while image **B** shows ISO 125 / DR100%. The JPEG in image **C** is the ISO 250 / DR200% version, and image **D** was taken with ISO 500 / DR400%.

The four JPEGs are clearly different regarding shadow and mid-tone brightness, because they must match their respective indicated ISO settings. Obviously, a JPEG taken at ISO 500, f/11, 1/400 sec. must look brighter than one taken at ISO 64, f/11, 1/400 sec. However, the underlying RAW data is the same in all four instances.

In many practical situations, correctly exposing to the important highlights of a scene results in a live view image that looks very dark in the midtones and shadows, which makes it difficult to compose and focus the shot. Using "JPEG settings for RAW shooters" can mitigate this issue, but sometimes it's just not enough. If that's the case, using an equivalent ISO/DR setting can help us out.

For example, the following three exposure settings are perfectly equivalent at the RAW level:

- f/2.8, 1/500 sec., ISO 125 / DR100%
- f/2.8, 1/500 sec., ISO 250 / DR200%
- f/2.8, 1/500 sec., ISO 500 / DR400%

The RAW data for these three shots is the same, only the JPEGs (and hence the live view) look quite different from each other. For example, the live view and JPEG of a f/2.8, 1/500 sec., ISO 500 / DR400% shot looks two stops brighter than the equivalent f/2.8, 1/500 sec., ISO 125 / DR100% version. However, the RAW data of these two shots is the same.

This gives you additional options. For example, you can *manually* expose your scene to its important highlights at ISO 125 / DR100% and then raise ISO one or two stops to 250 or 500, while at the same time changing the DR setting to DR200% or DR400%, respectively. *Increasing* RAW and JPEG ISO two stops from 125 to 500 and *decreasing* only RAW ISO two stops by selecting DR400% leaves the RAW data unchanged (+2−2=0). The only thing that has become brighter is the live view and the JPEG from the camera.

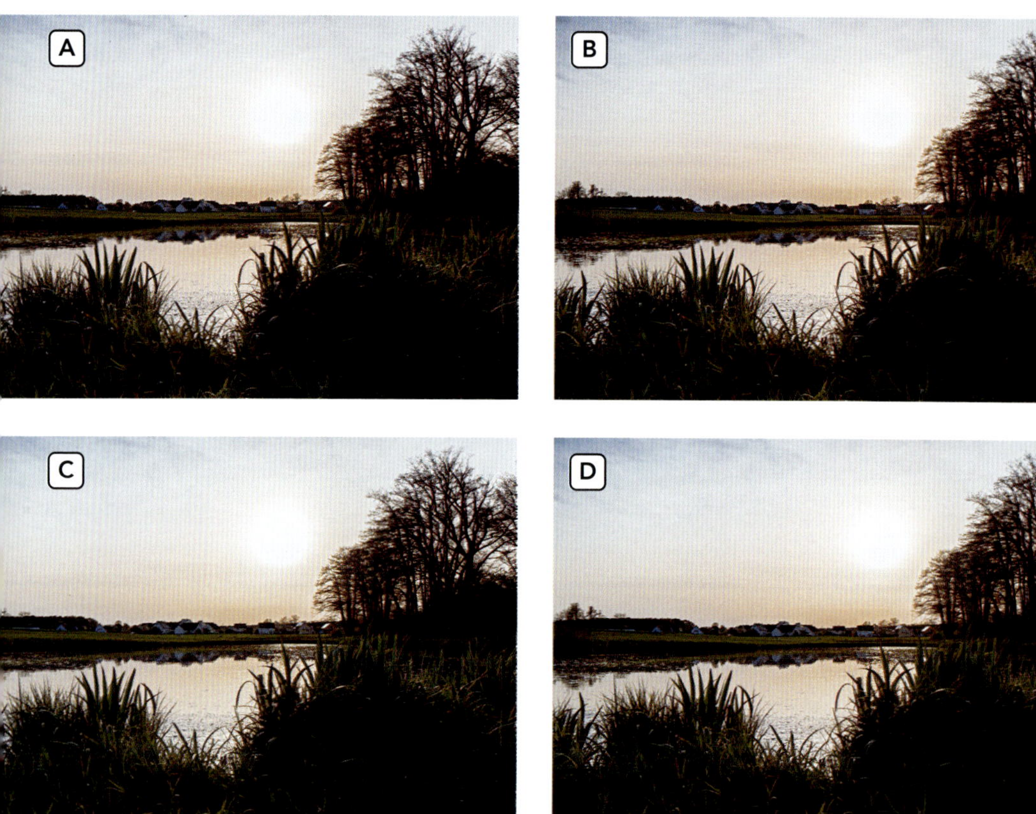

Fig. 62: ISO equivalence illustrated: This example shows the four shots from our previous illustration, all taken with the same exposure settings: aperture f/11 and shutter speed 1/400 sec. This time, however, I processed the RAW files of the four images in Adobe Lightroom and applied the same development settings to all of them—with the exception of the exposure slider, which was adjusted to compensate Lightroom's import exposure pull or push that is automatically applied to the RAW data based on the indicated ISO/DR setting.

The Lightroom-processed results from the shots taken with ISO L (64) / DR50% (image **A**, Lightroom exposure slider +3 EV), ISO 125 / DR100% (image **B**, exposure slider +2 EV), ISO 250 / DR200% (image **C**, exposure slider +1 EV) and ISO 500 / DR400% (image **D**, exposure slider 0 EV) look exactly the same. This isn't at all surprising because the RAW data *is* indeed the same.

This discovery can be of tremendous practical benefit if you intend to make the most of your camera's ISO-less sensor and push its dynamic range capabilities to the limit.

The best way to use the DR function for shooting scenes with very high dynamic range is to expose in manual mode M. Here's how to proceed:

- Set manual mode M and make sure the exposure preview for manual mode is enabled (SET UP > SCREEN SET-UP > PREVIEW EXP./WB IN MANUAL MODE > PREVIEW EXP./WB).

- Deploy "JPEG settings for RAW shooters" by selecting film simulation Eterna, Highlight Tone −2, and Shadow Tone −2. This step is optional but may be beneficial if the contrast of a scene is very high.

- Set DR100% and manually expose the high-contrast scene to protect important highlights. Use the RGB histogram with the live overexposure warning ("blinkies") and set an exposure that is just rich enough that some of the important highlights in your scene begin to blink. Remember that this is about protecting the *important* highlights. Feel free to overexpose parts of your scene that aren't worth saving, like the sun in a backlit daylight scene.

- Now that your exposure to the scene's critical highlights is manually set and locked, the live view may look too dark to comfortably frame the scene. So, let's add the DR function to the mix. First, increase ISO as needed by either one or two full stops (1 or 2 EV). Then neutralize this ISO change by also increasing DR by the same amount (either DR200% or DR400%). For example, you can raise ISO from 125 to 500 (i.e., a two-stop ISO *increase* applied to the RAW, the live view, and the JPEG) while also raising DR from DR100% to DR400% (i.e., a two-stop ISO *decrease* that is applied only to the RAW file, but not to the live view and the JPEG).

- Having completed the previous step, the RAW remains as it was, but the live view looks either one or two stops brighter than before. That's great for demanding, high-contrast scenes, because not only can we perfectly expose to their important highlights, but we can also still see what's going on in those dark parts of the scene.

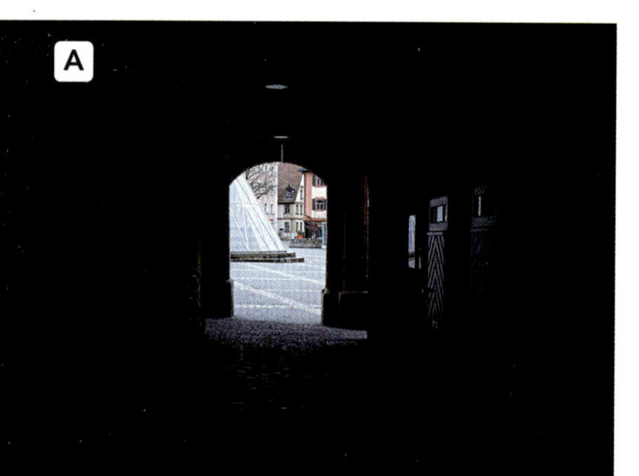

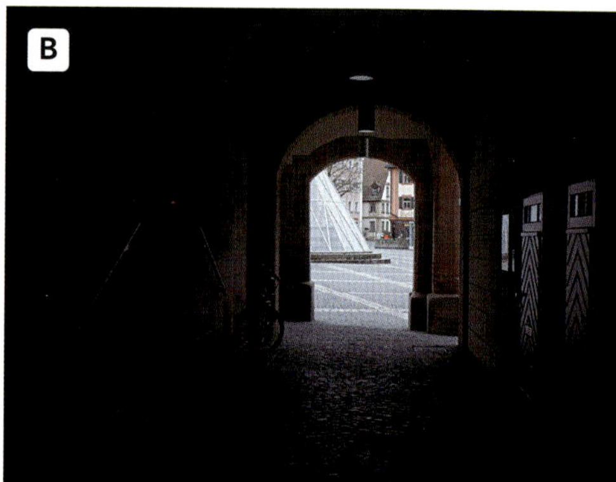

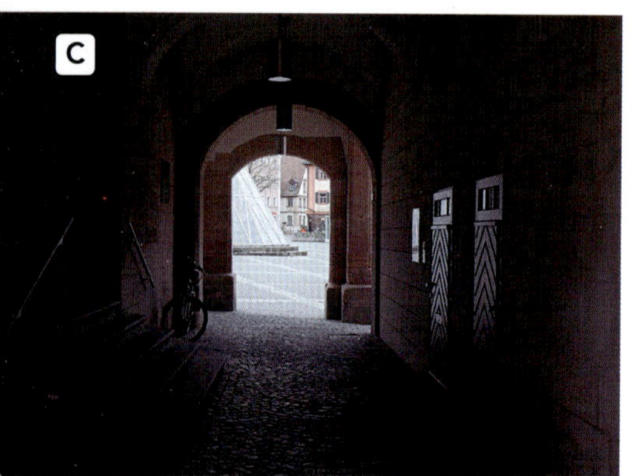

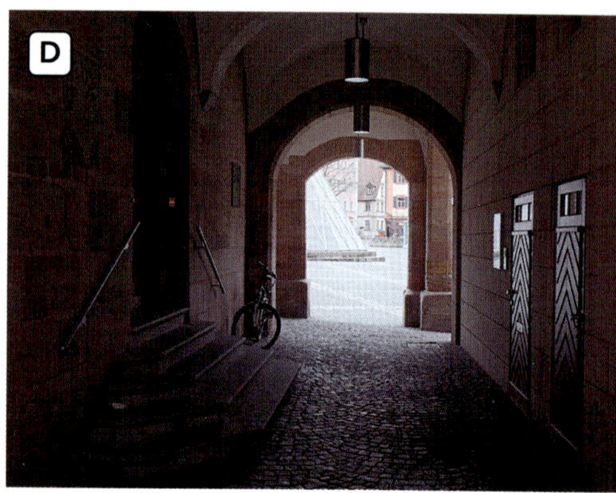

Fig. 63: This **high-contrast example** was shot at f/7.1 and 1/30 sec. in manual exposure mode. Image **A** shows the scene as it looked with Provia factory settings and base ISO 125. Image **B** shows the same image, but now with "JPEG settings for RAW shooters": film simulation Eterna, Shadow Tone –2, and Highlight Tone –2. While these are perfect settings for *exposing* a high-contrast scene toward its important highlights, the live view still looks a tad too dark to comfortably *frame* the scene. Luckily, we now know what to do. We can increase ISO / DR in tandem by one stop to ISO 250 / DR200%

(image **C**) or two stops to ISO 500 / DR400% (image **D**) to get a brighter live view (and brighter JPEG) without affecting the perfect RAW exposure that was already determined and set using the base ISO 125 / DR100% live view from image A.

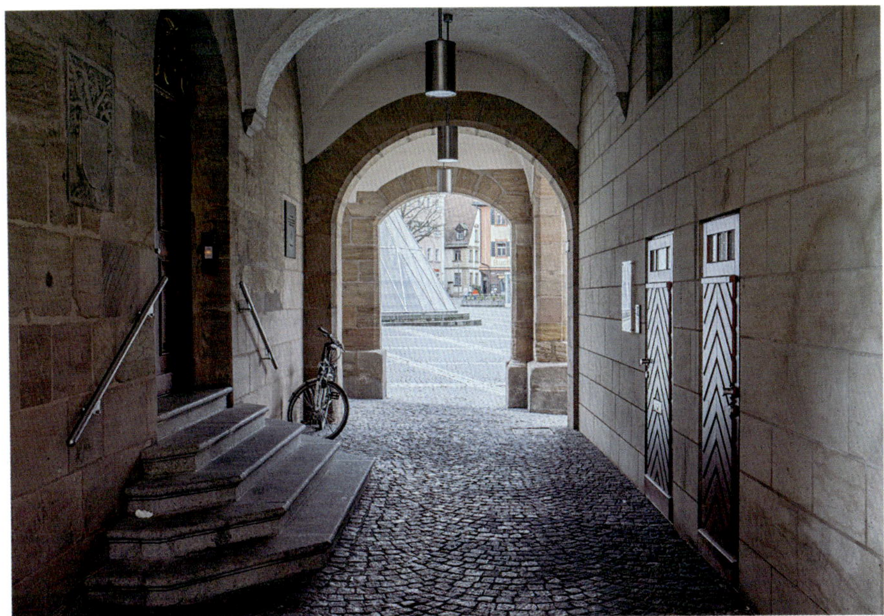

Fig. 64: This example shows the previous image after processing (tone mapping) the RAW file in Adobe Lightroom.

Using manual mode **M** to expose high-contrast scenes is highly recommended because you can easily split the process into two stages. First, you determine and set the correct exposure to protect important highlights of the scene using DR100% and "JPEG settings for RAW shooters." After the exposure is set, you can concentrate on brightening the live view to a more useable level by increasing ISO one or two stops while also raising DR to either DR200% or DR400%. With the brighter live view, you can easily compose the scene, focus it, and take the shot at the right moment. Not only can you now see what's going on in the shadows and midtones of the scene, the camera's auto white balance will also do a better job when it's not fishing in the dark. This is an accurate, reliable, and straightforward process, and I use it frequently with great success.

As an alternative to raising ISO and DR in tandem (which brightens the live view without affecting the RAW exposure), you can also expose high-contrast scenes in manual mode **M** and then turn off the exposure preview after determining the correct exposure. Here's how it works:

- Set manual mode **M**, DR100%, and turn *on* exposure preview (SET UP > SCREEN SET-UP > PREVIEW EXP./WB IN MANUAL MODE > PREVIEW EXP./WB).

- Like before, expose toward the important highlights of your scene and set a suitable exposure (ISO, aperture, and shutter speed).

- If the live view appears too dark, turn *off* exposure preview in manual mode (SET UP > SCREEN SET-UP > PREVIEW EXP./WB IN MANUAL MODE > OFF) and take your shots. The easiest way to do this is by assigning the manual exposure preview function to an Fn button or T-Fn gesture.

Turning off exposure preview in manual mode forces the live view to behave like it was in one of the three auto-exposure (AE) modes **P**, **A**, or **S**: the live view image will automatically change its brightness toward a middle-gray exposure (depending on the scene and the selected exposure metering method), but without affecting the actual exposure of the shot.

Using this rather simple procedure may sound quite appealing, but it has one major drawback: the JPEGs of your shots are still recorded rather dark (exposed to the highlights), making it difficult, or impossible, to immediately check critical focus and other details. You'd first have to push each image in the built-in or an external RAW converter. If you take a lot of images using this method, it can become quite a chore to browse through all your dark images and select the keepers.

<table>
<tr><td>DR versus DR-P</td><td>TIP 58</td></tr>
</table>

In addition to the DR function with its DR-Auto, DR100%, DR200%, and DR400% options, the X100VI also features a function called DR-P, which stands for Dynamic Range Priority.

If you activate DR-P in the IMAGE QUALITY SETTING menu, it replaces the classic DR function, so you can't use both functions together. It's either the one or the other. Setting DR-P to anything but OFF automatically overrides and cancels your DR settings.

The AUTO, WEAK, and STRONG options of DR-P correspond to the DR-Auto, DR200%, and DR400% settings of the DR function, while OFF relays control back to whatever regular DR settings you have selected. This also means that DR-P WEAK and DR-P STRONG have the same minimum ISO requirements as DR200% and DR400%.

So, what exactly is the difference between DR-P and DR? It's rather mundane: DR-P *combines* regular DR settings with different contrast settings into a package. For example, DR-P WEAK combines DR200% with HIGHLIGHT TONE −2 and SHADOW TONE −2. Correspondingly, DR-P STRONG results in an image that combines DR400%, HIGHLIGHT TONE −4, and SHADOW TONE −4. (These two −4 settings aren't available in the menu, but the camera can still access them internally.)

Please note that DR-P AUTO will record a shot with either DR-P WEAK or DR-P STRONG, but never with DR-P OFF. The live view in DR-P AUTO always represents a DR-P WEAK setting, even if DR-P STRONG is eventually used and recorded. Hence, never use DR-P AUTO when you want to use the live view or live histogram to determine the exposure.

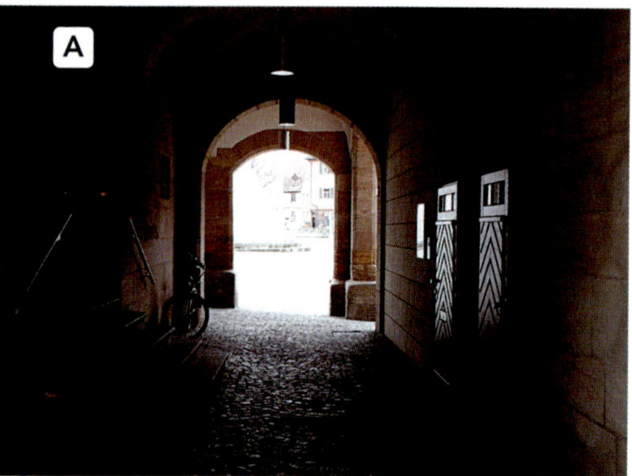

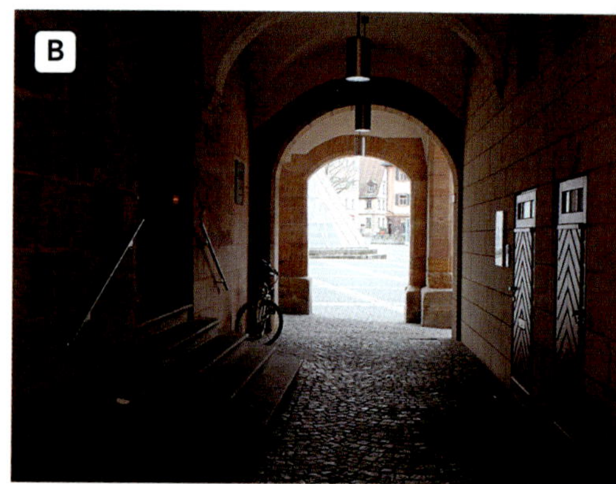

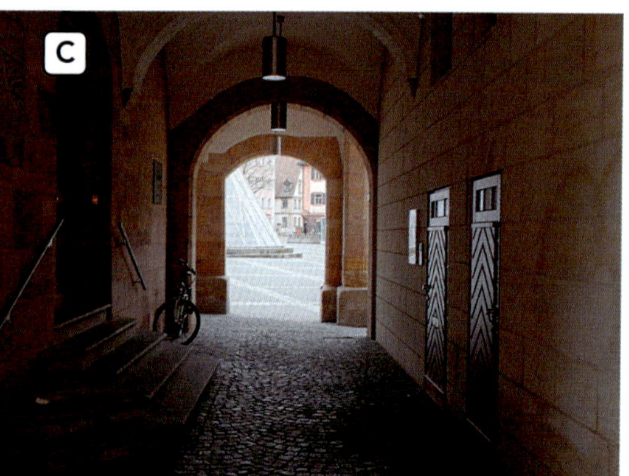

Fig. 65: This **Dynamic Range Priority** comparison shows straight-out-of-camera JPEGs of our familiar high-contrast scene (f/7.1, 1/30 sec., ISO 500, Classic Chrome) with DR-P OFF / DR100% (**A**), DR-P WEAK (**B**), and DR-P STRONG (**C**) settings.

Shooting RAW, you can change your mind later and reduce or remove DR-P from a newly generated JPEG in the camera's built-in RAW converter. Select the image in playback mode and press the Q button to access the RAW conversion menu, then scroll to D RANGE PRIORITY and select a different DR-P setting. Selecting OFF automatically enables the DYNAMIC RANGE and TONE CURVE menu items, where you can adjust dynamic range and contrast settings independently from each other.

Using the built-in RAW converter, you can only *reduce* dynamic range of newly created JPEGs, not add to it. For example, if you shot an image with DR-P STRONG, you could later reduce DR-P to WEAK or (with DR-P OFF) select either

DR400%, DR200% or DR100%. However, shooting with DR-P WEAK only leaves you with DR-P OFF and DR200% or DR100% as editing choices. DR-P STRONG or DR400% won't be available.

Instead of editing images with the Q button using the camera display or EVF, you can also use the free FUJIFILM X RAW STUDIO [43] software to revisit RAW files stored on your PC and create new JPEGs with different contrast settings.

Using DR-P for high-contrast daylight scenes	TIP 59

The global custom settings make it difficult to quickly switch between standard settings and "JPEG settings for RAW shooters" because they not only encompass JPEG settings but pretty much all camera settings. This is a problem when you only want to change JPEG settings but not everything else.

With custom settings out of the picture, is there another quick way to handle high-contrast scenes in the live view? Yes, there is! Let's assume the most common case, which is daylight scenes that can be exposed to the critical highlights at the camera's base ISO setting of 125. Here's how you prepare your camera:

- Set your X100VI to manual mode **M**.

- Set ISO to 500.

- Set DR-P to STRONG.

- Set ISO back to 125. The camera will automatically revert to DR100%.

- Select PROVIA or another film simulation that you like for your scene or topic. There's no need to employ specific "JPEG settings for RAW shooters" such as ETERNA and TONE CURVE (SHADOW TONE / HIGHLIGHT TONE) reduced to −2.

Preparing your camera like this makes exposing and shooting quite easy and straightforward:

- Expose for the critical highlights of your scene at ISO 125 by setting your desired aperture and selecting a shutter speed that doesn't clip bright parts that you want to keep. Use the live RGB histogram with blinkies to find this exposure.

- If the WYSIWYG image in your live view looks good, you can now take the shot.

- However, if it looks too dark, increase ISO from 125 to 250. Do not change aperture or shutter speed. The camera will automatically switch to DR-P WEAK and display a brighter live view. If that brightness is enough for you to compose and take the shot, do so now.

- However, if the live view still looks too dark, increase ISO further from 250 to 500. Do not change aperture or shutter speed. The camera will now automatically switch to DR-P STRONG and display an even brighter live view image with little contrast and allow you to compose the contents of even challenging high-contrast scenes. Take the shot at your convenience.

- When you are done shooting that scene or subject, switch ISO back to 125. The camera will automatically revert to DR100% and you are good to go to measure the exposure of your next subject.

Fig. 66: This **demanding sunset scene** was shot and processed entirely inside my X100VI, exposing with f/11 and 1/400 sec. Image **A** shows how I exposed the scene to preserve the critical highlights with PROVIA default settings at base ISO 125 / DR100%. Image **B** shows how I composed and took the shot with ISO-equivalent settings at ISO 500 / DR-P STRONG (still using PROVIA and f/11, 1/400 sec.), and image **C** is a straight-out-of-camera JPEG from reprocessing the RAW file of image B in-camera with the following settings changes: film simulation ASTIA, WB 5900K, WB SHIFT R: +1 / B: +2, COLOR +4, HIGH-ISO NR −1 and CLARITY +3.

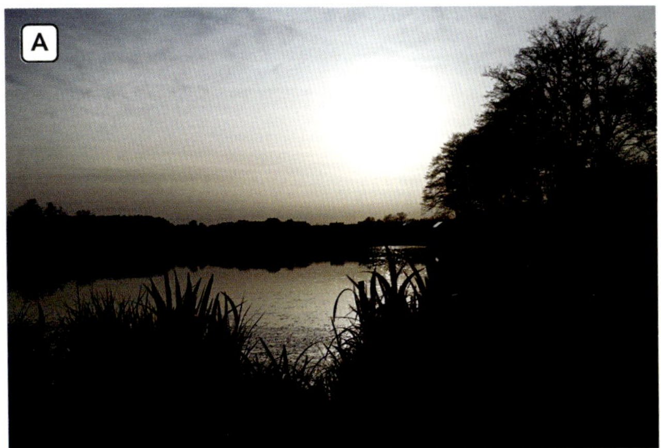

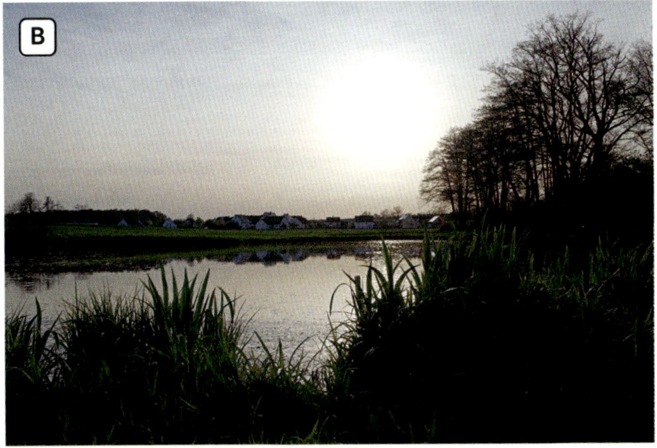

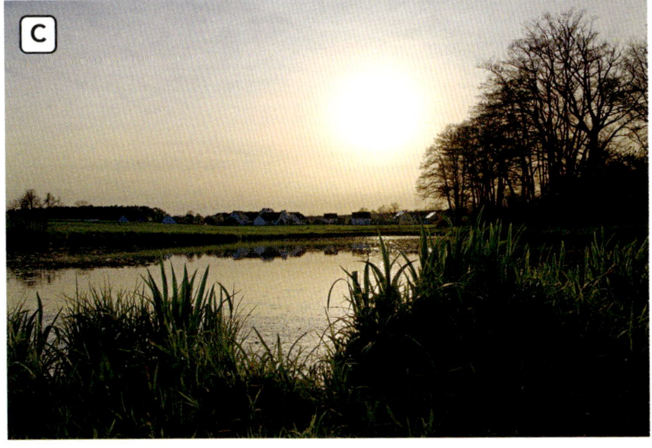

This simple method uses ISO-equivalent ISO/DR-P combinations to produce a live view and JPEGs that contain and capture much more dynamic range than "regular" JPEGs. An added benefit of this are RAW files that are much more flexible than regular DR100% RAW files when you want to process them in-camera with the built-in RAW converter. Even though the RAW image data itself doesn't change with ISO-equivalent settings, the RAW *metadata* does. A shot with DR-P STRONG in the metadata gives you more options: For example, you can reprocess it with DR-P WEAK, DR-P OFF / DR400%, DR-P OFF / DR200%, or DR100%. You can also combine these settings with PUSH/PULL exposure changes of up +3 EV and down to −2 EV.

In other words: Shooting with ISO 500 / DR-P STRONG instead of ISO 125 / DR100% (and otherwise identical exposure settings) gives you much more freedom with in-camera RAW conversions. Your built-in JPEG engine becomes more powerful and can handle high-contrast scenes that would otherwise be impossible to grasp with JPEGs created in-camera.

TIP 60	Dual conversion gain and how to use it

We already know that your X100VI uses a base ISO of 125. However, there's also what's called "dual conversion gain"—a second (higher) base ISO level. In our case, this additional base ISO level is automatically activated when you set ISO 500 (or higher) at DR100%.

Dual conversion gain (DCG) reconfigures the sensor for low-light use: read noise is further reduced, which means you can extract additional dynamic range in situations with very little light.

Normally, you wouldn't care about dual conversion gain because the camera is performing everything automatically. There is no "on/off" switch or menu: simply set a minimum of ISO 500 / DR100% (or ISO 1000 / DR200%; or ISO 2000 / DR400%) and dual conversion gain will be active.

You can make use of this second DCG ISO level in the same way you use base ISO 125 to extract as much dynamic range from high-contrast scenes as possible. However, in this case, we are talking about situations with very little light; scenes that one would usually expose with very high ISO settings such as 6400, 12800, or even 25600.

Instead of setting these high ISO values, you can just as well set the camera to ISO 500 / DR100% (or to equivalent ISO-level settings of ISO 1000 / DR200% or ISO 2000 / DR400%) and shoot away, while protecting as many highlights as possible. Of course, you can also use DR-P WEAK instead of DR200%, or DR-P STRONG instead of DR400%.

Dual conversion gain results in a small noise advantage. It's not much, but it can be essential in situations where you must push shadows up several stops during RAW processing, or when you need to take images at very high ISO levels like 12800.

In shooting situations that require high ISO levels, you can use ISO-equivalent DR-P settings based on your camera's dual conversion gain level of ISO 500:

- Set your X100VI to manual mode **M**.

- Set ISO to 500, which is your camera's DCG level.

- Set DR100% and DR-P OFF.

- Select PROVIA or another film simulation that you like for your scene or topic. There's no need to employ specific "JPEG settings for RAW shooters" such as ETERNA and TONE CURVE (SHADOW TONE / HIGHLIGHT TONE) reduced to −2.

After this preparation, you can measure the exposure and start shooting:

- Expose for the critical highlights of your scene by setting your desired aperture and selecting a shutter speed that doesn't clip bright parts that you want to keep. Use the live RGB histogram with blinkies to find this exposure.

- If the WYSIWYG image in your live view looks good, you can now take the shot.

- However, if the live view looks too dark, increase ISO from 500 to 2000 and select DR-P STRONG. This will considerably brighten the live view and the associated JPEGs. Do not change aperture or shutter speed. Take the shot at your convenience.

- When you are done shooting that scene or subject, switch ISO back to 500 and select DR-P OFF and DR100%. You are now good to go to measure the exposure of your next subject.

Hint: If your scene is very dark, make sure to select EVF/LCD LOW LIGHT PRIORITY in SET UP > POWER MANAGEMENT > EVF/LCD BOOST SETTING and enable BOOST mode in SET UP > POWER MANAGEMENT > PERFORMANCE.

TIP 61	Using the DR function for high-key photography

High-key photography [44] delivers images with tones that mostly occupy the right half of the histogram. High-key images can be achieved by lighting a scene brightly and uniformly with little differences in contrast, and then overexposing the scene by one or two stops. This results in images with a bright, clean, and joyful look. This is why high key is often used for product shots, portraits, and advertising.

Normally, high-key photographs require suitable low-contrast lighting. If the contrast is too strong, a bright exposure of the darker tones will lead to blown highlights.

To be suitable for high key, most of your scene must fit into the right half of the histogram. If that's not the case, there are two options: you can either reduce the contrast of the scene by applying fill light (like a flash), or you can apply appropriate tone mapping (pushing the shadows and midtones while protecting the highlights) during RAW conversion.

Thanks to the DR function, the second option is also available in-camera. This means that you can generate JPEGs with a high-key look directly in your X100VI.

Here's how:

- Set the camera to manual exposure mode **M** and turn off Auto-ISO, so aperture, shutter speed, and ISO can be set manually. Make sure to set the dynamic range to DR100%.

- Expose the scene as usual to protect critical highlights that you do not want to blow. The live view and live histogram are your friends. Set aperture, shutter speed, and ISO accordingly. Take a test shot to be sure that the scene is exposed as brightly as possible without any blown critical highlights.

- Now double your ISO setting (for example, from ISO 125 to ISO 250) and change the dynamic range setting from DR100% to DR200%. Don't change your aperture and shutter speed, though!

- In the live view and live histogram, your scene will be looking brighter. Take a shot with these new settings and inspect the resulting high-key JPEG in your camera's playback mode.

As far as the RAW data is concerned, it makes no difference whether you shoot the very same scene with ISO 125, DR100%, f/5.6, and 1/1000 sec., or with ISO 250, DR200%, f/5.6, and 1/1000 sec. Even ISO 500, DR400%, f/5.6, and 1/1000 sec. would result in the same RAW data all over again. However, you will see a huge difference in the corresponding straight-out-of-camera JPEGs: shadows and midtones will appear increasingly bright (high key), but the brightest highlights will be protected: this is the X100VI's built-in tone mapping at work.

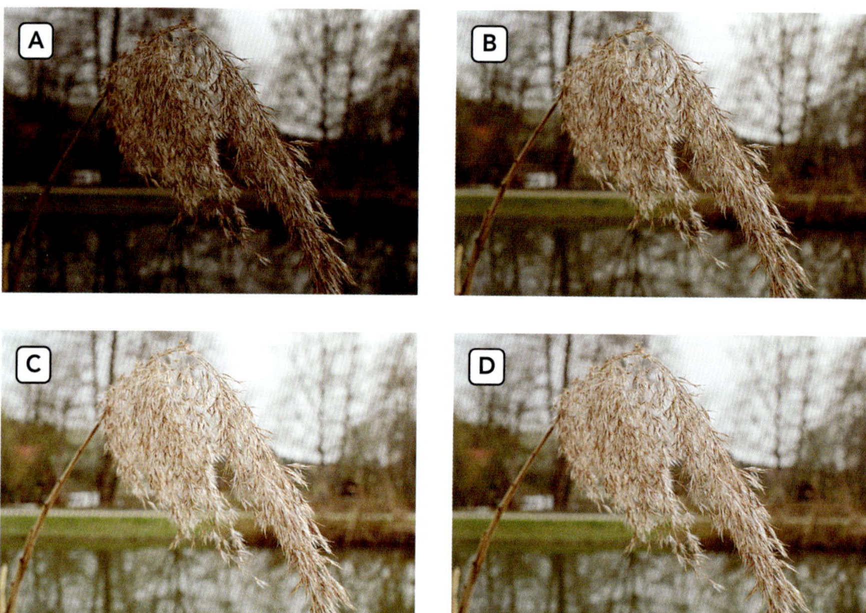

Fig. 67: Turning the DR function into a **virtual high-key studio**: Image **A** illustrates a regular exposure at ISO 125, DR100%, f/5.6, and 1/250 sec. The exposure was designed to protect the sky in the background. Image **B** is the same scene shot at ISO 250, DR200%, f/5.6, and 1/250 sec. The RAW data remains the same. However, the JPEG's histogram has shifted to the right, but without blowing bright highlights. Image **C** goes a step further and shows a version of the shot with ISO 500, DR400%, f/5.6 and 1/250 sec. Too much? You can always fine-tune such results in the camera's built-in RAW converter, for example, by changing the contrast (HIGHLIGHT TONE and SHADOW TONE settings) along with the exposure (PUSH/PULL PROCESSING). Image **D** is an example for this: It is based on image C, but with HIGHLIGHT TONE –0.5, SHADOW TONE –0.5, and PUSH/PULL –1/3 EV.

Tone mapping and tonality compression can also be used to improve portraits. It can reduce contrast and harsh shadows on faces that are illuminated by a single light source, such as the sun. With our high-key technique, dark shadows under the eyes and nose can be lifted without blowing the bright parts of the skin. At the same time, the tone mapping and highlight tone compression make skin blemishes almost disappear.

Creating HDR images   **TIP 62**

A popular method of capturing high-contrast scenes is HDR photography. HDR means High Dynamic Range: multiple images of a scene are taken at different exposure levels and then they are merged into a single image with extended dynamic range. The merging process can be facilitated in your RAW converter (Adobe Lightroom, Capture One Pro), or with specialized software, such as Photomatix Pro by HDRsoft.

Here's a procedure that you can use to quickly generate three different exposures of a single scene:

- Put the camera on a tripod or a similar device.

- Connect a remote shutter release or set the self-timer to 2 seconds to avoid camera shake.

- Set the camera to manual exposure mode **M** and select AE BKT in the DRIVE button menu.

- Set AE BKT (auto exposure bracketing) to three shots with a variation of +3 FRAMES with a STEP of 3 EV (SHOOTING SETTING > AE BKT SETTING > FRAMES/STEP SETTING).

- Choose a low ISO setting (such as base ISO 125). Don't use extended ISO L, though!

- Deactivate any DR expansion by setting the dynamic range to DR100% and DR-P to OFF.

- Select a suitable aperture for your scene and use manual focus.

Having prepared the camera for HDR, you can now capture the actual images:

- Expose to the critical highlights, manually focus the scene and press the shutter release. Make sure to either use a remote shutter release or the self-timer. The camera will now record three images ranging from 0 EV to +6 EV.

This procedure results in three different exposures that you can merge using the HDR software of your choice. The resulting image will have an additional dynamic range of 6 EV.

<table><tr><td>TIP 63</td><td>Using the built-in HDR function</td></tr></table>

The HDR function of the X100VI resides in the DRIVE button menu. To activate it, press the DRIVE button and select one of the HDR modes: AUTO, 200%, 400%, 800%, or 800%+.

Fujifilm's HDR feature follows a concept that is very similar to its long-established DR function. It adds highlight dynamic range by exposing one shot darker than indicated by the EXIF data, live view, and camera settings. Additionally, it reduces shadow noise by also adding a brighter exposure. The main difference between HDR and DR is that DR works with a single shot, whereas HDR works with three frames: one "master frame" that is exposed with the selected and indicated settings, and two additional frames that are exposed darker/brighter than the master frame.

In HDR mode, the camera merges the three differently exposed frames to produce a composite JPEG or TIFF file with enhanced highlight dynamic range and less shadow noise. It also saves a container-style RAW file that includes the RAW data of the three differently exposed shots. As a result, HDR-RAF files are roughly three times the size of a regular single-shot RAF file.

- HDR AUTO automatically selects either 200%, 400%, or 800% based on the contrast range of the scene in the live view. I don't recommend using this setting.

- HDR 200% expands the highlight dynamic range of the scene by one stop and adds one stop of shadow noise mitigation (±1 EV). The JPEG result will look very similar to using DR200% with the same (or equivalent) exposure settings (aperture, shutter speed, ISO).

- HDR 400% expands the highlight dynamic range of the scene by two stops and adds two stops of shadow noise mitigation (±2 EV). The JPEG result will look very similar to using DR400% with the same (or equivalent) exposure settings (aperture, shutter speed, ISO).

- HDR 800% expands the highlight dynamic range of the scene by three stops and adds three stops of shadow noise mitigation (±3 EV). There is no equivalent DR setting in the X100VI. However, if you still use an older X-series compact camera with a 2/3-inch EXR sensor (like the X10, XF1, or X-S1), you can achieve similar results by setting this camera to DR800%.

- HDR 800%+ works like HDR800 but adds additional shadow dynamic range (and a small amount of additional highlight dynamic range) to the JPEG by flattening the tone-curve during internal RAW processing. It also appears to internally change the CLARITY setting.

My preferred HDR capture setting is HDR 800%+, usually in concert with a low-contrast film simulation like ETERNA or PRO NEG. STD. I recommend HDR 800%+ because it encompasses HDR 800%, HDR 400%, and HDR 200%. This means that you can convert an HDR 800%+ shot to HDR 800%, HDR 400%, or HDR 200% anytime later using your camera's internal RAW converter.

Please note that this is a one-way street: It's *not* possible to change a shot taken with HDR 200% to HDR 400%, or to reprocess an HDR 800% image as HDR 800%+ after the fact. However, you can always reprocess an HDR 800%+ image as HDR 800%, HDR 400%, or HDR 200%, including changing the film simulation, SHADOW/HIGHLIGHT contrast, and CLARITY settings in the process. The sky's the limit.

Here's how you prepare your X100VI for HDR shooting:

- Set the camera to manual exposure mode **M** and make sure that RAWs *and* JPEGs are recorded simultaneously (IMAGE QUALITY SETTING > IMAGE QUALITY > FINE+RAW).

- Please check that the exposure preview in manual exposure mode is enabled (SET UP > SCREEN SET-UP > PREVIEW EXP./WB IN MANUAL MODE > PREVIEW EXP./WB).

- Make sure that the RGB histogram with "blinkies" (visual overexposure warning) can be activated by pressing one of your camera's Fn buttons. Personally, I have assigned this function to Fn1.

- It's vital that the Natural Live View is *disabled* (SET UP > SCREEN SET-UP > NATURAL LIVE VIEW > OFF).

- To make things easier, set the film simulation to ETERNA (IMAGE QUALITY SETTING > FILM SIMULATION > ETERNA). You can also set HIGHLIGHTS and SHADOWS to −2 in the TONE CURVE menu (IMAGE QUALITY SETTING > TONE CURVE).

- To measure the exposure of your high-contrast scene, select a *regular* shooting mode, e.g., DRIVE button menu > STILL IMAGE and DR100% (IMAGE QUALITY SETTING > DYNAMIC RANGE > DR100%). Do **not** yet set the camera to HDR mode, yet!

Since this is also my recommended "RAW shooter" setup for regular, non-HDR photography, nothing is new so far. To measure and set the exposure of a scene for HDR-mode photography, you can follow these steps:

- Set a manual exposure that preserves the critical highlights of the scene. If possible, use the camera's ISO 125 base setting. If you need a higher ISO setting, I recommend the X00VI's dual conversion gain setting of ISO 500. Press Fn1 to activate the RGB histogram and the "blinkies", then set the brightest possible manual exposure (aperture and shutter speed) that doesn't blow important highlights of the scene. In other words: Make sure that critical highlights of your scene don't blink in the live view. To be accurate and useful, this determination requires a DR100% setting and a disabled Natural Live View. Also make sure that you are in a regular non-HDR shooting mode.

- After setting the "perfect" exposure for the critical highlights, decrease the shutter speed by *three* full stops to compensate the camera's shutter speed increase in HDR 800%+ mode. For example, when your measured exposure for the highlights was 1/250 sec. at f/8 and ISO 125, change it now to 1/30 sec., f/8, and ISO 125.

- Select HDR 800%+ mode (DRIVE button menu > HDR).

- Press the shutter button to take the shots. Hold the camera very still or use a tripod. In our example, the camera will take three frames with different exposures ranging between 1/4 sec. and 1/250 sec., with 1/30 sec. as the indicated master exposure. The three exposures will be saved in an HDR-RAF container file, and the camera will also create a composite HDR-JPEG file with enhanced dynamic range.

HDR-JPEGs exhibit a small crop because the camera requires extra space to realign the three individual frames, hinting that Fuji's HDR function is meant to be suitable for handheld shooting. However, whenever possible, you should use HDR in tandem with a tripod.

Please remember that HDR 800% and HDR 800%+ result in a minimum shutter speed that is six stops slower than your initially measured exposure for the critical highlights of your scene, so camera shake and/or motion blur can become an issue.

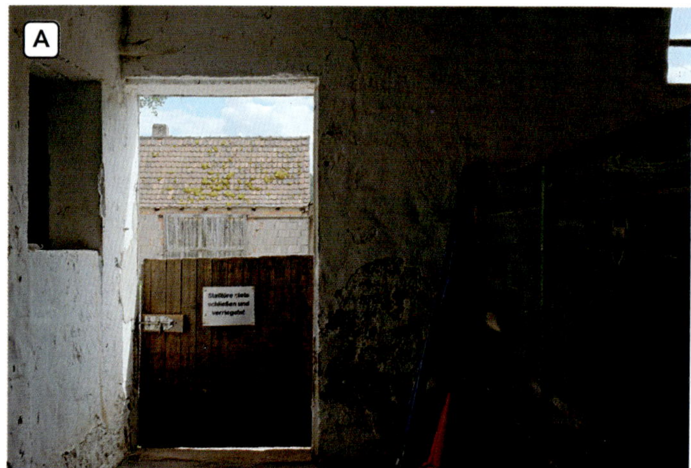

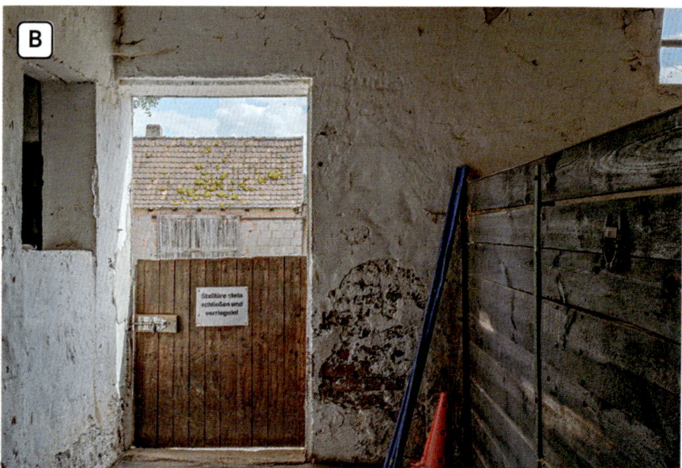

Fig. 68: Fuji's **HDR mode** takes three shots at different exposure levels: one shot at the set exposure, and two darker/brighter shots to protect highlights and reduce shadow noise. In HDR 800% and HDR 800%+ mode, the darkest frame is recorded three stops darker than the indicated exposure level. To compensate, I manually decreased the shutter speed three stops. Image **A** shows the straight-out-of-camera HDR 800%+ JPEG shot with the CLASSIC CHROME film simulation.

Using the built-in RAW converter, you can also save HDR composites as "16-bit" TIFF files and further process them with any software. In this case, I used Adobe Lightroom to turn the straight-out-of-camera HDR 800%+ CLASSIC CHROME TIFF into a punchier shot (image **B**).

An HDR 800%+ ETERNA composite can look like an ungraded F-Log video recording. Like F-Log, HDR 800%+ ETERNA provides a flat profile with maximum tonality, which makes it suitable for further post-processing. In this context, our best option is to reprocess the HDR 800%+ RAF using the camera's built-in RAW converter (PLAYBACK MENU > RAW CONVERSION) and save it in the 16-bit TIFF format. To retain as much fine detail as possible, you can also set NOISE RE-DUCTION to −4 in the RAW conversion menu.

A flat "16-bit" TIFF from the X100VI only contains 10 actual bits of tonality per color channel. This translates to 1024 brightness levels for red, green, and blue. Practically, this is perfectly sufficient because of the "flatness" of the file. You can further process (or "color grade") flat HDR 800%+ TIFFs in pretty much any image processing software.

As mentioned before, you can reprocess the original HDR 800%+ RAF in your camera with different parameters to alter the result. For example, you can increase the contrast by changing the film simulation from ETERNA to PROVIA or CLASSIC CHROME, or by downgrading HDR 800%+ to HDR 800% and at the same adjusting the settings for CLAR-ITY, HIGHLIGHT TONE, and SHADOW TONE to your taste. To make this procedure more comfortable, I recommend using Fuji's free X RAW STUDIO [45] software to remotely control the camera's built-in RAW converter. That way, you can safely store your HDR-RAF files on your PC or Mac.

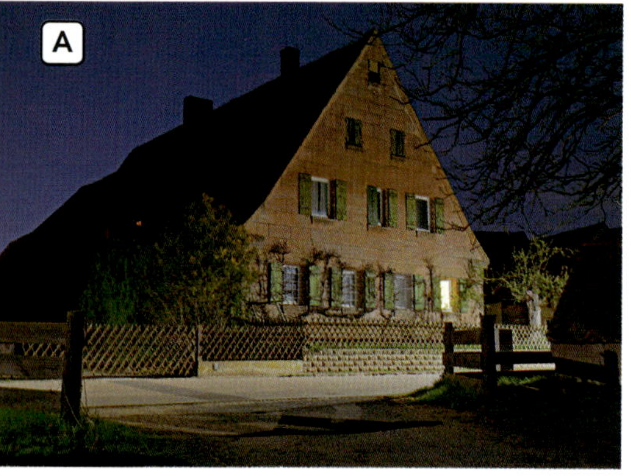

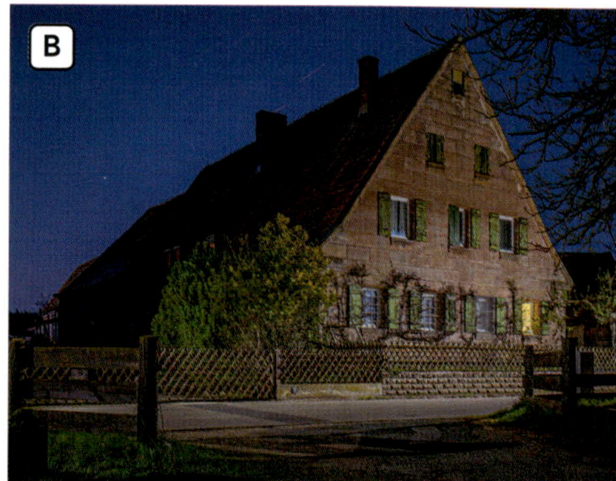

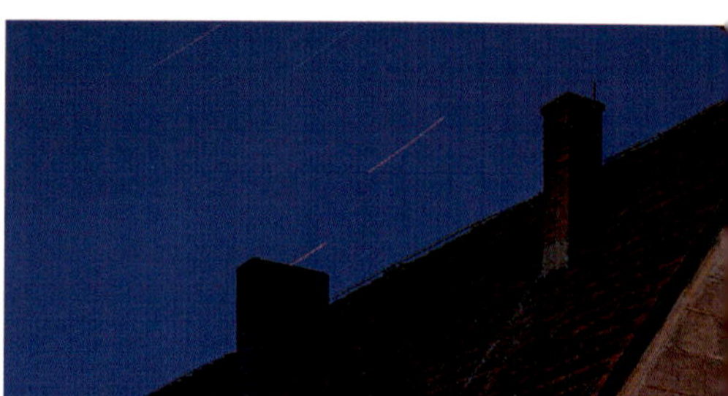

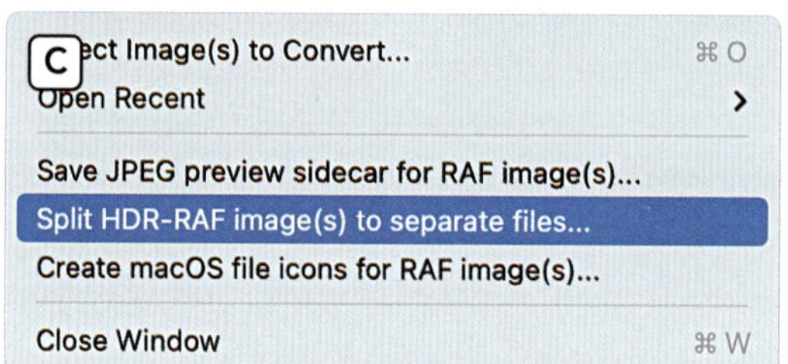

Fig. 69: Here's another X100VI HDR example that illustrates the **limits of the internal HDR processing**. Exposed to the highlights and processed with ETERNA, the contrast of the scene was still too much for HDR 800+. Even worse, the camera's internal HDR processing was unable to handle the star trails properly: they appear interrupted, courtesy of the three different exposures that make up the composite (image **A**).

Can we do better? Yes! Image **B** shows the same HDR shot but processed in Adobe Lightroom using its internal HDR-DNG photo merge feature. Since Lightroom and Capture One can't properly handle the HDR-RAF files of Fujifilm cameras (they only use one of the three embedded exposures), I had to first extract the three embedded RAW files and turn them into individual RAFs. Luckily, this could be easily performed with the **Iridient X-Transformer** app and its extraction function in the File menu (image **C**).

The built-in HDR function is an alternative to more conventional HDR methods. The traditional method is recording different RAW files through exposure bracketing and merging them into an HDR-DNG file. The industry standard here is Adobe Lightroom, with HDR RAW file merging capabilities that are superior to those of Capture One Pro.

With the help of Iridient X-Transformer [46], you can easily transform an HDR-RAF into three regular RAF files and process/merge them in Adobe Lightroom. This means that you get the best of both worlds:

- You can use the HDR function of your X100VI to create in-camera JPEGs with enhanced dynamic range. You can do this either methodically (as described above) or intuitively. As for using the HDR function intuitively, you should know that only fixed settings of HDR 200 and HDR 400 are correctly represented in the live view (WYSIWYG). This means that HDR Auto, HDR 800 and HDR 800+ don't have a proper WYSIWYG live view representation.

- If you feel the in-camera results of the HDR function aren't satisfactory, you can extract the three individual exposures with X-Transformer and process them like a traditional HDR exposure bracketing series in Adobe Lightroom or Capture One.

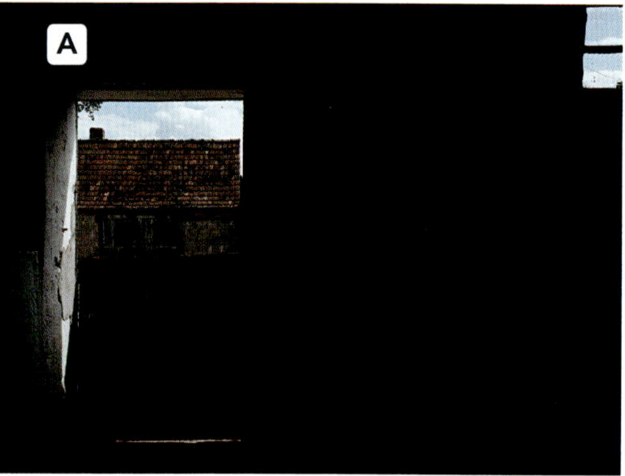
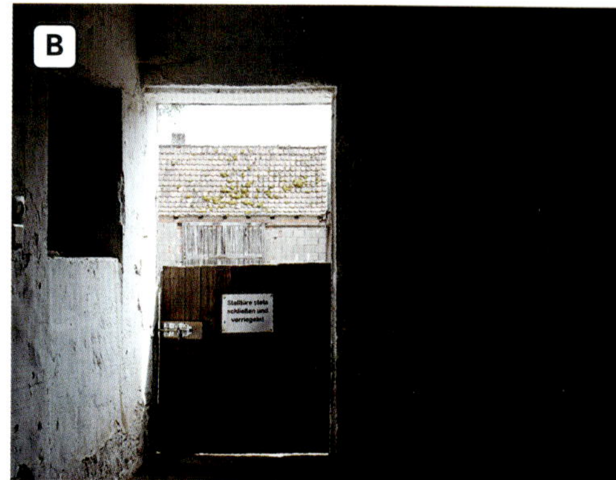
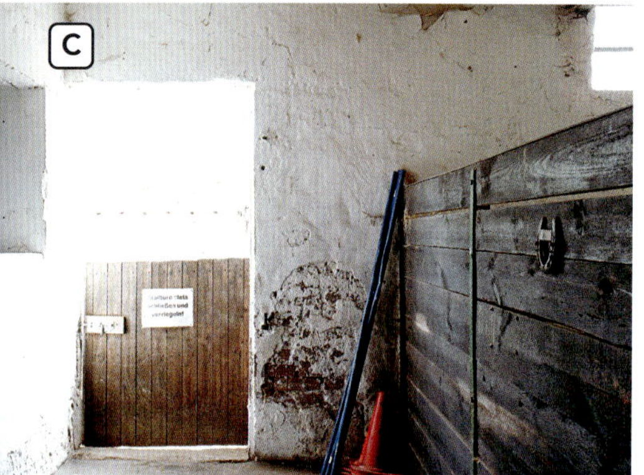
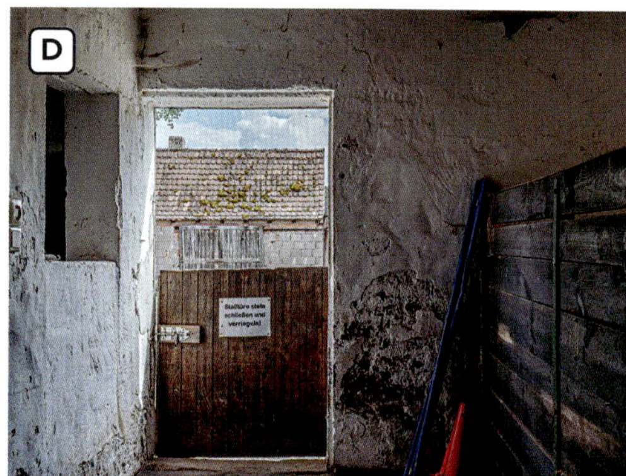

Fig. 70: Using **Iridient X-Transformer**, I extracted the three embedded exposures from the HDR-RAF of our previous example and saved them as separate RAF files. Images **A**, **B**, and **C** show them with the CLASSIC CHROME film simulation. The exposure difference between the shots is indeed 3 EV.

I used Adobe Lightroom's **HDR Photo Merge** tool to merge the three extracted RAF files into an HDR-DNG and processed it with Classic Chrome (image **D**). This method is more flexible than creating a TIFF image in-camera and then refine that TIFF in Lightroom or similar post-processing apps. Lightroom's HDR-DNG also shows less mandatory cropping, so you retain a larger field of view.

Using the electronic shutter — TIP 64

The electronic shutter (ES) of the X100VI allows shutter speeds as fast as 1/180,000 sec. This can be useful in situations with wide-open aperture in bright light because it can serve as an alternative to the camera's built-in ND filter.

You can set which shutter type the camera is supposed to use in SHOOTING SETTING > SHUTTER TYPE. There are three options:

- **MS**: The camera only uses the mechanical leaf shutter. This is the default setting and my recommended standard setting.

- **ES**: This setting switches the X100VI to its electronic shutter with available shutter speeds between 15 minutes and 1/180,000 sec., and ISO settings between 125 and 12800. You cannot fire a flash when the ES is in use.

- **MS+ES**: In this mode, the camera combines both shutter types. It will automatically use the ES for shutter speeds faster than the maximum supported shutter speed for the selected aperture. Flash photography is only possible within the envelope of the mechanical shutter (theoretically up to 1/4000 sec.)

To set shutter speeds faster than 1/4000 sec., you can set the shutter speed dial to **T** and access all available shutter speeds with the rear command dial in 1/3 EV steps.

Please note that even at 1/180,000 sec, the electronic shutter needs fractions of a second to capture all image contents. This effect, known as rolling shutter, can lead to weird distortions when you are taking pictures of fast-moving subjects. In addition, image quality can deteriorate when the ES is used in concert with pulsing or flickering artificial light sources. The long readout time and the rolling shutter are also responsible for the restrictions regarding flash photography.

Since the electronic shutter is completely silent, the camera is generating an artificial shutter sound when the ES is in use. The nature and volume of this sound effect can be set in SET UP > SOUND SET-UP, where you can also switch it off entirely.

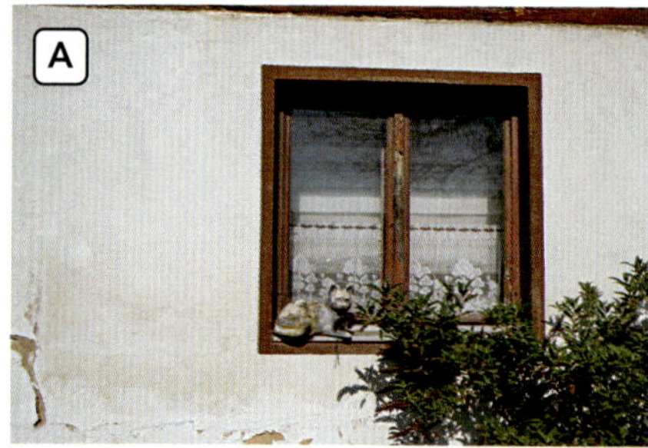

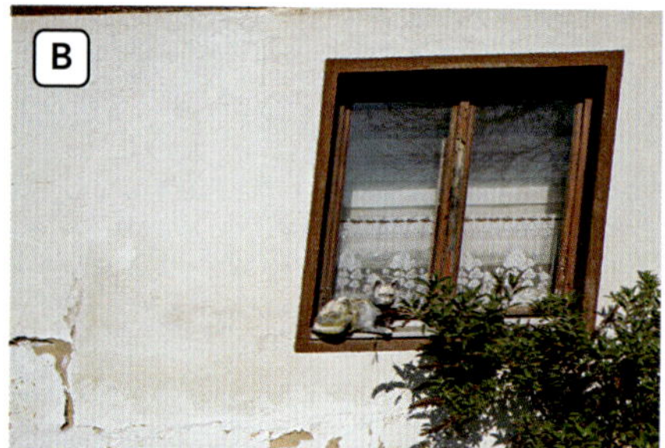

Fig. 71: The electronic shutter (ES) is a practical option for shots taken with fast apertures in bright light, when the maximum mechanical shutter speed simply isn't fast enough to avoid overexposure. However, the slow readout speed leads to **rolling shutter effects** such as banding (in concert with flickering light sources like LED lights) or distortion (with moving subjects or when you are panning the camera).

This example shows the same panning motion with the mechanical shutter (**A**) and the electronic shutter (**B**). Both images were taken with a shutter speed of 1/4000 sec. and with the camera swiftly panning from left to right. The distortion of the rolling shutter is clearly visible in image B.

TIP 65	The leaf shutter: pros and cons

Unlike most DSLRs and mirrorless system cameras, which rely on focal plane shutter mechanisms, the X100VI employs a leaf shutter that is built into the lens. Leaf shutters are different from focal plane shutters in several ways:

- Leaf shutters reside in the lens, close to the aperture, and they operate almost silently. In fact, the shutter in the X100VI is so silent that the camera emits an *artificial* shutter sound which can be switched off with SET UP > SOUND SET-UP > MS ELECTRONIC SHUTTER VOLUME > OFF. Leaf-shutter cameras like the X100VI are ideal in situations that require silent operation, like shooting on a movie set or in a theater.

- Due to their construction, leaf shutters offer slower maximum shutter speeds than modern focal plane shutters. In the X100VI, the maximum shutter speed of the mechanical shutter depends on the set aperture: the wider the aperture, the slower the maximum shutter speed. Between f/2 and f/2.5, the maximum shutter speed is 1/2000 sec., between f/2.8 and f/3.2 it's 1/2500 sec., between f/3.6 and f/4 it's 1/3200 sec., and between f/4.5 and f/16 it's 1/4000 sec.

- You can manually set "illegal" mechanical shutter speeds between the recommended maximum shutter speed and 1/4000 sec. in exposure modes **S** and **M**. The cameras will honor these settings and display the shutter speed in red, indicating that there may be issues such as subpar bokeh or exposure inaccuracies. In modes **A** and **P**, the camera won't use mechanical shutter speeds that are faster than the maximum shutter speed for the set aperture. In these modes, a red shutter speed indicates an overexposure warning.

- If your exposure requires a shutter speed beyond the mechanical maximum for the set aperture, you can either use the electronic shutter (set shutter mode ES or MS+ES) or deploy the built-in ND filter. The ND filter will reduce the incoming light by four aperture stops (EV). Example: If your exposure requires 1/4000 sec. at f/2 and ISO 125, deploying the ND filter will change this requirement to 1/250 sec. at f/2 and ISO 125—well within the limits of the mechanical leaf shutter.

- Unlike focal-plane shutters, leaf shutters can synchronize with flash lights at high speed—without energy-consuming high-speed sync (HSS). Even the tiny built-in flash of your X100VI can perfectly synchronize with the leaf shutters at shutter speeds as fast as 1/2000 sec.

<table><tr><td>**TIP 66**</td><td>Using flicker reduction features</td></tr></table>

Is it safe to use the mechanical shutter in situations with pulsing artificial light? The answer is yes *and* no. Because pulsing light sources have the nasty habit of continuously going on and off, the scene (your subject) is illuminated with varying amounts of light that fluctuate 100 or 120 times per second along with the phase frequency of the electric AC grid. Even in manual exposure mode **M**, shooting the same scene multiple times with the same exposure settings can result in inconsistently exposed images, depending on your shutter speed and how lucky you are to randomly catch a brighter or a darker portion of the pulsating light.

While this flicker phenomenon is invisible to the human eye, your camera will be affected by it as soon as you select faster shutter speeds. In such cases, the camera can record only a random portion of the light's pulsating on/off cycle.

This is where **flicker reduction** comes into play. You can find it under SHOOTING SETTING > FLICKER REDUCTION.

When you take a shot, flicker reduction forces your camera's exposure to coincide with cyclic peaks of the AC current phase. In other words, shots are delayed until the pulsating light happens to illuminate the scene with maximum brightness. With flicker reduction, your series of exposures will look uniformly bright.

In a world of pulsing energy-saving light sources and LED lights, flicker reduction is an essential feature. However, make sure to use it only in situations that require its magic. In natural daylight (or artificial light that doesn't pulse), flicker reduction is not only useless; it will also slow down your camera.

The X100VI offers two options for flicker reduction: FIRST FRAME and ALL FRAMES. ALL FRAMES corresponds to the regular FLICKER REDUCTION ON setting in older X camera models, meaning the camera is synchronizing with the line frequency before every single shot it takes, even during high-speed bursts that will inevitably be slowed down because of this. FIRST FRAME only performs this analysis before the first shot of a burst. This is my standard setting; I regard it as a good compromise.

Flicker reduction is not available in concert with the electronic shutter (ES). You can only use it with the mechanical shutter (MS). In MS+ES mode, flicker reduction is automatically disabled if the camera switches to the electronic shutter.

The X100VI incorporates an additional flicker reduction setting that can help you synchronize your shutter speed with pulsating light from LEDs and other sources: SHOOTING MENU > FLICKERLESS S.S. SETTING. If you turn this option ON, your manual shutter speed settings change in a few ways: Your minimum shutter speed is now 1/50 sec., and you can fine-tune the shutter speed in fractional increments to harmonize it with flickering light sources. This option only works in exposure modes M and S. It is also available in concert with the electronic shutter.

Using Multiple Exposure mode	TIP 67

Multiple Exposure overlays up to nine individual shots and creates a composite JPEG or HEIF file. It also saves single RAW files of each shot, so you can also process and overlay the individual shots externally on your computer. You can activate the function with DRIVE button menu > MULTI EXPOSURE, then choose one of the overlay options (ADDITIVE, AVERAGE, LIGHT, DARK).

The live view shows you the progress of your multi exposure series. This is very helpful for composing overlay images and once again provides true WYSIWYG. However, the result is just one JPEG or HEIF file that cannot be replicated in-camera with different parameters, so make sure to select the image size and quality settings that you need before taking the overlay shots. Of course, you can always process and overlay the RAW files in Photoshop or a similar app.

TIP 68	Adv. Filters: exposing with creative filters

Advanced Filters are a collection of creative effect filters. Gimmicks, you may rightfully say, but they can be fun to play with. To access the filters, press the DRIVE button and select Adv. > ADVANCED FILTER. After pressing OK, you can select one of 13 filter options.

Here's the good news: Adv. Filter doesn't just create a JPEG or HEIF file showing the effect, it also saves a RAW file that you can revisit later to generate a "real" image without fancy filter effects. You can do so using the built-in RAW converter or an external RAW converter like Lightroom. That said, there are two things that you should keep in mind:

- Depending on the selected filter option, Adv. Filter also adjusts the auto-exposure of your shot. For example, LOW-KEY will expose a scene much darker than HIGH-KEY. This means that depending on the filter you choose, the exposure of the RAW file will also change. To rule out exposure changes due to a specific filter selection, you can use manual exposure mode **M**.

- The RAW file that is created along with the effect JPEG cannot be used to create other Adv. Filter effects because the camera's built-in RAW converter doesn't offer any Adv. Filter options. You can only use the built-in RAW converter to create "regular" JPEG, HEIF, or TIFF images.

| Motion panoramas | TIP 69 |

PANORAMA works like the panorama function in your smartphone: while you pan the camera in a horizontal or vertical motion, the X100VI takes a series of images and stitches them together in a panoramic JPEG file. After selecting PANORAMA in the DRIVE button > Adv. menu, you can choose between two angle sizes (M and L), and you can specify the direction of your panning motion (left, right, up, and down). You can use a vertical motion horizontally by holding the camera upright.

Here are a few tips for getting the best results with motion panoramas:

- Since PANORAMA results in only a JPEG file (no RAW), JPEG parameters such as white balance and film simulation must be set *before* taking the shots.

- Exposure, white balance, and focusing remain constant during the recording of a panorama. This applies to all focus modes (AF-S, AF-C, and MF). That's why it's important to set a focus distance and depth of field that work for the entire panoramic scene.

- Panoramas tend to extend over a wide area with varying light conditions and strong changes in contrast. In such cases, it's smart to shoot with an extended DR setting, such as DR200% or DR400%. In addition to that, the exposure should be set in a way that suits the entire panoramic image, not just a small part of it. The edges of a panorama are rarely representative; it's usually better to base your exposure on the main part of the image in the middle. Panorama works with all four exposure modes, so shooting it in manual mode **M** may be the smartest option. Please note that Panorama only works with multi metering.

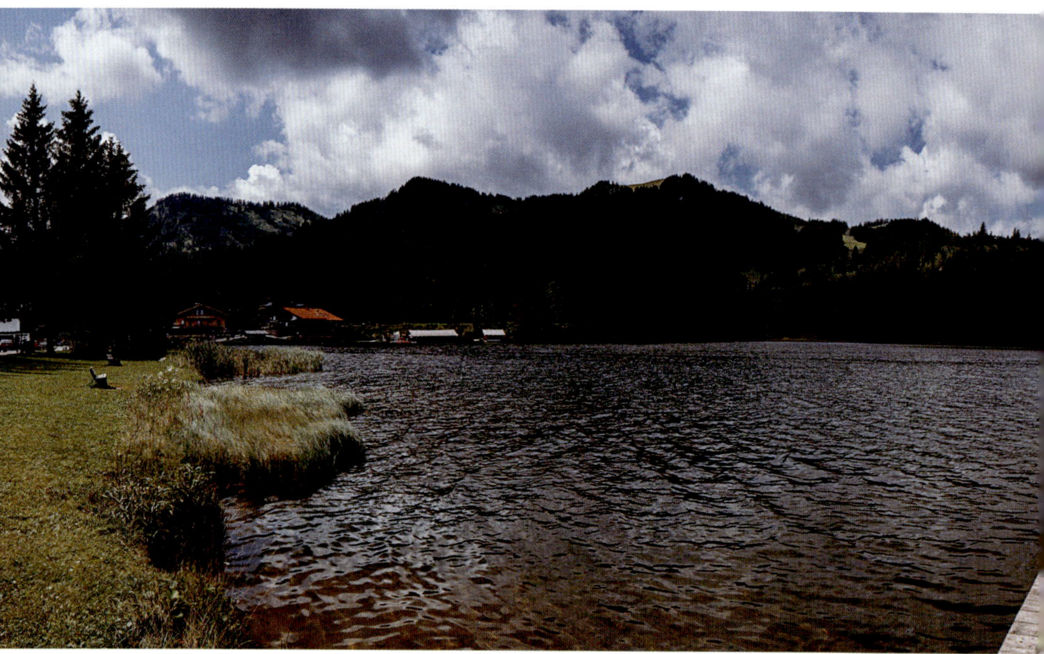

Fig. 72: PANORAMA is a "quick and dirty" method to produce panorama JPEGs. It's like shooting panoramas with a smartphone, and to be honest, modern smartphones often do a better job. If you are into high-quality results, let me propose an alternative: **shoot the panorama manually shot by shot and merge the RAW files** with software like Adobe Lightroom. For this example, I took 14 single overlapping handheld shots (holding the camera upright and using the 3D level) and merged the RAW files into a Lightroom Pano-DNG that could then be processed in Lightroom like a single RAW file.

- If you decide to *not* manually set exposure, white balance, and focus, point the camera toward a representative part of the panoramic scene, then lock focus, exposure, white balance, and DR by half-pressing the shutter button. Then pan to the point where you'd like to start the panning action (while holding the shutter button half-depressed), press the shutter button fully, and start panning. Don't forget that SHUTTER AE must be set to ON to lock the exposure of the panorama by half-pressing the shutter.

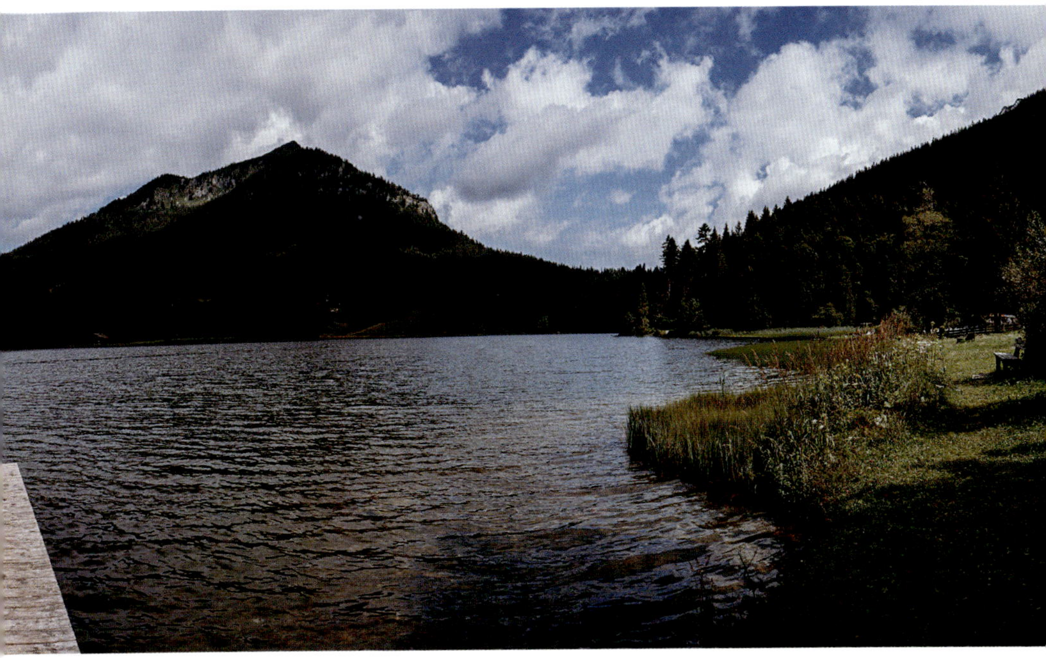

■ Avoid scenes that contain a lot of motion. Moving objects (people, vehicles, etc.) can lead to ghosting artifacts, which is when moving objects (partially) appear in more than one spot of the final panorama.

■ Keep a healthy distance to the panoramic scene. Don't shoot panoramas in close quarters. Also make sure that you have sufficient depth of field. Wide-angle lenses are better suited for this job than normal or telephoto lenses, so the 23mmF2 lens in your X100VI is usually a good fit.

■ Make sure that the shutter speed is fast enough to avoid motion blur from panning. Don't pan too fast!

■ Always pan with the EVF (camera held to your eye), not with the LCD display (arms stretched out in front of you).

■ While panning, stand parallel to the panoramic scene and always stand on level ground.

- Try to ignore the time delay that may occur between the currently recorded image and what's displayed in the EVF. Keep panning the camera in a smooth motion until the camera stops taking frames.

- If available, use a tripod and make sure the camera is leveled to the horizon.

- Immediately check your finished panorama in the camera's viewfinder after you have captured it. Look out for stitching errors and ghosting artifacts. Do this while you are still on location, not at home when it's too late to reshoot a panorama that went awry.

2.4 FOCUSING WITH THE X100VI

The X100VI features a hybrid autofocus system that combines CDAF and PDAF. CDAF, PDAF, and hybrid AF? It can be quite confusing.

- **CDAF** means **C**ontrast **D**etection **AutoFocus** and is a standard in mirrorless cameras. CDAF is available throughout the entire sensor area (117 or 425 AF frames in Single Point mode or 117 AF frames in Zone and Wide/Tracking mode). It works quite precisely but is not particularly fast.

- **PDAF** means **P**hase **D**etection **AutoFocus** and used to be the standard AF in DSLRs. Since the X100VI is mirrorless, its PDAF works directly on the sensor and covers almost its entire area. PDAF is fast and particularly good at tracking moving subjects. It can predict where a moving object will be a split second from now, a feature that can be quite useful when you shoot in burst mode.

- **Hybrid AF** means that the camera automatically chooses and combines available AF methods (CDAF or PDAF) for the current subject and the current light conditions.

| CDAF and PDAF: what's the difference? | TIP 70 |

Both AF methods offer distinct qualities that can be useful during your daily shooting:

- CDAF focuses on surfaces and works best with areas that offer a lot of contrast. CDAF doesn't work well for a solid white or black wall, but for a checkered wall, it works great. It's the same with clothing: solid colors may be tough, but patterned clothes work wonderfully. CDAF operates with a trial-and-error approach: it keeps adjusting the focus until it finds the distance setting with the utmost contrast. CDAF doesn't directly go to the optimal focus distance. This results in heightened autofocus motor activity and visible focus hunting while the AF iterates back and forth until it finds the optimal focus position.

- PDAF loves focusing on edges, especially vertical edges (or horizontal ones if you hold the camera upright). Unlike CDAF, PDAF can directly determine the distance to an object, so there's no need for focus hunting. This is why PDAF is considerably faster.

- Both methods depend on sufficient light to work with maximum efficiency. The brighter a scene is and the more contrast it has, the better the AF will work. Because all lenses are darker near the edges than they are at the center (this effect is called vignetting), in poor light, the autofocus may work less efficiently with focus frames that are located far off center.

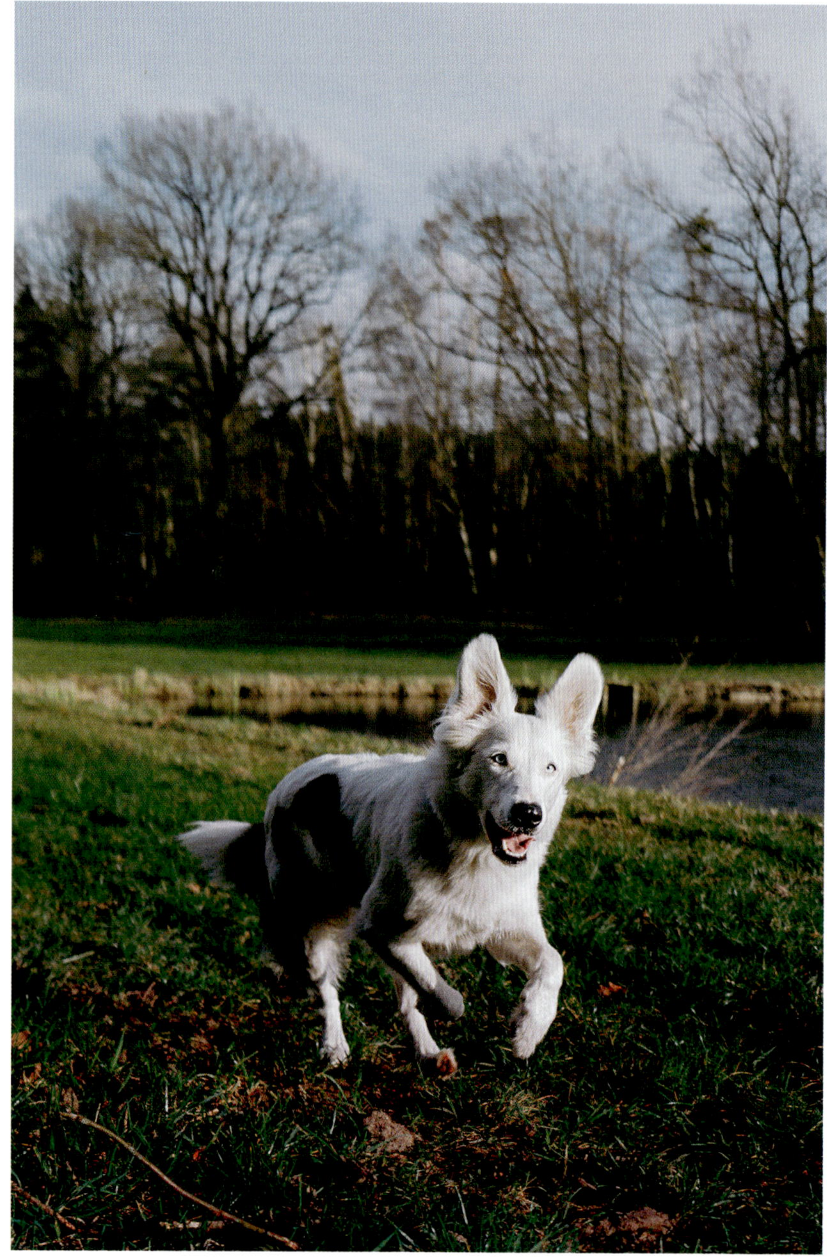

Fig. 73: Tracking fast-moving subjects like this running dog is a job for the **phase detection autofocus** (PDAF).

<table><tr><td>AF-S or AF-C?</td><td>**TIP 71**</td></tr></table>

Your X100VI features two basic AF modes that can be selected with the focus mode selector at the side of the camera:

- **AF-S (AF Single) is meant for stationary subjects**. When you half-press the shutter button, the camera will focus on the object covered by the active AF frame and lock the distance (as long as you keep the shutter button half-pressed). You can then either fully press the shutter button to take the shot, or you can take your finger off the shutter release and try again.

- **AF-C (AF Continuous) is meant for moving subjects**, especially those that move toward or away from the camera. When you half-press the shutter button, the camera starts focusing on the object covered by the active AF frame and continuously adjusts the distance to the moving object while you keep the shutter button half-pressed.

While AF-C focuses using the set working aperture, AF-S can open the aperture beyond the working aperture to improve the AF performance in poor light. This also improves the focusing accuracy due to the reduced depth of field caused by the wide-open aperture.

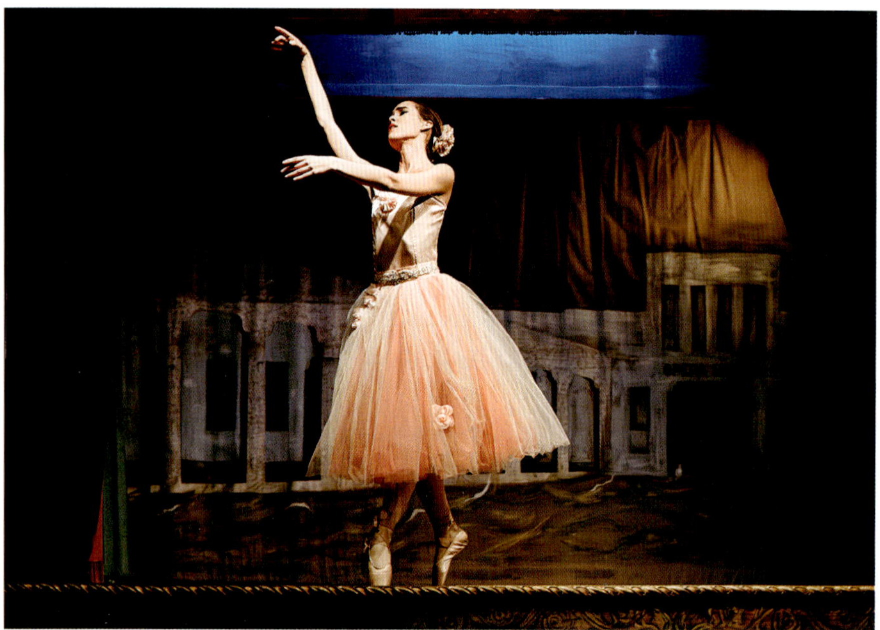

Fig. 74: When shooting with **AF-C in poor light**, it helps to keep the aperture wide open.

> **TIP 72** Single Point AF vs. Zone AF vs. Wide/Tracking AF

AF/MF SETTING > AF MODE lets you choose between SINGLE POINT, ZONE, or WIDE/TRACKING autofocus. The X100VI also offer an ALL option, which lets you seamlessly select one of the three AF modes simply by changing the size of the focus frame or zone. I recommend setting your camera to ALL.

- **Single Point AF** mode is my recommended AF setting for most applications. In this mode, you can manually select one of up to 425 available focus frames. Try to avoid old habits like using only the center frame in concert with the focus-and-recompose [47] technique. It's better to *first* compose the shot and *then* select a suitable AF frame that covers the part of the image you want to be in perfect focus. This helps you avoid focus errors that invariably occur when you pan the focus plane. Such focus errors may be irrelevant with long focal lengths and small aperture openings (larger depth of field) but focus errors can be quite unpleasant with wide-angle lenses, a wide aperture opening (small DOF), and in situations with a short distance between the camera and the subject. Single Point AF can be used in concert with both AF-S and AF-C.

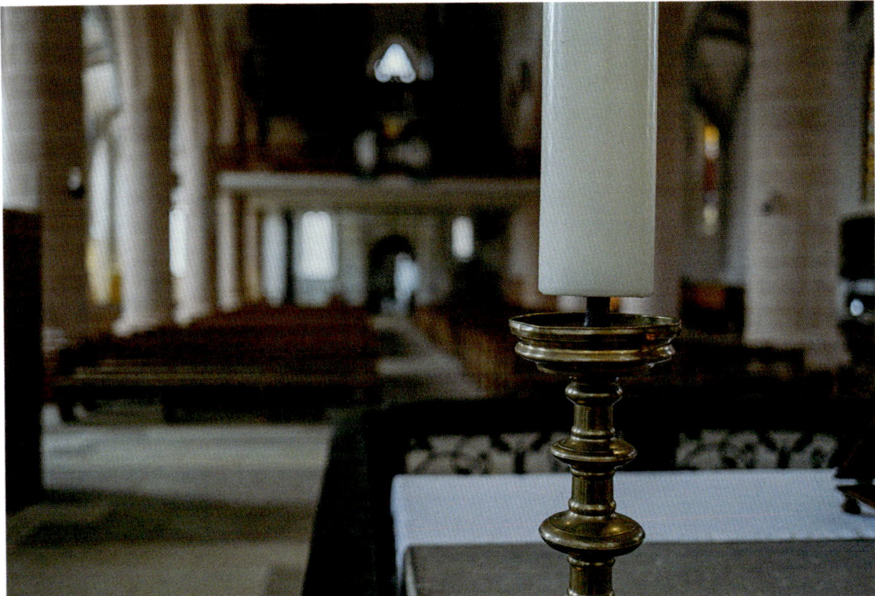

Fig. 75: Shooting with **little depth of field**, you can't afford to use a focus-and-recompose habit because it would quickly lead to soft results that appear out of focus. Instead, compose the shot, and then focus using a single focus frame that covers the part of the image that is supposed to be in focus.

■ You can think of **Zone AF** as an extension of Single Point AF. Basically, an AF zone is a particularly large AF frame that consists of a matrix of smaller AF points. Zones are available in three default sizes that cover 3 × 3, 5 × 5, or 7 × 7 out of a total of 117 AF points. If that doesn't suit you, you can also define three custom zone sizes and shapes to better match the size and shape of your subject. Like Single Point AF frames, AF zones can be moved around within the image area. Since they are larger than focus frames, AF zones make it easier to focus on moving subjects. In Zone AF mode, the camera will usually start looking for something to focus on in the center (crosshairs) of the selected zone and will then expand its search toward the edges of the zone until it finds a target. Like Single Point AF, Zone AF works in concert with either AF-S or AF-C.

- When you combine **Wide/Tracking AF** mode with **AF-S**, you get *Wide AF* mode. The camera scans the entire image frame and automatically selects several focus frames. It's a bit like rolling dice, since the camera is simply looking for areas it can easily focus on. It doesn't know what's important in a scene. This changes when Wide/Tracking is used in concert with **AF-C**: this results in *Tracking AF*, which offers real 3D tracking of moving objects; that is, objects that not only move toward or away from the camera, but also left, right, up, and down within the image frame. To track such an object, select Wide/Tracking and AF-C and pick one of the available AF points. Make sure the selected point covers the moving object you want to track. Half-press the shutter button to start the tracking process. While you keep the shutter button half-pressed, the camera will automatically follow the selected subject as it moves across the image area.

TIP 73	Correct focus stick configuration

For the best results, you must configure the focus stick in a way that's different from the factory default setting. *Without these settings, many of the tips and procedures in this book will not work, so please make sure that we are all on the same page.*

To adjust the focus stick configuration, press and hold the focus stick until the FOCUS LEVER SETTING configuration menu appears. Now select the following options:

- PUSH > EDIT FOCUS AREA. This setting ensures that pressing the focus stick takes you to the FOCUS AREA screen where you can adjust the size and position of the focus frames. You can also quickly change the AF mode, given that AF mode ALL has been selected in the AF/MF SETTING > AF MODE menu.

- TILT > DIRECT AF POINT SELECTION. This setting allows you to directly move the focus frame or zone around simply by tilting the focus stick. This is the easiest way to adjust the position of the focus frame or guide the face/eye detection and subject detection systems.

Selecting an AF frame or AF zone	TIP 74

The X100VI allows you to use the focus stick or the touchscreen to select a focus frame or zone. Make sure that the focus stick is configured as described in the previous tip.

- Pressing the focus stick opens the FOCUS AREA screen, where you can reposition the focus frame or focus zone by tilting the stick in any direction. You can change the size of the frame or zone by turning the front or rear command dials. In AF mode ALL, doing so also changes the AF mode (Single Point, Zone, Wide/Tracking). In the FOCUS AREA screen, pressing the rear command dial resets the size of the zone or frame to their default values. Pressing DISP/BACK centers the position of the AF frame or zone.

- You can also *directly* move the focus frame or zone around simply by tilting the focus stick without pressing it first. This is the easiest way to adjust the position of the focus frame. However, to have additional options like changing the size of the frames, you must first press the focus stick to get to the actual FOCUS AREA screen.

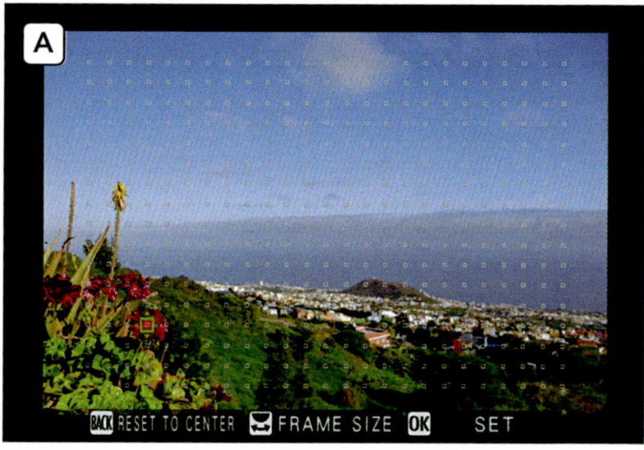

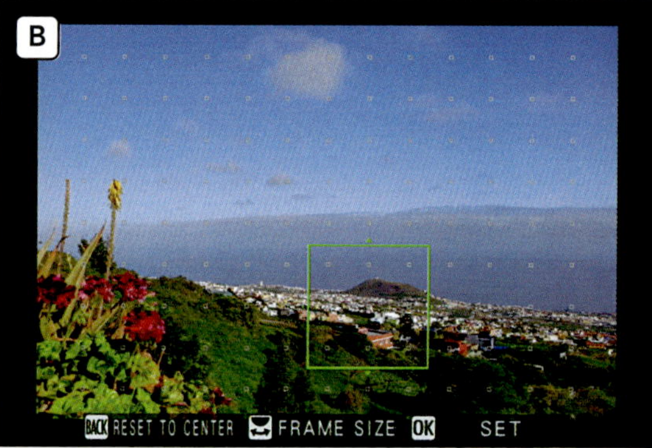

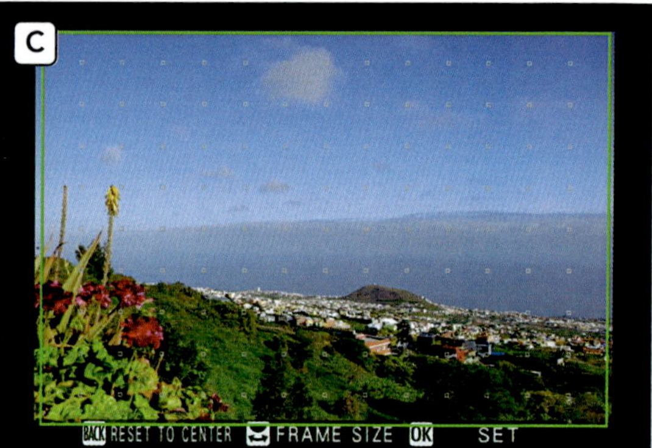

Fig. 76: Pressing the focus stick opens the **FOCUS AREA screen**, where you can select a focus frame or AF Zone and change their sizes. Using the convenient AF mode ALL, changing the size cycles through AF modes Single Point AF (**A**), Zone AF (**B**), and Wide/Tracking AF (**C**).

You can also use the touchscreen to change the position of a focus frame or zone. Make sure the touchscreen-AF interface is set to AREA mode, and then tap anywhere on the screen to select an AF area or zone.

You can even use the touchscreen like a trackpad to change the position of the focus frame or zone when you are looking through the viewfinder. You can select the active trackpad area with SET UP > BUTTON/DIAL SETTING > TOUCH SCREEN SETTING > EVF/OVF TOUCH SCREEN AREA SETTINGS.

Of course, for all of this to work, the touchscreen must have been enabled in the first place, so make sure that SET UP > BUTTON/DIAL SETTING > TOUCH SCREEN SETTING > *(camera symbol)* TOUCH SCREEN SETTING is set to ON.

Choosing a suitable AF frame or AF zone size	TIP 75

The X100VI offers 117 or 425 different AF frames in Single Point AF, and each frame comes in six sizes. You can change the size of an AF frame by pressing the focus stick and turning one of the command dials left or right to decrease or increase the frame size.

AF frame size affects the efficiency of CDAF and PDAF. A basic rule to follow is: *Make your AF frame as large as possible and as small as necessary.*

This is why:

- With a larger AF frame size, the camera has more to work with and a better chance to find contrast in a target, especially when the light conditions aren't optimal. There's also a better chance the camera will be able to use the faster PDAF method. When PDAF isn't possible, the camera will fall back to the slower CDAF.

- With a smaller AF frame size, the autofocus becomes more accurate. A small AF frame gives you better control over *exactly* what the camera is focusing on. Avoid AF frame sizes that are larger than the part of your image that needs to be in focus. For example, if your AF frame is larger than the head of the person you are focusing on, there's a chance that the camera will instead focus on the background behind them, especially if that background contains a lot of contrast.

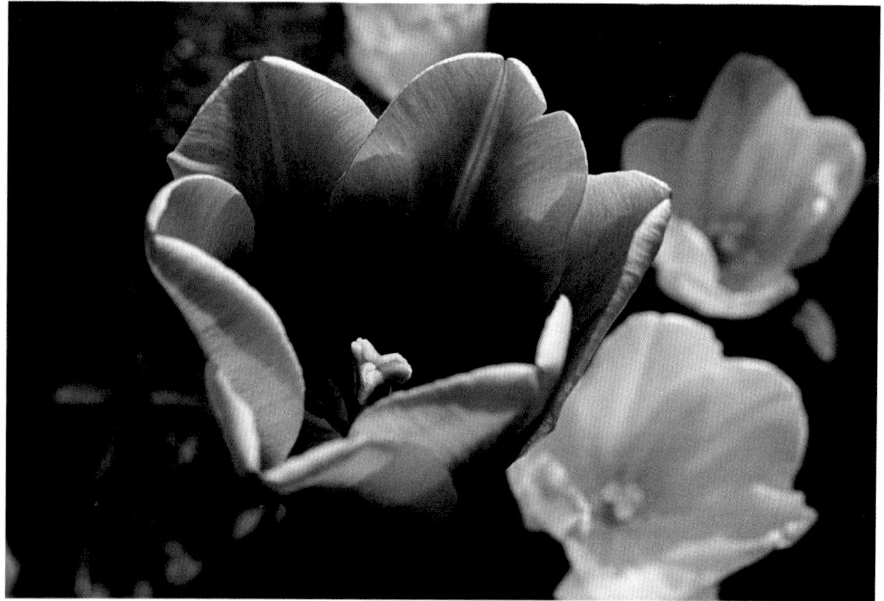

Fig. 77: To get tiny parts of an image in perfect focus, it's best to choose a **small AF frame** size (SOOC JPEG).

In a similar fashion, you can change the size of AF zones by pressing the focus stick and then turning the command dial left or right. You have a choice of three default AF zone sizes: 3 × 3, 5 × 5, or 7 × 7 out of 117 frames. Additionally, you can define three custom zone sizes to match your focus target's size and shape.

Since we can regard AF zones as very large AF frames, the same rules apply. Larger zones are more convenient, and they potentially offer a faster AF response, but they are also potentially less accurate than smaller zones. Hence the availability of three user-defined custom zone sizes that can better match a subject's shape and avoid unnecessary overhead.

Manual focus and DOF zone focusing	TIP 76

Manual focus (MF) mode offers several focus aids:

- A magnification tool with several magnification levels.
- Focus peaking (Focus Peak Highlight) with two strength levels and optional colors.
- Digital split image.
- Digital microprism.
- An electronic distance scale with depth-of-field bars.
- Instant AF: autofocus in MF mode that is triggered by pressing the AEL/AFL button in manual focus mode.

The electronic distance scale can help you define a focus zone with a predetermined depth of field (DOF). The X100VI offers two DOF scales: a *pixel-based* scale (recommended) and a *film-format based* scale (not recommended). If you opt for PIXEL BASE in AF/MF SETTING > DEPTH-OF-FIELD SCALE, everything inside the DOF zone will look pixel-sharp even when the image is magnified to a 100% view. Please don't confuse manual zone focusing with Zone AF—they are completely different things.

Here's a zone-focusing example using the 23 mm lens manually set to 5 m and stopped down to f/11. The DOF bars will show a depth-of-field zone that begins at around 4 m and ends at around 9 m. This means everything located within this zone (between 4 and 9 m) will appear equally in-focus in the final image. You only must make sure that your subject is inside that zone when you press the shutter button.

A special case of manual zone focusing is when setting the hyperfocal distance [48]. This is the distance setting with the maximum DOF (all the way to infinity). Again, the electronic DOF scale can be very helpful: you can manually set the distance where the blue DOF bar on the right touches the infinity mark. For example, with the 23 mm lens set to f/16, the hyperfocal distance is located at approximately 10 m, with the pixel-sharp DOF zone extending from approximately 5 m to infinity.

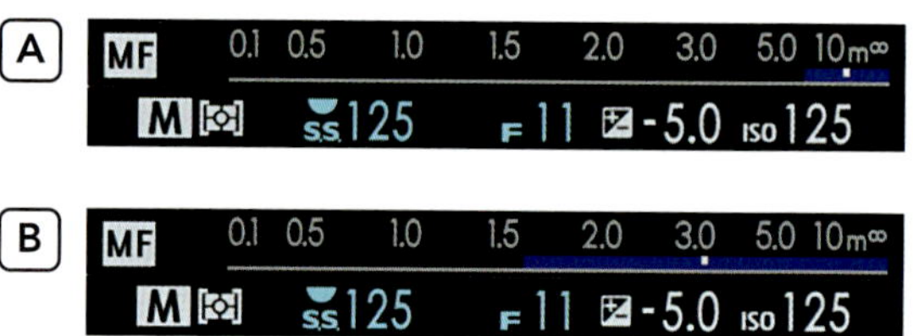

Fig. 78: Setting the **hyperfocal distance** with the electronic distance and DOF scale: instead of focusing on a predetermined distance, manually change the focus distance until the DOF bar touches the ∞ mark on the right end of the scale. This gives you the hyperfocal distance for a given aperture and focal length. This illustration shows the hyperfocal distance of the 23 mm at f/11 for both the PIXEL BASIS option (**A**) and FILM FORMAT BASIS option (**B**).

Please note that depth of field is very much dependent on the circle of confusion (CoC) [49]. Fujifilm uses a very conservative CoC that guarantees pixel-sharp results even when the DOF zone is viewed at 100% magnification on a computer screen. Fuji is literally using the sensor's physical resolution limit as a benchmark. In PIXEL BASIS mode, everything that's located inside the electronic DOF zone will be rendered as sharp as the sensor can resolve it. In the age of pixel peeping, this is as good as it can get.

The FILM FORMAT BASIS option of the DOF scale is based on a much less conservative circle of confusion that is several aperture stops more generous than the PIXEL BASIS scale. You can change the scale to FILM FORMAT BASIS (and hence use a less conservative scale with all your lenses) in AF/MF SETTING > DEPTH-OF-FIELD SCALE. However, I want to reiterate that I do not recommend this setting. Instead, I recommend using the PIXEL BASIS scale.

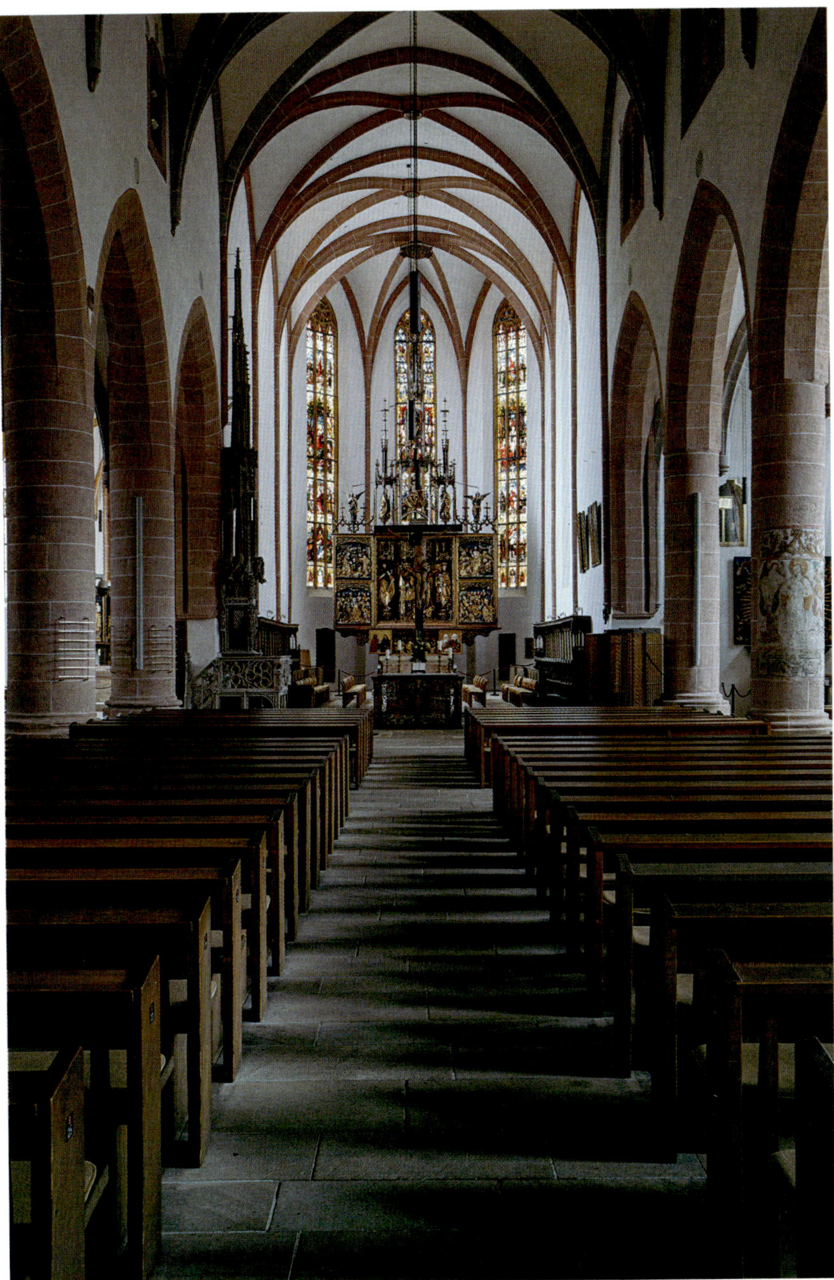

Fig. 79: This shot was manually focused by setting the **hyperfocal distance** on the camera's electronic PIXEL BASIS focus distance scale.

<table><tr><td>TIP 77</td><td>**Manual focus assistants**</td></tr></table>

The X100VI features several MF assistants:

- **Focus Peaking** (or Focus Peak Highlight) emphasizes the edges of objects when they are in focus.

- **Digital Split Image** tries to simulate the split image indicator of manual focus SLRs. It works best with vertical edges (or horizontal edges when the camera is held in portrait orientation).

- **Digital Microprism** simulates a microprism that used to be popular in the manual-focus SLR days.

To quickly switch between the available MF assistants, press and hold the rear command dial for about a second while you are in MF mode. For this to work, FOCUS CHECK must have been assigned to the rear command dial Fn button.

You can watch a short video [50] demonstrating different manual focus assistants. There's also a video demonstrating the "real thing": actual analog split image and microprism focusing with an old Minolta SLR [51].

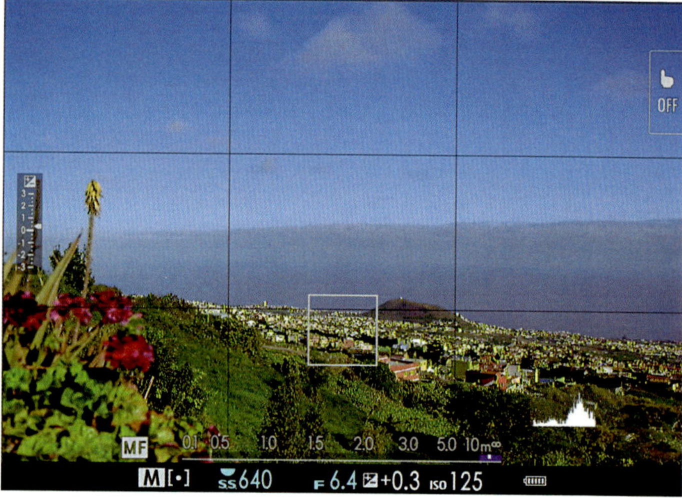

Fig. 80: Focus peaking is my favorite among the available manual focus aids. In this example, I opted for yellow outlines to indicate the areas of the scene that are in focus.

Selecting AF/MF SETTING > INTERLOCK MF ASSIST & FOCUS RING > ON automatically activates the selected MF assistant when the focus ring is turned. After a short period of inactivity, the MF assistant is then automatically disabled again. My personal recommendation for this setting is ON. I use it in concert with focus peaking.

Using the Focus Check magnifier tool	TIP 78

The magnifier tool is helpful for checking if the focus is spot-on. Press the rear command dial (either in AF-S/Single Point AF or in MF mode) to magnify the area that is targeted by the selected focus frame. Of course, this assumes the rear command dial is operating with its default FOCUS CHECK Fn button assignment.

You can change the magnification level by turning the rear command dial. You can also combine focus check with any MF assistant (focus peaking, digital split image, and digital microprism). Please note that in digital split image and digital microprism mode, only *one* magnification level is available.

By selecting AF/MF SETTING > FOCUS CHECK > ON, the magnifier tool is *automatically* activated when you turn the manual focus ring of the lens in MF mode. You can immediately cancel any automatic focus check by half-pressing the shutter button.

There are up to 425 different focus frames available in manual focus mode. The active frame indicates which part of the image will be magnified when focus check is activated. As usual, you can change the active frame with the focus stick or touchscreen.

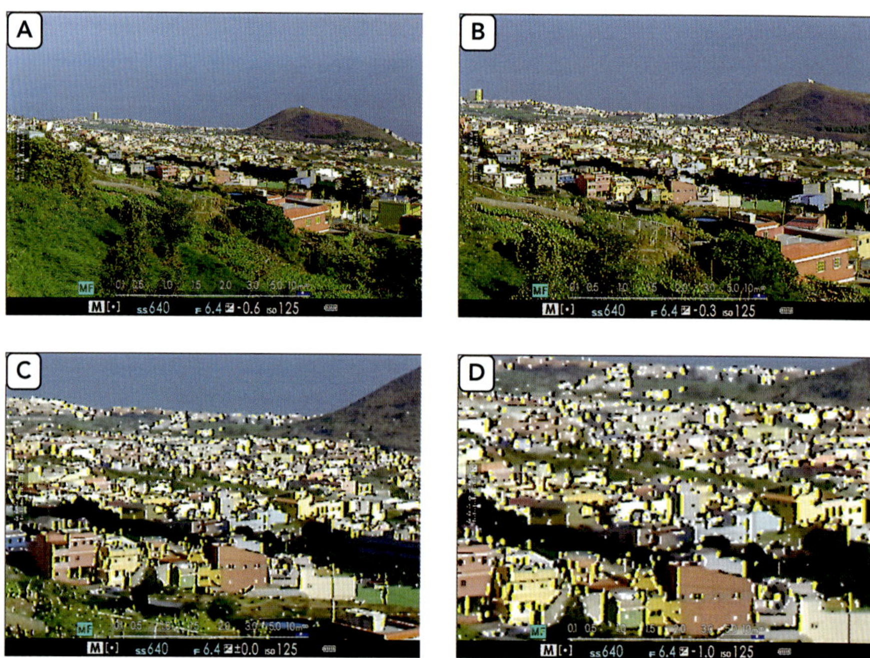

Fig. 81: The X100VI offers several **magnification levels**. To make things easier, the magnification can be combined with focus peaking. You can also move the magnified area with the focus stick or touchscreen while Focus Check is zoomed into the frame.

Please note that Focus Check is not available in AF-C mode, or when Pre-AF has been turned on.

TIP 79	Using Instant AF-S and Instant AF-C

Instant AF must be initiated with an Fn button and is only available when the designated Fn button has been tasked with either AF-ON, AF LOCK ONLY or AE/AF LOCK. Personally, I recommend using the AEL/AFL button with an AF-ON assignment for Instant AF. To check or change the Fn button assignment in your camera, press and hold the DISP/ BACK button until the Bluetooth & FUNCTION (Fn) SETTING screen appears.

Instant AF allows you to autofocus the camera in manual focus mode by pressing the AEL/AFL button. Instant AF always works with a wide-open aperture. Like the regular autofocus, its efficiency depends on the size of the selected focus frame.

Instant AF is the most precise AF method available, but it is a bit slower than the camera's regular autofocus. It can be combined with conventional manual focusing: you can use Instant AF to quickly autofocus on an object, and then manually fine-tune the focus by turning the focus ring and using MF assistants like the magnifier and focus peaking.

Instant AF normally functions like AF-S, but you can also set it to continuous focus with AF/MF SETTING > INSTANT AF SETTING > AF-C. In this mode, Instant AF will track the subject distance with AF-C while you keep the AEL/AFL button pressed in manual focus mode.

Unlike regular AF-C (that focuses with the working aperture), Instant AF-C can focus with a wide-open aperture, making it an option for stage and concert photography with moving subjects in poor light, where you want to shoot with AF-C and a stopped-down lens. Just keep the AEL/AFL button pressed for continuous instant autofocus as you press the shutter button at the right moment.

Note that Instant AF-C stops focusing when you half-press the shutter button. To avoid unnecessary time lags between focusing and shutter release, it's best to first activate Instant AF-C by pressing and holding the AEL/AFL button (or any other designated Instant AF button) to continually focus and then *fully press* the shutter button to take a shot. In other words: skip the half-press and go all the way.

 Using AF+MF

AF+MF allows you to manually focus in AF mode by turning the focus ring, all while holding the shutter button half-pressed. Select AF/MF SETTING > AF+MF > ON to enable this feature.

Here's how it works:

- Autofocus on your subject as usual in AF-S or AF-C mode by half-pressing the shutter button.

- Once the autofocus has been confirmed (green square[s]) or not confirmed (red AF warning), keep the shutter button half-pressed and rotate the focus ring of your lens to *manually* adjust the focus distance until you are satisfied. If focus peaking is enabled, it will automatically engage when the focus ring is rotated and manual focus (MF) kicks in. You can also use the Focus Check function (AF/MF SETTING > FOCUS CHECK > ON) to automatically magnify the focus area when you turn the focus ring. For this to work, make sure that AF-S and Single Point AF are set. You can also combine Focus Check magnification with focus peaking. Turn the rear command dial to change the magnification factor and press the rear command dial to manually enable/disable the live view magnification. Remember that all this must be performed while you hold the shutter button half-pressed, so this might require some practice.

- When you are happy with your manual focus adjustments, fully press the half-pressed shutter button to take the shot.

At first glance, the MF component of AF+MF may look like your regular manual focus, but it's not. While genuine MF is performed at a wide-open aperture, the MF part of AF+MF is performed at the selected working aperture. That's because the shutter button is half-pressed, so the camera has already been primed to take the shot with minimal shutter lag.

This also means the EVF/LCD will display a live view image that shows the actual depth of field of the resulting image, and focus peaking will show a larger area as being in focus when you stop down the lens. This can make it more difficult to nail your manual focus adjustment.

*Important: Switching on AF+MF in the menu internally sets both the AF-S and the AF-C PRIORITY SELECTION to RELEASE priority. This means that the camera may not focus correctly in AF-S mode if you swiftly and fully press the shutter release button (basically skipping the half-press phase and the autofocus confirmation). In AF-C mode, the camera may take a larger number of misfocused images, especially in combination with burst shooting. For this reason, I strongly recommend **not** using AF+MF in the X100VI.*

Pre-AF: a relic of the past	TIP 81

Pre-AF brings the AF-C of first-generation Fujifilm X cameras (like the X-Pro1) to modern models like your X100VI. With Pre-AF set to ON, the camera will continuously focus on whatever is covered by the active AF frame, even when the shutter button is *not* half-pressed.

Pre-AF burns plenty of power because the autofocus in the lens is always working. On the other hand, using it can potentially result in a quicker AF response, and it can help face/eye detection and subject detection find a target. Remember to pack a few extra batteries if you intend to use this function. I usually set AF/MF SETTING > PRE-AF to OFF.

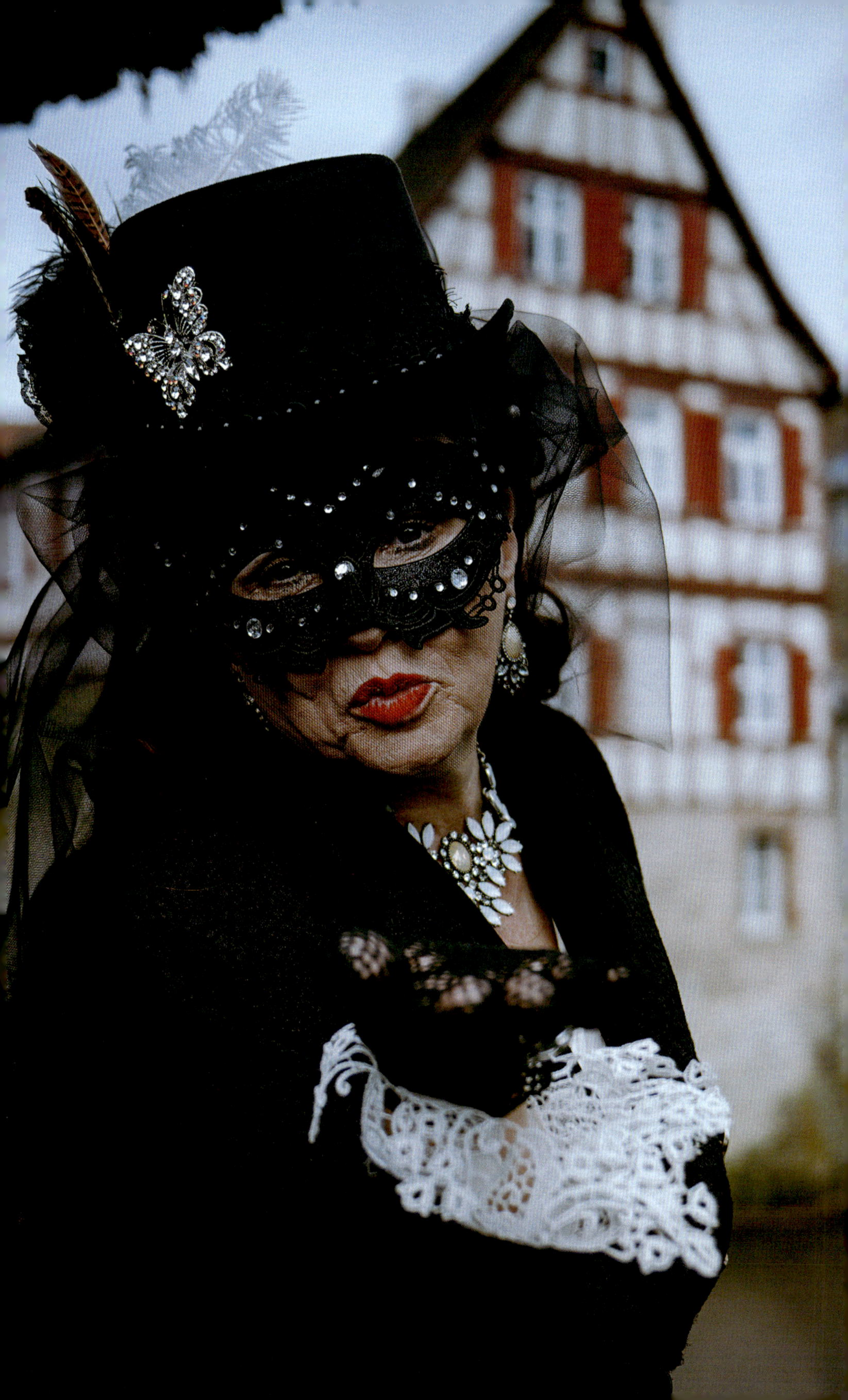

| Using face/eye detection and subject detection | TIP 82 |

Face detection and subject detection are combined autofocus and exposure metering modes. They even affect auto white balance. You can activate face/eye detection with AF/MF SETTING > FACE/EYE DETECTION SETTING > FACE DETECTION ON and picking one of the four eye detection options.

Here's what it does:

- The camera scans the scene and detects human faces, heads, and bodies. It automatically focuses on one of the detected subjects when the shutter button is half-pressed. When more than one face or person is detected, the camera tends to focus on the one that's closest to the focus frame (or zone) of the underlying autofocus mode. This person/head/face/eye will be highlighted with a white frame.

- Face detection and subject detection use a custom version of weighted multi metering that can put a bias on the selected subject. It may also influence the camera's auto white balance.

Face detection and subject detection are both a blessing and a curse. They are a blessing when they work because they focus directly on a subject or object and make sure that they are "correctly" exposed. It's a curse when the detection goes wrong because it doesn't just mean the focus might miss its mark; it may also mess up your exposure metering and change your auto exposure.

The good news is that in many cases, face and subject detection work. For example, face detection works with people who only show their profiles to the camera, persons wearing glasses, and even persons that turn away from the camera. In such cases, face detection will focus on the head or on the entire body.

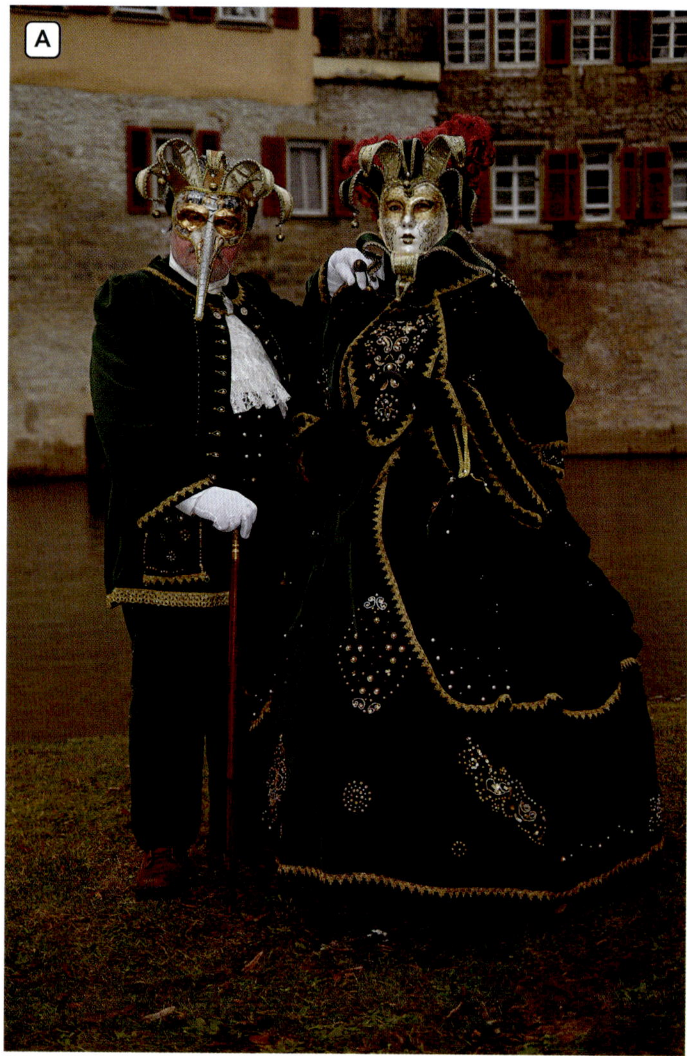

Fig. 82: Face detection is great for scenes with one or more people looking at (or showing their profile to) the camera. Fifth-generation X cameras like the X100VI feature enhanced face and subject detection that's based on machine learning. For example, the face/eye detection algorithm can also detect and direct the autofocus to the head, torso, or entire body of a person. It's also quite robust when it comes to unusual cases, like this SOOC JPEG of a masked couple (image **A**). A look at the decoded metadata reveals what the face detection algorithm identified as viable target areas (image **B**).

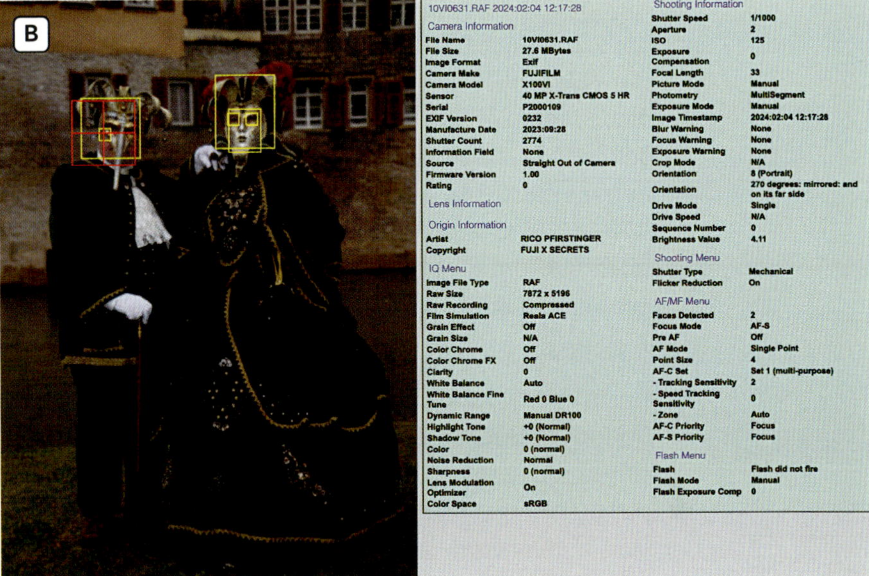

Here are a few helpful tips regarding face and subject detection:

- If you want to take face detection and subject detection exposure metering out of the equation (and I highly recommend that you do), you can set the camera to manual exposure mode **M**. While the *metering* will still be affected in this mode, the *exposure* itself will not.

- Spot, center-weighted, and average metering aren't available when face or subject detection are active. The camera is always using a derivate of multi metering.

- When face or subject detection fail to detect a suitable target in the scene, the camera will automatically fall back to the selected regular AF mode: Single Point, Zone, or Wide/Tracking. At the same time, exposure metering reverts to regular multi metering.

- Face and subject detection can and should be assigned to function (Fn) buttons or Touch-Fn gestures.

- Face detection and subject detection cannot be active at the same time. It's either one or the other. However, you can regard face/eye detection as simply another subject detection mode. There's no difference in camera behavior between face/eye detection and the six subject detection options (ANIMAL, BIRD, AUTOMOBILE, MOTORCYCLE&-BIKE, AIRPLANE, TRAIN). That said, FACE/EYE DETECTION offers additional options such as selecting the left or right eye or switching off eye detection altogether.

- Subject detection will only detect the currently selected subject type. For example, if you select MOTORCYCLE&-BIKE, the camera will not look for and detect trains, cars, planes, or animals. However, it may very well detect a person riding a bike and focus on their head, helmet, or face. If they come close enough, the camera may even focus on that person's eye.

- Fujifilm is always enhancing and expanding the face and subject detection functions to make them more useful and effective. For example, BIRD mode now also detects insects, and AIRPLANE mode detects helicopters and drones.

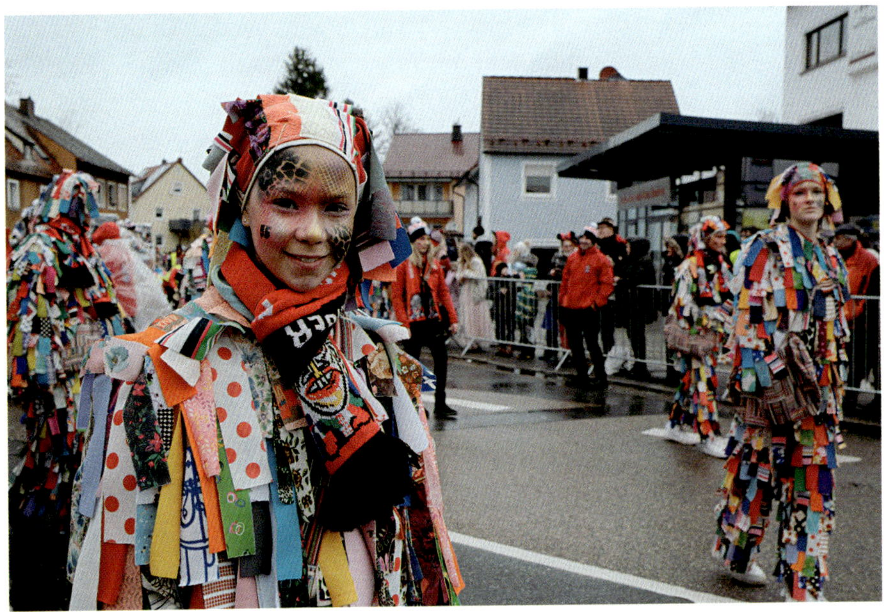

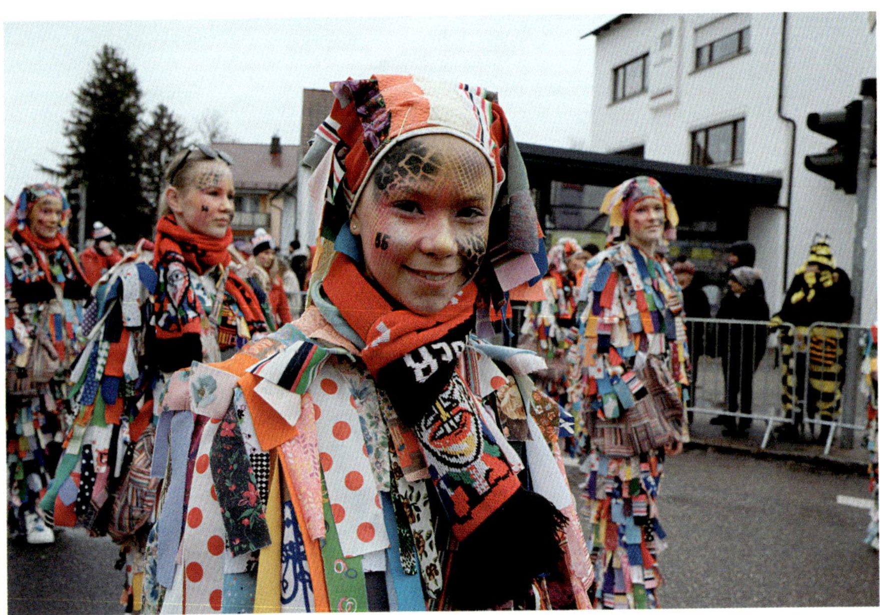

Fig. 83: If **persons are moving** around, the X100VI can track their faces with AF-C and face/eye detection (SOOC JPEGs).

Face detection accuracy can be improved with the optional eye detection feature. To activate it, select either LEFT EYE PRIORITY or RIGHT EYE PRIORITY. You can also select EYE AUTO to make the camera focus on the eye that's closest to the camera or select EYE OFF to deactivate eye detection during face detection.

In the live view, the camera will highlight a detected eye with a small square and will focus on it when you half-press the shutter button. I usually set this function to EYE AUTO. You can then toggle between the left or the right eye by assigning RIGHT/LEFT EYE SWITCH to an Fn button or T-Fn gesture of your liking.

Important: Face/eye and subject detection aren't available when the optical viewfinder (OVF) is in use! If you use the OVF with active face/eye/subject detection, your X100VI will automatically revert to the underlying autofocus mode and regular multi metering.

| TIP 83 | Face/subject detection and the underlying fallback auto-focus mode |

With face and subject detection, the underlying fallback AF mode is the autofocus mode that is selected when you activate face detection or subject detection on top of it:

- Single Point AF
- Zone AF
- Wide AF (in concert with AF-S)
- Tracking AF (in concert with AF-C)

Face/subject detection AF and the underlying AF mode work together in two ways:

- The size and the position of the focus frame (Single Point AF), the focus zone (Zone AF) or the tracking frame (Tracking AF) determine the area and vicinity where face detection and subject detection are looking (and not looking) for suitable targets. It also determines on which of multiple suitable targets to focus. For example, if face detection finds a group of three people, the camera will focus on the face that's closest to the position of the underlying focus mode's focus frame.

- If face detection or subject detection fail to find or track a target for whatever reason, the autofocus automatically reverts to the underlying AF mode: Single Point AF, Zone AF or Wide/Tracking AF.

Based on the above, here are a few tips on how to use face/subject detection in concert with underlying AF modes:

- To make the camera scan the entire image frame for subjects, you can select Wide AF as your underlying AF-S mode. In AF-C, the widest scan area is provided with Zone AF and a centered 7x7 zone.

- To direct face or subject detection to a *specific* subject in your frame, you can use Single Point AF or Zone AF with a small or regular frame size and position that frame close to your chosen subject.

- Always remember that the autofocus will use the position and size of the underlying AF mode's focus frame or zone when no subject can be detected, or when subject tracking is interrupted or fails. The underlying AF mode is your fallback AF mode. For example, when you are shooting portraits with face/eye detection in AF-S, you might want to select a small Single-AF frame as your fallback AF mode and position that frame over the face or (if possible) an eye of your subject.

- If a face or subject has been detected and you half-press the shutter button in AF-C mode, the camera will keep tracking the selected subject no matter what until you release the shutter button. Of course, if subject tracking fails, the camera will fall back to the underlying autofocus mode. If your underlying AF mode is Tracking AF, the autofocus will store and track the pattern that occurs at the position where face or subject detection tracking stopped working. This means that when you are tracking moving subjects in AF-C mode, it can be a good idea to use Tracking AF as your underlaying AF mode. In this case, Tracking AF will take over at the position where face or subject detection have lost the target.

■ Face and subject detection are meant to make your life easier. But *easier* isn't always *better*. In many situations and with some practice, you may do a better job than the camera—not only detecting suitable subjects, but also positioning a perfectly sized focus frame on them. This is especially true for stationary subjects that can be shot in AF-S mode. I use subject detection mostly in scenarios where I cannot always keep a regular focus frame or zone trained on a moving subject. However, I am always selecting a suitable fallback AF mode and trying to keep the focus frame or zone of the fallback mode on target in case the camera's "smart" subject tracking fails. In other words: Don't rely too much on the camera to do your job.

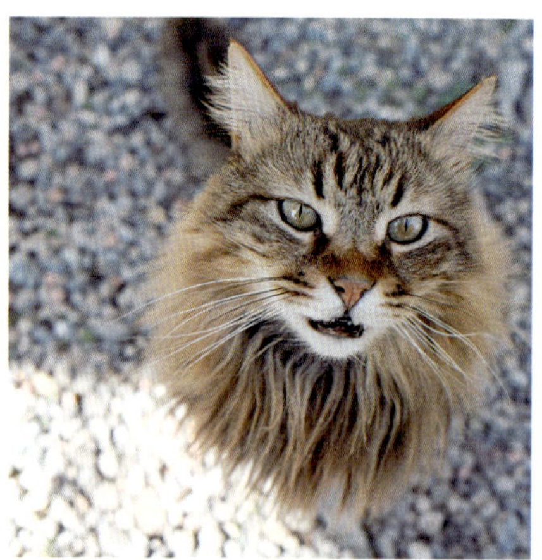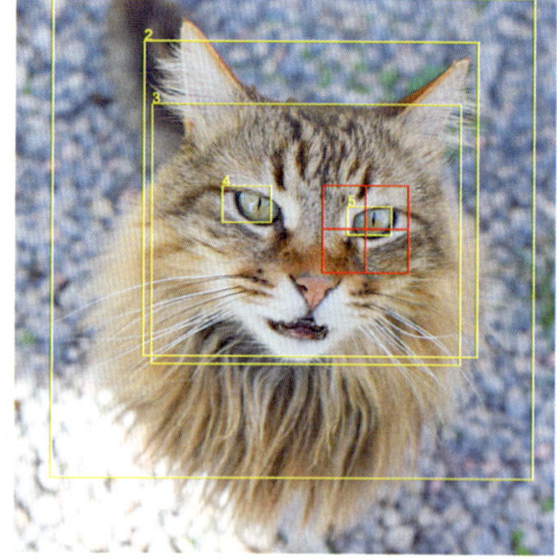

Fig. 84: This SOOC JPEG of a cat was shot with **ANIMAL subject detection**. As a safety, I used Single Point AF as my fallback autofocus mode, pointing the focus frame at one of the eyes. However, as you can see in the second image, the subject detection algorithm found plenty of target options by itself.

| Using AF-ON (back-button focusing) | TIP 84 |

AF-ON brings back-button focusing to your X100VI, a common practice among DSLR users. Simply put, AF-ON assigns the autofocus to a function button. Press that button, and the camera starts focusing. Release it, and the focusing stops at the current focus position—until you press the AF-ON button again.

In other words: AF-ON performs the same autofocus function as half-pressing the shutter button (assuming that SHUTTER AF ON is set in the SET UP > BUTTON/DIAL SETTING menu). In AF-S mode, pressing AF-ON will perform a single focus search and lock the distance. In AF-C mode, AF-ON will continuously focus on a target as the button is kept pressed (just like half-pressing the shutter button).

In the X100VI, the AF-ON function is not pre-assigned, so it's your job to connect it to an Fn button. The obvious choice here is the AEL/AFL button. To check or change the Fn button assignment in your camera, press and hold the DISP/BACK button until the Bluetooth & FUNCTION (Fn) SETTING screen appears.

You can press and hold AF-ON (= the AEL/AFL button) while you simultaneously press the shutter release button. Here's what happens:

- In AF-S mode, pressing and holding AF-ON will focus the camera and lock that focus while AF-ON is held, so simultaneously half-pressing or pressing the shutter button won't interfere with your locked focus.

- In AF-C mode, pressing AF-ON means that the camera keeps tracking your target as long as AF-ON is pressed and held.

- In manual focus (MF) mode, AF-ON turns into Instant AF.

If you are a "religious" back-button-AF user, you may find it more comfortable to entirely disable the shutter release button's AF functionality by selecting SET UP > BUTTON/DIAL SETTING > SHUTTER AF > OFF for AF-S and/or AF-C. After that, AF-ON will be the only available method to autofocus in AF-S or AF-C mode.

TIP 85	Focusing in poor light

Low light can lead to poor contrast along with more photon noise, making it more difficult for the camera to find and lock the correct autofocus distance. However, the amount of light (and hence noise) that reaches the sensor depends not only on the brightness of a scene, but also on the brightness of the lens. Luckily, the 23mmF2 lens in your X100VI is a good performer, and its brightness doesn't decrease when you attach a WCL or TCL.

The autofocus works best good light and contrast. When the light is poor, it's vital to target surfaces with contrast and, if possible, use a larger AF frame size. You can also generate light—the camera's AF assist lamp can illuminate a subject to help the autofocus find better contrast. Be aware that the AF assist lamp can be easily blocked by an attached lens hood. Watch out for this and remove the lens hood if necessary. Since the AF assist lamp tends to concentrate on the center of the image, it works best in concert with one of the more central AF frames. To use the AF assist lamp, make sure to set AF/MF SETTING > AF ILLUMINATOR > ON.

An alternative to using the AF assist lamp is using a flashlight to temporarily illuminate a subject. If you are indoors, you can try turning on the lights in the room for a moment and using AF-Lock or AF-On to lock the focus. Just make sure to meter and set the exposure *after* the lights are off again.

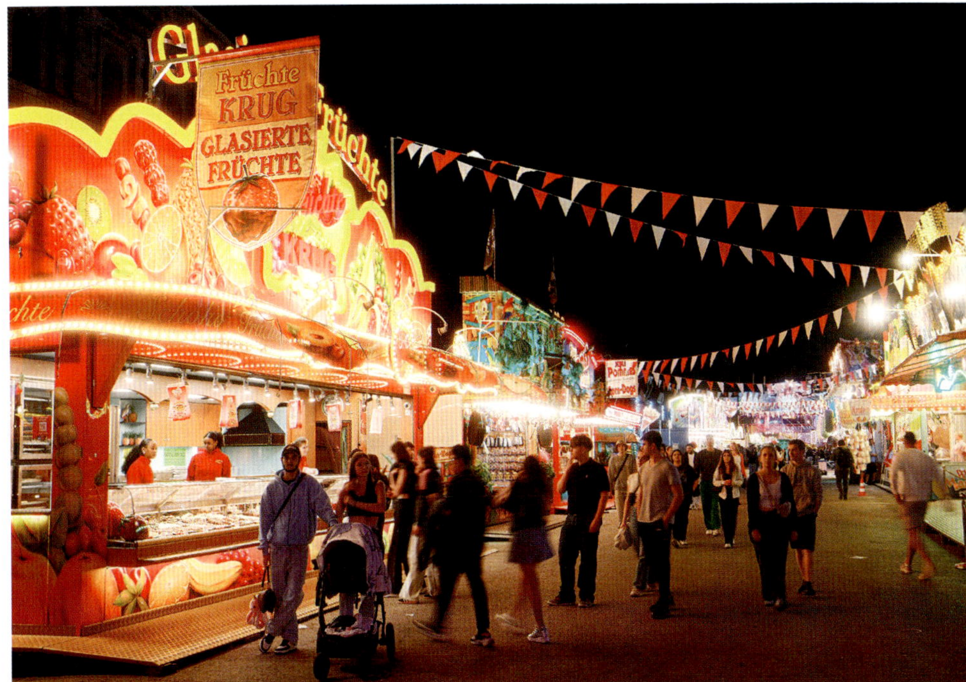

Fig. 85: Shooting at night is a joy with the X100VI. With its powerful IBIS, I found that can shoot handheld using slow shutter speeds down to 1/2 sec. In AF-S mode, stopping down the lens in low light doesn't degrade the AF performance because unlike AF-C, the camera can open the aperture during the focusing process.

This SOOC JPEG was shot with 1/10 sec. at f/8 and ISO 500 / DR400%.

Important: If you intend to stop down the aperture of your lens in poor light, make sure to use either AF-S or manual focus with Instant AF-S or Instant AF-C as your focusing mode. Why? Because Instant AF always focuses wide open. Try to avoid regular AF-C, because this mode will usually focus with (or closer to) your stopped-down working aperture, which will make things more difficult for your camera because less light will reach the sensor.

<table><tr><td>**TIP 86**</td><td>**Macro: focusing at close distances**</td></tr></table>

The biggest challenge with shooting macro is the lack of depth of field (DOF) [52]. The slightest movement may cause the shot to be out of focus. That's why macro photography is usually performed using a tripod and manual focus, often with Instant AF, Focus Check (magnifier tool), and focus peaking. It's vital not to recompose after the focus has been set. To get a visual impression of the current DOF, you can half-press the shutter (make sure SHUTTER AE is ON) or assign PREVIEW DEPTH OF FIELD to one of your Fn buttons.

Macro shots usually require you to stop down the lens to increase the DOF. Since this can result in slower shutter speeds, it's important to make sure the subject isn't moving too fast or out of the focus plane. Shooting a close-up of a flower in the wind may not yield excellent results.

If you don't want to use manual focus for close-up shots, you can also focus automatically. Here's how:

■ Due to the parallax effect at close distances, don't use the OVF for macro shots. Instead, use the EVF or LCD.

■ Set AF-S and Single Point AF and select a small AF frame size.

■ Reposition the small AF frame to exactly cover the part of the image you want to be in focus. Quickly take the shot after you half-press the shutter—don't recompose.

■ You can check your focus with the magnifier tool before taking a shot by pressing the rear command dial. After doing so, you can change the magnification factor by turning the command dial.

■ Try not to shoot handheld; it's better to use a tripod.

- Stop down the lens and visually check the depth of field by half-pressing the shutter button or using the DOF preview function (remember that function can be assigned to any Fn button).

- Make sure there is sufficient light and try to shoot subjects that don't move in and out of the focus plane.

The 23mmF2 lens of your X100VI isn't a typical macro lens. Due to its minimum focus distance of approximately 10 cm, your options are limited as far as very small subjects are concerned. To further decrease the minimum focus distance of the lens, you can add an inexpensive diopter lens with a 49 mm thread. Like reading glasses, these lenses are available in different strengths (typically +1 to +4). However, getting even closer also means that you can easily scare away living subjects such as insects.

Another option to tighten the frame is attaching a TCL-X100(II) to increase the focal length from 23 mm to 33 mm without changing the minimum focus distance. That said, the high resolution of the X100VI offers plenty of crop potential, so you can also magnify your subject simply by cropping it after-the-fact.

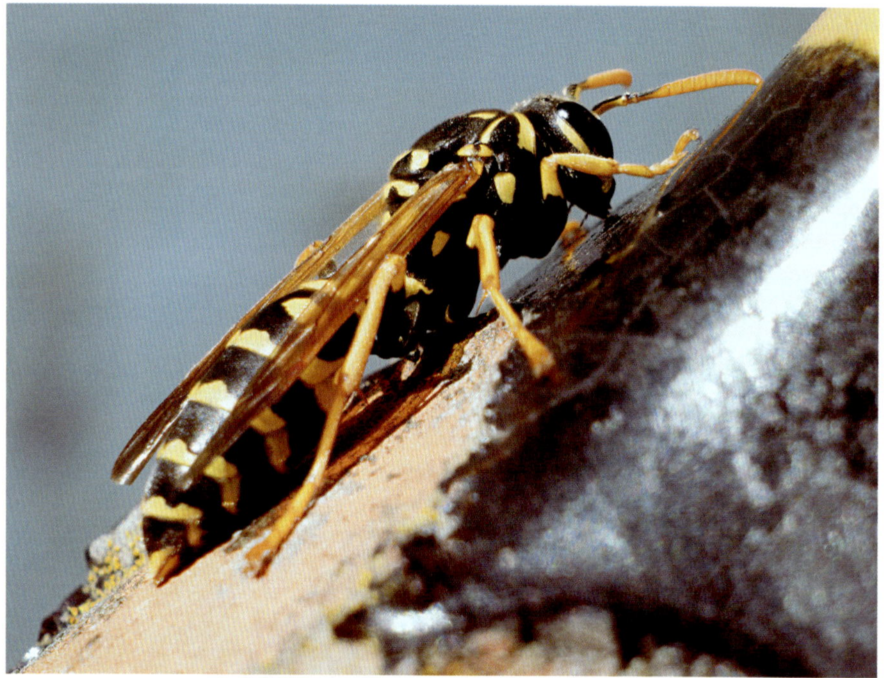

Fig. 86: Macro shots can be quite challenging due to their lack of DOF. This is why a tripod is highly recommended. That said, hand-held shots like this example are possible, as well. In this case, I didn't even need a diopter lens to decrease the focus distance—simple cropping did the job (23 mm, ISO 125, 1/125 sec., f/7.1).

TIP 87	Focus Bracketing

The need for greater depth of field (DOF) is a common issue for macro and landscape photographers. With increasing sensor resolution, diffraction blur [53] becomes a serious limitation. To avoid visible diffraction with your 40 MP APS-C sensor, you should avoid stopping down much beyond f/8.

For macro and landscape photographers, stopping down the lens to f/16 often isn't an option due to quality considerations. Not to mention that even at f/16, the depth of field would still not be sufficient in many macro situations.

What to do? There is a popular solution among ambitious photographers called *focus bracketing*, where multiple images are taken at various focus distances. The shots are later merged (i.e., *stacked*) into a single image that displays increased depth of field. The series of individual source images can be merged in Photoshop or in other specialized software such as Helicon Focus [54]. This technique is referred to as *focus stacking* [55].

Focus bracketing helps you automate the generation of the source material you need for focus stacking. To configure focus bracketing in your X100VI, select SHOOTING SETTING > FOCUS BKT SETTING and choose MANUAL or AUTO.

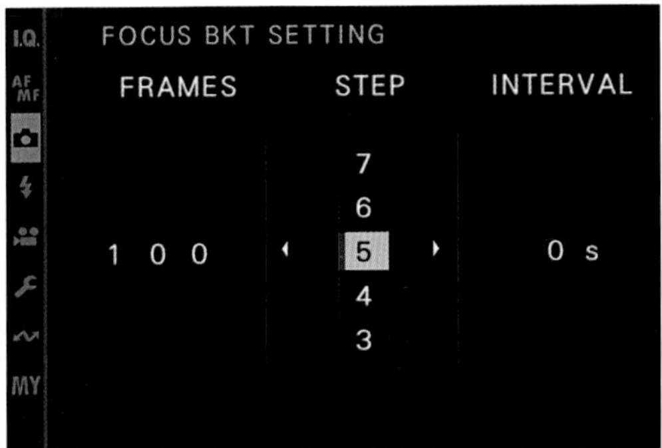

Fig. 87: The manual **focus bracketing configuration screen** allows you to set the number of frames the camera should automatically take (FRAMES), the relative focus distance difference between individual shots (STEP), and the pause between individual shots (INTERVAL). The latter is useful so that the camera can settle down after each shot to avoid shutter-induced vibration—which is hardly an issue considering the X100VI has a tiny, quiet leaf shutter. However, you may need a longer interval in concert with flash light to give the flash sufficient time to recharge between shots. To eliminate any possible shutter vibration, you can also select electronic shutter (ES).

To initiate manual focus bracketing, it's best to select MF and manually focus on the nearest point of the subject you want to have in perfect focus. It's also recommended to stop down the lens to its sweet spot. For the X100VI, an aperture setting between f/4.5 and f/6.4 appears to be quite optimal.

Depending on your needs and time restraints, you can experiment with various step settings. Make sure the camera is in FOCUS BKT mode (FOCUS BKT must be selected in the DRIVE button menu). To start the sequence, press the shutter button. The camera will take the set number of images or stop when it reaches infinity—whatever occurs first.

When the camera has finished recording the source images, you can merge them in Photoshop or in specialized focus-stacking software like Helicon Focus.

Sounds cumbersome? It is! Luckily, your X00VI also features an *automatic* focus bracketing mode, where you can manually set a starting point (the closest focus distance) and an end point (the furthest focus distance) for a given scene or subject. The camera will then automatically take the required number of shots at varying distance settings to cover the area between the start point and the end point. All that's left for you to do is specify the shooting interval between consecutive bracketing shots. With the leaf shutter of the X100VI, you can safely pick a shooting interval of zero without suffering shutter shock vibration.

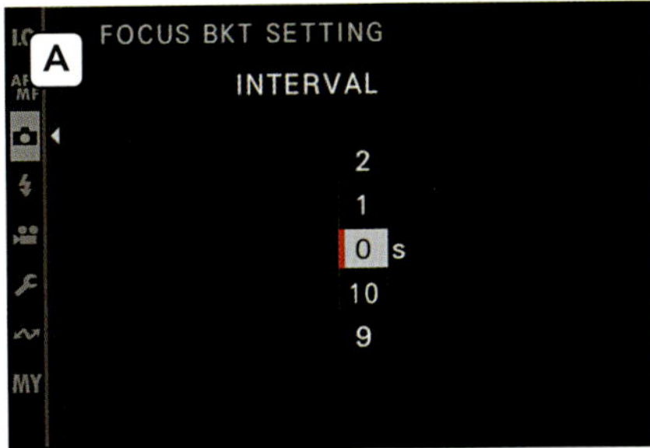

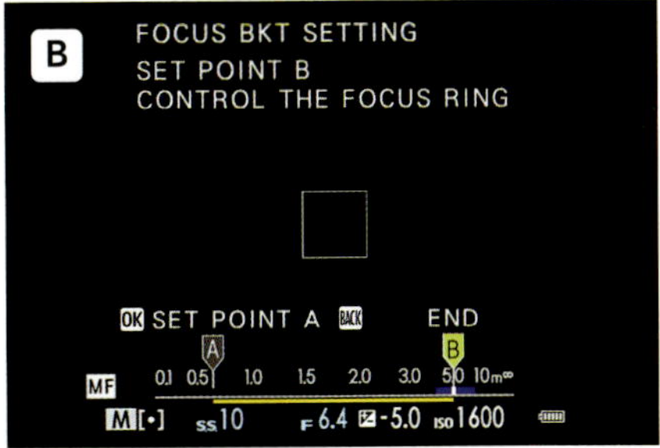

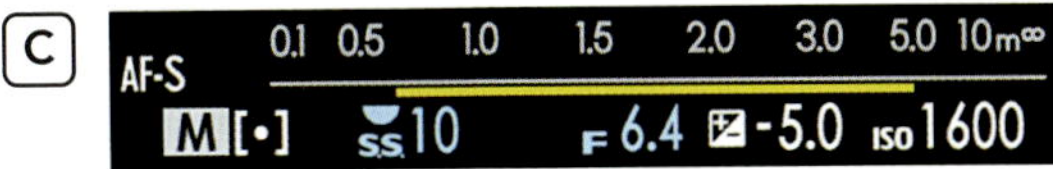

Fig. 88: Focus Auto Bracketing facilitates the image acquisition process and automatically captures the number of shots that are required to cover a user-defined distance range. In your X100VI, the focus bracketing settings menu is hidden under SHOOTING SETTING > FOCUS BKT SETTING > AUTO, followed by different settings pages.

After selecting AUTO as your focus bracketing mode, the camera opens the next settings page where you can specify the INTERVAL. This is the time lag between consecutive acquisition shots. Your options range from 0 to 10 seconds. Ideally, you should select a zero interval to mitigate the risk of subject motion blur (**A**). If you are using a flash, make sure that the interval is long enough to give your flash sufficient time to recycle between shots.

After setting and confirming the INTERVAL time, the next FOCUS BKT SETTING screen (**B**) prompts you to manually set the focus bracketing range and asks you to enter corresponding "A" (near) and "B" (far) points. This is performed by turning the manual focus ring of your attached lens. Sadly, this process is not very intuitive: The camera asks you to toggle between the "A" and "B" points with the OK button and to confirm your finished range setting with the BACK button. To facilitate the range setting process, you can use a manual focus assistant like focus peaking, so make sure to enable it in the AF/MF SETTING > MF ASSIST menu before entering the FOCUS BKT SETTING process. You can also use the magnifier tool to zoom in and out.

Having set and confirmed your focus bracketing range, the camera will now display a yellow line below the live view's distance scale that indicates the bracketing distance range (**C**).

Once everything is set up properly, you can just press the shutter release button and the camera will automatically record the required number of shots that cover the preset focus distance range based on the current aperture setting.

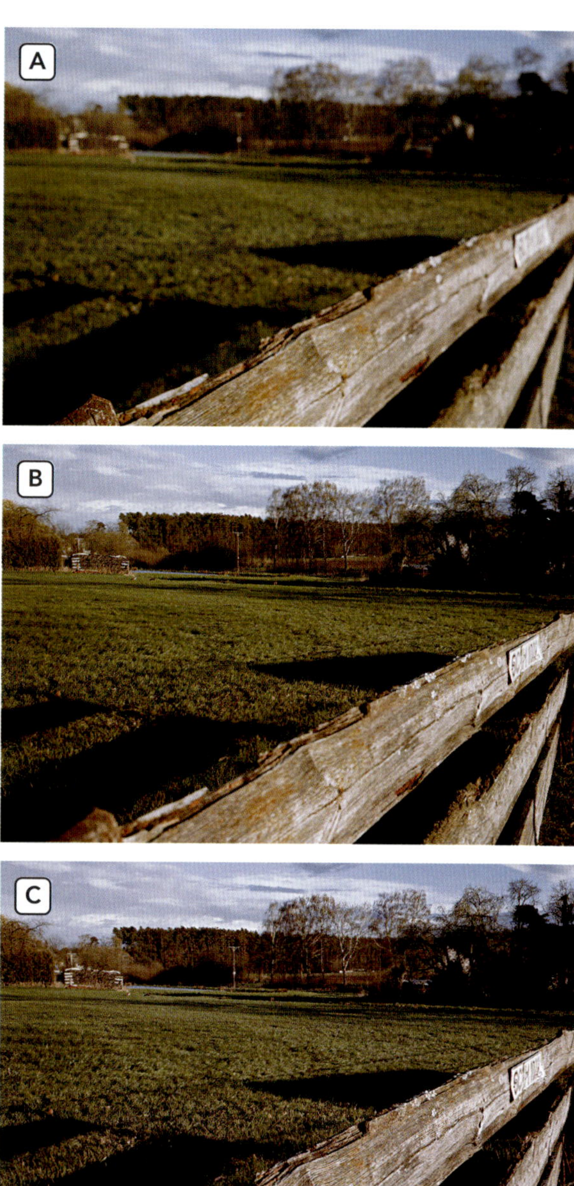

Fig. 89: I used **AUTO focus bracketing** for this landscape shot. Image **A** shows the near point, image **B** the far point of my focus bracketing series. Image **C** shows the result after merging (stacking) the 35 acquired RAF files with Helicon Focus software and exporting

a linear DNG file that I could process in Lightroom with the same RAW development settings that I used for individual shots out of the bracketing series.

23 mm, ISO 125, f/5.6, 1/250 sec., tripod, auto focus bracketing, zero interval, mechanical shutter

Limiting the autofocus range	TIP 88

By limiting the autofocus range, you can make sure that the camera is literally focusing on "where the action" is, ignoring possible distractions. This can speed up the focusing process and avoid misfocused images.

Go to AF/MF SETTING > AF RANGE LIMITER and select a range preset or select/set define a CUSTOM focus range. This range definition process works just like the auto focus bracketing range definition process described above. The active AF limit is then indicated by a yellow line below the focus distance scale in the live view.

Important: *Activating subject detection or face/eye detection overrides (disables) any selected camera-based AF range limit, meaning the camera will use the full AF range.*

Select AF/MF SETTING > AF RANGE LIMITER > OFF to disable the autofocus range limiter.

Focusing on moving subjects (1): the autofocus trick	TIP 89

Consider these "rules:" use AF-S (Single) for stationary subjects; use AF-C (Continuous) for subjects that move toward or away from the camera. However, as usual, there are no rules without exceptions. Meet the so-called "autofocus trick" or "shutter mash" technique. It employs AF-S to focus on moving subjects and has been an option since the early days of the X100 Classic and the X-Pro1. Here's how:

- Set the camera to AF-S and single shot drive mode (STILL IMAGE).

- Make sure that Boost mode is switched on and that AF/ MF SETTING > RELEASE/FOCUS PRIORITY > AF-S PRIORITY SELECTION is set to FOCUS.

- Use Single Point AF or Zone AF. Select an AF frame or zone position and size that cover the part of the moving subject you want to be in focus.

- Set a suitable exposure and make sure the shutter speed is fast enough to avoid unwanted motion blur. Some action shots require shutter speeds of 1/1000 sec. or faster.

- Follow the moving subject in the viewfinder, making sure the selected AF frame or AF zone always covers the part of the subject that needs to be in focus. Do *not* half-press the shutter button!

- *Fully* press the shutter button in one swift motion when you want to take the shot. The camera will need some time to focus, so make sure the focus frame remains positioned on the moving subject while the camera is focusing. As soon as the camera can lock the focus, it will automatically take the shot.

The AF trick, also known as *shutter mash*, is based on the camera's autofocus priority logic. When you release the shutter, the camera *first* attempts to lock the focus and *then* takes the shot. Since the delay between having locked the focus and releasing the shutter is very short, the moving subject ends up being in focus most of the time. This means the AF trick works best with aperture settings that offer sufficient depth of field, and with subjects that don't move too quickly toward the camera.

A negative aspect of this method is the delay between fully pressing the shutter button and the camera taking the shot. This makes it challenging to hit decisive moments and requires some amount of foresight from the photographer.

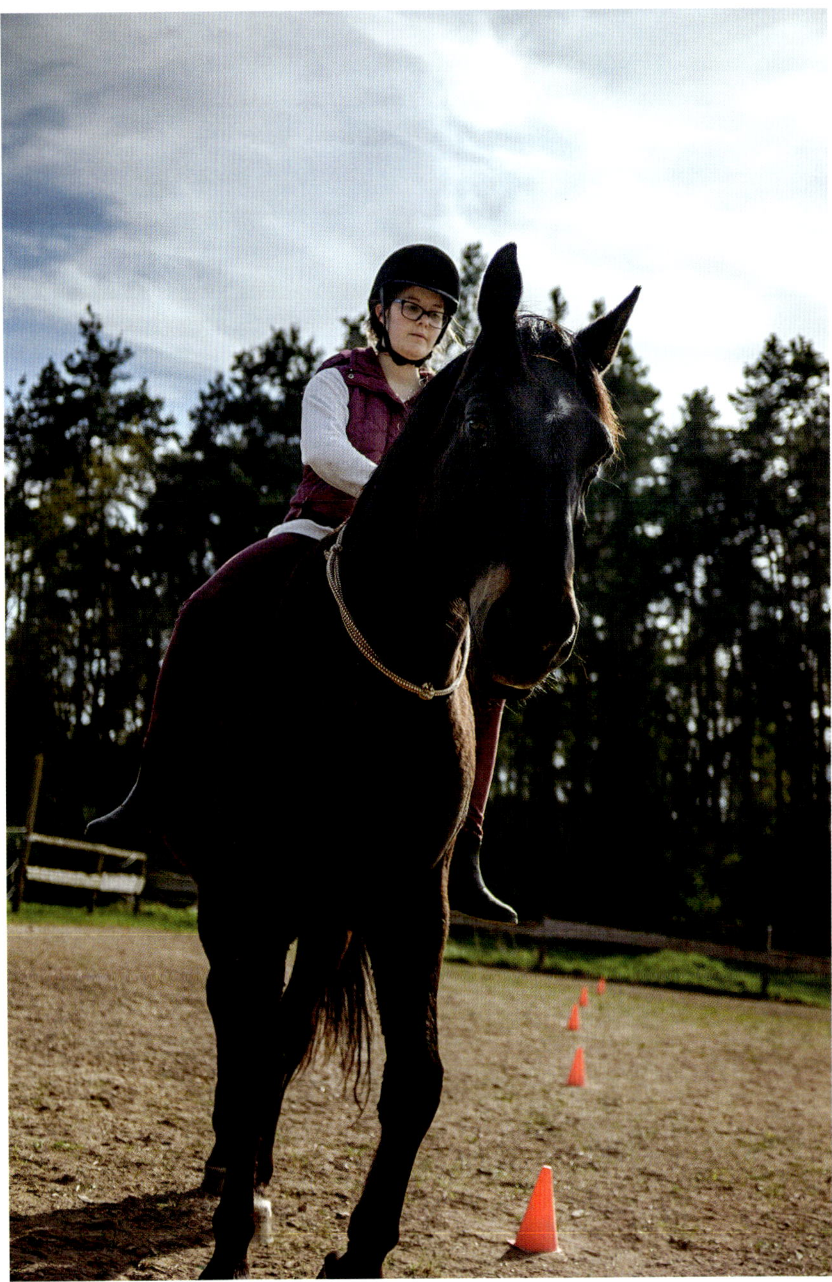

Fig. 90: A moving horse captured using the autofocus trick or **shut-ter mash technique**.

The autofocus trick has been around for more than a decade. Initially, it was the *only* way to autofocus on moving subjects with X cameras. Of course, this has changed over the years, and the shutter mash technique has now taken a back seat compared to other methods that involve AF-C, including 3D subject tracking. Mirrorless cameras have come a long way.

However, this ancient method is still useful. Imagine you are shooting portraits, a landscape, or a city view in AF-S mode. Suddenly, you encounter an unexpected moving subject, like a bird, a moving vehicle, or a running person that looks interesting. There's no time to switch focus modes. You must take the shot immediately, or the opportunity will be lost. In those scenarios, the autofocus trick can be quite helpful because you don't have to change any settings. Just point the AF-S focus frame or zone at the target and fully press the shutter button, while following the target with the focus frame until the camera takes the shot.

TIP 90	Focusing on moving subjects (2): the focus trap

Setting up a focus trap is about manually pre-focusing on a location that a moving object will eventually pass through. This method can be useful with sports and other activities that run along a pre-determined course, track, street, trail, etc.

This is how it works:

- Set the camera to manual focus (MF).

- Pre-focus on the location where you want to capture the moving subject. Select an aperture with sufficient depth of field (DOF) to make sure all relevant parts of the object will be in focus.

- Half-press the shutter button when the moving subject is approaching the location you have in focus. The camera will lock the exposure and set the working aperture (assuming SHUTTER AE is ON).

- Fully press the shutter button as soon as the subject is about to cross the in-focus location.

There's only a very small shutter lag between half-pressing and fully pressing the shutter button. Depending on how fast the subject is moving, it may be necessary to fully press the shutter button a split second before the subject has reached the pre-focused position.

Alternatively, you can set the camera to high-speed burst mode, increasing the chance that one or two frames will successfully capture your fast-moving subject as it crosses your focus trap.

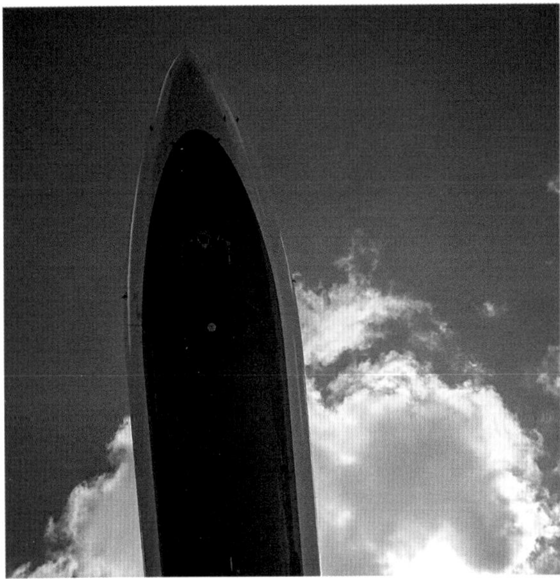

Fig. 91: Focus trap: To capture this landing Airbus A330 as it was flying over me at only a few meters, timing was essential. Instead of using autofocus, I pre-focused the lens with sufficient depth of field and waited for the right moment with my camera primed and the shutter half-pressed. At the decisive moment, I fully-pressed the shutter button. I also used the camera's optical viewfinder. This ruled out any live view lag and provided a bright optical image of the subject.

You can also trap moving subjects in a preset focus zone. Stop down your lens enough to create a sufficiently large DOF zone, and then wait until a subject enters the zone. This method is often used by street photographers who can't afford to miss the decisive moment.

A variant of this method is panning [56] the camera with a slow shutter speed and a small aperture (plenty of DOF). The slow shutter speed makes sure that the background is blurred while the subject remains in focus.

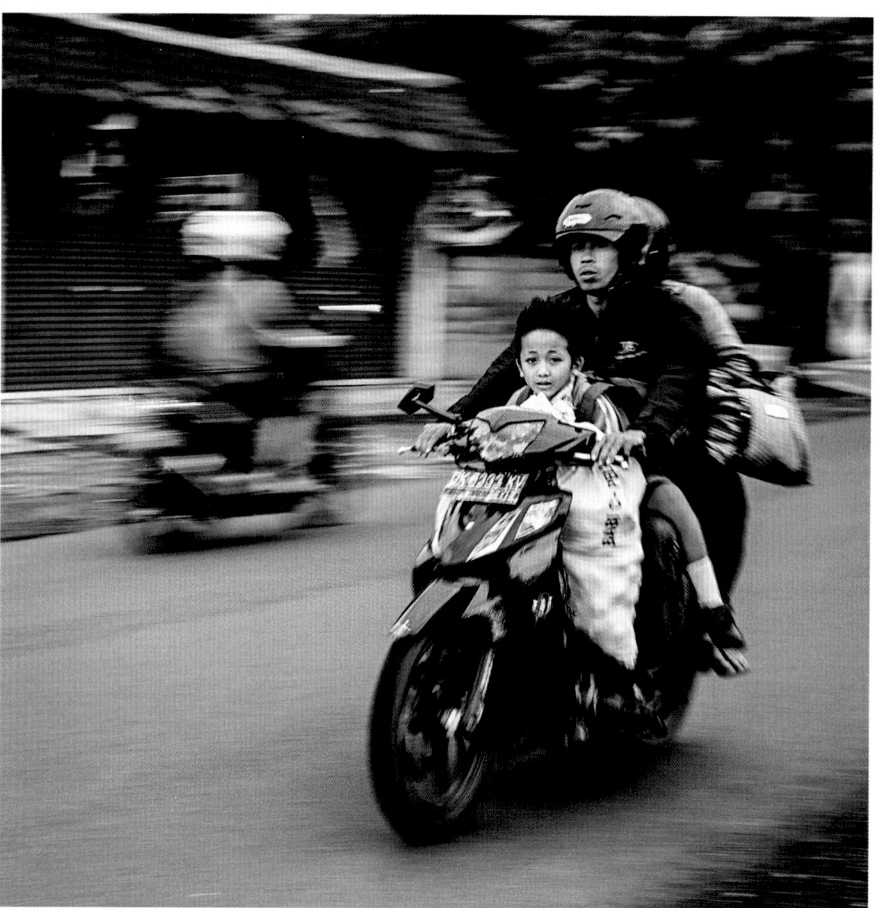

Fig. 92: Isolating a subject by **panning** can be performed with either manual focus (using a focus trap zone) or with AF-C.

<table><tr><td>Focusing on moving subjects (3): AF-C tracking using Single Point AF, Zone AF, or Tracking AF</td><td>TIP 91</td></tr></table>

Predictive PDAF (phase detection autofocus) allows you to track moving subjects in three-dimensional space. Since the camera can calculate the movement of the subject, it can automatically pre-focus on the predicted distance and compensate for any inherent shutter lag.

The X100VI features predictive PDAF that covers almost the entire sensor area, so you don't have to restrict the positioning of your AF frames or zones.

Let's start with the **Single Point AF** and **Zone AF** modes:

- Set the focus to AF-C and make sure Boost mode is set.

- Set the camera to burst mode (DRIVE button). I recommend a CL setting of 6 fps that displays a real-time live view image between shots.

- Use the mechanical shutter to avoid the rolling shutter artifacts of the electronic shutter.

- Select a suitable autofocus frame or zone size. Since PDAF covers the entire sensor area of the X100VI, there are no restrictions regarding size and position of the AF frame or zone.

- Position the selected AF frame or AF zone to directly cover the subject or the part of the subject you want in focus. Half-press the shutter button, and the camera will start tracking the subject covered by the AF frame or AF zone.

- Keep the shutter button half-pressed as you follow the moving subject with the selected AF frame or AF zone.

- Fully press the shutter button when you want to start taking the series of exposures. The actual burst speed (frame rate) depends on how well the camera can track the subject. As the camera is taking pictures, keep the selected AF frame or AF zone trained on the part of your image that is supposed to be in focus. This may be challenging at first, so practice is important.

In principle, AF-C tracking also works in single shot mode (DRIVE button mode STILL IMAGE). In this case, the camera takes a single frame when the shutter button is fully pressed and then ends the tracking.

As an alternative to tracking moving subjects using Single Point and Zone AF, you can use **Tracking AF** mode in concert with AF-C. This mode enables real 3D tracking; meaning the camera isn't merely tracking a subject's changing distance from the camera (z-axis), but it also tracks its left/right (x-axis) und up/down (y-axis) movements inside the image frame.

Here's how it works:

- Set the focus mode to AF-C and make sure that Boost mode is active.

- Set the camera to **Tracking AF** and select a slow burst mode (CL).

- Select one of the available tracking AF points. The point you select will serve as a starting point for your tracking action, so position it in a way that suits your composition.

- To identify your target, make sure the selected AF point covers the object you want to track and then half-press the shutter button. While you keep the shutter button half-pressed, the camera will use pattern recognition to automatically follow the object as it moves around in the frame (or as you move the camera).

- Fully press the shutter button and keep it pressed to take pictures at the selected burst rate. The camera will continue exposing images until you release the shutter button.

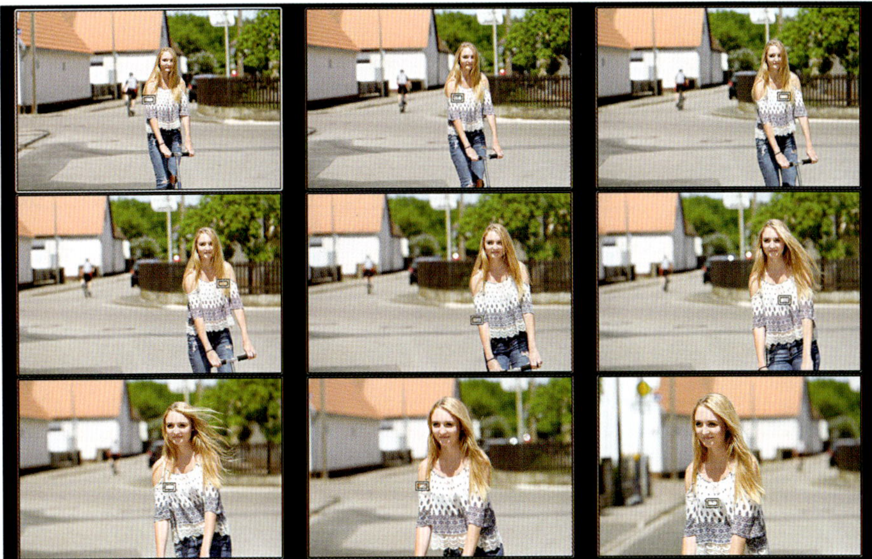

Fig. 93: AF-C in concert with **TRACKING AF and burst mode** can track a subject in 3-dimensional space. To accomplish this, the camera is using pattern recognition to follow the designated subject as it moves.

Performance-wise, AF-C tracking mode has long been a weakness with many X cameras. This has changed for the better with newer models like your X100VI. The same is true for AF-C tracking with face detection and subject detection. The X100VI offers much-improved AF-C tracking in concert with these modes.

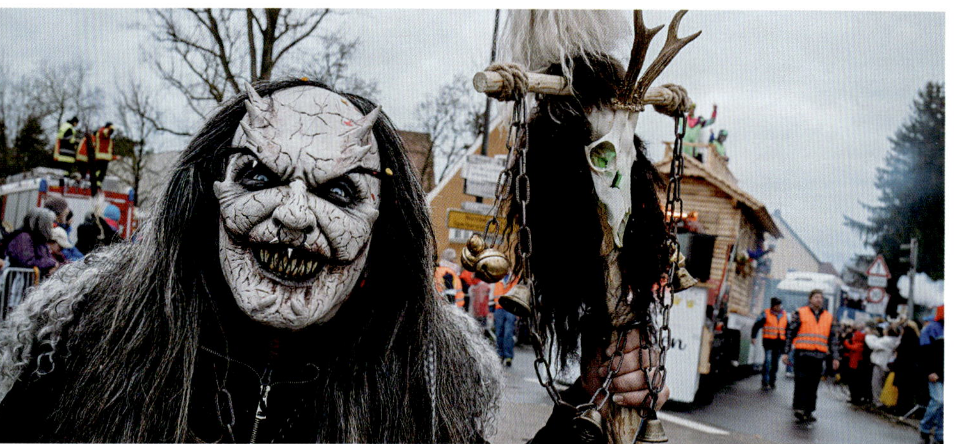

Fig. 94: AF-C in concert with **face detection** has traditionally been a weakness of older X-series cameras. However, modern bodies like the X100VI offer reliable face- and eye-detection tracking, as demonstrated by this rather unconventional example.

| TIP 92 | Tracking AF vs. face/eye and subject detection tracking |

Combining Wide/Tracking AF mode with AF-C will get you Tracking AF. Combining face/eye detection AF or subject detection AF with AF-C will get you something very similar. So, what are the differences?

- Tracking AF requires *you* to identify the target and show it to the camera by pointing the focus frame at it. When you half-press the shutter button, the camera will "learn" the color/contrast pattern beneath the focus frame, memorize it, and focus on it. As long as you keep the shutter button half or fully depressed, the focus frame follows that pattern around the image area, providing the auto-focus system continuously with a target to focus on.

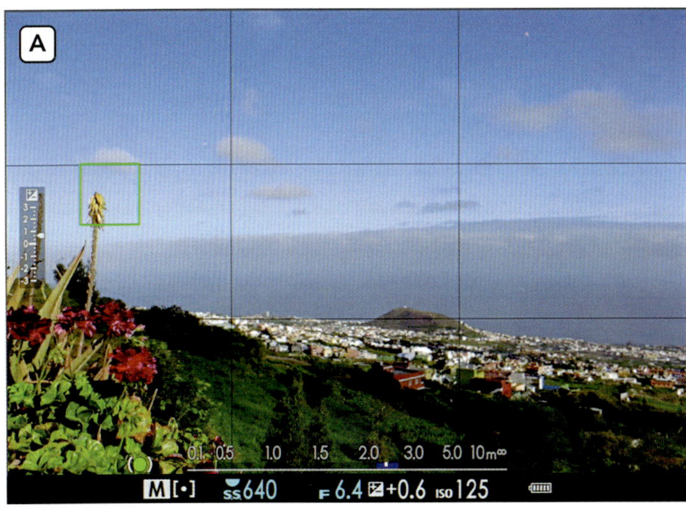

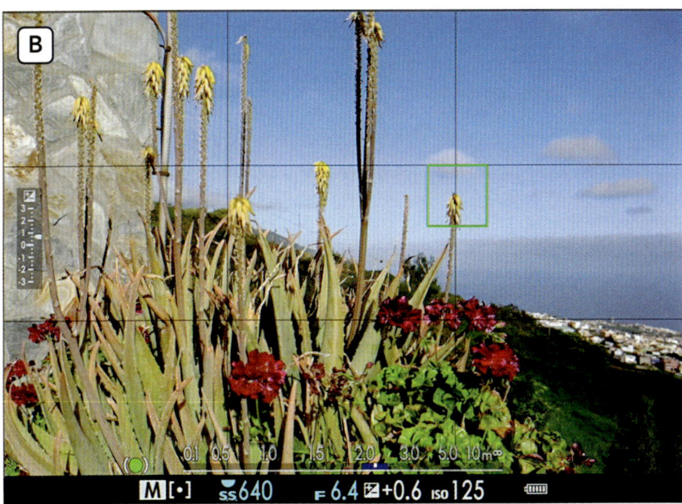

Fig. 95: In **Tracking AF**, you are identifying the target by pointing the focus frame at it and half-pressing the shutter button (**A**). When the target moves around the frame (or when you move the camera and reframe the target, like in this example), Tracking AF will stay on the target and focus on it for as long as you keep the shutter button half-depressed (**B**).

- Face/eye detection and subject detection combined with AF-C basically does the same as regular Tracking AF. The main difference is that the camera identifies suitable targets (faces, animals, cars, etc.) that are in the vicinity of the focus frame. By changing the size and position of the underlying focus frame or focus zone, you can direct the system to a different target, or you can select one of multiple available targets. When you half-press the shutter button, the camera memorizes the selected target and starts focusing on it. As long as you keep the shutter button half or fully depressed, the selected subject will be followed throughout the entire image area, providing the autofocus system continuously with coordinates to focus on.

Due to the similarity between these modes, it may sometimes be a good idea to select Tracking AF as your underlying fallback AF mode and select face/eye detection or subject detection on top of it. This way, the camera will use face/eye tracking or subject tracking for suitable targets but can automatically fall back to regular Tracking AF if a subject target has been (temporarily) lost. In that case, Tracking AF will take over and continue tracking the target starting right at the position where face/eye detection or subject detection have lost theirs.

<table><tr><td>TIP 93</td><td>Using AF-C custom settings</td></tr></table>

The X100VI features three parameters that allow you to customize the AF-C's behavior for a specific task or application:

- **Tracking Sensitivity** (TS) specifies whether the camera should switch its focus to a different subject or retain its current focus to wait for the subject to reappear. This control is useful when the subject you are focusing on disappears behind an obstacle or goes out of the frame, or when you aim at a new target with a different distance. Selecting 0 (zero) makes the camera switch its focus immediately to the new distance, while choosing 1–4 progressively extends the time it will retain the "old" focus distance. Technically speaking, tracking sensitivity 0 will not predict an autofocus target's position when it's temporarily lost or obscured by something else. Tracking sensitivity settings of 1, 2, 3, and 4 will predict a lost or obscured target's position for another approximately 0.4 seconds, 0.7 seconds, 1.0 second, and 1.3 seconds, respectively, before the AF-C locks onto the new target distance.

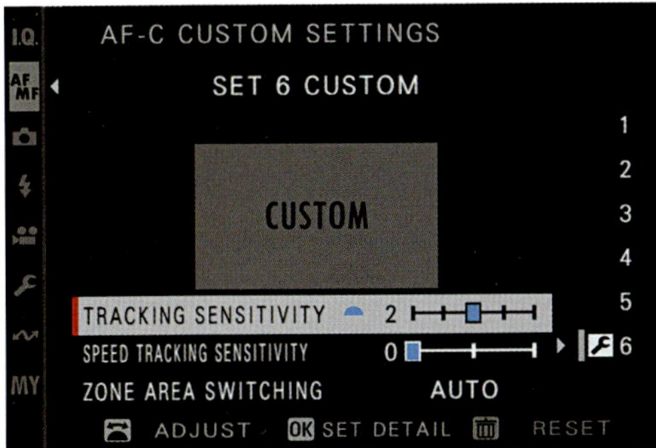

Fig. 96: By selecting a higher **TS setting**, the camera will wait a moment or two before it switches the continuous autofocus to a new target distance. The default setting is 2, which means the camera will give you about 0.7 seconds to re-aim the focus frame or zone back on your subject after you have lost sight of it. Higher TS settings are useful in situations where you want to track a specific subject with as little interference as possible.

- **Speed Tracking Sensitivity** (STS) controls the camera's tracking characteristics based on changes to the subject's speed. Selecting 0 (constant speed), the camera expects a steady movement when it predicts the subject's distance. Select 1 or 2, and the camera takes speed changes more and more into account when it's predicting subject movement, making it suitable for suddenly accelerating or decelerating targets, like race cars.

- **Zone Area Switching** (ZAS) is available only in Zone AF mode and specifies which part of the focusing zone should be given focusing priority. CENTER maintains focus on the center of the zone. FRONT switches the focus to the closest subject (or the closest part of a subject) anywhere inside the zone area, which (in concert with a TS setting of 0) is great for immediately capturing new targets that suddenly move into a zone. AUTO tracks the subject you first focused on as long as it remains inside the zone area.

The X100VI offers several presets that cover typical AF-C shooting scenarios. Select AF/MF SETTING > AF-C CUSTOM SETTINGS, and then pick one of the following available parameter sets:

- **SET 1:** MULTI PURPOSE is the default setting and is our general AF-C setting. It's a great choice for situations where you don't have a clear understanding of how a specific custom setting could improve the AF-C performance. Its parameter settings are TS 2, STS 0, and ZAS AUTO.

- **SET 2:** IGNORE OBSTACLES & CONTINUE TO TRACK SUBJECT keeps the focus on a subject even when it has temporarily left the frame or has been obscured by obstacles. This can be useful for following a specific target with the camera and ensuring that the target isn't dropped when it's temporarily obscured by people, trees, or other obstacles that obscure the line of sight to your target. Its parameter settings are TS 3, STS 0, and ZAS CENTER.

- **SET 3:** FOR ACCELERATING/DECELERATING SUBJECT is your typical racetrack mode. It takes changing relative speeds of subjects moving toward the camera into account. Whenever you have targets that accelerate or decelerate in relation to your camera position, this mode can be useful. Its parameter settings are TS 2, STS 2, and ZAS AUTO.

- **SET 4**: FOR SUDDENLY APPEARING SUBJECT allows the camera to instantly focus on a subject that enters the focusing area, with priority given to any object (or any part of it) that is closest to the camera. It is ideal for subjects that suddenly appear in the focusing frame. Its parameter settings are TS 0, STS 1, and ZAS FRONT. This setting is typically used in concert with Zone AF.

- **SET 5**: FOR ERRATICALY MOVING & ACCEL./DECEL. SUBJECT is suitable for subjects that are moving at varying speeds in different directions, coming in and out of the focusing area. It is optimized for shooting field sports like soccer or tennis. Of course, this also applies to playing kids or dogs. Its parameter settings are TS 3, STS 2, and ZAS AUTO.

- **SET 6**: CUSTOM stores your own setting for the three AF-C subject-tracking parameters: TRACKING SENSITIVITY (TS), SPEED TRACKING SENSITIVITY (STS), and ZONE AREA SWITCHING (ZAS). Use this preset to manually create optimized settings for the specific movement characteristics of your subject.

Focus Priority vs. Release Priority	TIP 94

Selecting focus priority for AF-S and AF-C can reduce the number of out-of-focus pictures on your memory card. Here is how to set it up:

- Set AF/MF SETTING > RELEASE/FOCUS PRIORITY > AF-S PRIORITY SELECTION > FOCUS to prevent the camera from taking the shot before it has finished focusing.

- Set AF/MF SETTING > RELEASE/FOCUS PRIORITY > AF-C PRIORITY SELECTION > FOCUS to make sure the camera takes pictures in AF-C mode (particularly in concert with burst mode) only when the autofocus can lock onto something. By default, the camera is set to release priority, following the motto, "better a misfocused shot than no image at all." Since I am no fan of misfocused shots, my camera is set to focus priority for both AF-S and AF-C.

Important: When AF+MF is ON, the camera will always use Release Priority for both AF-S and AF-C, even if the respective menu setting says Focus Priority. This can lead to misfocused images because the camera can now take pictures before the autofocus has finished its job.

TIP 95	Using Pre-Shot ES

Pre-Shot ES is a "time machine" that allows you to capture moments you just missed. It only works in concert with the electronic shutter (ES) and high-speed burst mode (CH). Pre-Shot ES takes advantage of the X100VI's electronic shutter and new processor, which allow for faster burst mode settings (10, 13, or 20 frames per second) that work with a 1.29x crop. You can also use 8.9 or 13 fps without a crop.

Pre-Shot ES compensates for the reaction time between recognizing a sudden event and pressing the shutter release button. With extremely quick subjects, that delay can cause you to miss your ideal moments.

In Pre-Shot ES mode, the X100VI starts recording and buffering images as you half-press and hold the shutter release button. As long as you keep the button pressed halfway down, the camera keeps recording images into its buffer. It will continue to refresh the buffered content (FIFO: first in, first out) so that you always have the most recent frames stored in the buffer.

When a sudden event happens and you fully press the shutter to capture it, the camera will not only take new images from that moment forward, it will also write the previously buffered images onto the memory card. It will continue to capture and write new images to the card while you hold the shutter release all the way down.

In effect, Pre-Shot ES allows you to go back in time and capture the moment or moments right *before* you fully pressed the shutter release button. Normally, those moments would be lost due to the inevitable reaction time of the photographer and camera. You can activate Pre-Shot ES with SHOOTING SETTING > PRE-SHOT ES > ON, but only when the camera is set to ES-only and CH high-speed burst shooting.

Since Pre-Shot ES only works in concert with the electronic shutter, it is subject to rolling shutter artifacts such as object distortion (when you are panning the camera or with subjects that move very fast) and an uneven exposure (banding) under pulsing artificial light. This rolling shutter effect may be more pronounced if you shoot without the 1.29x crop.

Using Sports Finder Mode	TIP 96

Sports Finder Mode adds a 1.29x crop to your resulting image. The crop is indicated through a bright white frame in the live view. Sports Finder Mode only works in concert with the mechanical shutter (MS). It can help you reduce your reaction time in situations with moving objects that suddenly appear in the live view, because it allows you to see beyond the final image frame. This is very much like the bright frame in the optical viewfinder of the camera.

In Sports Finder Mode, the camera's AF tracking extends beyond the indicated bright frame, making it possible to track objects that are outside the active image area. This is also why I am covering this feature here in the focus section of this book and not in the section about the viewfinder.

You can activate Sports Finder Mode with SHOOTING SETTING > SPORTS FINDER MODE > ON. As mentioned, it adds a 1.29x crop to the image. Please note that unlike using the digital teleconverter or a non-standard image format (like 1:1), this mode also crops the RAW data.

2.5 WHITE BALANCE, JPEG SETTINGS, RECIPES, AND RAW CONVERSION

A significant feature of all X-series cameras is their ability to set white balance [57] and JPEG parameters before *and* after you take a shot, thanks to the built-in RAW converter. This gives you full control over the look of your JPEGs that are generated in your camera.

You can set your JPEG settings in advance, using "film recipes" or your own favorite settings. However, it's not necessary to anticipate and set the "perfect" settings for each shot or subject in advance because you can always generate different JPEG, HEIF, or TIFF versions of a shot with the internal RAW converter—anytime and anywhere. For example, you could create a version with bold Velvia colors, or a black-and-white version with strong contrast, minimal noise reduction, and attractive grain. With access to the RAW file, you can change all JPEG parameters after the fact. You can use the RAW file to create as many different-looking JPEGs, HEIFs, or TIFFs as you want.

Using the built-in RAW converter in the playback menu is quite simple because it offers the same functions that are available in shooting mode.

JPEG and RAW converter settings—an overview	TIP 97

Here's an overview of camera functions that you can apply to a photo before *and* after you take the shot:

IMAGE QUALITY SETTING menu	RAW CONVERSION menu
(Exposure Comp. Dial)	PUSH/PULL PROCESSING
IMAGE SIZE	IMAGE SIZE
IMAGE QUALITY	IMAGE QUALITY
SELECT JPEG/HEIF	FILE TYPE
DYNAMIC RANGE	DYNAMIC RANGE
D RANGE PRIORITY	D RANGE PRIORITY
FILM SIMULATION	FILM SIMULATION
WHITE BALANCE	WHITE BALANCE
(incl. WB SHIFT)	WB SHIFT
COLOR	COLOR
SHARPNESS	SHARPNESS
TONE CURVE (HIGHLIGHTS)	TONE CURVE (HIGHLIGHTS)
TONE CURVE (SHADOWS)	TONE CURVE (SHADOWS)
HIGH ISO NR	HIGH ISO NR
GRAIN EFFECT	GRAIN EFFECT
MONOCHROMATIC COLOR	MONOCHROMATIC COLOR
COLOR CHROME EFFECT	COLOR CHROME EFFECT
COLOR CHROME FX BLUE	COLOR CHROME FX BLUE
SMOOTH SKIN EFFECT	SMOOTH SKIN EFFECT
CLARITY	CLARITY
COLOR SPACE	COLOR SPACE
HDR MODE (DRIVE button menu)	HDR MODE
DIGITAL TELE-CONV. (SHOOTING SETTING menu)	DIGITAL TELE-CONV.

In X RAW STUDIO, the tone curve settings for highlight and shadow contrast are named HIGHLIGHT TONE and SHADOW TONE. This is just a different naming convention for TONE CURVE (HIGHLIGHTS) and TONE CURVE (SHADOWS).

Notable differences between shooting mode and after-the-fact RAW conversion in playback mode affect only a few items in this list:

- **Exposure corrections** made *before* you take a picture can affect aperture, shutter speed, and ISO. **Push/pull processing** applied *after* you have taken a picture affects only the ISO amplification. Effectively changing the ISO via push/pull processing also doesn't change the nominal ISO value in the EXIF data [58] of the generated JPEGs. Instead, Push/Pull processing in the internal RAW converter has the same effect as moving the exposure slider in external RAW conversion software, such as Lightroom, Silkypix, or Capture One.

- *Before* you take an image, you can select from four **dynamic range** options: AUTO, DR100%, DR200%, and DR400%. DR200% exposes the RAW file one ISO stop darker than indicated; DR400% exposes it two ISO stops darker. DR-Auto automatically selects either DR100% or DR200%. *After* you have taken an image, you can still select different DR settings in the internal RAW converter. However, you can only *reduce* the DR after the fact; you cannot increase it. If you are working on a RAW file that was recorded with DR400%, you can reprocess it to create JPEGs with DR400%, DR200%, or DR100%. A DR200% RAW file can be reprocessed with DR200% or DR100%, but not DR400%. And a DR100% RAW file can only be reprocessed with DR100%. The same restrictions apply to the D RANGE PRIORITY settings STRONG, WEAK, and OFF.

Additionally, the RAW conversion menu offers options to change the HDR mode and the digital teleconverter setting. Again, you can only *downgrade* these settings after the fact. For example, if you recorded an image in HDR 800%+, the RAW conversion menu lets you downgrade this setting to HDR 800%, HDR 400%, or HDR 200%. If you shot it in HDR 400%, you could only downgrade to HDR 200%.

In a similar fashion, if you shot with the digital teleconverter, you could turn it off after the fact in the RAW conversion menu. However, you cannot *add* the digital teleconverter later.

| Basic white balance options | TIP 98 |

The correct white balance ensures that neutral (white or gray) areas of an image appear without color tints, regardless of the light conditions. At the same time, the results are usually not supposed to look clinically neutral. Your X100VI masters this task quite well, so you can rely on the Auto white balance setting to get it right most of the time.

However, "most of the time" is not "all the time." There are instances when the white balance is off, or when you *want* it to be off. For example, you may want to emphasize a sunset with a warmer white balance. In such cases, it makes perfect sense to manually set the white balance in advance or after the fact.

The X100VI offers a variety of options to manually set the white balance, as follows:

- Several white balance presets for typical situations, such as sunny weather (Fine), cloudy skies (Shade), and tungsten light (Incandescent).

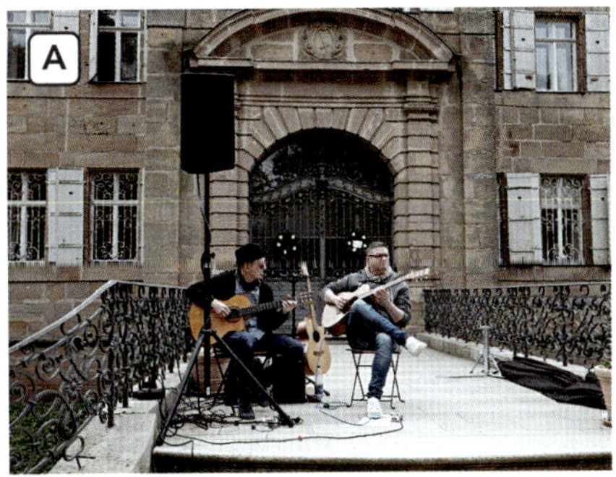

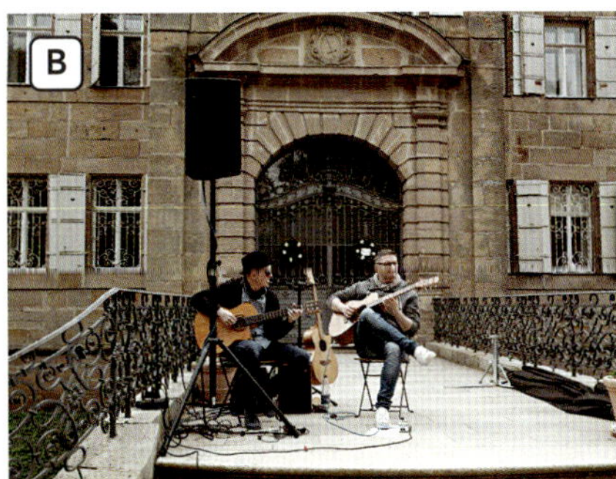

Fig. 97: AUTO white balance isn't always right or suitable, especially with artificial ambient light. However, you can adjust white balance later with the built-in, or an external, RAW converter. In this case of two straight-out-of-camera JPEGs, a simple white balance preset change in the camera from AUTO (**A**) to SHADE (**B**) did the job and created a warmer look with just one click in X RAW STUDIO. All other settings remained the same.

- A Kelvin option to manually set the color temperature.

- Custom white balance that meters a white or neutral surface (like a white wall) under the current light conditions. This way, the camera can adjust the white balance to make the surface appear neutral. The X100VI features three independent slots for your custom WB settings.

- You can also bias the camera's AUTO white balance to prioritize either the mood of a scene (AUTO AMBIENCE PRIORITY) or to achieve a more neutral result (AUTO WHITE PRIORITY).

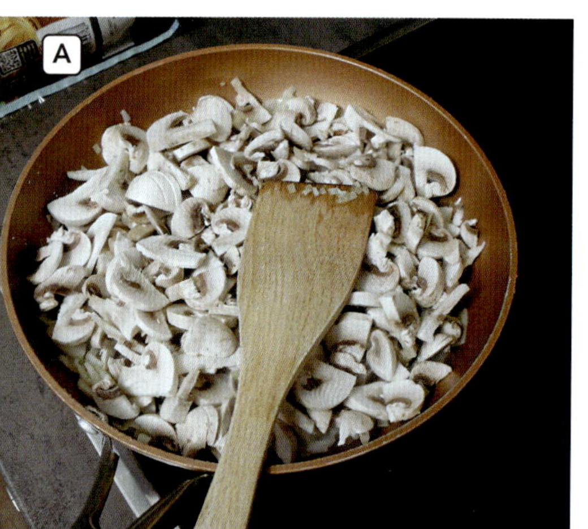

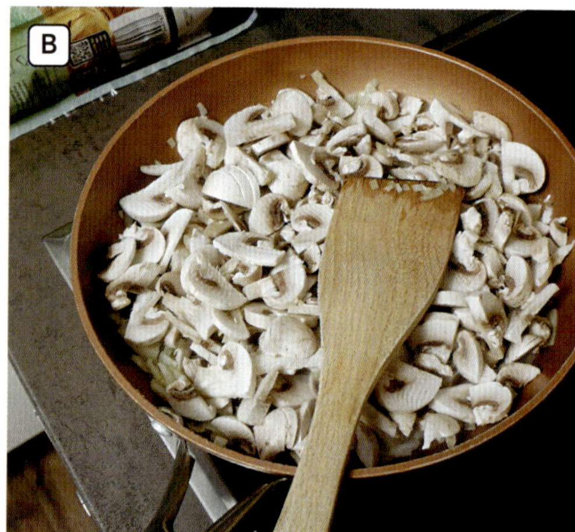

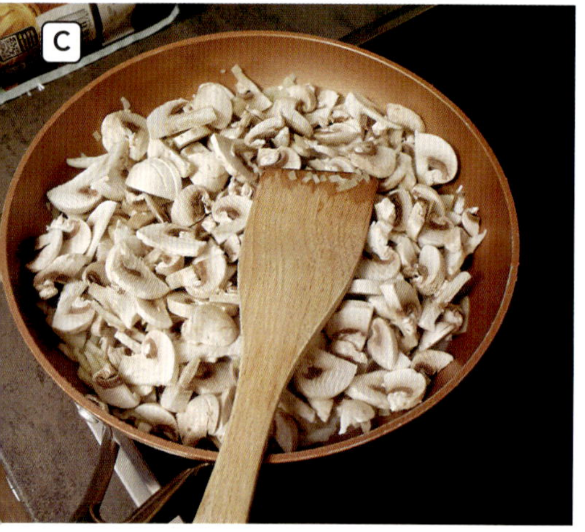

Fig. 98: In the X100VI, **AUTO white balance** encompasses three menu options: AUTO WHITE PRIORITY, the regular AUTO mode, and AUTO AMBIENCE PRIORITY. This example with straight-out-of-camera JPEGs shows the difference between AUTO WHITE PRIORITY (**A**), regular AUTO white balance (**B**), and AUTO AMBIENCE PRIORITY (**C**).

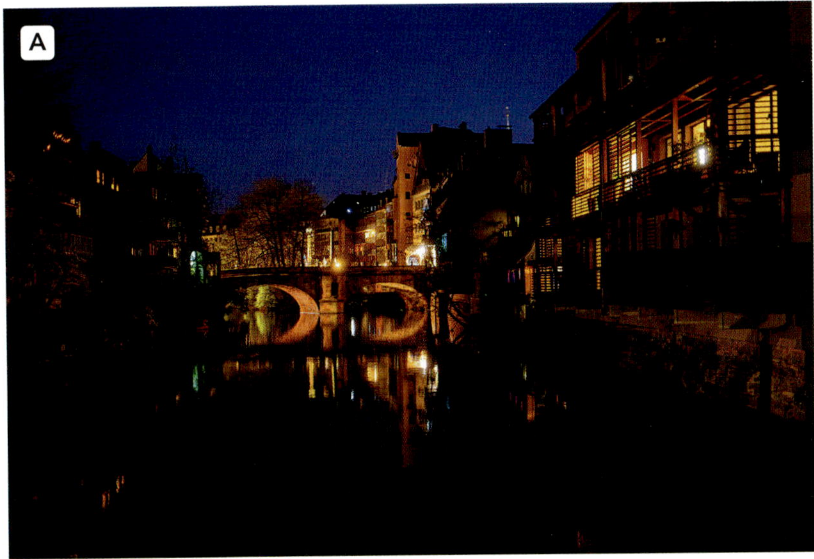

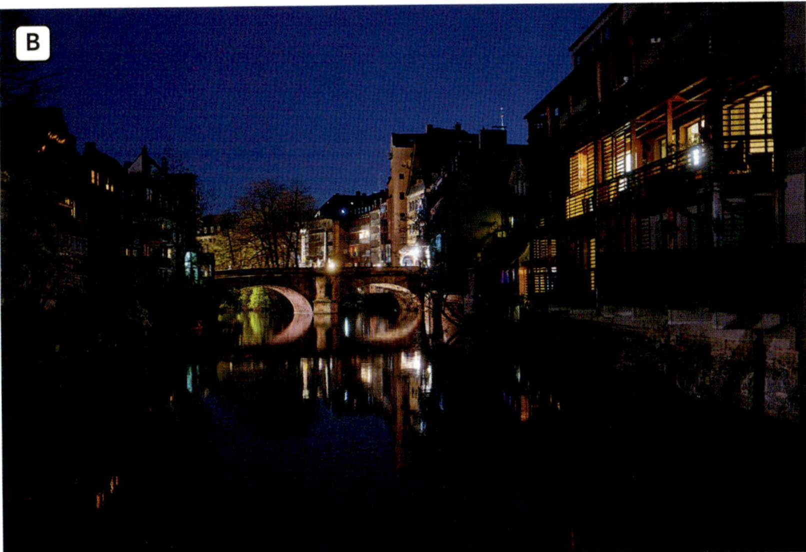

Fig. 99: Two versions of the same shot processed with **different white balance settings**. Image **A** shows the WB Auto setting; image **B** shows the same shot after a manual white balance adjustment in Lightroom. While white balance can also be adjusted with the camera's built-in RAW converter, extensive changes like this one may be easier to accomplish with external RAW conversion software.

<table><tr><td>TIP 99</td><td>Custom white balance: a little effort can go a long way.</td></tr></table>

This function is only available *before* you take a shot, because you are metering the white balance of the actual scene. Custom white balance allows you to calibrate the camera's white balance toward a part of your scene you want to appear neutral in the final image.

Here we go:

- Select IMAGE QUALITY SETTING > WHITE BALANCE > CUSTOM. The X100VI allows you to set and save three different custom white balance settings in the camera (CUSTOM 1–3).

- Point the camera toward a surface you want to use as a neutral reference—for example a white wall or a gray card [59]. Make sure the surface is large enough to be fully covered by the white balance metering frame in the viewfinder. Move closer to your subject if you need to.

- Fully press the shutter button to meter and set the new custom white balance. The live view will change accordingly and will simulate the adjusted color temperature. If you are happy with the result, confirm it by pressing the OK button.

You can use the same procedure with a firing flash unit. In this case, the custom white balance will meter the mix of light from the flash with the ambient light that hits your neutral reference surface.

Don't worry! You are under no obligation to use the custom white balance later during RAW conversion. It's simply one of many options, and you can always adjust it later as you please. For example, you can use the built-in RAW converter with a manual KELVIN setting or select one of the white balance presets (FINE, SHADE, FLUORESCENT LIGHT 1-3, INCANDESCENT, and UNDERWATER). You can even apply AUTO white balance anytime later because the camera will always save its automatic white balance reading for later use by the internal RAW converter. This includes the AUTO white balance options for AMBIENCE PRIORITY and WHITE PRIORITY.

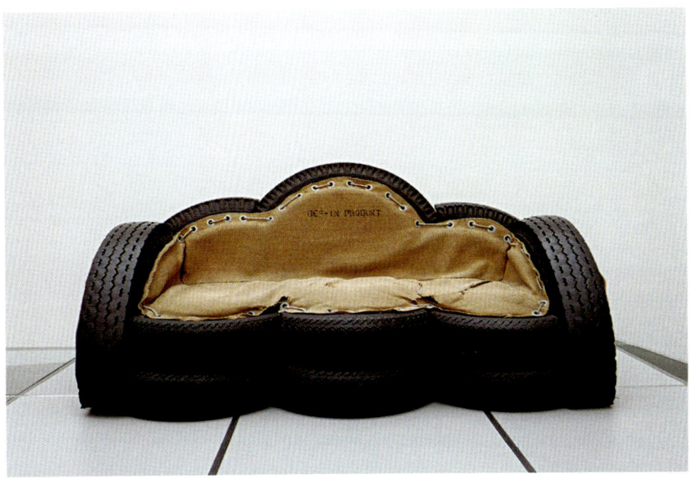

Fig. 100: A **custom white balance** setting was used to take this shot. The wall behind the sofa served as a neutral reference.

Changing color tints with WB SHIFT	TIP 100

WB SHIFT lets you correct (or introduce) a color tint in any shot. You can adjust the color tint as an addition to any white balance setting—either before you take a shot, or in the built-in RAW converter.

You can individually set a *different* white balance shift for each of the camera's white balance options (Auto, Kelvin, WB presets, and Custom white balance settings). You can do this by adjusting the setting between green and red on the X-axis and between yellow and blue on the Y-axis of the display that automatically appears when you select one of the white balance options.

I recommend a neutral setting here to avoid confusion. As mentioned before, there's a different white balance shift setting for each of the white balance options, meaning the camera can store up to a dozen white balance shift settings at once. This makes it too easy to forget a previously set correction, which is why I recommend introducing white balance shift only during RAW conversion, or when you are shooting with specific film simulation "recipes."

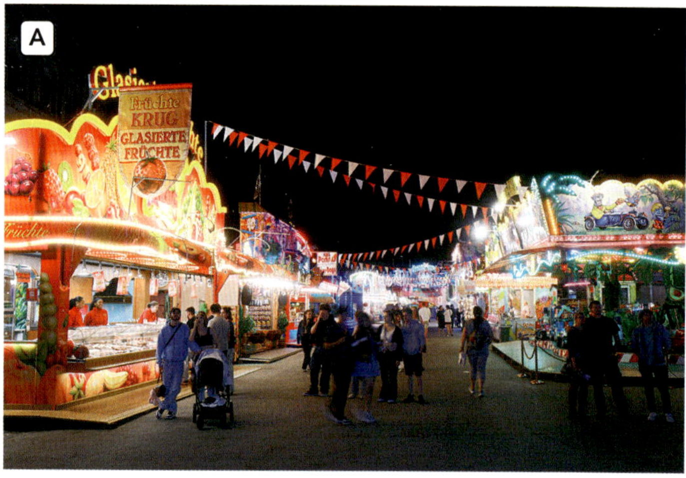

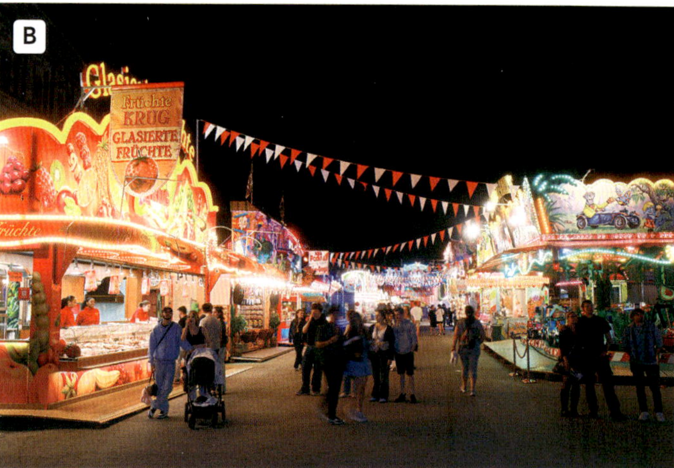

Fig. 101: WB SHIFT in action: Image **A** shows a straight-out-of-camera image (SOOC JPEG) without a white balance shift. Image **B** is the same shot, again straight out of camera and the same white balance color temperature setting, but with an additional WB SHIFT of RED +5 and BLUE –4.

Shifting the white balance is an integral part of retro-style film recipes that are particularly popular with users of X100 series cameras. In most cases, there's a positive shift on the RED axis (X) and a negative shift on the BLUE axis (Y).

Important: *When you process a RAW file externally with Lightroom or similar software, any WB Shift settings that were active when you took the image will usually be disregarded. However, Capture One Pro is an exception to this rule and honors WB Shift settings automatically.*

White balance and monochrome images	TIP 101

You may think white balance adjustments don't affect black-and-white images because monochrome shots only consist of neutral shades of gray. However, your white balance settings still affect the *underlying* color information that your monochrome conversion is based on.

Black-and-white photography is color photography with an additional dimension of complexity. This added dimension is determining how specific grayscale brightness levels are derived from specific colors. Since your white balance settings affect the colors of the underlying shot, they also affect the gray tones of the color-to-monochrome conversion.

Black-and-white images can be created either in-camera (with the MONOCHROME and ACROS film simulations) or externally with RAW conversion software such as Lightroom or Capture One. When you set your X100VI to ACROS or MONOCHROME, it is still recoding RAW *color* images, which are then converted into black-and-white JPEGs, HEIFs, or TIFFs.

Knowing this, you can manipulate the look of your black-and-white conversions by changing the white balance during RAW conversion—either in-camera or externally in your post-processing software. With the built-in RAW converter, you can use one of the white balance presets, or you can select a manual Kelvin setting between 2500K and 10000K.

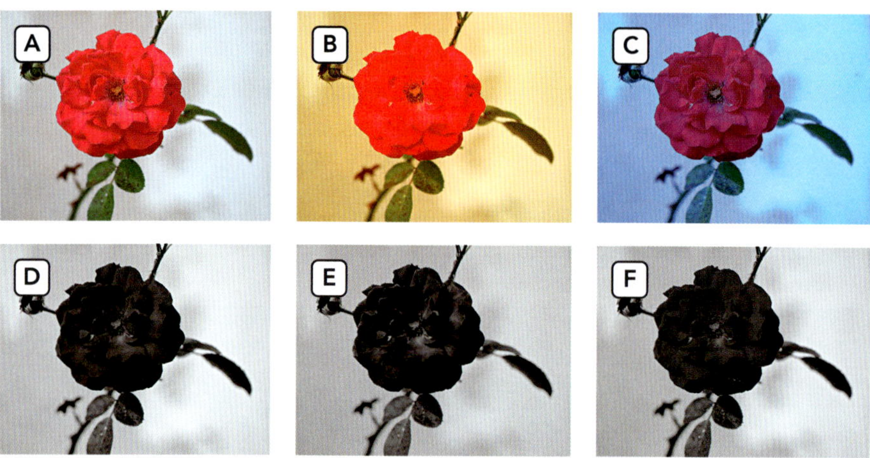

Fig. 102: White balance and monochrome: In the upper row, this illustration shows the same color image with Auto white balance (**A**), a 2500K setting (**B**), and a 10000K setting (**C**). The lower row (**D**, **E**, **F**) exhibits monochrome conversions of the above images; all three made with a MONOCHROME+G FILTER film simulation and a SHADOW TONE +4 setting using X RAW STUDIO. The various underlying white balance settings have a visible impact on the appearance of the monochrome conversions.

TIP 102	Using film simulations

The importance of film simulations for the overall look of a JPEG is often underestimated. Film simulations influence color grading, color saturation, dynamic range, and contrast in the resulting JPEG files. Picking a film simulation should always be the first step when adjusting JPEG parameters. As with all JPEG settings, film simulations have no effect on the actual RAW file (the digital negative). They only affect the JPEGs, HEIFs, and TIFFs that are generated in the camera (the digital prints).

Here are the available film simulation options:

- PROVIA is the standard, all-purpose setting. The name reminds us of Fuji's popular Provia slide film.

- VELVIA is a very contrast-heavy, color-saturated derivate of the legendary Fuji Velvia slide film. It's mostly used for landscape and nature shots and is rather unsuitable for portrait work.

- ASTIA is a color slide film derivate with softer highlights and pleasing skin tones. It's often used for portraits but can also work with landscape shots that feature vegetation and blue sky.

- CLASSIC CHROME reminds us of the golden era of color magazine photography. The distinctive look of Classic Chrome is equally suitable for landscapes and portraits.

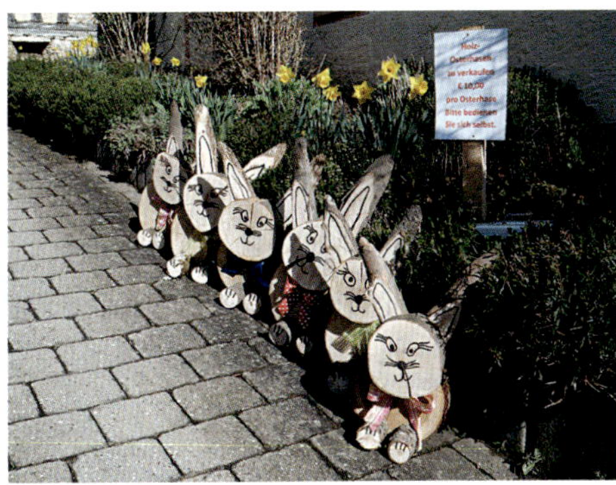

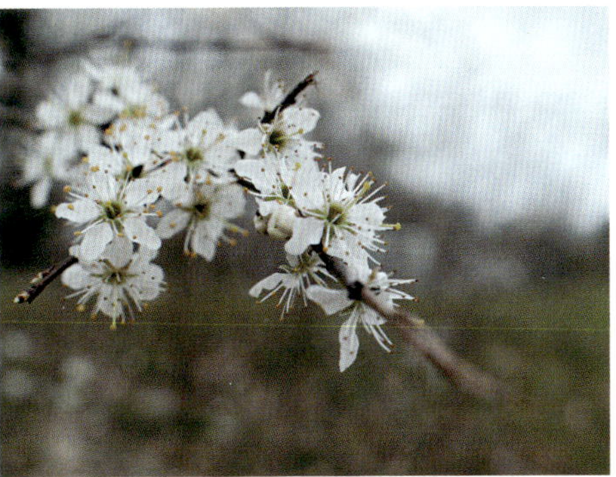

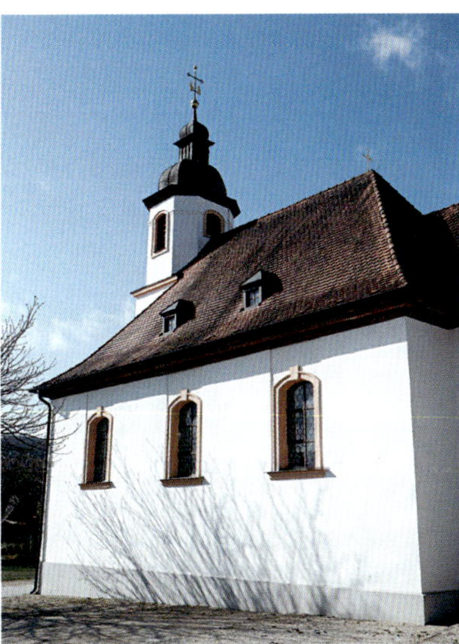

Fig. 103: The timeless documentary look of **CLASSIC CHROME** has earned it much popularity in a very short time.

- REALA ACE is Fujifilm's 20th film simulation and based on the color negative film with the same name. Like Provia, it's an all-purpose option, but with brighter and more detailed shadows, punchier midtones and vivid highlights. This makes it a great option for landscape shots that require plenty of dynamic range yet shouldn't look dull.

- PRO NEG. HI is derived from a professional color negative film that was specifically made for portraits. It delivers accurate and pleasing skin tones with nice contrast and adds some punch to the image without adding too much color saturation to faces.

- PRO NEG. STD is a rather neutral film simulation. Featuring flat contrast, subdued colors, and high dynamic range, it can look dull at first, but the JPEGs are usable for further post-processing. Fuji recommends this film simulation for studio portraits with a flash setup.

- CLASSIC NEG. is based on Fujifilm's popular Superia color negative film. It features a quite unique look with distinct green and red tones.

- NOSTALGIC NEGATIVE is like Pro Neg. Std, but with warmer tones and a more vintage look. I specifically like it for fall colors and to mitigate strong contrasts.

- ETERNA is the most neutral film simulation. Though Eterna was designed as a flat and desaturated film simulation for video production, it's also our preferred low-contrast, high dynamic range profile for RAW photography.

- ETERNA BLEACH BYPASS is a desaturated and much more contrasty version of ETERNA. It delivers a gritty, cinematic look.

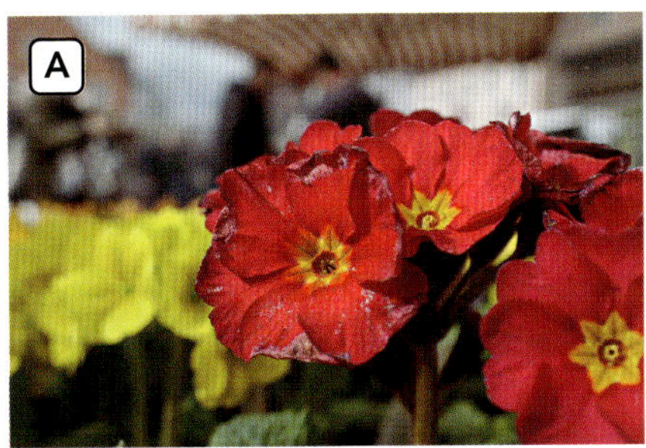 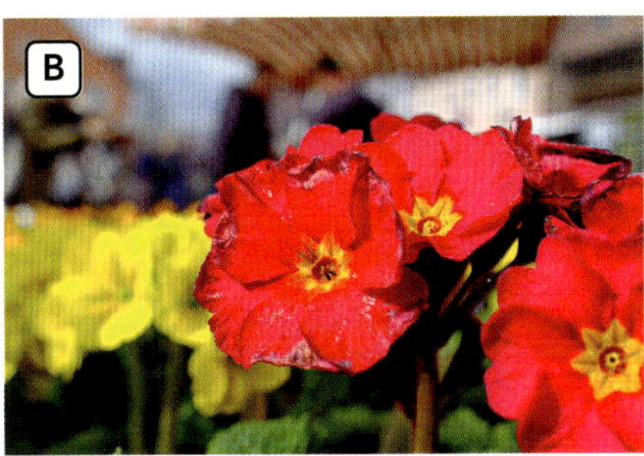

Fig. 104: Antagonists: ETERNA and VELVIA illustrate the spectrum of Fuji's various film simulation modes. Image **A** shows the ETERNA version of a shot, image **B** its VELVIA cousin.

- MONOCHROME is Fuji's standard black-and-white conversion. Black-and-white photography is based on assigning specific gray levels to specific colors of a scene. To increase the contrast, many photographers combine MONOCHROME with increased SHADOWS and HIGH-LIGHTS settings in the TONE CURVE menu. Additionally, noise reduction is often decreased to reveal more detail and display more noise, which gives the appearance of film grain.

- MONOCHROME+Ye FILTER adds a digital yellow filter to the black-and-white conversion. This typically results in a slight increase of contrast because yellow parts of the scene will be represented by brighter gray tones.

- MONOCHROME+R FILTER adds a red filter to the black-and-white conversion. This means that skin tones will become brighter, which will camouflage reddish skin impurities. Conversely, blue skies will be darkened, adding contrast between clouds and the sky.

- MONOCHROME+G FILTER adds a green filter to the black-and-white conversion. This filter will add texture to skin tones and can potentially emphasize imperfections.

- SEPIA results in a sepia-toned monochrome JPEG for a vintage-looking touch.

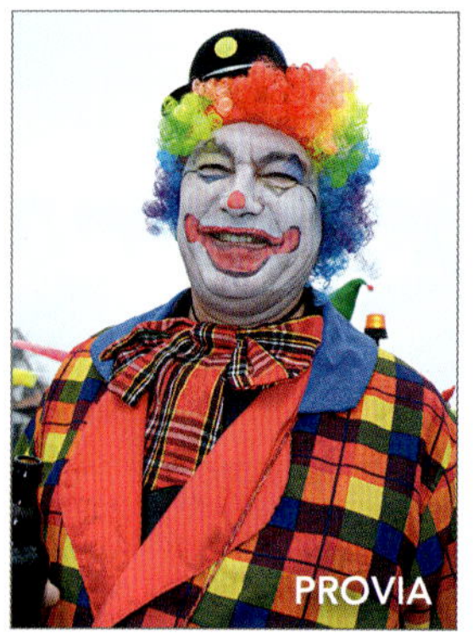

PROVIA

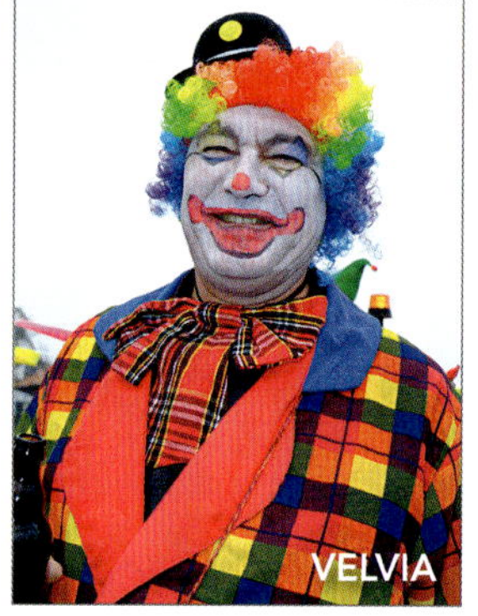

VELVIA

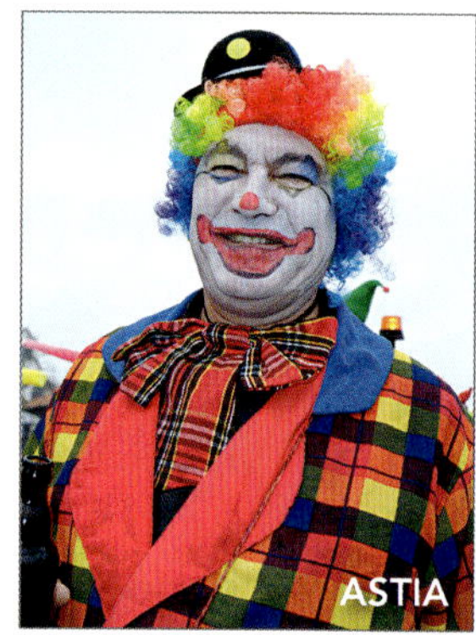

ASTIA

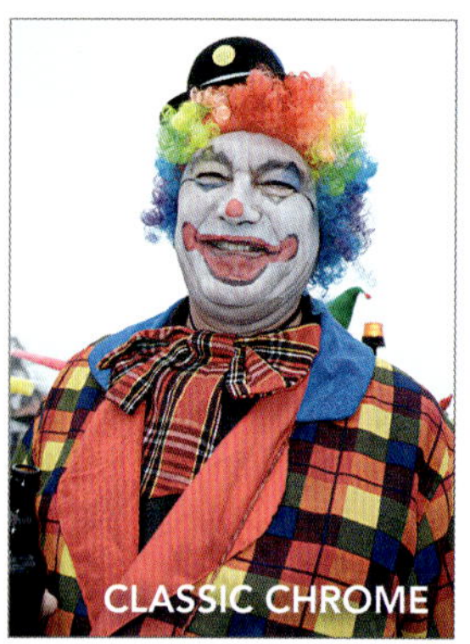

CLASSIC CHROME

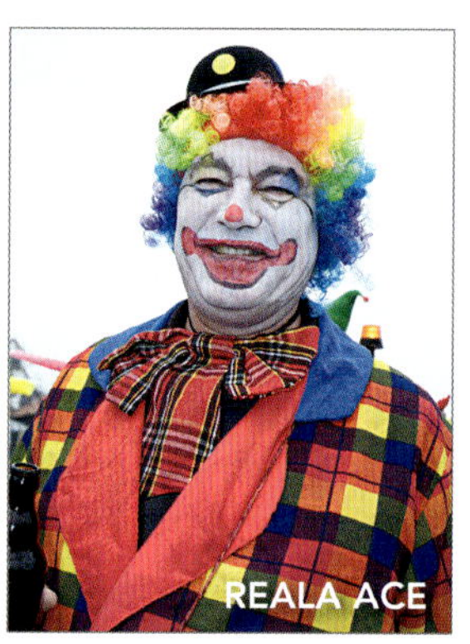

REALA ACE

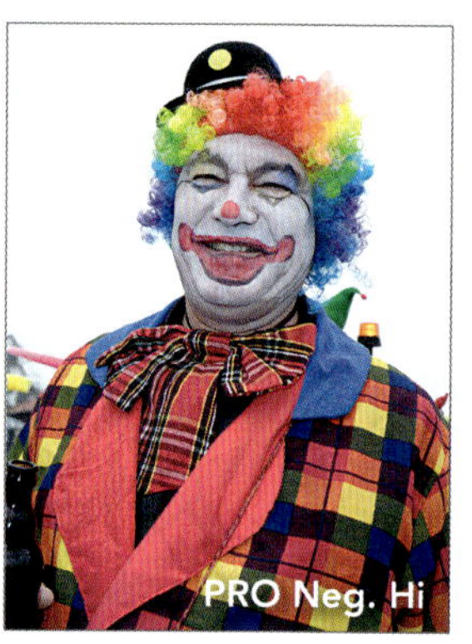

PRO Neg. Hi

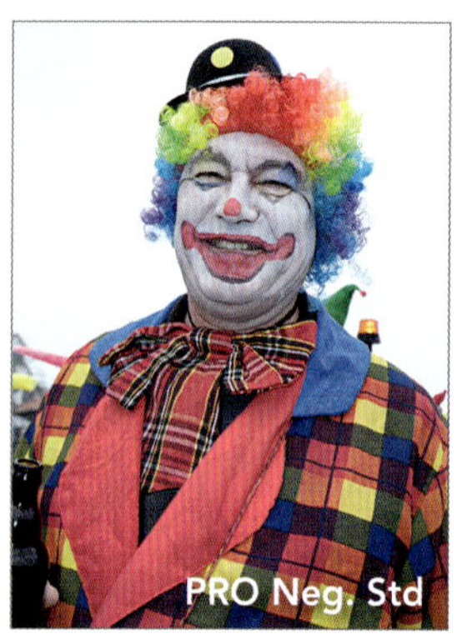

PRO Neg. Std

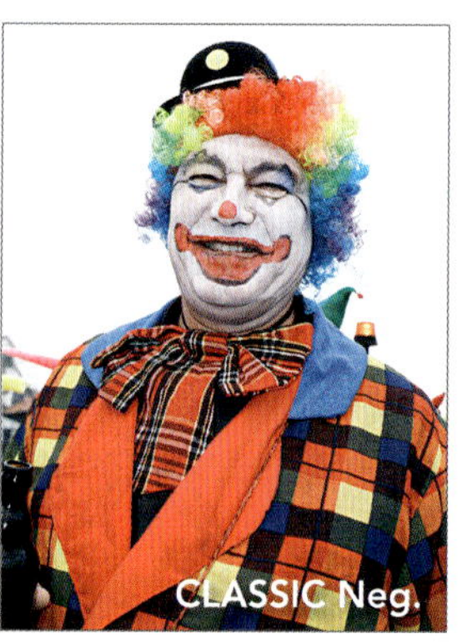

CLASSIC Neg.

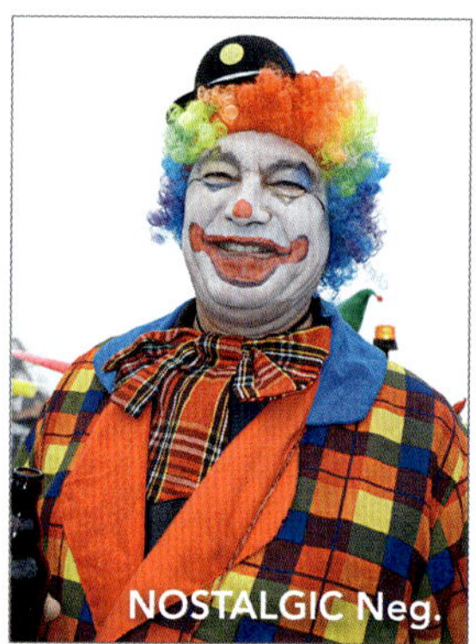

NOSTALGIC Neg.

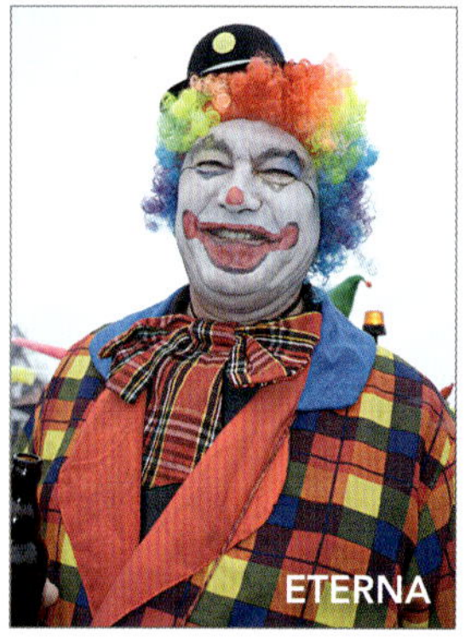

ETERNA

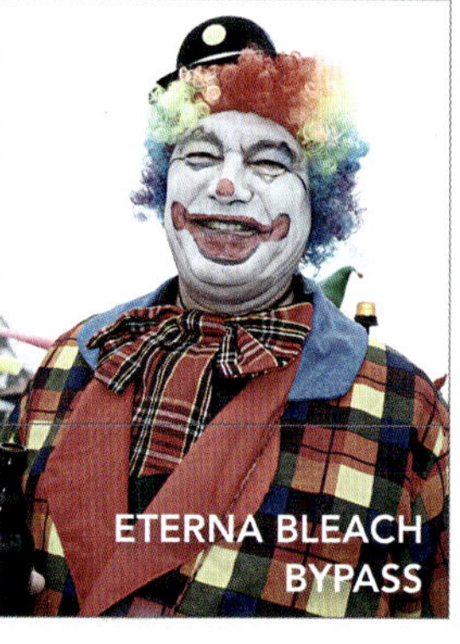

ETERNA BLEACH
BYPASS

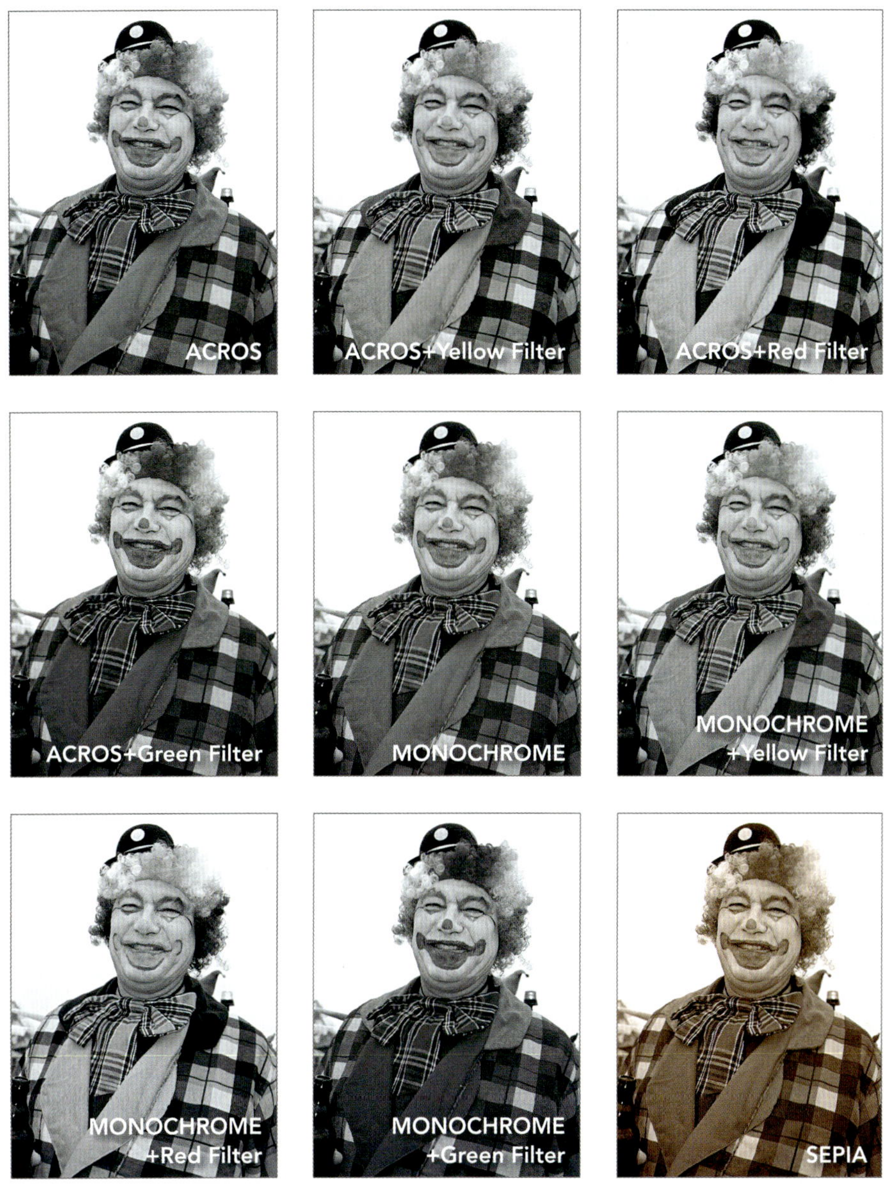

Fig. 105: Comparing all 20 film simulations: These two sets of straight-out-of-camera JPEGs illustrate the same shots in all 20 film simulations that are available in the X100VI.

See also the set on the following pages.

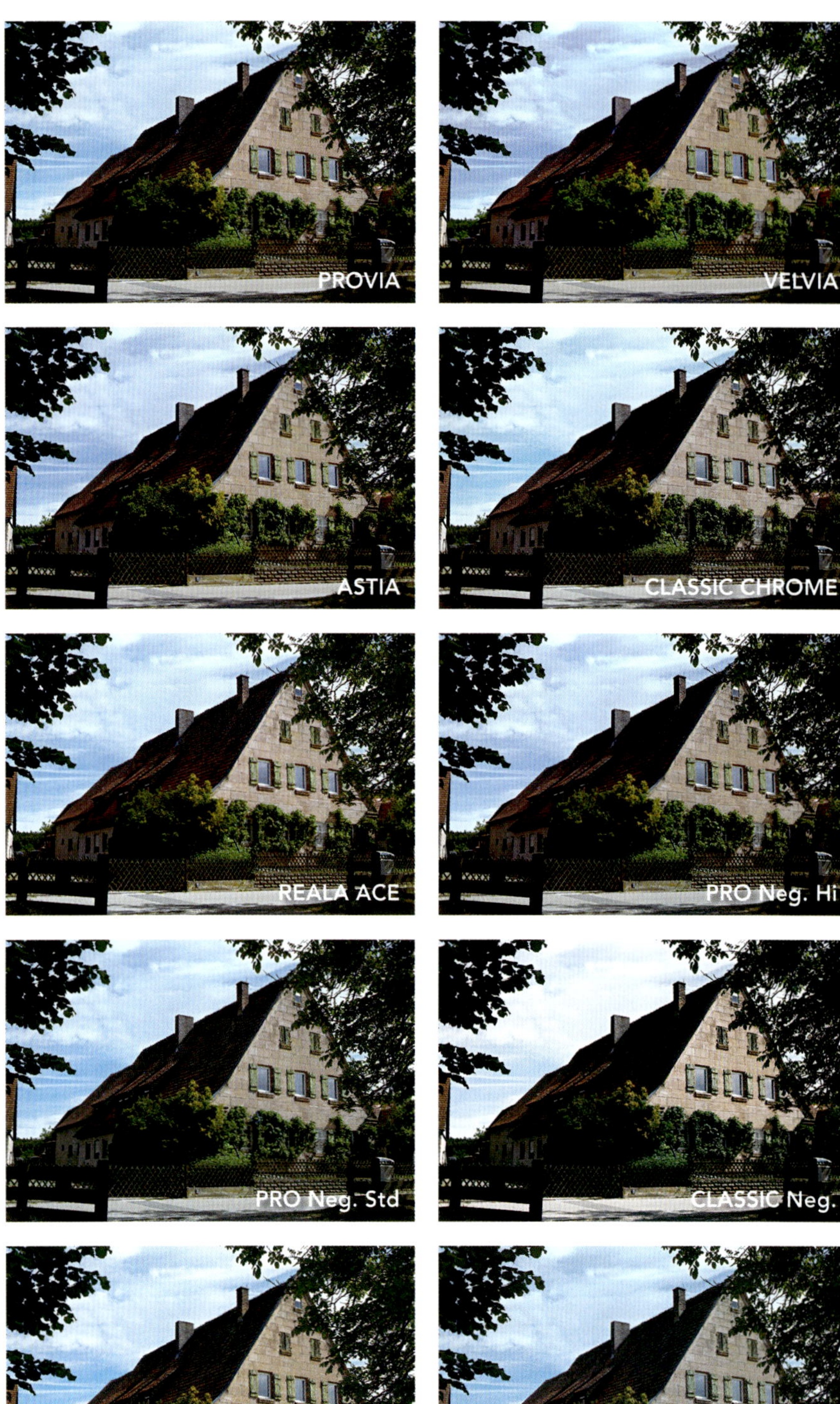

PROVIA
VELVIA
ASTIA
CLASSIC CHROME
REALA ACE
PRO Neg. Hi
PRO Neg. Std
CLASSIC Neg.
NOSTALGIC Neg.
ETERNA

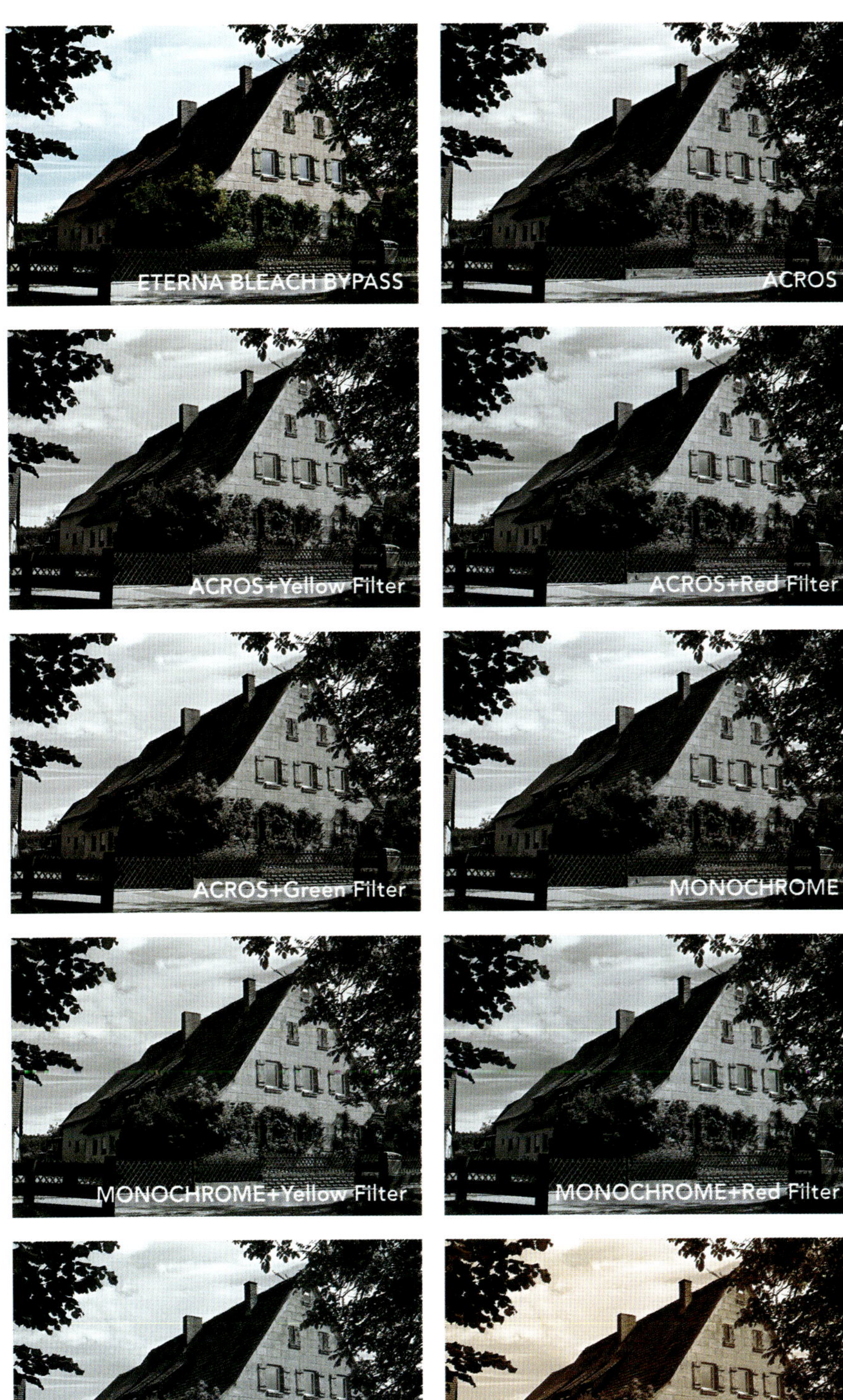

ETERNA BLEACH BYPASS
ACROS
ACROS+Yellow Filter
ACROS+Red Filter
ACROS+Green Filter
MONOCHROME
MONOCHROME+Yellow Filter
MONOCHROME+Red Filter
MONOCHROME+Green Filter
SEPIA

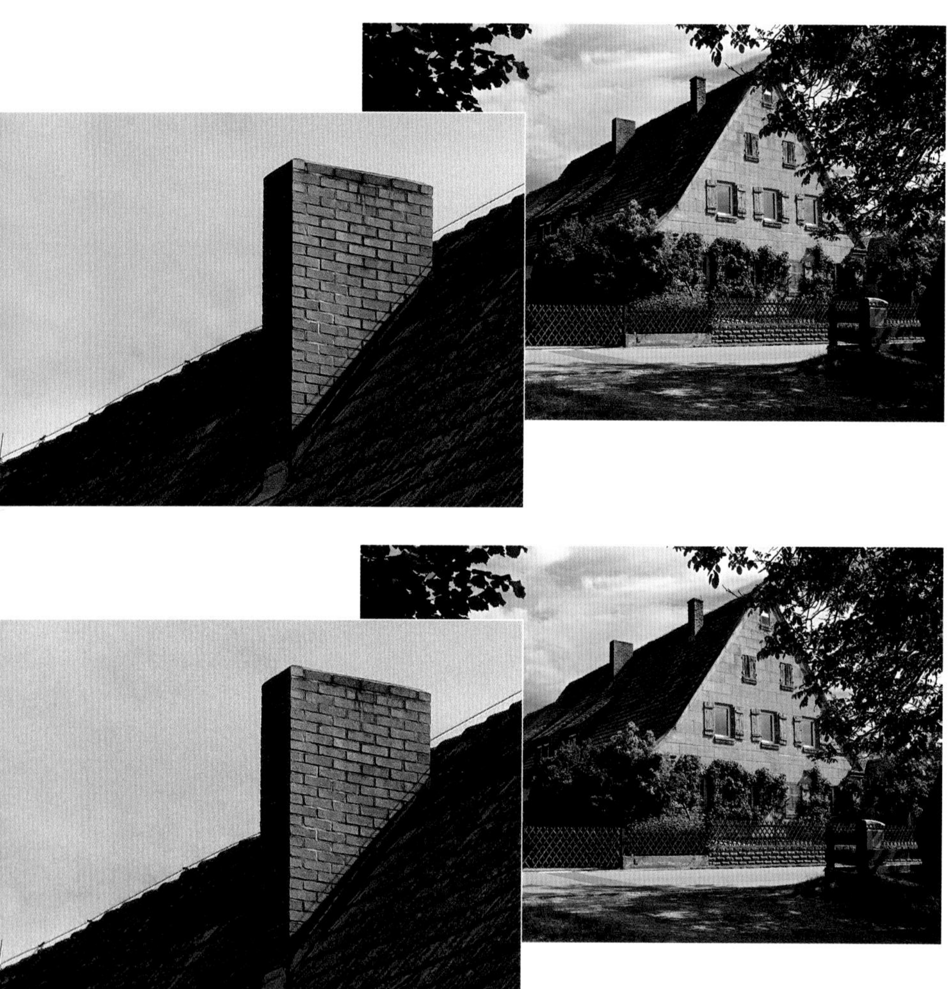

Fig. 106: ACROS has quickly become a favorite among X-series users. These SOOC examples illustrate ACROS noise shaping at different ISO settings: ISO 125 (image **A**), ISO 1000 (image **B**), ISO 8000 (image **C**), and ISO 25600 (image **D**). In all cases, noise reduction was set to –4.

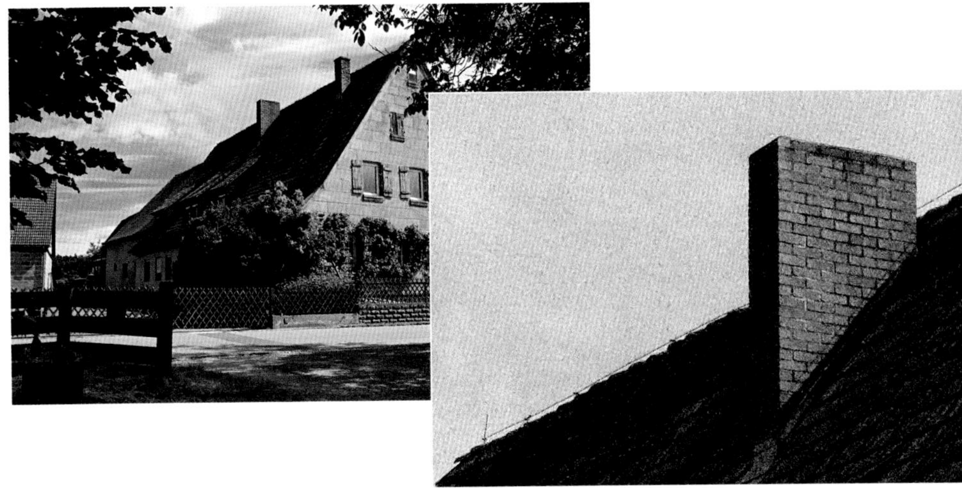

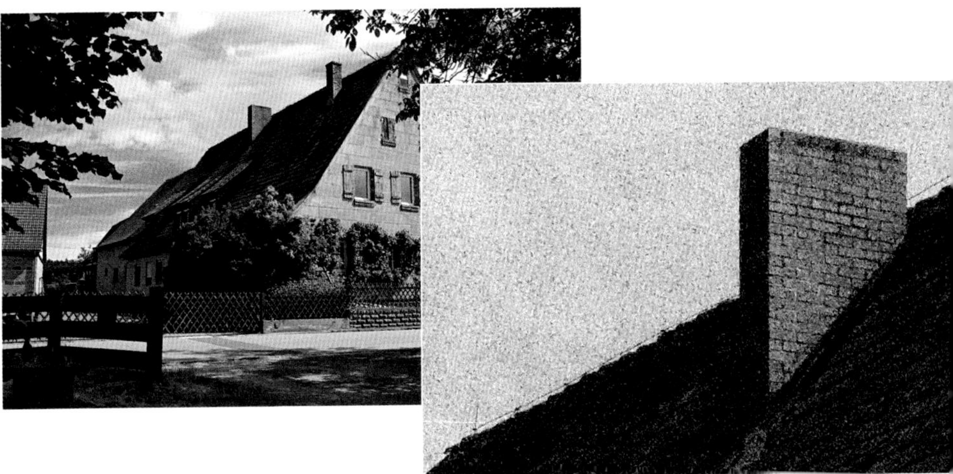

■ ACROS is a more sophisticated alternative to the regular MONOCHROME settings and is available in four versions: no filter, or with either a yellow, red, or green filter. It reminds us of Fujifilm's analog Acros film and offers a quite filmic look. This is partly because ACROS includes a noise-dependent analog film grain simulation that transforms regular image noise into analog-looking grain.

The noise-dependent analog film grain simulation of ACROS is based on innovative noise shaping technology. To make the grain visible, your image must contain some noise, so it's best to set in-camera noise reduction to a minimum (−4). Even at base ISO, there's already a subtle difference between ACROS and the regular MONOCHROME film simulation—if you set noise reduction to −4 to give the noise-shaping algorithm something to work with.

The best way to learn about film simulations is to experiment and compare the various options for yourself. The easiest way to do so is with the camera's internal RAW converter. Take a RAW file and process it with different film simulations, then compare the results on your computer monitor.

You can use the free X RAW STUDIO [60] software to control your camera's built-in RAW converter from your Mac or Windows PC. X RAW STUDIO conveniently works with RAW files that are stored on your computer but uses your camera and its image processor to perform the actual conversion work.

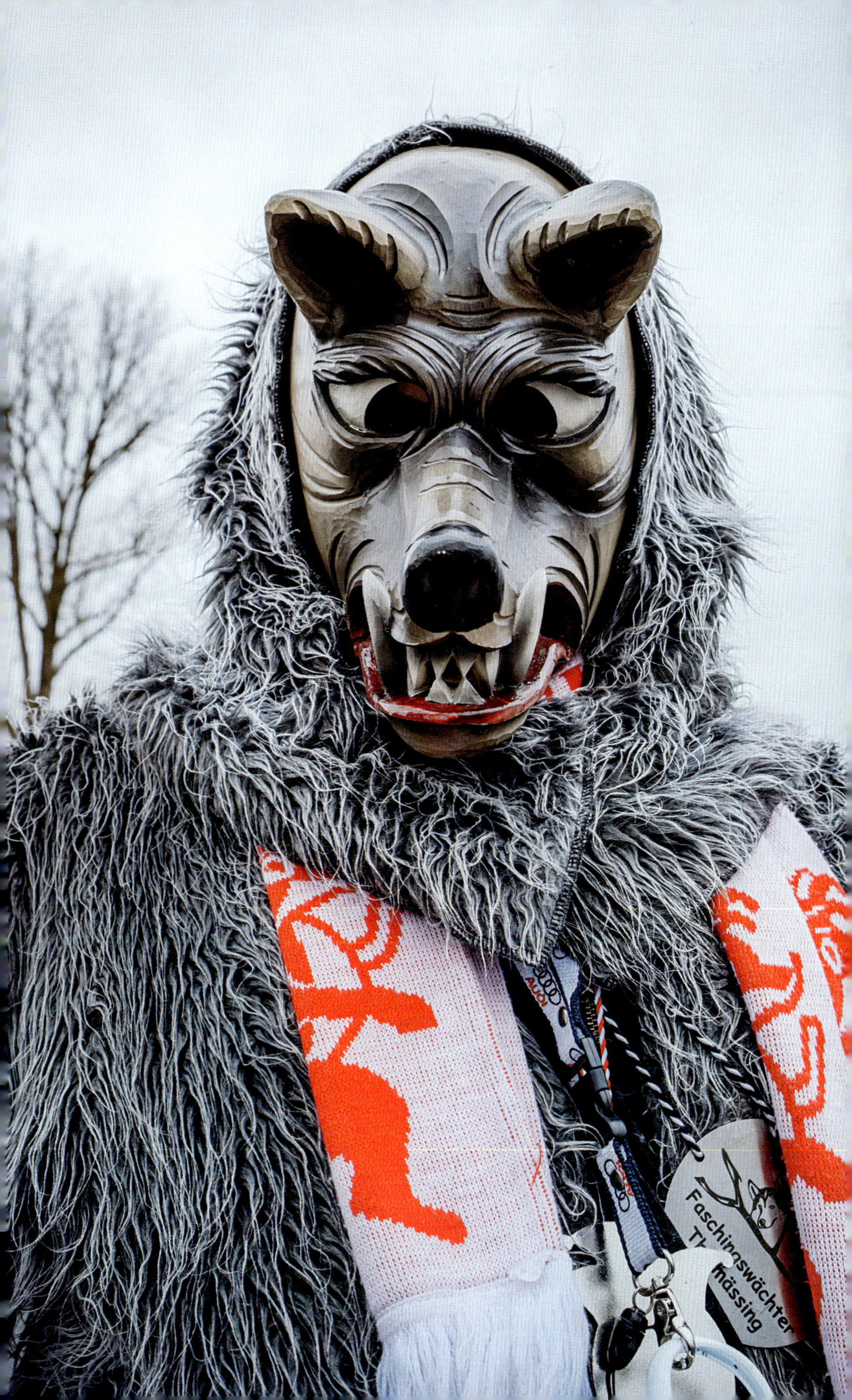

Faschingswächter
Ty
mässing

<table><tr><td>**TIP 103**</td><td>**Using the GRAIN EFFECT**</td></tr></table>

Fujifilm is all about great film simulations with an organic look. In this context, adding "analog film grain" to a digital image can be useful to achieve a more natural look with enhanced micro contrast.

GRAIN EFFECT offers three settings (OFF, WEAK, and STRONG) that can be combined with two grain sizes (SMALL and LARGE). It adds a layer of randomized, simulated film grain to the image and can be used with all film simulations.

Please note that I do *not* necessarily recommend using GRAIN EFFECT in concert with the ACROS film simulation—it would mix two different grain effects. After all, ACROS already brings its own noise-dependent grain to the table. That said, if you are using ACROS with low ISO settings, the grain from ACROS noise shaping may not be sufficient to achieve a desired "analog look", so adding more grain with GRAIN EFFECT may be required.

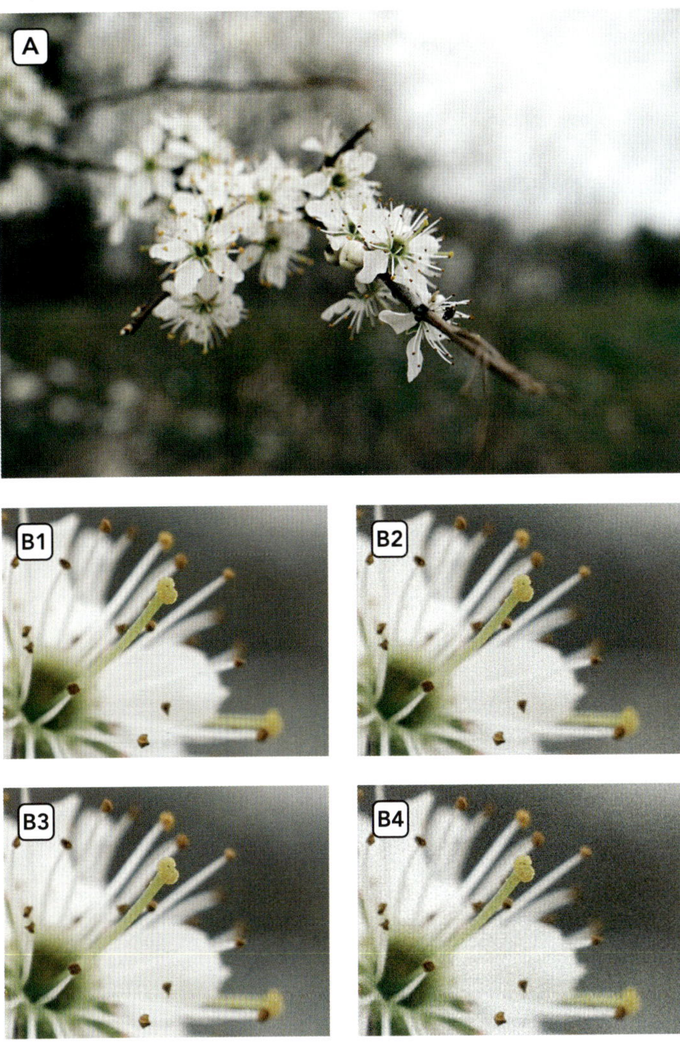

Fig. 107: Starting with the X-Pro3, Fujifilm has enhanced the **GRAIN EFFECT** with additional options. In addition to the Roughness setting (WEAK / STRONG), there's now also a Size setting to choose between SMALL and LARGE grain. This leaves us with four different combinations that are illustrated with these SOOC examples. Image **A** shows the entire scene with a GRAIN EFFECT LARGE / STRONG setting. Image **B** displays four magnified crops. SMALL / WEAK (**B1**), SMALL / STRONG (**B2**), LARGE / WEAK (**B3**), LARGE / STRONG (**B4**).

To preserve detail, adding grain should always be performed in concert with a noise reduction setting of −4.

TIP 104   Contrast settings: adjusting highlights and shadows

A useful feature of the X100VI is its ability to independently set the contrast [61] for dark and bright parts of a JPEG image using the HIGHLIGHT TONE and SHADOW TONE settings of X RAW STUDIO. This corresponds to the TONE CURVE setting (with options HIGHLIGHTS and SHADOWS) in the IMAGE QUALITY SETTING and the camera's RAW conversion menu. These settings can also be used to extend a JPEG's dynamic range by lifting dark shadows or softening bright highlights. To increase the overall contrast of a shot, you can increase both parameters in tandem. To reduce the overall contrast, decrease the value for both parameters.

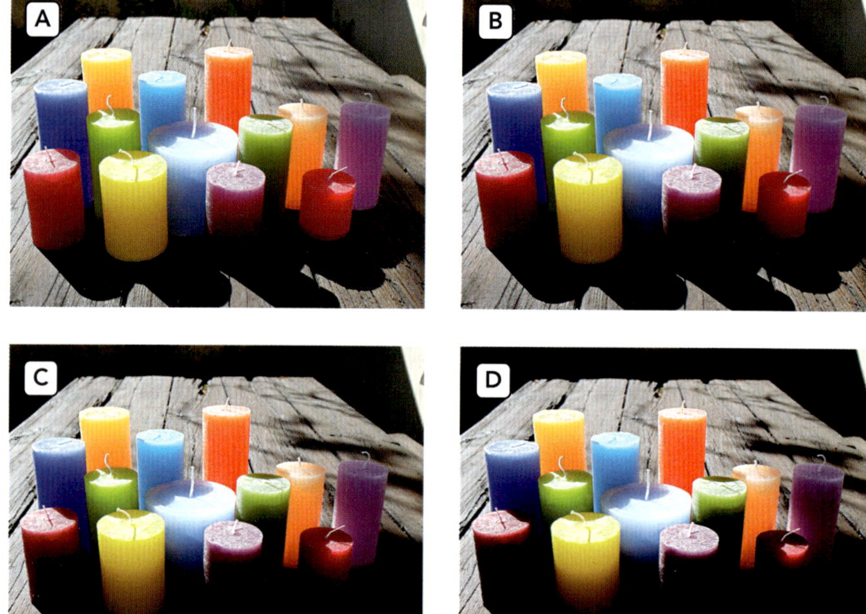

Fig. 108: Comparing **Shadow Tone** or **Tone Curve (Shadows)** settings of a PROVIA image: Image **A** shows a SHADOW TONE –2 version; image **B** shows a neutral 0 setting, image **C** displays the RAW file processed with SHADOW TONE +2, and image **D** shows the maximum of SHADOW TONE +4. Shadows and dark midtones change, but the highlights remain untouched.

It's worth mentioning that increased contrast also enhances the impression of image sharpness and color saturation. This demonstrates that JPEG parameters always work in concert with each other.

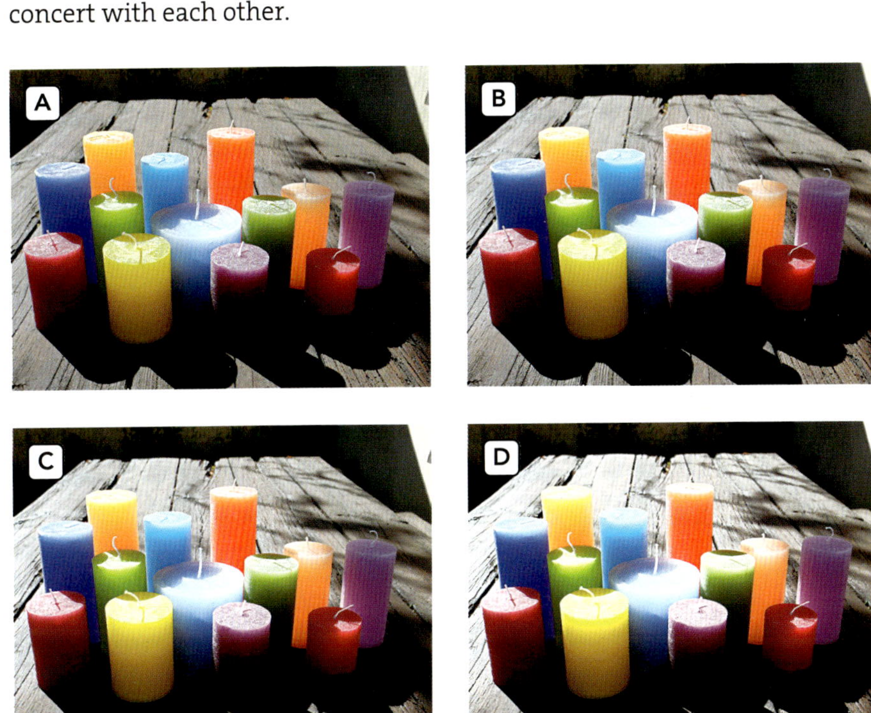

Fig. 109: Comparing **Highlight Tone** or **Tone Curve (Highlights)** settings: Image **A** shows the HIGHLIGHT TONE –2 version of a PROVIA image; image **B** shows the same RAW file processed with a neutral 0 setting, image **C** displays the image with HIGHLIGHT TONE +2, and image **D** shows the maximum highlight contrast setting of +4. Changing the highlight contrast leaves the shadows and darker midtones untouched.

Color saturation	TIP 105

After picking a suitable film simulation mode, you still might want to change the color saturation [62] of an image. You can do so with the COLOR setting.

Too much color saturation can obscure texture and details. For example, VELVIA is a very saturated film mode that may sometimes require a reduction in color saturation.

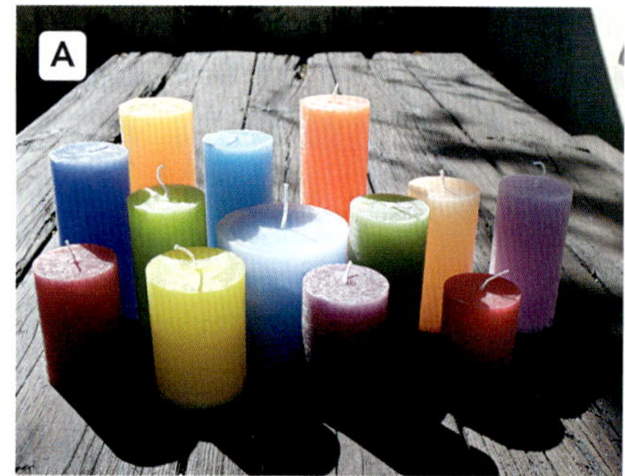
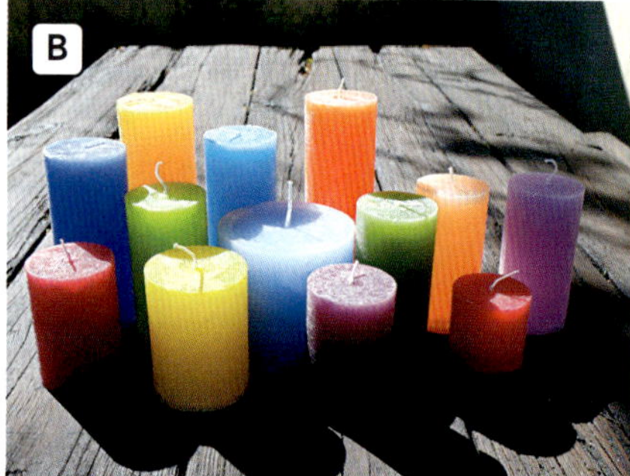

Fig. 110: Color saturation: Image **A** shows a PROVIA version with COLOR –4; image **B** shows the same RAW file processed with COLOR +4.

TIP 106	The COLOR CHROME EFFECT

COLOR CHROME EFFECT is a calculation-heavy process that adds depth to saturated colors in an image. There are three settings: OFF, WEAK, and STRONG. It can be applied in concert with any film simulation and only affects the red and green channel components of the image.

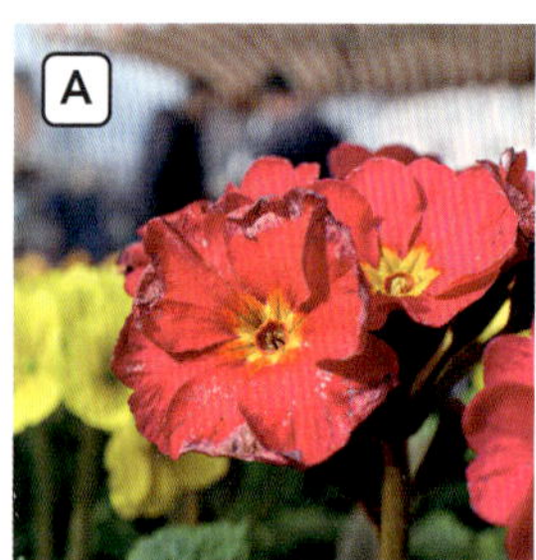
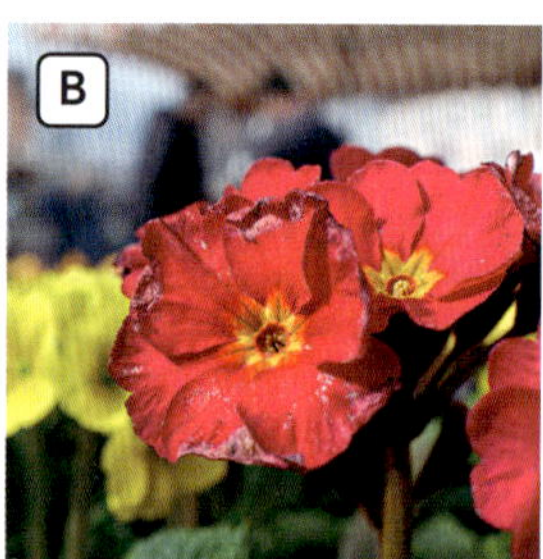
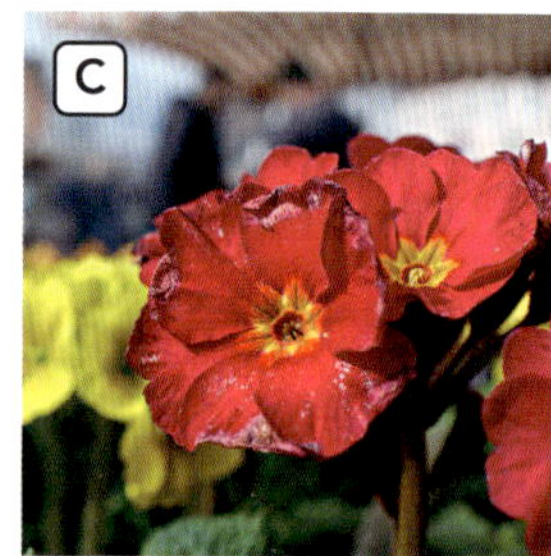

Fig. 111: This SOOC example illustrates how a saturated PROVIA JPEG image (**A**) is changed by adding a COLOR CHROME EFFECT > WEAK (**B**) and STRONG (**C**) setting.

COLOR CHROME FX BLUE works just like COLOR CHROME EFFECT but only affects the blue parts of your image. For example, you can use it to emphasize a blue sky.

To affect all colors in your image, you can combine both Color Chrome Effect options.

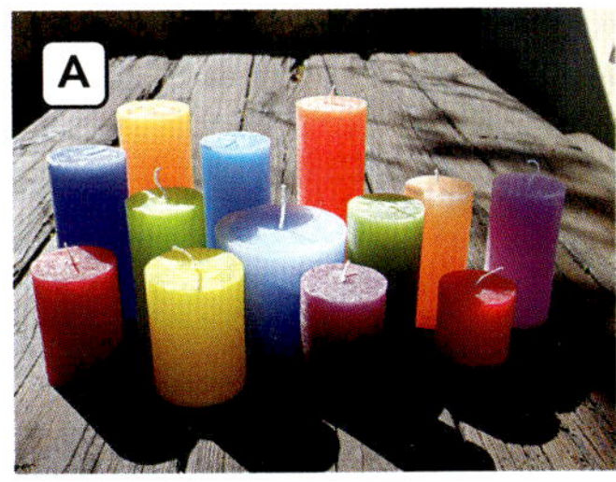
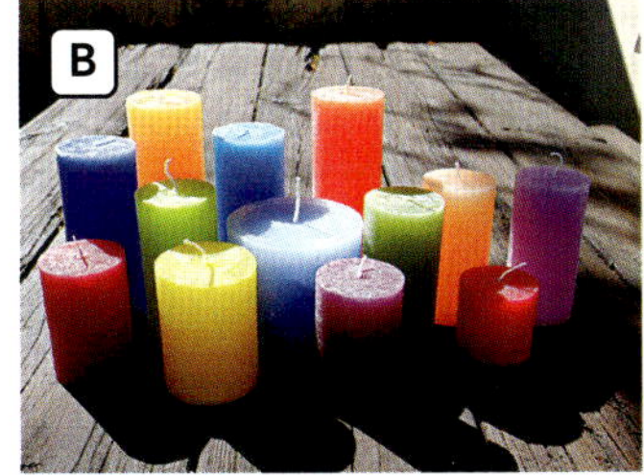
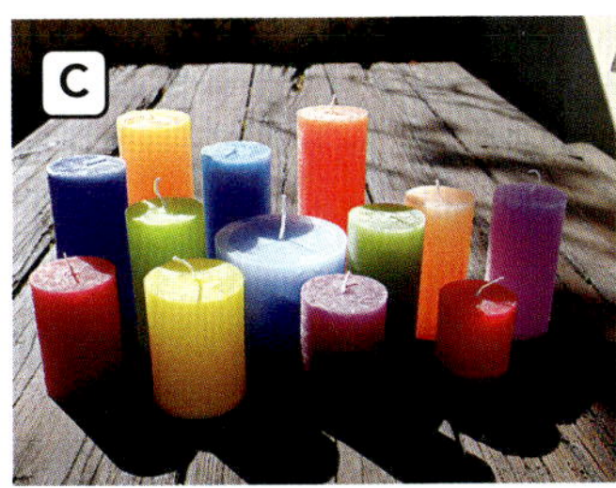

Fig. 112: This example shows ASTIA SOOC JPEGs with COLOR CHROME FX BLUE > OFF (**A**), WEAK (**B**), and STRONG (**C**).

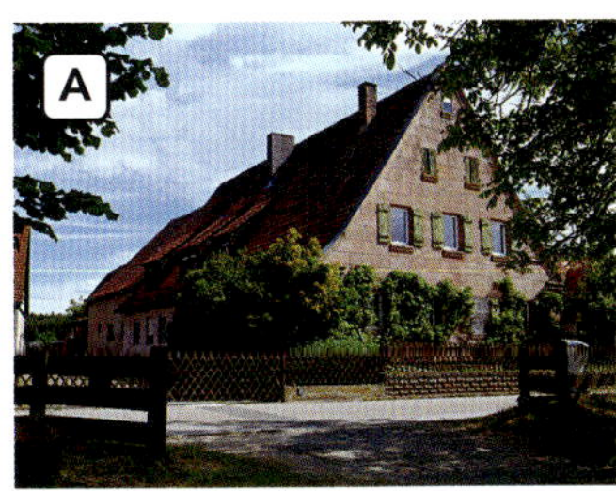
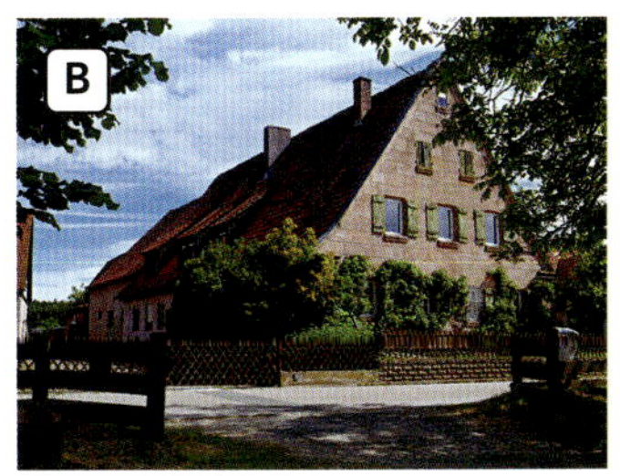
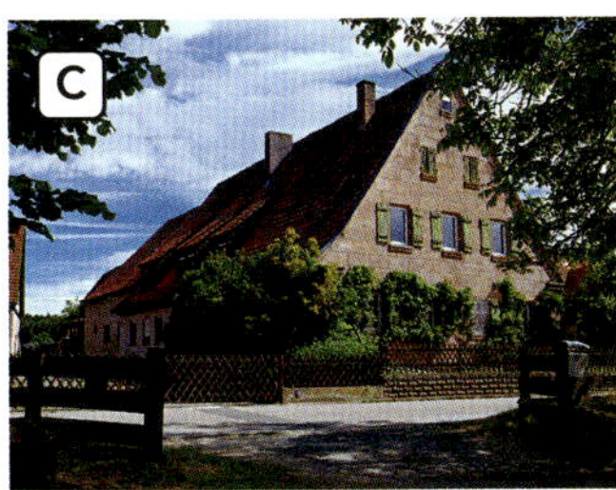

Fig. 113: A popular application of COLOR CHROME FX BLUE is adding contrast to a blue sky with clouds, like in this ASTIA SOOC example with COLOR CHROME FX BLUE > OFF (**A**), WEAK (**B**), and STRONG (**C**).

<table>
<tr><td>TIP 107</td><td>MONOCHROMATIC COLOR: adding color tints to mono-chrome images</td></tr>
</table>

In many cases, printed black-and-white photos aren't just black and white, but they contain a warm or cool color tint. Even in photographic books, it's a common printing practice to add at least one color to monochrome pictures to increase the range of tones that can be realized during the printing process.

The X100VI lets you add a color tint to ACROS and MONO-CHROME images. With the MONOCHROMATIC COLOR setting, you can change the neutral look of black-and-white images with a Warm/Cool adjustment on the vertical axis and a Magenta/Green adjustment on the horizontal axis.

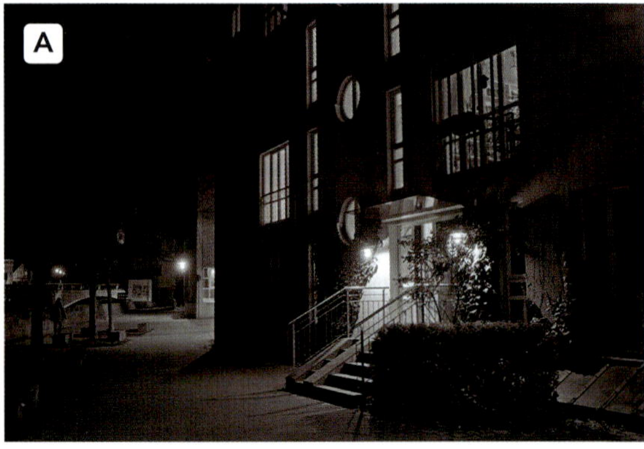

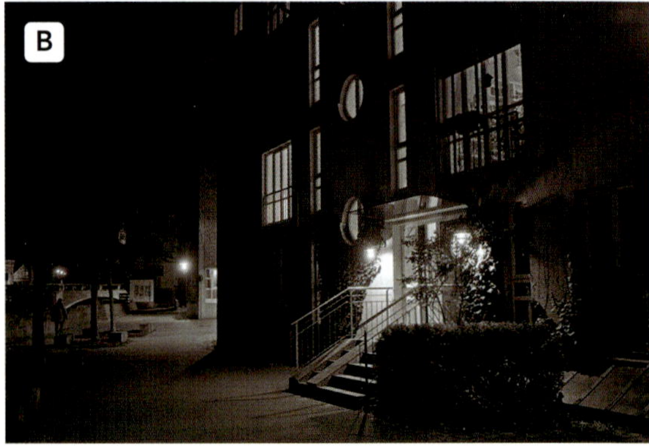

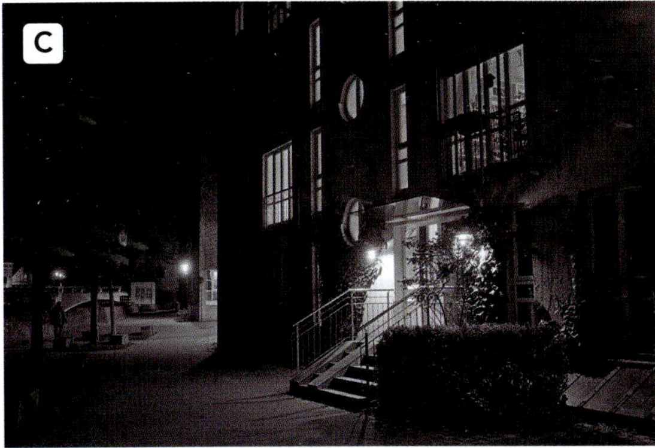

Fig. 114: This SOOC example illustrates the effect of the MONO-CHROMATIC COLOR setting on black-and-white shots: Image **A** shows an ACROS image with a neutral setting of 0. Image **B** is the same shot, but with Warm/Cool set to +2 and Magenta/Green to –1. Image **C** shows a variant with Warm/Cool –2 and Magenta/Green –2.

Using the SMOOTH SKIN EFFECT	TIP 108

High-resolution cameras like the X100VI can sometimes reveal "too much" detail, particularly when it comes to human skin in portrait shots. Of course, you can always get rid of blemishes in your external RAW conversion software or with programs like Photoshop. However, there's an easy way to get smoother skin in-camera: use the SMOOTH SKIN EFFECT.

This function is available in two strengths: WEAK and STRONG. Personally, I recommend using the WEAK option because STRONG can lead to "plastic skin." That said, it's certainly a matter of taste, and there are also significant cultural differences as to what amount of skin smoothing is desirable.

Please note that SMOOTH SKIN EFFECT doesn't just affect human faces and skin tones but your entire image, so it's possible that other fine details are smoothened by this effect, too.

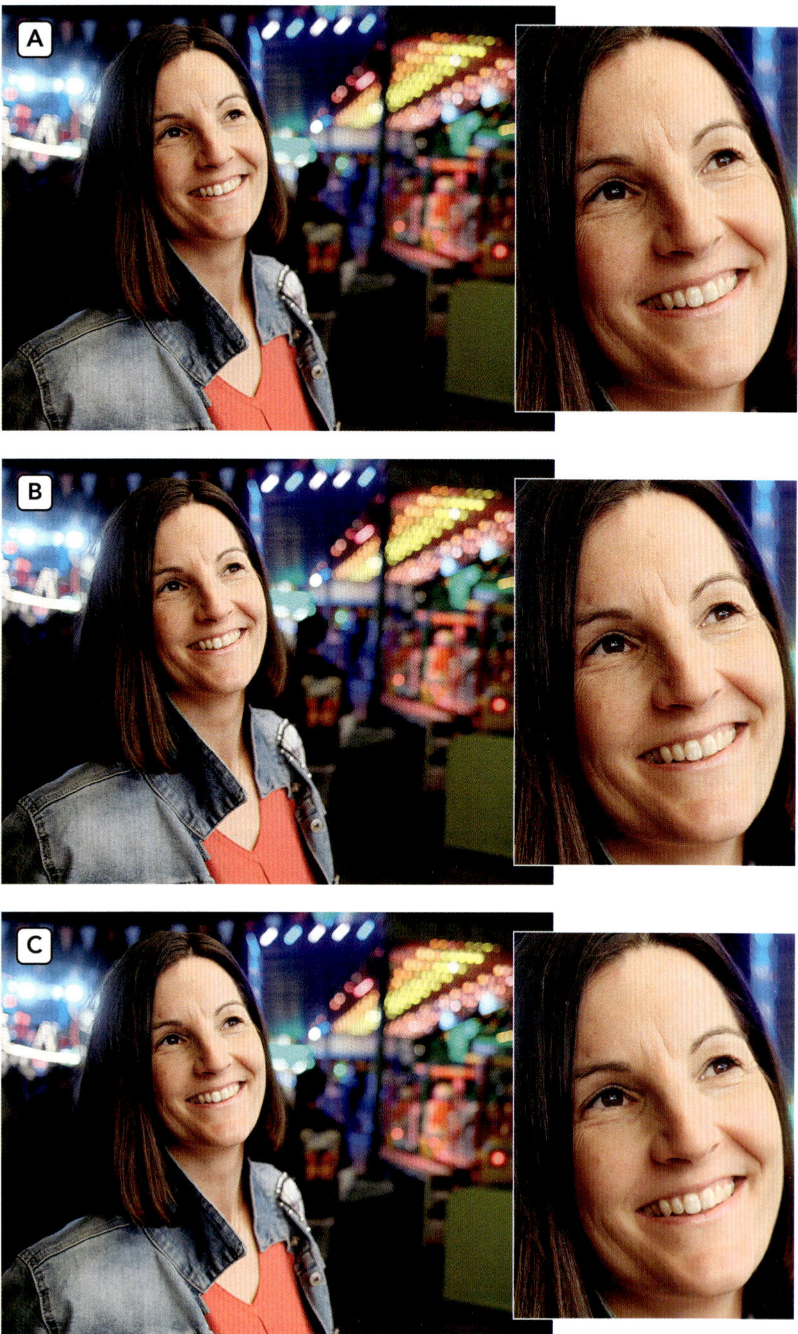

Fig. 115: This SOOC example shows the same portrait in three different versions: SMOOTH SKIN EFFECT OFF (**A**), WEAK (**B**), and STRONG (**C**).

Be careful with CLARITY!	TIP 109

CLARITY enhances or reduces the micro-contrast in your image. Basically, micro-contrast is the contrast (brightness difference) between neighboring pixels. More micro-contrast adds more grit and perceived sharpness (like a dehazing effect); reducing micro-contrast makes the image look softer and dreamier. The X100VI lets you adjust the micro-contrast in 11 steps (−5 to +5), with 0 being the neutral default setting.

CLARITY should preferably be applied after-the-fact with the built-in RAW converter, not during your actual shooting. In other words: CLARITY should be set to 0 (zero) in the IMAGE QUALITY SETTING menu.

Here's why: CLARITY significantly slows down your camera. It may take up to two seconds to process and save a single image. Consequently, CLARITY is not available in concert with burst mode and bracketing modes. Using any of these modes will automatically reset CLARITY to zero. To save you all this trouble, it's better to apply clarity after the fact, for example with X RAW STUDIO, where you can also try out different strength settings and see their effect.

I understand that CLARITY settings other than zero are often part of "film simulation recipes" that are particularly popular with users of X100 series cameras. So, if you insist on using film recipes with non-zero CLARITY settings during shooting, that's perfectly okay. Just know and remember that these settings will be ignored in concert with CL and CH burst shooting and all bracketing modes. And don't be surprised when your X100VI becomes really slow in single shot mode.

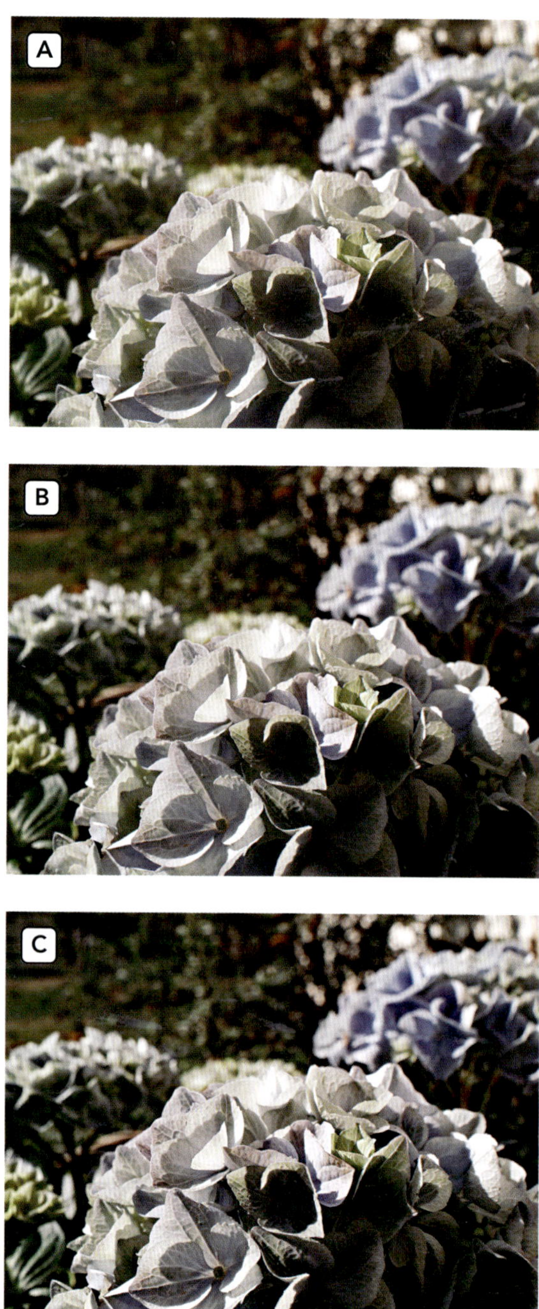

Fig. 116: This SOOC example shows the same image with CLARITY set to –5 (**A**), neutral 0 (**B**), and +5 (**C**).

Please note that CLARITY is unavailable when you are shooting in the HEIF format. This restriction includes after-the-fact HEIF conversions using the built-in RAW converter, either directly in the camera or via X RAW STUDIO.

Color space: sRGB or Adobe RGB?	TIP 110

A color space [63] is a way of organizing available colors. The X100VI offers two options: sRGB [64] and Adobe RGB [65]. Both color spaces contain the same *number* of colors, but not the *same* colors—their gamuts [66] are different.

Adobe RGB covers a larger gamut than sRGB because its colors are optimized for CMYK printing. On the other hand, sRGB is optimized for computer monitors and all kinds of high-resolution displays, such as HD and UHD TVs, smartphones, and tablets. Since Adobe RGB encompasses a wider gamut than sRGB, the gaps between neighboring colors and tones are larger because both color spaces contain the same number of colors. Adobe RGB must spread out this number of colors over its larger gamut. This larger gamut (compared to standard sRGB) is why Adobe RGB is also known as an "extended" color space.

Users often misunderstand and assume that "extended" means "better." It does not. The additional colors in Adobe RGB are only useful if you intend to print your JPEG or TIFF files with a commercial CMYK printer. This requires a calibrated workflow and a wide-gamut monitor that can display the entire Adobe RGB gamut. However, many computer monitors can only display the sRGB gamut. Using Adobe RGB on such a monitor would be like working with half-closed eyes because you wouldn't be able to see many of the colors you are using.

For most users (including me), sRGB is the best choice of color space. Images rendered in this color space can be viewed, processed, and printed on a wide variety of devices without unpleasant surprises. In any case, you should calibrate your computer monitor with hardware like Datacolor's Spyder. Uncalibrated screens will not give you an accurate representation of the colors in your images.

Important: The COLOR SPACE setting in your X100VI only affects the JPEGs and TIFFs that are created inside your camera. It also affects the live-view image—and since the LCD display and the EVF only support sRGB, it would be a bad idea to shoot with Adobe RGB. The result would be a mismatch between what you see and what you get. WYSIWYG would be broken. Hence, always select sRGB in the IMAGE QUALITY SETTING menu!

COLOR SPACE is a JPEG setting, so it doesn't affect RAW data. RAW files have no defined color space, yet. The color space is set when you export an image after processing the RAW. This also means that you can export the same image in different versions, using different color spaces.

Please note that Adobe RGB isn't available in concert with the HEIF format.

<table><tr><td>TIP 111</td><td>Working with the built-in RAW converter</td></tr></table>

The quickest way to access the built-in RAW converter in your X100VI is to select a RAW image in playback mode and press the Q button. The RAW converter in your camera serves two main purposes:

- You can create various versions of a shot, for example, a colorful Velvia version and a gritty black-and-white version of the same image. Not sure what's best or what you want? Quickly create multiple versions with different film simulations and varying JPEG settings, and then sort them out later on your computer screen.

- You can improve your images after the fact. Since it's hard (if not impossible) to guess and set the perfect JPEG settings for each shot in advance, it's more convenient to adjust these parameters later when you have time to look at your results. You can easily change parameters like white balance, color saturation, contrast settings, sharpness, or noise reduction. You can also adjust the exposure and try various film simulations.

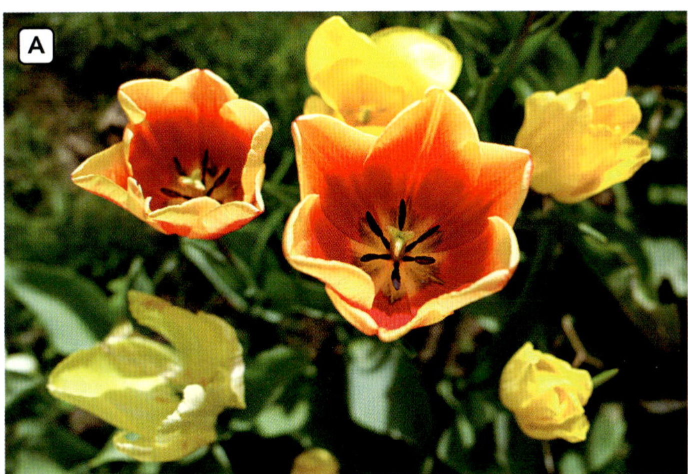

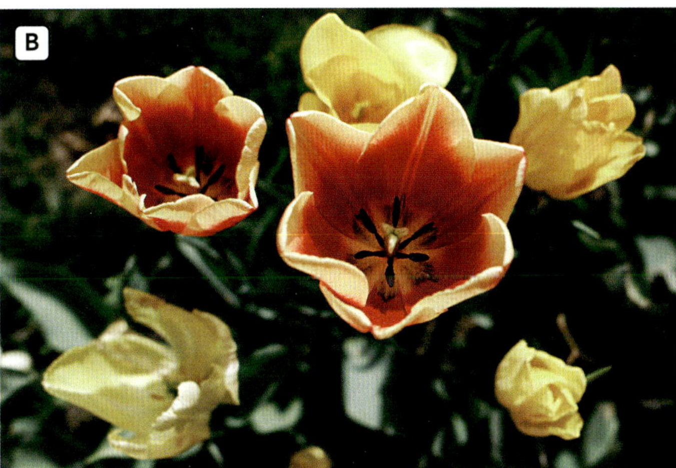

Fig. 117: Using the **built-in RAW converter** to change the look of a shot: image **A** shows the scene as it was recorded with the camera's default settings. Image **B** is the same shot processed with adjusted JPEG settings.

Here are a few things you can accomplish with the built-in RAW converter:

■ Use PUSH/PULL processing to brighten (*push*) underexposed shots or darken (*pull*) overexposed images.

■ Use the TONE CURVE settings (SHADOW TONE and HIGHLIGHT TONE) to selectively adjust the contrast of dark or bright parts of your image. It's perfectly adequate to combine these functions with PUSH/PULL processing.

■ Adjust the color saturation of your photos with the COLOR parameter. Reducing the color saturation can recover texture when one or more of the color channels appear oversaturated.

■ Diminish NOISE REDUCTION to preserve more texture.

■ Add or remove micro-contrast with CLARITY, beautify skin with the SMOOTH SKIN EFFECT, deepen colors with a COLOR CHROME EFFECT, add film grain with the GRAIN EFFECT, or tint black-and-white images with MONO-CHROMATIC COLOR.

■ Adjust the white balance using one of the presets or a Kelvin value to make your images look warmer or cooler. Use WB SHIFT to correct or introduce a color tint.

■ Picked the wrong color space? No problem! Just reprocess the shot with the correct color space.

■ You can always *reduce* DYNAMIC RANGE, D RANGE PRIORITY, or an HDR setting. You can also *remove* a previously set DIGITAL TELECONVERTER, and you can *change* the IMAGE SIZE and aspect ratio, the IMAGE QUALITY (NORMAL or FINE), or the exported FILE TYPE (JPEG, HEIF, TIFF 8-bit, and TIFF 16-bit). Please note that TIFF 16-bit is really just a 10-bit file, and so is HEIF.

To process RAW files that have already been transferred to a computer, you can use the free X RAW STUDIO application as a remote-control interface for your camera's built-in RAW converter.

By the way: Your X100VI cannot process RAW files from other X-series models. For example, the built-in RAW converter of your camera cannot process RAW files that were taken with an X-H2 or X-T5. However, you can process RAW files that were shot with a different X100VI camera.

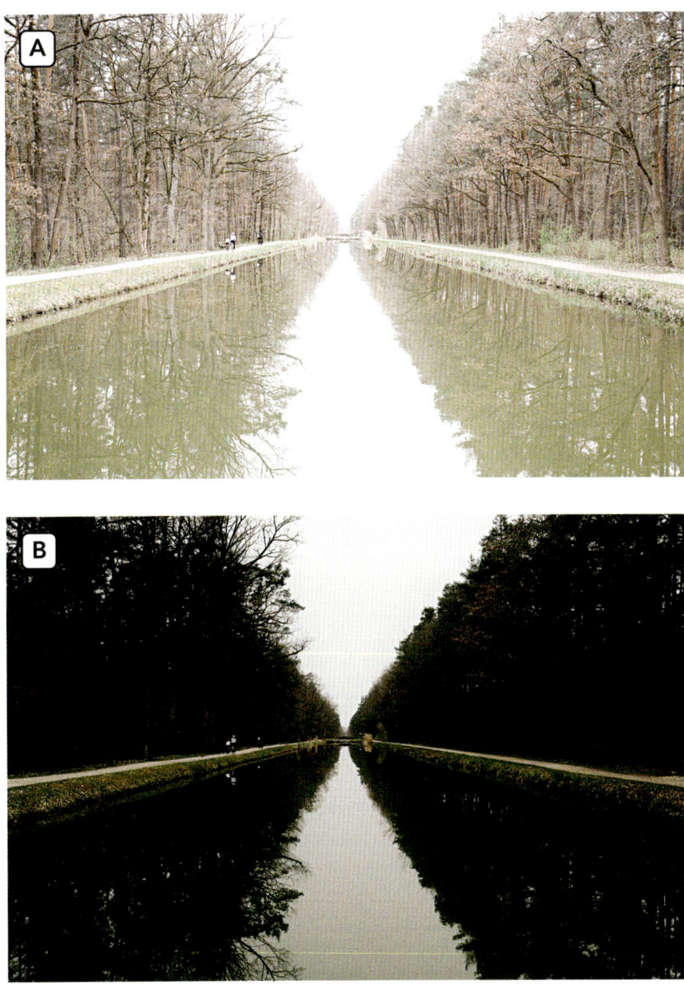

Fig. 118: You can also use the built-in RAW converter to **correct a shot**. Image **A** shows an overexposed sample shot that was recorded with Classic Neg. and DR400%. Image **B** is the same shot reprocessed in-camera with adjusted settings.

<table>
<tr><td>TIP 112</td><td>Working with X RAW STUDIO</td></tr>
</table>

The built-in RAW converter is a practical tool for on-the-fly RAW conversions while you are in the field. You can use your camera's LCD or EVF display (I recommend the latter) to create new and improved JPEGs from RAW files that are saved on the memory card in your camera.

But what if your RAW files have already been transferred to a computer? Instead of copying them back to a card and processing them in-camera, there's a better and more comfortable way: FUJIFILM X RAW STUDIO.

X RAW STUDIO is a free download for Windows and macOS [67]. Don't confuse it with a stand-alone RAW converter, though. Basically, X RAW STUDIO is a PC/Mac-based remote-control and user interface for the built-in RAW converter of your X100VI. This means that X RAW STUDIO cannot function without your camera, which must be tethered to your Mac or PC with a USB data cable.

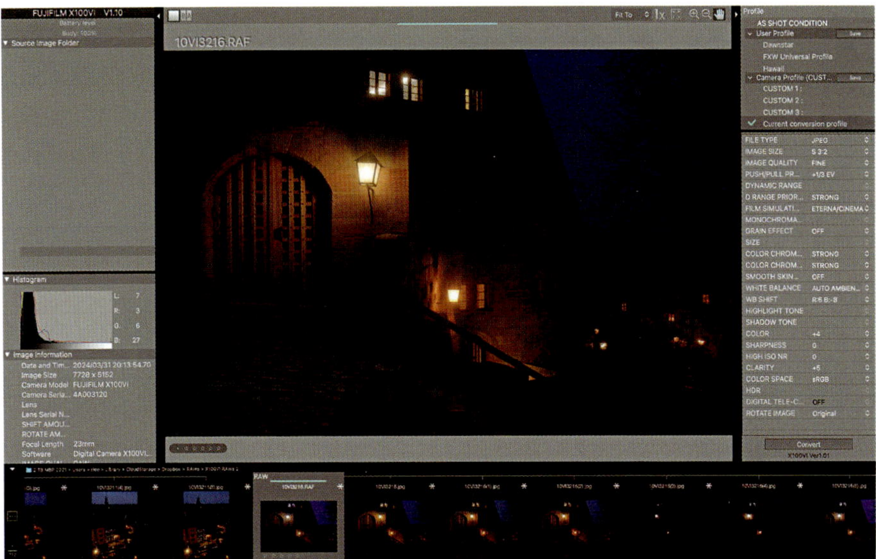

Fig. 119: FUJIFILM **X RAW STUDIO** is a simple way to remotely control the built-in RAW converter of your camera and use it to process RAW files that are stored on your Windows PC or Mac. The free app sends RAW files from your computer to the camera via a USB-C connection, where they are processed to "in-camera JPEGs" that are immediately returned to your PC. You get the best of both worlds: the ease of use of a computer interface (with a larger display and convenient storage for all your images) is combined with the processing power and image quality of your camera's internal RAW converter.

Set-up your camera to work with X RAW STUDIO by selecting NETWORK/USB SETTING > CONNECTION MODE > USB RAW CONV./BACKUP RESTORE, and then connect it to your Mac or PC via USB while X RAW STUDIO is running. Operating the software is mostly self-explanatory, but feel free to consult Fuji's online manual [68].

Since it runs on a computer, X RAW STUDIO offers a more comprehensive user interface than the stand-alone converter in your camera. You can copy and paste development settings from one image to others, and you can set-up and save development presets (film simulation recipes) for later use. Batch processing of multiple RAW images is also no problem.

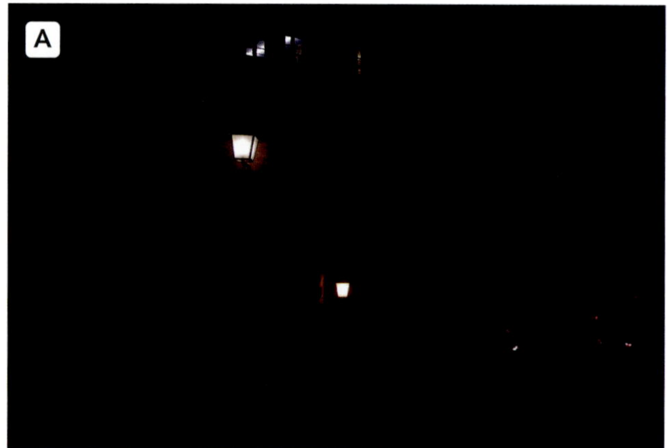

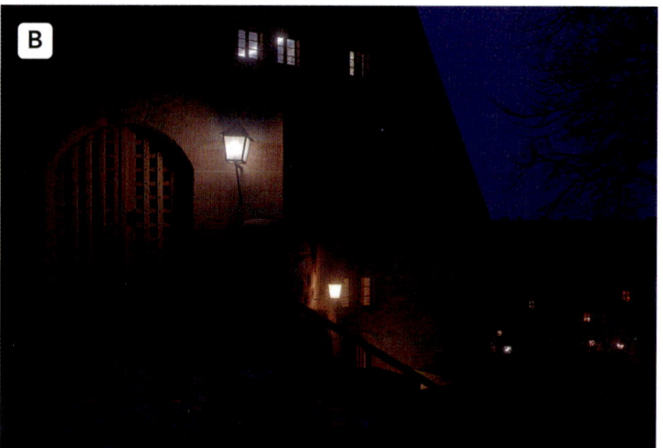

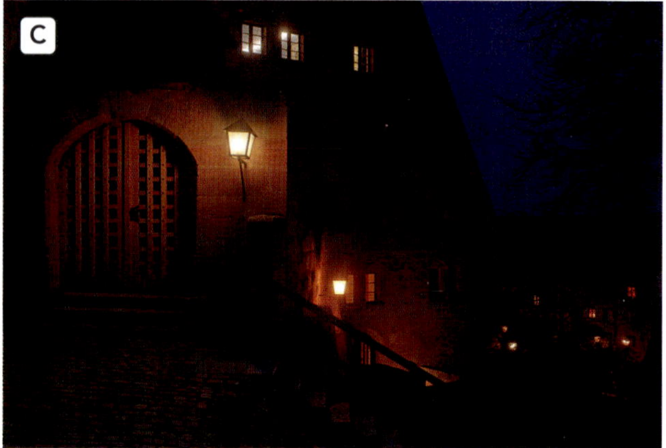

Fig. 120: X RAW STUDIO offers a straightforward workflow. After connecting the X100VI to your Mac or PC, you begin with selecting a RAW image from your computer's hard drive, then apply various JPEG setting changes. You can also adjust the exposure with PUSH/ PULL PROCESSING, decrease DR, DR-P, HDR, and teleconverter settings and change the aspect ratio and output size of the result.

Here's a typical workflow example. Image **A** shows a night shot as I exposed it with the camera's default settings: PROVIA, DR100% and a manual exposure for the critical highlights that resulted in a handheld IBIS shot with 1/6 sec. and f/5.6 at base-ISO 125. Obviously, this JPEG image—and the corresponding WYSIWYG live view—are too dark. It is virtually impossible to frame the shot with the electronic viewfinder.

Well, we know what to do. Image **B** shows the same image— still with 1/6 sec. at f/5.6, but with ISO-equivalent settings: ISO 500 and DR-P STRONG. I also exchanged PROVIA for the less contrasty ETERNA film simulation. This image was easy to frame in the live view, so I took the shot. Please note that a Tiffen Glimmerglass 1 filter was attached to the lens to add diffusion.

After transferring the images of the day from the camera to my Mac, I opened X RAW STUDIO to apply some JPEG setting magic. Image **C** shows the above shot with these adjustments: PUSH/ PULL +1/3 EV, DR-P STRONG, ETERNA, COLOR CHROME EFFECT STRONG, COLOR CHROME FX BLUE STRONG, WB AUTO AMBI- ENT PRIORITY, WB SHIFT R: +6; B: –8, COLOR +4, and CLARITY +5.

Working with film simulation recipes	TIP 113

One of the attractions of the X100VI is its ability to deliver images that look like film, without cumbersome external processing. Combining film simulations with specific JPEG settings such as white balance, WB shift, highlight and shadow contrast, sharpness, noise reduction, clarity, color saturation, color chrome effects, and grain can lead to quite distinctive looks. These looks are often referred to as *recipes*, and many of them have been designed to mimic popular analog film emulsions.

You can find hundreds of different Fujifilm X recipes online. The most popular source is Fuji X Weekly [69]. I can highly recommend it as a starting point to get familiar with recipes. Just by experiencing how they impact your images, you can learn a lot from using third-party recipes.

Recipes aren't black boxes containing some secret sauce. They are fully disclosed combinations of JPEG and DR settings that deliver a certain look. Try different combos and make your own changes to better understand the inner workings of your camera's JPEG engine. Soon, you may be able to come up with your own recipes. You will also be able to make informed adjustments to your JPEG settings depending on the subject and how you want to present it.

You can store different recipes in the seven custom settings (C1–C7) in the IMAGE QUALITY SETTING menu. However, since the custom settings of the X100VI are global settings that contain more parameters than just JPEG settings, you must be careful that the remaining settings also fit your shooting situation.

An alternative solution is to apply recipes after the fact using the X RAW STUDIO software that allows you to store and apply a virtually unlimited number of recipes under its User Profile tab. With the Camera Profile tab, you can even copy recipes to and from the custom settings of your connected camera by right-clicking on an item in the list of recipes (User Profiles) or custom settings (Camera Profiles).

To successfully use X RAW STUDIO, your images must be available as RAW files on your Mac or PC. If you want to apply third-party recipes without limitations, your shots should have been recorded with DR400%. Simple reason: Many popular recipes ask for DR200% or DR400%, and higher DR settings can only be applied to RAW files that were recorded with a DR setting that was at least as high. Example: You cannot apply DR200% or DR400% to a RAW file that was shot with DR100%. Personally, I sometimes take it even further and shoot with DR-P STRONG because DR-P STRONG encompasses *all* DR *and* DR-P settings, giving me the freedom to apply all of them after-the-fact.

If you are shooting with higher DR or DR-P settings, be careful to correctly expose the image to preserve critical highlights. Luckily, the WYSIWYG live view, live histogram, and blinkies of the X100VI usually work with fixed DR and DR-P settings, so you can still rely on the histogram and blinkies. Don't set the camera to DR-Auto or DR-P Auto, though.

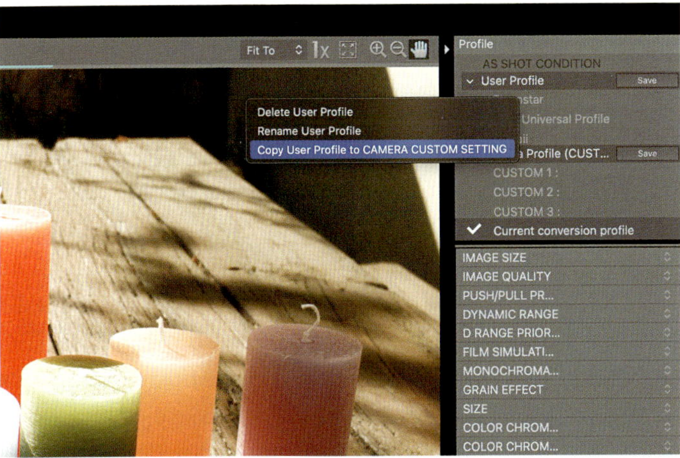

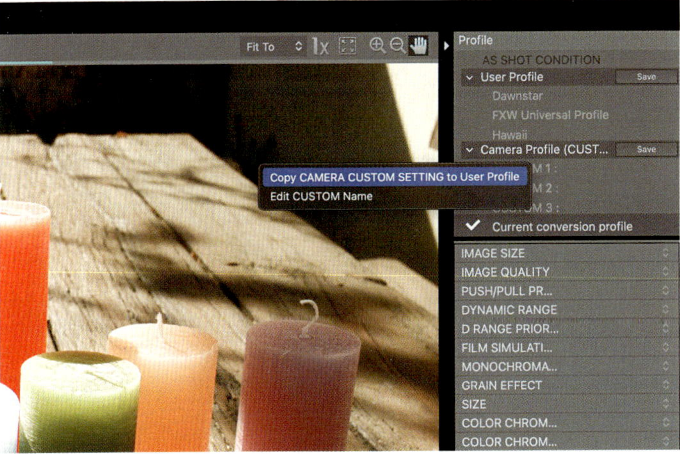

Fig. 121: X RAW STUDIO allows you to store and apply as many **recipes** (User Profiles) as you like. You can also copy a recipe *into* a custom setting slot of your connected camera or copy a recipe *from* the camera into X RAW STUDIO's User Profiles. Simply right-click on one of the Profiles to view these options.

| TIP 114 | Achieving that "retro look" |

One of the reasons for the popularity of X cameras is their ability to deliver images that bear the look of analog film prints or slides—and to do so straight-out-of-camera (SOOC).

Let's be clear: You can pretty much use any modern digital camera to generate images with a grainy retro look. Just process the RAW files in software like Adobe Lightroom using a decent preset pack that replicates the look of legendary analog film emulsions. Personally, I have been using Lightroom presets from Really Nice Images (RNI) [70] for many years.

Fujifilm X cameras like the X100VI make it possible to produce similar results as straight-out-of-camera JPEGs, and websites like Fuji X Weekly [71] provide hundreds of "recipes" that are supposed to do in-camera what preset packs can do in Adobe Lightroom or Capture One Pro.

Again, let's be clear: Using Lightroom or Capture One in concert with good film presets offers far more processing freedom than using an in-camera recipe to create a JPEG—just like an analog negative in the hands of a capable lab technician offers more flexibility than a Polaroid or Instax snapshot.

However, Fujifilm Instax is tremendously popular. Why? Because it's fun! And so is taking retro pictures with your X100VI! Here are a few pointers that will make it easier for you to create your own analog film recipes.

Using the X100VI with factory default settings and standard film simulations like Provia or Reala Ace delivers a clean, contemporary look with sharp details, little noise, balanced colors, nice contrast and a neutral white balance.

You don't want that? Here are some typical JPEG setting changes that can result in the coveted "retro look":

- The most popular retro film simulations are Classic Chrome, Classic Neg. and, to a lesser degree, Nostalgic

Neg. These film simulations come pre-loaded with retro colors and tonality, making it easy to turn them into SOOC JPEGs that resemble classic analog film.

- Changing and/or shifting the white balance is a major factor when it comes to achieving images that look retro and nostalgic. Almost all recipes apply a white balance shift, mostly with a positive Red and a negative Blue value. Some recipes also rely on white balance presets (like Shade) or a fixed Kelvin setting to provide a warmer or cooler appearance.

- Many retro film recipes demand higher DR settings such as DR200% or DR400%. This leads to a softer, more film-like highlight clipping. Often, these higher DR settings arrive in concert with a recommended positive exposure compensation.

- Retro recipes usually ask for non-standard highlight and shadow contrast settings. For example, a recipe that asks for DR400% and a brighter exposure (positive exposure compensation) may compensate for this by adding more shadow contrast in the TONE CURVE (SHADOWS) menu.

- Most film recipes set noise reduction to the minimum of −4 and add some grain effect.

- To achieve an analog look, it's useful to decrease sharpening. Did you know that sharpening also affects the crispness of the Grain Effect? Hence, less is more: Many retro recipes ask for a negative sharpening setting.

- Old prints often look desaturated, so reducing the color saturation is a frequently used recipe ingredient. The desaturation can be countered with some measure of the Color Chrome Effect and/or Color Chrome Blue Effect.

- Clarity is another helpful tool. A negative value reduces the micro-contrast to produce the softer look of older prints or slides.

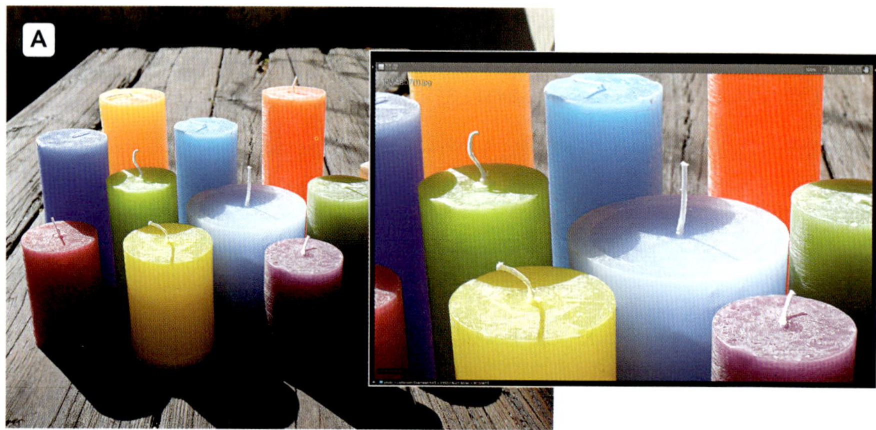

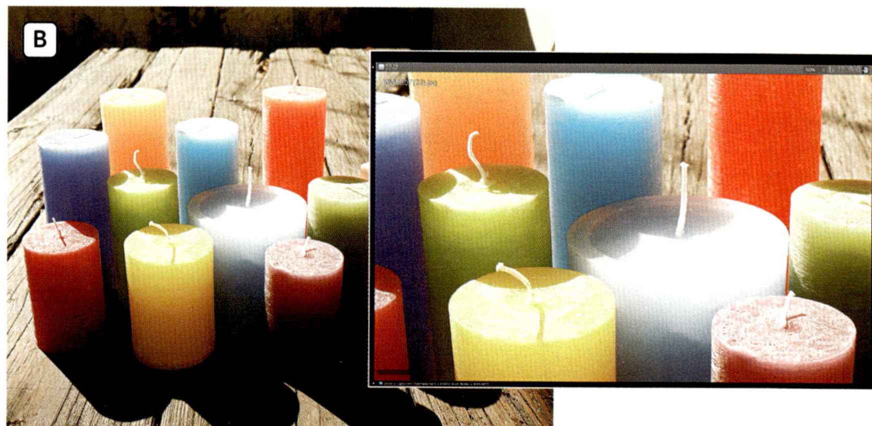

Fig. 122: In this SOOC example, image **A** shows a test shot with Provia factory settings and neutral Auto white balance. Image **B** is the same image, but with these **retro JPEG setting modifications**: film simulation Classic Neg., Grain Effect Strong & Large, Color Chrome Effect Weak, White Balance preset Shade, WB Shift to Red: +3 and Blue: –5, Shadow Tone (Tone Curve Shadows) –2, Color –2, Sharpening –3, Noise Reduction –4, and Clarity –2. The other JPEG settings remained neutral, but I applied a 1/3 EV Push to brighten the overall result. I conveniently used X RAW STUDIO to make these changes.

2.6 FLASH PHOTOGRAPHY

Flash photography means taking a double exposure. The lighting in a flash shot always consists of two components: ambient light and flash light.

- The **ambient-light** component is metered like a regular non-flash exposure. The camera is metering the scene with multi, average, center-weighted, or spot metering, while the selected auto exposure mode (**P**, **A**, or **S**) automatically selects suitable exposure parameters based on your adjustment of the exposure compensation dial. As usual, the live view and live histogram are your friends. You can also set the exposure of the ambient-light component manually in mode **M**, which is my preferred method in almost all situations. Basically, exposing the ambient-light component works exactly like exposing a scene without flash.

- The **flash-light** component can be automatically metered and adjusted by the camera to match the overall exposure. To accomplish this, the X100VI employs a so-called TTL metering system. TTL stands for Through The Lens. It means that the flash light is entering the camera through the lens before it's metered with the image sensor. This happens with the help of a weaker pre-flash that is emitted solely for metering purposes. You can bias the strength of the automatic flash-light component either on the FLASH FUNCTION SETTING page, or directly on external Fujifilm TTL flash units like the EF-X20. Please note that while the live view, live histogram and blinkies provide a preview of the ambient-light component, they completely ignore the flash-light component that will be added to the final image. Personally, I rarely use TTL flash and prefer to set the power of the flash-light component manually.

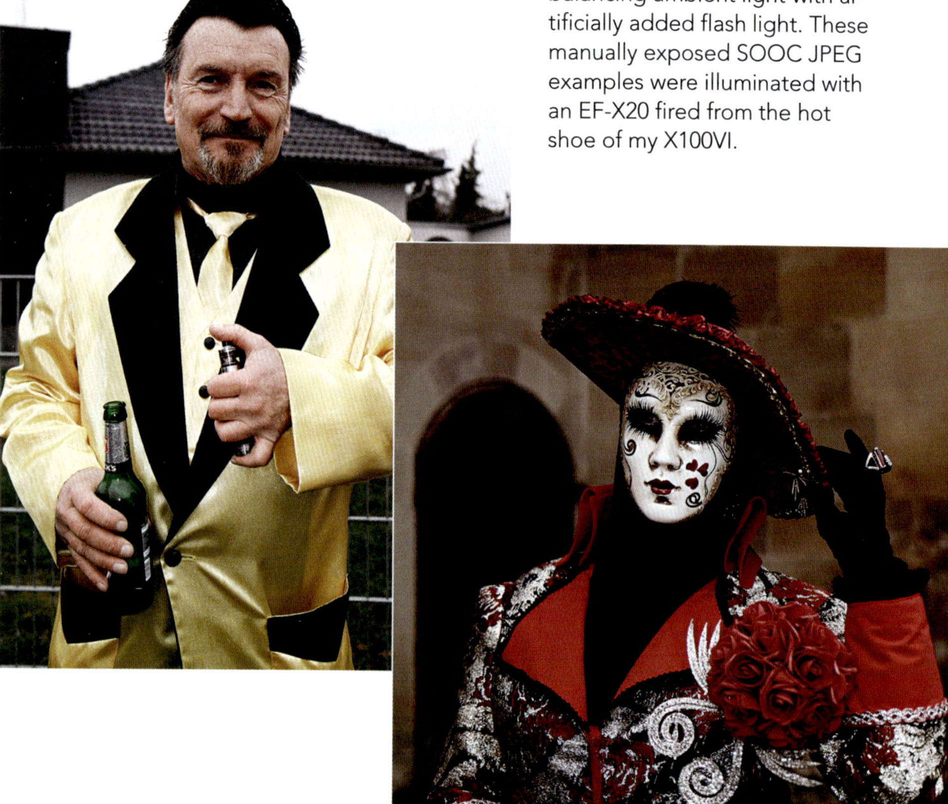

Fig. 123: In many cases, **flash photography** is about balancing ambient light with artificially added flash light. These manually exposed SOOC JPEG examples were illuminated with an EF-X20 fired from the hot shoe of my X100VI.

Besides Fuji and Fuji-compatible TTL flash units, you can also use generic third-party flash units. Pretty much everything that fits onto the hot shoe works. Using generic third-party flash units means that TTL flash metering is no longer available, so you must manually set the flash energy output. You can also use automatic flash units that use their own built-in light sensor to automatically measure and adjust the flash output.

Understanding flash modes TIP 115

The TTL flash logic in your X100VI supports several flash modes that can be selected in the Quick menu or on the FLASH SETTING > FLASH FUNCTION SETTING page.

- TTL FLASH AUTO is only available in mode **P** and automatically fires an available flash unit if the camera decides it's necessary. It's a silly mode, since you probably know better than your camera whether you want to use a flash. When the flash is firing, it works just like regular TTL, which is our next mode.

- TTL STANDARD always fires an active flash unit. This setting is available in all four exposure modes (**P**, **A**, **S**, and **M**). In modes **P** and **A** (where the camera's auto exposure determines the shutter speed), the slowest available shutter speed is 1/60 sec., meaning more distant parts of the scene that cannot be illuminated by the flash-light component may be underexposed.

- TTL SLOW SYNC. works like standard TTL but allows slower shutter speeds than 1/60 sec. to better capture the ambient-light component. This can be helpful when the light is poor, and you still want to capture more of the background. This setting is only available in exposure modes **P** and **A**. However, in concert with AUTO-ISO, this mode will only go slower than 1/60 sec. if AUTO-ISO has reached the ISO ceiling set with MAX. SENSITIVITY *and* the AE-determined shutter speed is slower than the MIN. SHUTTER SPEED setting. Hence, I recommend *not* using AUTO-ISO in concert with TTL SLOW SYNC. flash photography.

- MANUAL FLASH works like TTL SLOW SYNC., but allows you to manually specify the light emission power. This setting is available in all four exposure modes (**P**, **A**, **S**, and **M**).

- COMMANDER uses the built-in flash as a trigger flash that releases external flash units that feature an optical sensor (like Fuji's EF-X20 and many third-party flash units). Please note that you must manually adjust the power of the triggered external flash. Don't forget that the commander flash is also emitting flash light that can affect the exposure of your scene, especially when you are shooting with high ISO settings. Commander is available in all four exposure modes (P, A, S, and M) in concert with the built-in flash.

- OFF makes sure that no flash is fired, even when a flash is switched on and connected to the camera.

- In the FLASH FUNCTION SETTING page, there is an option to specify whether the flash is supposed to fire on the FRONT (1st) or REAR (2nd) curtain. This option is available in all flash modes, and it is relevant for shooting moving subjects at slow shutter speeds. Since flash photography is a double exposure, it makes a difference whether the flash is fired at the beginning or at the end of a longer exposure.

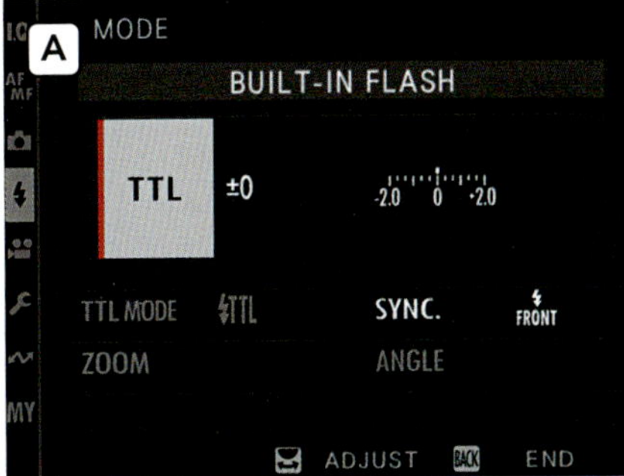
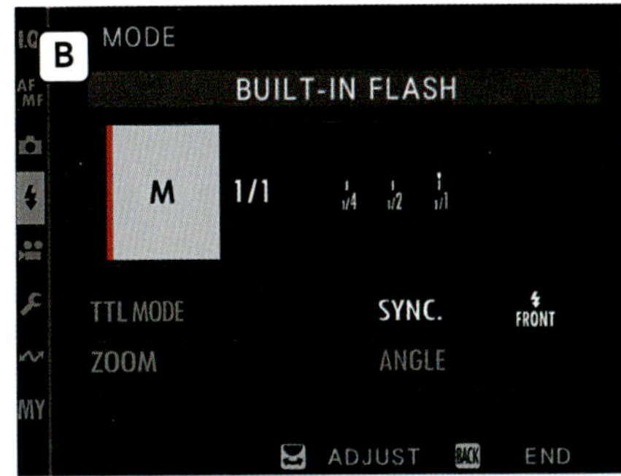
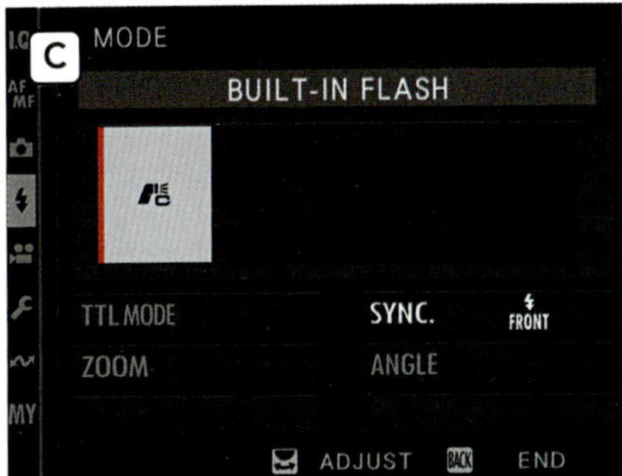
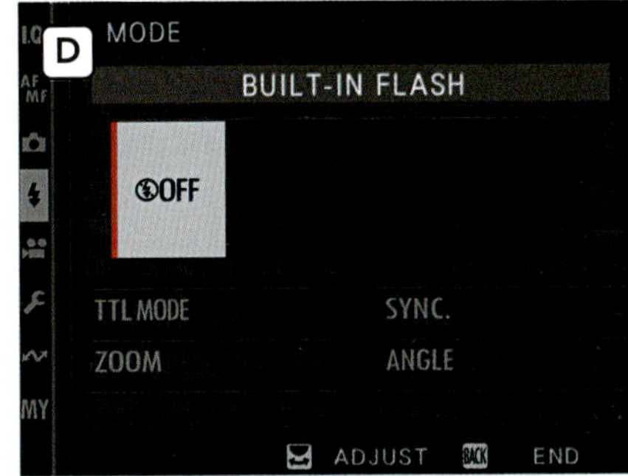

Fig. 124: The FLASH FUNCTION SETTING PAGE lets you **control flash parameters** such as flash mode, sync. mode, and flash exposure compensation. Even for the tiny built-in flash, you can choose between several modes: TTL (auto flash exposure, image **A**), M (manual flash exposure, image **B**), and Commander (image **C**). OFF disables all camera flash functions (image **D**).

Important: To use a generic shoe-mount flash (with mid-contact sync.) on the X100VI instead of its built-in flash, you must select FLASH SETTING > BUILT-IN FLASH > OFF.

Controlling the ambient-light component	TIP 116

When you are metering a scene with your X100VI, you will quickly realize that it doesn't make any difference whether the flash is turned on or off while doing so. The metering result will always be the same. In other words, the X100VI is metering the ambient-light component always in the same way, with or without flash. In case you choose to use a flash, the flash-light component will simply be *added* to the ambient-light component.

This is important because it tells us that we don't have to fear some camera voodoo that may or may not influence the metering of the ambient light as soon as we switch on a flash. Instead, we can be certain that the camera's metering will always deliver consistent results. This also means that it's *our* job to balance both light components; for example, we can reduce the ambient-light component to make room for more flash light in the composite exposure.

Typically, if you want to use the flash as a fill-in light to brighten a dark foreground (such as a backlit person), you wouldn't have to change much, since the flash-light component would brighten the dark foreground simply by filling in the light that's missing. However, if you use the flash on a scene that's already fully exposed by natural light, the camera's TTL flash metering would conclude that no additional light is necessary. A forced flash would still fire, of course, but with minimal output; it would either be almost invisible, or it may lead to an overexposed end result. To emphasize the flash-light component, reduce the exposure of the ambient-light component.

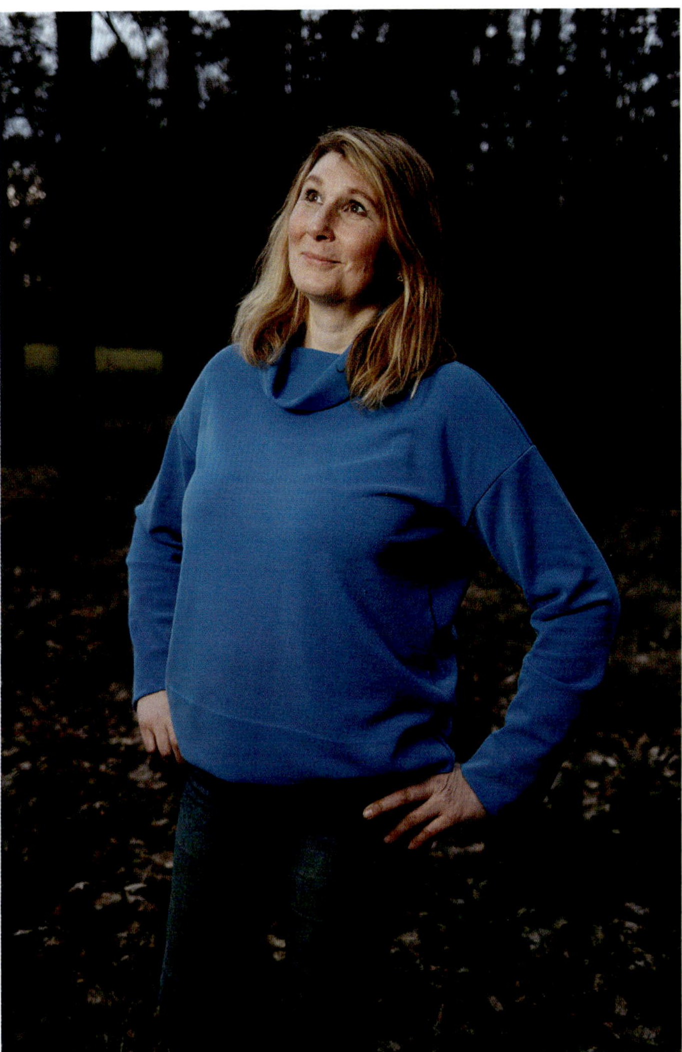

Fig. 125: In this SOOC JPEG example, reducing the **ambient-light component** to darken the background left more room for the flash-light component.

Here's how it works:

- You can control the exposure of the ambient-light component either with the exposure compensation dial or by setting an appropriate manual exposure (ISO, aperture, shutter speed). Less ambient light will prompt the TTL flash metering to add a stronger flash-light component, since the TTL flash system will always try to deliver balanced results. Changing the exposure compensation dial has no direct effect on the flash component of the shot; it only affects the exposure of the ambient-light component.

- To control the ambient-light component in manual mode **M** using the live view and the live histogram, make sure to set SET UP > SCREEN SET-UP > PREVIEW EXP./WB IN MANUAL MODE > PREVIEW EXP./WB.

- In a studio setting, you often want to minimize the ambient-light component and illuminate your subject entirely with flash light. In such cases, I recommend small aperture settings (large aperture numbers), base ISO 125, and a fast shutter speed. The fastest official flash synchronization speed of the X100VI is 1/2000 sec., but some flash units won't be that fast, especially when fired at full power and/or with a wireless transmitter. To compose a scene with very little ambient light in mode **M**, set SET UP > SCREEN SET-UP > PREVIEW EXP./WB IN MANUAL MODE > OFF. Otherwise, it will be hard to make out anything in the electronic viewfinder.

- Sometimes the fastest available (or usable) flash sync speed will still overexpose the ambient-light component, even at base ISO 125. Yes, you could stop down the aperture, but this might negate the purpose of achieving a nice subject-to-background separation with little depth of field. In such a case, it's useful to deploy the camera's built-in neutral density filter to reduce the amount of light that hits the sensor by four stops.

- Like the DR function, flash light is often used to reduce contrast between a darker subject and a brighter background. You can combine both features, which may be useful if the background—when viewed isolated from the foreground—still contains so much contrast that DR expansion is required. Think of a night scene with city lights, streetlamps, and bright billboards in the background. In such a scenario, a flash could illuminate a person standing in the foreground, while the DR function (DR400%) would help capture the colors and textures of the city lights. DR400% is also useful when you are illuminating scenes with subjects that expand deep into space and don't have an equal distance to the camera. In such cases, DR400% will give subjects that are closer to the flash light an additional overexposure protection of 2 EV which can be retrieved during external RAW conversion of your shot.

- The previously discussed 1/60 sec. minimum shutter speed limit in modes **P** and **A** and normal sync. can lead to an underexposed ambient-light component. Please note that the camera will not issue an underexposure warning—it assumes that the missing ambient light is compensated by the flash-light component. Of course, this won't be the case in many practical shooting situations. Still, the shutter speed limit can be useful because it prevents shaky or blurred backgrounds in hand-held shots. This isn't an issue when using a tripod, so you could circumvent the limit by selecting TTL SLOW or by manually setting a slow shutter speed in **S** or **M** mode.

- Ambient light and flash light frequently exhibit different color temperatures, which makes it difficult to find a white balance setting that suits all parts of the image. Luckily, some RAW converters (like Lightroom) allow selective white balance editing in an image. Another method is to use a gel filter in front of the flash unit to warm or cool the flash light to better match (or contrast with) the ambient light.

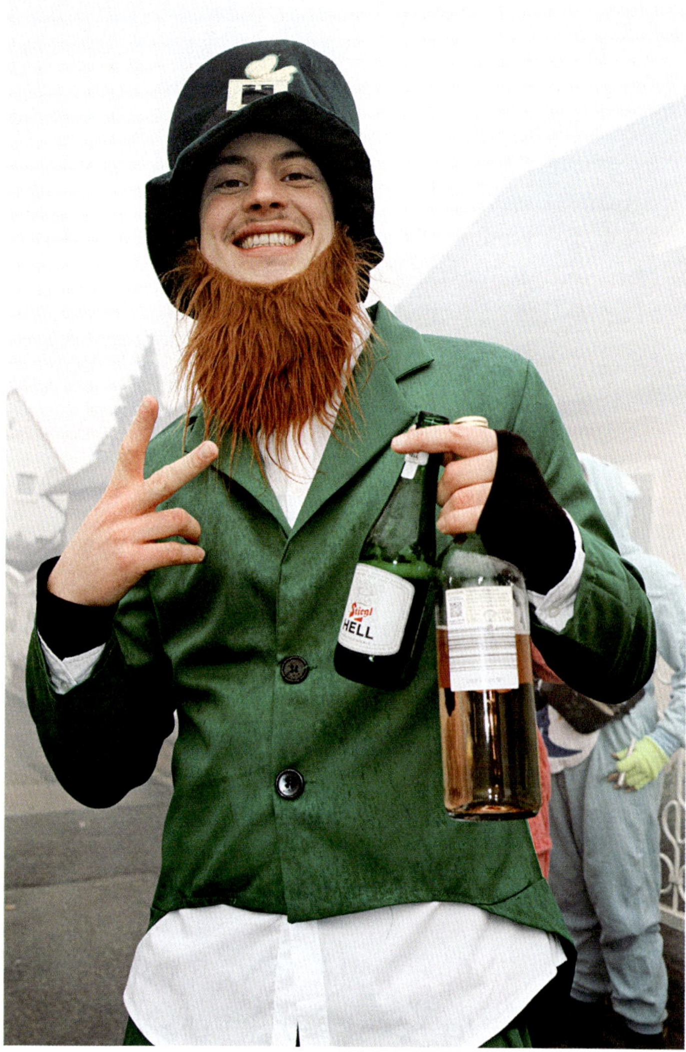

Fig. 126: With plenty of ambient light, the **flash-light component** takes a backseat. In this SOOC JPEG example, it mostly added a spark to the eyes. Even though this image was shot with the EF-X20, the built-in flash is also quite useful for this kind of application.

<table><tr><td>Controlling the flash-light component</td><td>TIP 117</td></tr></table>

If the flash-light component of your image turns out too bright or dark, you can bias the camera's TTL flash system:

- To bias the flash-light component of your shot, you can adjust the flash exposure compensation in the camera on the FLASH SETTING > FLASH FUNCTION SETTING page or on most external TTL flash units. Combining the in-camera flash compensation with an additional compensation setting on the flash unit itself can sometimes add-up both corrections, depending on the flash unit you are using.

- You will often get nicer-looking results by bouncing the flash off the ceiling, which makes the flash light look softer. Of course, bouncing the flash light requires much more power, so you may need a stronger flash. It's also worth noting that bouncing the flash from a colored surface will tint the light accordingly.

- To add a tint or change the color temperature of your flash light, you can attach colored gel filters in front of your reflector. The color temperature of unfiltered flash light usually corresponds to regular daylight.

- The range of your flash unit depends on the set aperture, the ISO setting, and (of course) the power setting. In TTL mode, the camera is automatically adjusting the light output of your flash, but many flash units (including the built-in flash of the X100VI) can also be set to manual. This way, you are the one setting the power output of the flash. In manual mode **M**, changing the shutter speed doesn't affect the brightness of the flash-light component of your shot. Hence, changing the shutter speed is a quick way to adjust the exposure of the ambient-light component without messing with your carefully balanced manual flash-light setup.

TIP 118 | **Front-curtain vs. rear-curtain flash synchronization**

Flash photographs are double exposures consisting of ambient light and flash light. When you shoot the ambient light with a slow shutter speed, there is the question of when the flash (with its much faster speed) should fire. Normally, the flash is fired at the *beginning* of an exposure with the shutter opening its FRONT (or 1st) curtain. However, if the REAR (or 2nd) curtain has been selected, the flash fires at the *end* of the exposure when the rear shutter curtain closes.

Naturally, moving objects change their position during the exposure of a shot. Synchronizing the flash with the rear curtain ensures that moving objects are frozen where they are positioned at the end of the exposure as opposed to at the beginning. This often results in the moving object appearing more natural in the image.

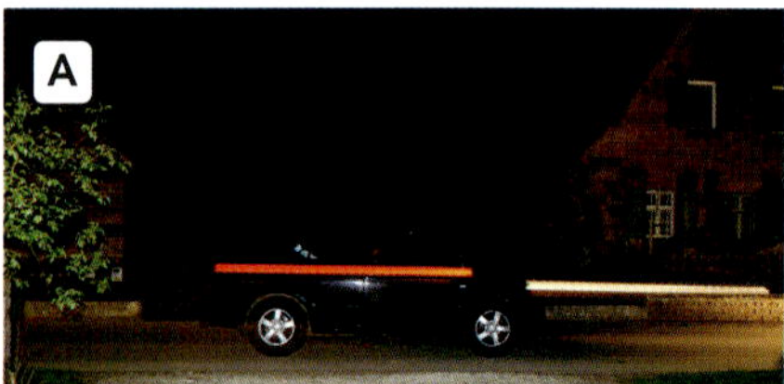

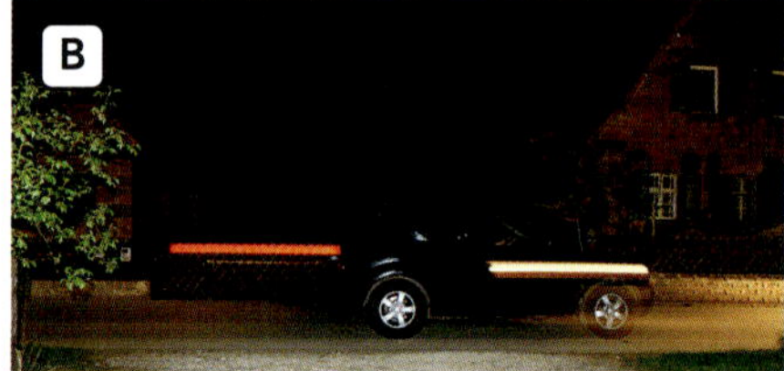

Fig. 127: Front- and rear-curtain sync: This example shows the same scene photographed with front-curtain sync (**A**) and rear-curtain sync (**B**). Image A shows how the flash freezes the moving vehicle at the beginning of the exposure, while image B shows it being frozen at the end of the exposure. The rear-curtain version looks more natural and avoids the false impression of the car moving backward. This is also a good example to examine the nature of flash photographs as double exposures. You can see how the slow shutter speed captures the moving vehicle as a blurry trail of light, while the fast flash instantly freezes parts of it.

Flash synchronization: what's the limit?   **TIP 119**

Officially, the fastest flash sync [72] speed of the X100VI is 1/2000 sec., but the X100VI will also offer and honor faster shutter speeds up to 1/4000 sec. in flash mode. However, there may be a price to pay: At maximum power, many flash units need between 1/200 sec. and 1/500 sec. to fully emit their energy. This means that with very fast shutter speed settings, a portion of the flash light wouldn't be recorded: the shutter would already have closed before the flash had finished emitting light.

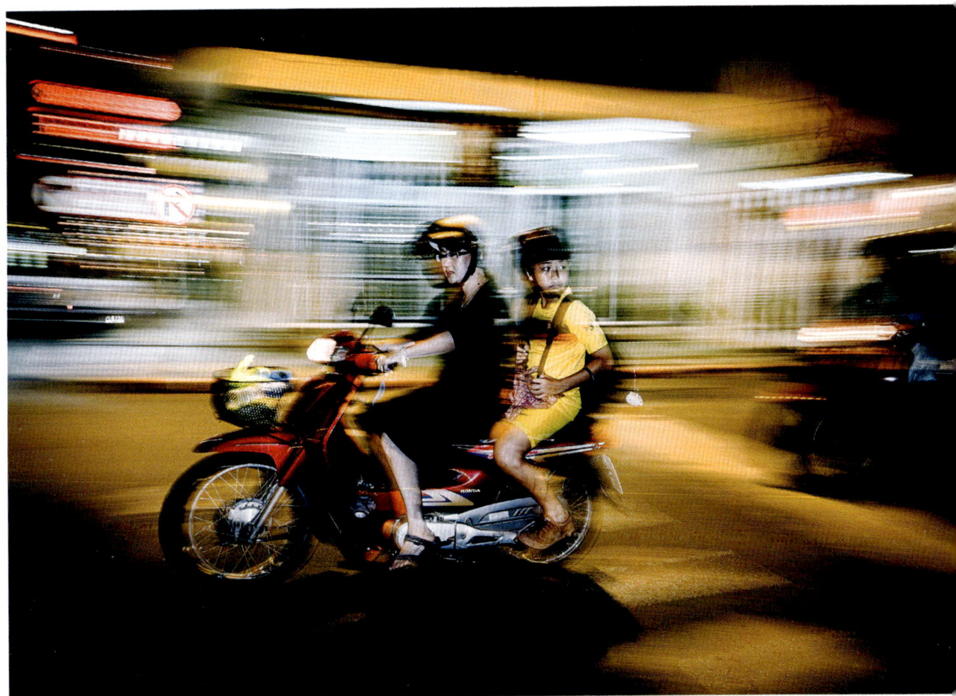

Fig. 128: It's possible to deliberately use a **very slow synch speed** to create a blurry background behind a more contoured flash-lit foreground.

Using wireless flash (TTL and manual) can impose further sync limits, because the transmitter on the camera must communicate with the off-camera flash. This latency takes time and can reduce the maximum *effective* sync speed of your setup. In my experience, light-based communication (such as Fujifilm's EF-X500) results in less latency than radio-based communication (like the Godox 2.4GHz system). If available, also make sure to set radio transmitters into leaf shutter mode. Typically, their factory setting will be optimized for regular focal plane shutters.

I recommend 1/500 sec. as a usable fastest sync speed for off-camera radio flash units operating at a higher power setting. With less output power, faster shutter speeds of up to 1/1000 sec. may also be possible.

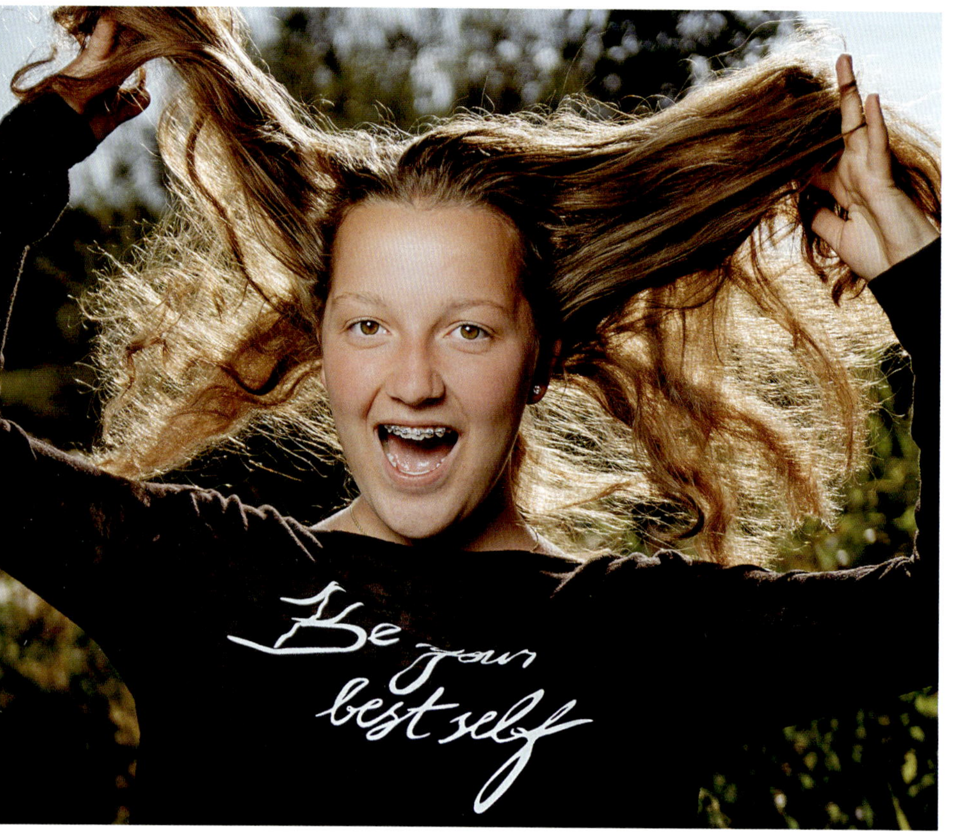

Fig. 129: This **wireless flash shot** was taken with a shutter speed of 1/800 sec. using a Godox X1TF radio transmitter and TT600 flash.

| Red-eye removal | TIP 120 |

If the flash and your subject share almost the same optical axis (a frequent occurrence with a hot-shoe flash), it can lead to the red-eye effect [73]: an unpleasant red reflection in the eyes.

If you pull up FLASH SETTING > RED EYE REMOVAL and then FLASH, the camera will emit a pre-flash prior to each shot that prompts your subject's pupils to contract, thus reducing or eliminating the red-eye effect.

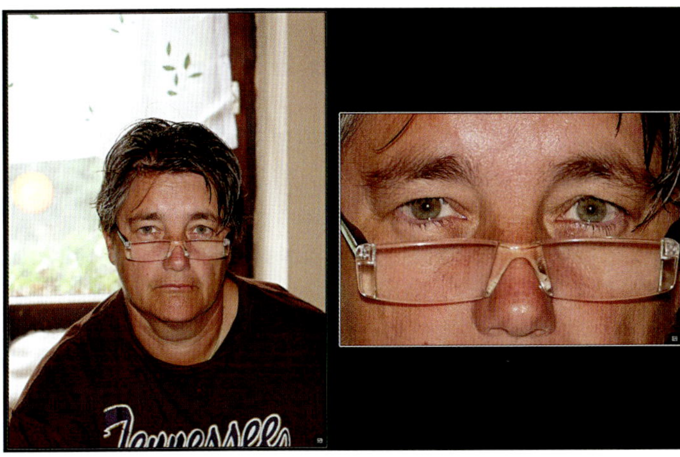

Fig. 130: The **red-eye removal** function emits a pre-flash that is bright enough to prompt your subject's pupils to contract.

| Using TTL-Lock | TIP 121 |

TTL-Lock works like AE-Lock. Where AE-Lock locks the exposure of the ambient-light component, TTL-Lock locks the exposure of the flash-light component. To use TTL-Lock, you must first assign it to one of your camera's Fn buttons. To do so, press and hold the DISP/BACK button until the Fn configuration screen appears.

TTL-Lock can work in one of two ways:

- Keep and lock the exposure of the most recent flash exposure when you press the TTL-Lock button (FLASH SETTING > TTL-LOCK MODE > LOCK WITH LAST FLASH).

- Meter the flash exposure with a metering flash when you press the TTL-Lock button and immediately lock the metered result (FLASH SETTING > TTL-LOCK MODE > LOCK WITH METERING FLASH).

TTL-Lock is practical in situations where you want to take more than one picture of the same scene and maintain a consistent flash output for the entire series. A typical method involves setting the LOCK WITH LAST FLASH option, and then taking a few test shots of the scene and applying flash exposure compensation until the result looks great. Now press TTL-Lock to lock and maintain this "perfect" flash exposure while you take additional pictures of the scene.

TTL-Lock also allows higher frame rates in burst mode. In this scenario, you will probably prefer the LOCK WITH ME-TERING FLASH setting. Pressing TTL-Lock will then meter scene and store the calculated flash exposure. As you then take images in burst mode, the frame rate will be faster because the camera doesn't have to emit and analyze a new metering flash before each frame. That said, make sure that your flash unit is powerful enough to keep up with the selected frame rate.

TIP 122	Perfect companion: the Fujifilm EF-X20

Fuji's TTL system flash EF-X20 was specifically designed for early retro-style cameras like the X-Pro1, but also works perfectly with the X100VI.

I use the EF-X20 as my main flash on the X100VI. It's small, lightweight and very easy to operate. All I need to do is turn the top dial to adjust the flash output. The EF-X20 illuminates the entire field of view quite evenly, and it is more powerful than it looks.

Its main downside is the long recycling time after emitting a full-power flash. However, with the leaf shutter of the X100VI, we hardly need full power. Shooting with apertures between f/2 and f/5.6 and using at least ISO 500 in concert with DR400%, typical portrait situations won't require full flash power. In fact, sometimes even the weakest "1/64" power setting may still be too much and lead to overexposed results if your subject is located close to the camera.

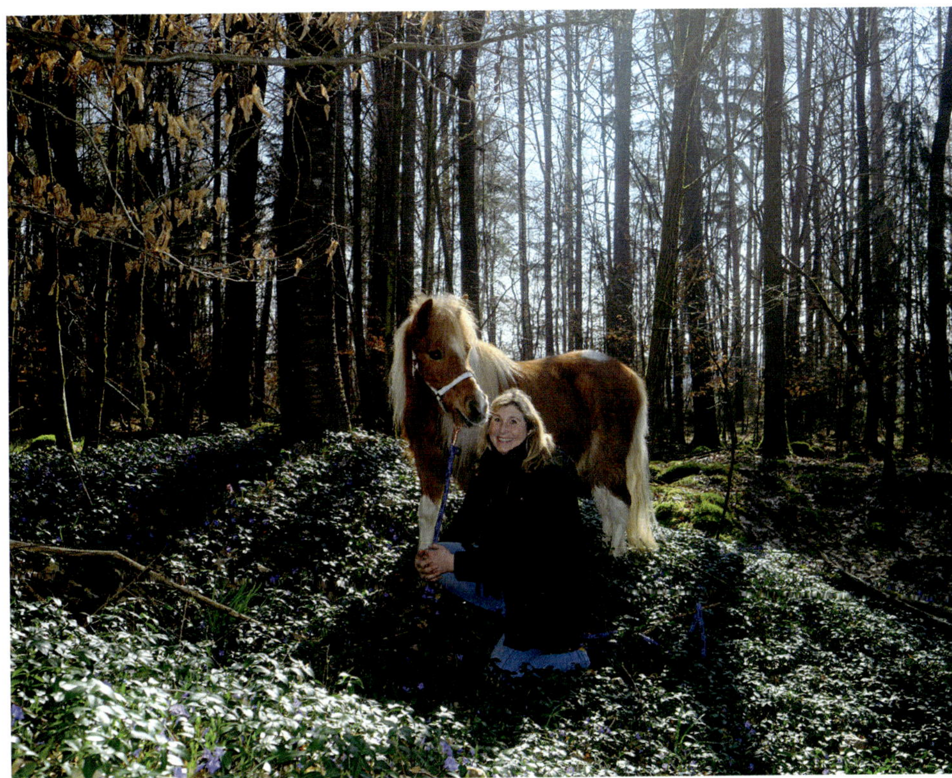

Fig. 131: The **EF-X20** may be small, but it's more capable than you might think. This SOOC JPEG illustrates how this tiny on-camera flash overpowered the sun for a backlit portrait shot at f/4 with 1/1000 sec. and ISO 500 / DR400%.

Besides using it as a TTL flash, you can also set its output power manually. You can even trigger it wirelessly with another flash, such as the camera's Commander flash:

- Set the flash mode for the built-in flash in your X100VI to COMMANDER.

- Move the mode switch on your EF-X20 to the N position.

- Manually set the desired flash output on your EF-X20. There are seven levels, from 1/1 (full power) to 1/64.

With this setup, the flash on your X100VI will wirelessly trigger the EF-X20. Please consider that the light emitted by the commander flash can still affect your image.

Fig. 132: An optically triggered **EF-X20** slave flash.

Sadly, the EF-X20 isn't produced anymore. Pre-owned units are highly sought-after and available online at premium prices that surpass the original list price. The flash is also popular with Leica users who use it as a shoe-mounted manual flash on M series cameras. Much like the X100VI, the EF-X20 has become kind of a "cult product".

Big brother: the Fujifilm EF-X500   **TIP 123**

The EF-X500 is Fuji's version of a professional flashgun, with wireless TTL control of several flash units (organized in up to three independent groups), stroboscope flash, and a secondary LED reflector that can be used as a catch light [74], a more powerful AF assist lamp, or a video lamp. For cameras with focal plane shutters, it also features FP high-speed sync to support shutter speeds of up to 1/8000 sec.

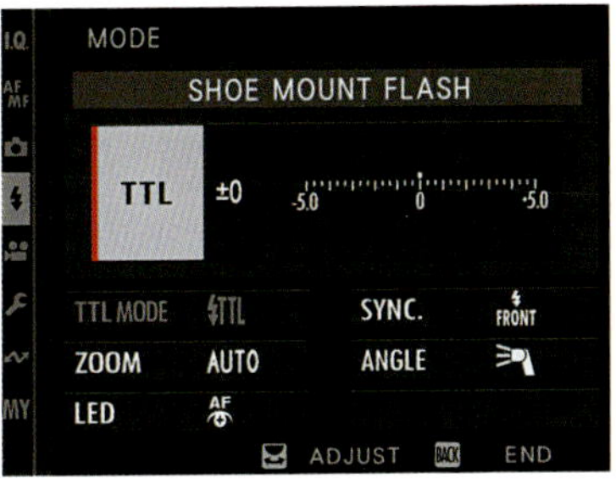

Fig. 133: With the fully featured **EF-X500** attached, the FLASH FUNCTION SETTING page of the X100VI adds several new items, including a reflector angle control and control of the secondary LED, which can be used as an AF assist lamp and/or a catch light.

You can use the EF-X500 as a single flashgun or as a commander / slave solution in setups with multiple wireless flash units. Communication between commander and slave units is light-based.

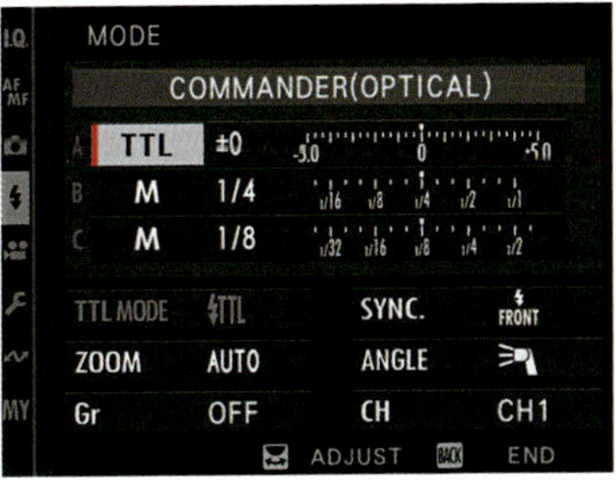

Fig. 134: In **TTL Commander** (master) mode, one EF-X500 can control multiple flashguns in three independent groups (A, B, C) via a light communication protocol. Each group can be controlled via direct TTL, a ratio of another TTL group, or fully manually.

While the EF-X500 has many great features and delivers good quality, there are also a few negative aspects to it:

- The flash is quite large, heavy, and expensive.

- Wireless TTL control is realized with outdated light signals instead of state-of-the-art radio transmission.

- Users must purchase and attach a heavy and expensive EF-X500 as a wireless master controller in optical Commander mode.

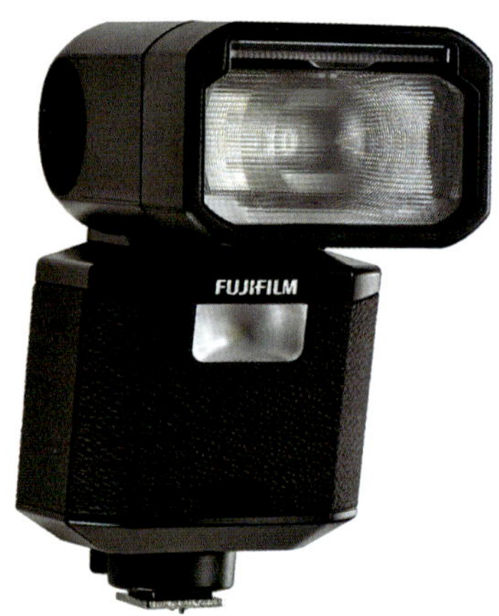

Fig. 135: The **EF-X500** is Fujifilm's pro flash and leans a bit to the large, heavy, and expensive side. However, I prefer it over the newer EF-60. The EF-60 is a rebranded Nissin flash that isn't as well-integrated into Fujifilm's flash system as the EF-X500.

TIP 124	Generic third-party flash units

Basically, you can use any modern flashgun from any vendor with your X100VI, if you are prepared to manually set its power. You can connect third-party flash units directly to the camera's hot shoe, or use a cable or a wireless (radio) triggering device.

The camera's TTL modes aren't available when you are using third-party flashes because the camera isn't *metering* the flash light, it's only *triggering* the flash. Again, the official maximum sync shutter speed is 1/2000 sec.

To use a generic shoe-mount flash (with mid-contact sync.) on the X100VI instead of the built-in flash, you must select FLASH SETTING > BUILT-IN FLASH > OFF.

TIP 125	Fujifilm-compatible third-party flash units

There's a growing number of affordable third-party flash units and systems that claim specific compatibility with

Fujifilm cameras, including TTL support and (in concert with focal plane shutters) high-speed sync.

Personally, I am invested in radio transmitters and external flash units from Godox. They offer a broad range of flash units that all adhere to the same radio transmission standard—from small speedlights to big studio flash units with up to 2400 Ws. Some of their radio transmitters for Fujifilm cameras also include a specific leaf shutter mode to enhance compatibility with the X100 series. If you already use Godox and are looking for a small and lightweight transmitter that fits nicely on the X100VI, I can recommend the stylish Godox X3F [75] with its optional touchscreen interface.

As much as I like the Godox system for off-camera work, I stick with Fujifilm's EF-X20 and EF-X500 as my preferred on-camera flash units. My reasoning is simple: The EF-X500 is the only on-camera flash that supports all features of Fujifilm's flash system. And the EF-X20 is simply the most convenient, best-looking and easy-to-use flash for the X100 series.

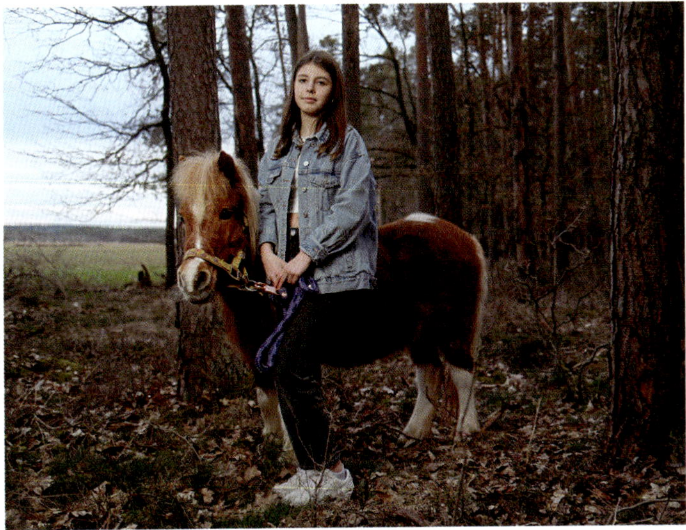

Fig. 136: Radio-controlled **external flash units** offer great flexibility in setting and modifying light. This SOOC JPEG was shot with a Godox AD200 strobe with a cheap shoot-through umbrella. The flash transmitter in the camera's hot shoe was a Godox XPro2IIF.

> **TIP 126** | "In your face" flash photography

Decades ago, during the film days, it was quite common to use a shoe-mounted flash for direct subject illumination. The flash light travelled flat into a person's face, sometimes with the added bonus of a red-eye effect. Of course, this lazy method was frowned upon by advanced photographers. Instead, it was recommended to bounce flash light off the ceiling or to use an untethered external flash.

Today, a rising number of younger photographers and content creators are not only rediscovering film and other analog media, but they are also reviving old techniques. Emitting flash light on the optical axis is an effective way to achieve a simple, direct retro look. The results look raw, unfiltered and spontaneous, and they are unlike typical smartphone images.

Here are a few tips for shooting with "in your face" flash:

- To avoid flash overexposure, I recommend setting the camera to DR400%. This also reduces skin reflections. If the result looks "too nice," you can always reprocess the shot with DR200% or DR100%.

- I usually shoot in manual mode **M** for all four exposure parameters: aperture, shutter speed, ISO, and flash output. If your flash supports TTL, feel free to use it for speed and convenience. However, be prepared for shots to turn out overexposed or underexposed. In any case, you should keep manual control over aperture, shutter speed, and ISO to stay on top of the ambient-light component.

- If you use a small flash unit or even the tiny built-in flash, you can extend its reach by opening the aperture and/or raising the ISO. Changing the shutter speed doesn't affect flash performance. Make sure to operate inside the practical sync speed margin of your flash unit. This means that your shutter speed must be slow enough to give the flash sufficient time to emit the set amount of light.

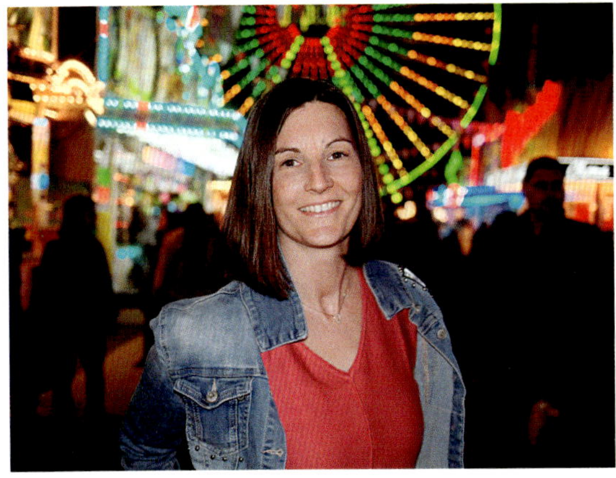

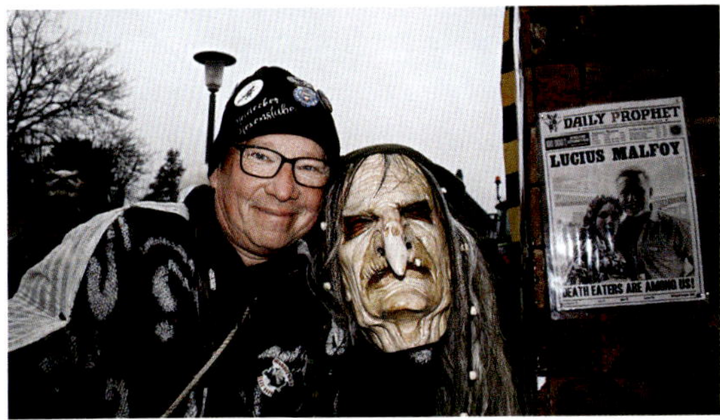

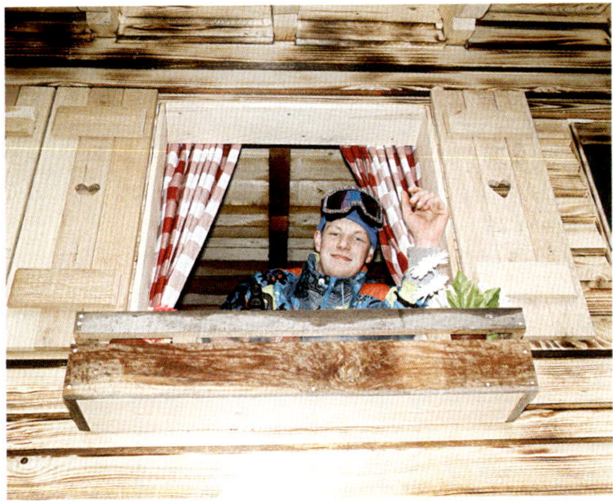

Fig. 137: These SOOC JPEG examples were shot with direct **"in your face" flash light** from an EF-X20 that was mounted on my X100VI. It's a blast from the past.

2.7 CONNECTIVITY

TIP 127	Using the XApp

Fuji's XApp works with wireless iOS and Android devices, and it allows you to remotely control your camera by providing a live view image and a touch-screen interface to set the focus point, change exposure parameters, and take a shot. The wireless connection is based on the camera's or smartphone's Wi-Fi capabilities.

To use the XApp, you must first download and install the free app on your smartphone or tablet. You can find download links and additional information online [76].

Among others, the XApp allows you to perform these tasks:

- Remotely trigger the camera via Bluetooth.

- Remote-control the camera via Wi-Fi, which includes having a live view window in the app.

- Review images and transfer them from the camera to your smartphone or tablet via Wi-Fi (RAW, JPEG, or HEIF).

- Review camera usage and activity data.

- Update the camera firmware.

- Save and restore complete sets of camera settings.

- Synchronize GPS data from your smartphone or tablet with your camera.

| Streaming the live view via HDMI | **TIP 128** |

The X100VI offers HDMI live streaming, meaning that the contents of the live view (electronic viewfinder or LCD) can be transmitted to a monitor, TV, or projector via the camera's HDMI output. All you must do is connect the camera's Micro-HDMI jack to a suitable monitor with a digital input (HDMI, DVI, etc.). Real-time streaming will start automatically once the connection is established.

This is a useful feature for workshops, product demonstrations, or professional productions, where customers can watch on a monitor what the photographer is seeing in the live view.

You can also use the HDMI live view output to connect the camera to an HD or 4K frame-grabber like Elgato Cam Link, which is then connected to your computer. With this setup, you can make videos and screenshots of the live view.

| USB video conferencing | **TIP 129** |

Personally, I use HDMI and Elgato Cam Link for video conferencing. However, there's an alternative way to set up the USB port for this task: Selecting USB WEBCAM in the NETWORK/USB SETTING > CONNECTION MODE menu allows you to stream video via the USB port to video conferencing software (like Zoom) on your computer.

2.8 ANYTHING ELSE?

Hopefully, this book has answered many of your questions that went beyond the user manual of your camera. However, this isn't the end: you can read my old X-Pert Corner blog, participate in Fuji X forums, join a virtual Fuji X Secrets workshop, or book personal 1:1 training via Zoom.

| TIP 130 | Forums, blogs, magazines, and workshops |

- High-resolution versions of selected images in this book are available on Flickr [77].

- At Fuji X Secrets [78], you will find articles and reviews covering specific features, firmware, and products for X-series cameras.

- My X-Pert Corner blog [79] covers a variety of topics about the Fujifilm X series. You will find everything from service articles that go beyond this book to "First Look" previews of cameras and lenses.

- There are two online forums that focus on Fujifilm's X series: The Original Fuji X Forum [80] and The Ultimate Fuji X Forum [81].

- I am a regular contributor of gear-related articles in FUJI-LOVE [82], a dedicated monthly online magazine for all things Fuji X.

- Books, blogs, and forums are great, but what about a more personal touch? You can book a personal 1:1 training session that can answer your Fujifilm X-related questions. Thanks to my virtual Zoom setup with two screens, live-view streaming, and 3.3K screen sharing with pixel-peeping quality, we can cover all topics, from gear via ISOless exposure and focusing to RAW processing. Anything goes.

ONLINE REFERENCES

Websites are not run by Rocky Nook and are subject to change without our knowledge.

If necessary, we will update these references. For an updated version of this reference list, please download the available document at:

www.rockynook.com/fuji-x100vi-online-references/

[1]   https://fujifilm-dsc.com/en/manual/x100vi/#gsc.tab=0
[2]   https://fujifilm-x.com/global/support/compatibility/cameras/x100vi/
[3]   https://fujifilm-x.com/global/support/download/firmware/cameras/x100vi/
[4]   https://fujifilm-x.com/global/support/download/
[5]   https://fujifilm-x.com/global/support/download/procedure-x-compact/
[6]   https://digitalcamera-support-en.fujifilm.com/digitalcameraengpcdetail?aid=000003848&_ga=2.49993830.1779550970.1677863511-1749972570.1672392523
[7]   https://digitalcamera-support-en.fujifilm.com/digitalcameraengpcdetail?aid=000003852&_ga=2.23844730.1779550970.1677863511-1749972570.1672392523
[8]   https://fujifilm-x.com/global/products/software/xapp/
[9]   http://en.wikipedia.org/wiki/Vignetting
[10]   http://en.wikipedia.org/wiki/Distortion_(optics)
[11]   https://en.wikipedia.org/wiki/Chromatic_aberration
[12]   https://en.wikipedia.org/wiki/Dark-frame_subtraction
[13]   https://fujifilm-x.com/global/support/download/software/x-acquire/
[14]   https://fujifilm-x.com/global/products/software/xapp/
[15]   https://fujifilm-x.com/global/support/download/software/x-raw-studio/
[16]   http://en.wikipedia.org/wiki/Raw_image_format
[17]   https://en.wikipedia.org/wiki/JPEG
[18]   https://fujifilm-x.com/global/support/download/software/raw-file-converter-ex-powered-by-silkypix/
[19]   https://en.wikipedia.org/wiki/WYSIWYG
[20]   https://en.wikipedia.org/wiki/Live_preview
[21]   https://en.wikipedia.org/wiki/Parallax#Parallax_error_in_photography
[22]   https://en.wikipedia.org/wiki/Zone_System
[23]   http://www.cambridgeincolour.com/tutorials/histograms1.htm
[24]   http://www.cambridgeincolour.com/tutorials/histograms2.htm
[25]   https://en.wikipedia.org/wiki/Depth_of_field

[26] https://en.wikipedia.org/wiki/Motion_blur
[27] https://en.wikipedia.org/wiki/Aperture_priority
[28] https://en.wikipedia.org/wiki/Aperture
[29] https://en.wikipedia.org/wiki/Depth_of_field
[30] http://www.cambridgeincolour.com/tutorials/diffraction-photography.htm
[31] https://en.wikipedia.org/wiki/Shutter_priority
[32] https://en.wikipedia.org/wiki/Shutter_speed
[33] https://en.wikipedia.org/wiki/Motion_blur
[34] https://en.wikipedia.org/wiki/Panning_(camera)
[35] https://en.wikipedia.org/wiki/Long-exposure_photography
[36] http://www.cambridgeincolour.com/tutorials/camera-shake.htm
[37] https://en.wikipedia.org/wiki/Bracketing
[38] https://en.wikipedia.org/wiki/Dark-frame_subtraction
[39] https://en.wikipedia.org/wiki/Neutral-density_filter
[40] https://en.wikipedia.org/wiki/Film_speed#Digital_camera_ISO_speed_and_exposure_index
[41] https://www.iridientdigital.com/products/xtransformer.html
[42] https://www.dxo.com/dxo-pureraw/
[43] https://fujifilm-x.com/global/products/software/x-raw-studio/
[44] https://www.diyphotography.net/lighting-high-key-and-low-key/
[45] https://fujifilm-x.com/global/products/software/x-raw-studio/
[46] https://www.iridientdigital.com/products/xtransformer.html
[47] https://digital-photography-school.com/the-problem-with-the-focus-recompose-method/
[48] https://en.wikipedia.org/wiki/Hyperfocal_distance
[49] https://en.wikipedia.org/wiki/Circle_of_confusion
[50] https://www.youtube.com/watch?v=7FR3l6S12JA
[51] https://www.youtube.com/watch?v=rnkib7FZ8S8
[52] https://en.wikipedia.org/wiki/Depth_of_field
[53] https://www.cambridgeincolour.com/tutorials/diffraction-photography.htm
[54] https://www.heliconsoft.com/heliconsoft-products/helicon-focus/
[55] https://en.wikipedia.org/wiki/Focus_stacking
[56] https://en.wikipedia.org/wiki/Panning_(camera)
[57] http://www.cambridgeincolour.com/tutorials/white-balance.htm
[58] https://en.wikipedia.org/wiki/Exif
[59] https://en.wikipedia.org/wiki/Gray_card
[60] https://fujifilm-x.com/global/support/download/software/x-raw-studio/
[61] https://en.wikipedia.org/wiki/Contrast_(vision)
[62] https://en.wikipedia.org/wiki/Colorfulness
[63] https://en.wikipedia.org/wiki/Color_space
[64] https://en.wikipedia.org/wiki/SRGB
[65] https://en.wikipedia.org/wiki/Adobe_RGB_color_space
[66] https://en.wikipedia.org/wiki/Gamut
[67] https://fujifilm-x.com/global/support/download/software/
[68] https://fujifilm-x.com/global/stories/fujifilm-x-raw-studio-features-users-guide/

[69] https://fujixweekly.com/fujifilm-x-trans-v-recipes/
[70] https://reallyniceimages.com/
[71] https://fujixweekly.com/
[72] https://en.wikipedia.org/wiki/Flash_synchronization
[73] https://en.wikipedia.org/wiki/Red-eye_effect
[74] https://en.wikipedia.org/wiki/Catch_light
[75] https://www.godox.com/product-a/X3.html
[76] https://fujifilm-x.com/global/products/software/xapp/
[77] https://www.flickr.com/photos/ricopfirstinger/sets/721777203
      19010857/
[78] https://fuji-x-secrets.net/
[79] http://www.fujirumors.com/category/x-pert/
[80] http://www.fujix-forum.com/
[81] http://www.fuji-x-forum.com/
[82] https://fujilove.com/

INDEX